Zombie Army

Studies in Canadian Military History
Series editor: Andrew Burtch, Canadian War Museum

The Canadian War Museum, Canada's national museum of military history, has a threefold mandate: to remember, to preserve, and to educate. Studies in Canadian Military History, published by UBC Press in association with the Museum, extends this mandate by presenting the best of contemporary scholarship to provide new insights into all aspects of Canadian military history, from earliest times to recent events. The work of a new generation of scholars is especially encouraged, and the books employ a variety of approaches – cultural, social, intellectual, economic, political, and comparative – to investigate gaps in the existing historiography. The books in the series feed immediately into future exhibitions, programs, and outreach efforts by the Canadian War Museum. A list of the titles in the series appears at the end of the book.

CANADIAN WAR MUSEUM
MUSÉE CANADIEN DE LA GUERRE

Zombie Army

The Canadian Army and Conscription in the Second World War

Daniel Byers

UBCPress · Vancouver · Toronto

25 24 23 22 21 20 19 18 17 16 5 4 3 2 1

Printed in Canada on FSC-certified ancient-forest-free paper (100% post-consumer recycled) that is processed chlorine- and acid-free.

Library and Archives Canada Cataloguing in Publication

Byers, Daniel Thomas, author
Zombie army : the Canadian Army and conscription in the Second World War / Daniel Byers.

(Studies in Canadian military history)
Includes bibliographical references and index.
Issued in print and electronic formats.
ISBN 978-0-7748-3051-5 (hardback). – ISBN 978-0-7748-3052-2 (pbk.)
ISBN 978-0-7748-3053-9 (pdf). – ISBN 978-0-7748-3054-6 (epub)
ISBN 978-0-7748-3055-3 (mobi)

1. Draft – Canada – History – 20th century. 2. Canada. Canadian Army – Recruiting, enlistment, etc. – World War, 1939-1945. 3. World War, 1939-1945 – Canada. I. Title. II. Series: Studies in Canadian military history

UB345.C2B94 2016 355.2'2363097109044 C2016-901342-1
C2016-901343-X

Canadä

UBC Press gratefully acknowledges the financial support for our publishing program of the Government of Canada (through the Canada Book Fund), the Canada Council for the Arts, and the British Columbia Arts Council.

Publication of this book has been financially supported by the Canadian War Museum.

Printed and bound in Canada by Friesens.
Set in Helvetica Condensed and Minion by Artegraphica Design Co. Ltd.
Copy editor: Matthew Kudelka
Proofreader: Dianne Tiefensee

UBC Press
The University of British Columbia
2029 West Mall
Vancouver, BC V6T 1Z2
www.ubcpress.ca

SALUTE TO A ZOMBIE[1]

[Sung to the tune of "My Darling Clementine"]

I'm a Zombie, I'm a Zombie,
I'm a Zombie. Yes, I am
I'd much rather be a Zombie
Than an Active Service Man.

I'm a Zombie, I'm a zombie,
I'm a Zombie, till I die.
Active Service makes me nervous,
So I'll never go and try.

I was a Zombie, I was a Zombie,
I was a Zombie, and it's right,
While in Col. Ralston's Army,
I'll never have to go and fight.

I was a Zombie, I was a Zombie,
I was a Zombie I'll allow.
Tired of BS., I put up a GS
So I'm in the army now.

So I joined Active Service,
Sailing over with the tide,
I can walk along the street now
And never have to go and hide.

Now come listen all you Zombies,
You drink our wine, you drink our beer,
But you won't turn G[eneral].S[ervice].
For a handcuffed volunteer.

That's the end of our story,
All you Zombies, Please take heed,
Why not join the Active Service,
Help us out, where ere there's need.

Contents

Tables and Figures

Tables

Figures

Acknowledgments

I HAVE BENEFITED FROM the contributions of many individuals who have aided me over the years in my research for this study, who have commented on drafts of one or more parts of it, and who in all cases have provided me with general advice and encouragement. In particular, I am grateful to a number of past and present archivists and historians from Library and Archives Canada, including Paul Marsden, Robert MacIntosh, Tim Dubé, Myron Momryk, Robert Fisher, and Tim Cook (now of the Canadian War Museum), and Carl Christie, Serge Bernier, and Stephen Harris of the Directorate of History and Heritage, Department of National Defence. George Henderson and the rest of the staff at the Queen's University Archives, along with that of the Provincial Archives of Nova Scotia (now Nova Scotia Archives), made it a pleasure for me to visit both Kingston and Halifax in the early years of my research, to view the papers of several former members of the federal Cabinet and other individuals. More recently, Carol Reid and others at the Military History Research Centre of the Canadian War Museum have been just as co-operative and helpful. Terry Copp, with whom I studied for six years at Wilfrid Laurier University (WLU), and Ron Haycock, for whom I worked as a research assistant for several years at the Royal Military College of Canada (RMC), have both been (and continue to be) major influences on me, both as an author and now as a professor of history – as has Carman Miller, my doctoral supervisor at McGill University, who provided me with much understanding, aid, guidance, and constructive commentary throughout the time that I spent completing my studies, as well as advice since then, for this book and other works. I would also like to thank former colleagues with whom I worked for several years as an instructor in the Department of History at RMC, and especially Roch Legault, who helped me prepare the earlier French-language version of part of this book that is listed at the end of these acknowledgments, Michael Hennessy, who provided me with a number of other very helpful suggestions in the early stages of drafting this book, generally, and Jane Errington, who as the Chair of the History Department provided me with much support in order to help me complete early work on it while I was also juggling teaching duties in Kingston. Other people have been kind enough to share aspects of their own research with me, or helped guide me to specific sources (or both), including Suzanne Morton of McGill University, Paul Dickson, who is the biographer of H.D.G. Crerar, and Hugh Halliday, who is an expert on all things related to the Canadian air force, military medals, and numerous other topics.

Along the way, I was also blessed with a number of good friends, all of whom shared many conversations with me about my work and assisted it in other ways. Among them are Ken Reynolds, Serge Durflinger, Marc Drolet, Lori McNulty, Catherine Cournoyer, and Tara Newell, all of whom were fellow students with me at McGill (although with some of whom I regret that I have lost touch since then), as well as Peter Nayler, whom I met at Library and Archives Canada in the early days of researching this topic, Bill Rawling of the Directorate of History and Heritage in Ottawa, and Rob Guertin, who has been a close friend since our earliest days as undergraduate students together at WLU. The latter two individuals have also gone above and beyond the call of duty many times by putting up with my staying at their homes during my various travels doing research and attending conferences. More recently, I have had the benefit of a wonderful group of colleagues with whom I teach in the Department of History at Laurentian University, both in Sudbury and especially at our Barrie campus, to all of whom I extend my thanks for their support and encouragement over the past few years.

Most recently, I have benefited from a similar range of support from Emily Andrew, Megan Brand, and everyone else at UBC Press, as well as its two anonymous peer reviewers, all of whose comments have without a doubt helped improve the final product that appears here. I would like to thank the Military and Strategic Studies / Security and Defence (Forum) program of the Department of National Defence, and the Social Sciences and Humanities Research Council of Canada for major awards that aided me in completing most of the research upon which this book is based, as well as McGill University and the Post-Graduate Students' Society of McGill for other early financial support. More recently, Laurentian University provided me with a generous start-up grant for new professors that enabled me to put the finishing touches on my research, and I received a sizable award from its Laurentian University Research Fund to help pay the costs of publication. Lastly, I am grateful to the Canadian War Museum for funding the very important series "Studies in Canadian Military History" of which I am now honoured that this book is a part, and in particular the series editor, Andrew Burtch. In the end, the strengths of my work reflect the countless contributions of all of the people listed above. Any errors or omissions that may remain are entirely my own.

NOTE: Some of the material in this book appeared in an earlier form in "Mobilising Canada: The National Resources Mobilization Act, the Department of National Defence, and Compulsory Military Service in Canada, 1940–1945," *Journal of the Canadian Historical Association* 7 (1996): 175–203; "Les << zombies >> du Canada: un portrait des conscrits canadiens et de leur expérience durant la Deuxième Guerre mondiale," *Bulletin d'histoire politique* 8(2–3) (printemps 2000): 184–204; and "Canada's Zombies: A Portrait of Canadian Conscripts and Their Experiences during the Second World War," in *Forging a Nation: Perspectives on the Canadian Military Experience*, ed. Bernd Horn (St. Catharines: Vanwell, 2002), 155–76.

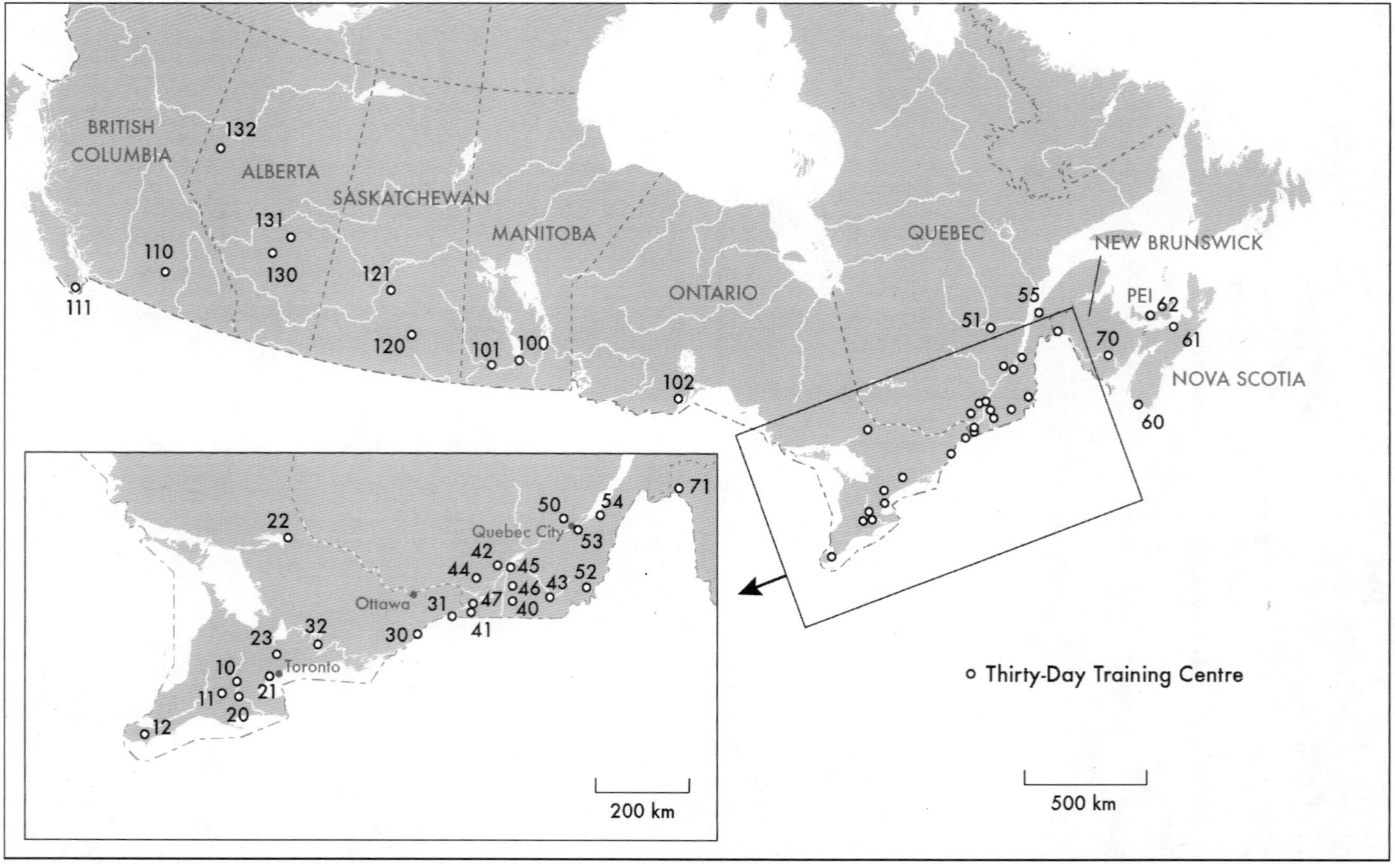

Figure 1 Thirty-Day Training Centres, October 1940. Map by Eric Leinberger.

Figure 1: Thirty-Day Training Centres, October 1940

Number	Location
10	Kitchener, Ontario
11	Woodstock, Ontario
12	Chatham, Ontario
20	Brantford, Ontario
21	Long Branch, Ontario
22	North Bay, Ontario
23	Newmarket, Ontario
30	Brockville, Ontario
31	Cornwall, Ontario
32	Peterborough, Ontario
40	Farnham, Quebec
41	Huntingdon, Quebec
42	Joliette, Quebec
43	Sherbrooke, Quebec
44	St.-Jérôme, Quebec
45	Sorel, Quebec
46	St.-Hyacinthe
47	Valleyfield, Quebec
50	Valcartier, Quebec
51	Chicoutimi, Quebec
52	Lac-Mégantic, Quebec
53	Lauzon, Quebec
54	Montmagny, Quebec
55	Rimouski, Quebec
60	Yarmouth, Nova Scotia
61	New Glasgow, Nova Scotia
62	Charlottetown, PEI
70	Fredericton, New Brunswick
71	Edmundston, New Brunswick
100	Portage la Prairie, Manitoba
101	Brandon, Manitoba
102	Fort William, Ontario
110	Vernon, British Columbia
111	Gordon Head, British Columbia
120	Regina, Saskatchewan
121	Dundurn, Saskatchewan
130	Red Deer, Alberta
131	Camrose, Alberta
132	Grande Prairie, Alberta

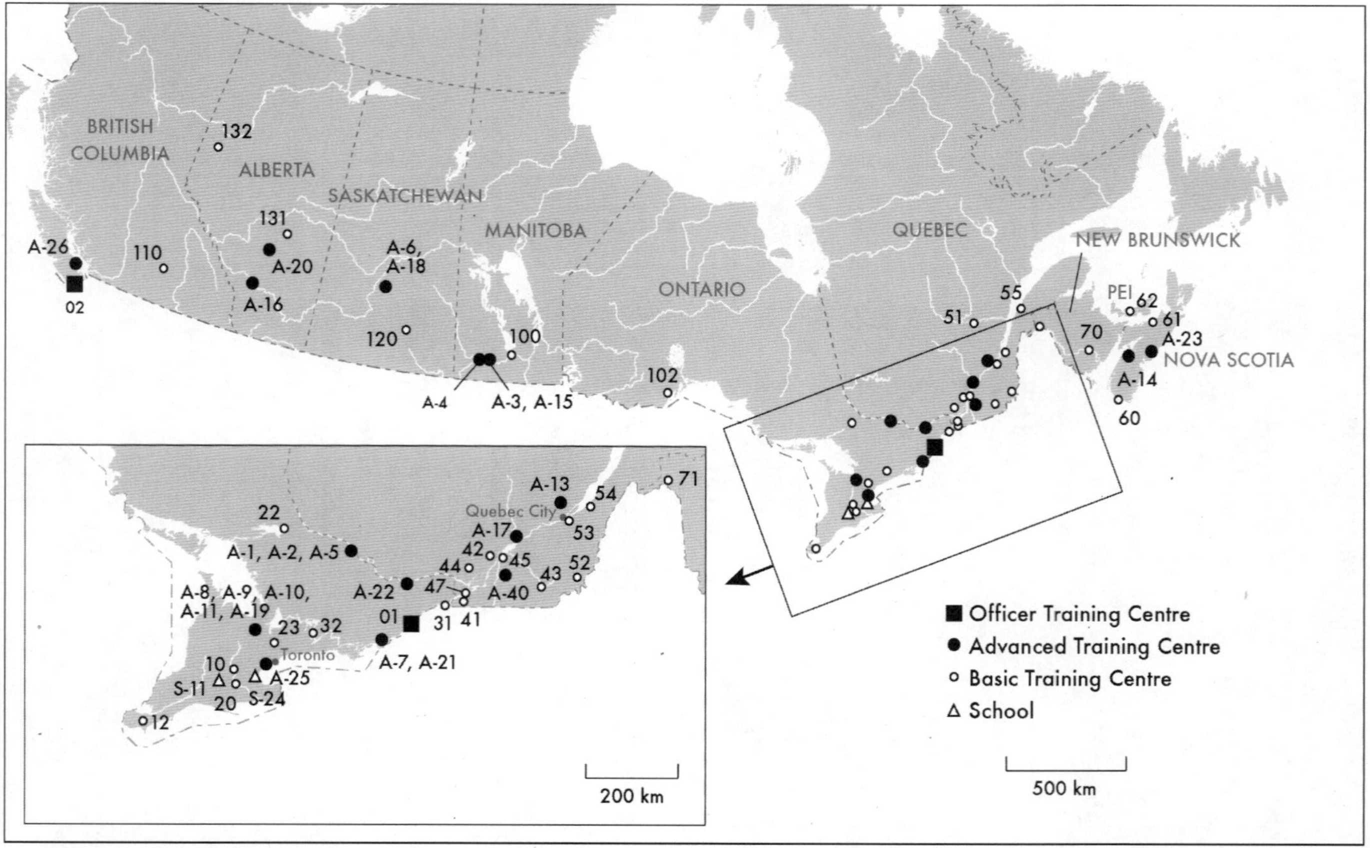

Figure 2 Army Training Centres in Canada, April 1941. Map by Eric Leinberger.

Figure 2: Training Centres in Canada, April 1941

Basic Training Centres

10	Kitchener, Ontario
12	Chatham, Ontario
20	Brantford, Ontario
22	North Bay, Ontario
23	Newmarket, Ontario
31	Cornwall, Ontario
32	Peterborough, Ontario
41	Huntingdon, Quebec
42	Joliette, Quebec
43	Sherbrooke, Quebec
44	St.-Jérôme, Quebec
45	Sorel, Quebec
47	Valleyfield, Quebec
51	Chicoutimi, Quebec
52	Lac-Mégantic, Quebec
53	Lauzon, Quebec
54	Montmagny, Quebec
55	Rimouski, Quebec
60	Yarmouth, NS
61	New Glasgow, NS
62	Charlottetown, PEI
70	Fredericton, NB
71	Edmundston, NB
100	Portage la Prairie, Manitoba
102	Fort William, Ontario
110	Vernon, BC
120	Regina, Saskatchewan
131	Camrose, Alberta
132	Grande Prairie, Alberta

Schools

S-11	(Driving & Maintenance) Woodstock, Ontario
S-24	(Trades) Hamilton, Ontario

Advanced Training Centres

A-1 (Artillery)	Petawawa, Ontario
A-2 (Artillery)	Petawawa, Ontario
A-3 (Artillery)	Shilo, Manitoba
A-4 (Artillery)	Brandon, Manitoba
A-5 (Engineering)	Petawawa, Ontario
A-6 (Engineering)	Dundurn, Saskatchewan
A-7 (Signals)	Barriefield, Ontario
A-8 (Armoured)	Camp Borden, Ontario
A-9 (Armoured)	Camp Borden, Ontario
A-10 (Infantry)	Camp Borden, Ontario
A-11 (Infantry)	Camp Borden, Ontario
A-12 (Infantry)	Farnham, Quebec
A-13 (Infantry)	Valcartier, Quebec
A-14 (Infantry)	Aldershot, NS
A-15 (Infantry)	Shilo, Manitoba
A-16 (Infantry)	Calgary, Alberta
A-17 (Machine Gun)	Trois-Rivières, Quebec
A-18 (Machine Gun)	Dundurn, Saskatchewan
A-19 (Service Corps)	Camp Borden, Ontario
A-20 (Service Corps)	Red Deer, Alberta
A-21 (Ordnance)	Barriefield, Ontario
A-22 (Medical)	Ottawa, Ontario
A-23 (Coast Defence)	Eastern Passage, NS
A-25 (Small Arms)	Long Branch, Ontario
A-26 (Small Arms)	Nanaimo, BC
A-40 (Administration)	St.-Hyacinthe, Quebec

Officer Training Centres

01	Brockville, Ontario
02	Gordon Head, BC

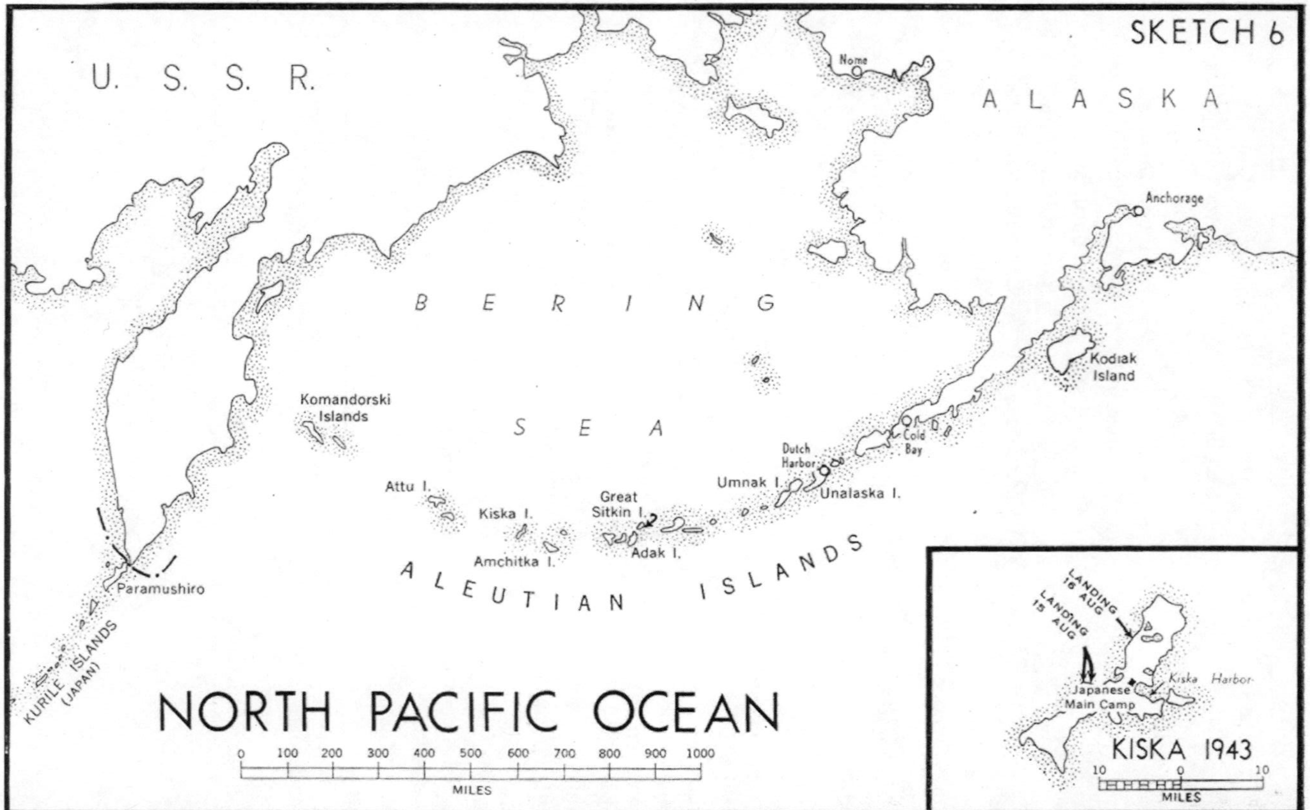

Figure 3 The Aleutian Islands and Canadian Landings on Kiska, August 15–16, 1943.
Source: C.P. Stacey, *Official History of the Canadian Army in the Second World War*, vol. 1: *Six Years of War: The Army in Canada, Britain and the Pacific* (Ottawa: Queen's Printer, 1955), 494.

Zombie Army

Introduction

DURING THE SECOND WORLD WAR, compulsory military service took on the longest, most comprehensive form that it has ever had in Canada. Under the authority of the National Resources Mobilization Act (NRMA) of June 1940, more than 150,000 men were compelled to undergo training and serve for up to four years on home defence duties in the Canadian army – over 15 percent of the total of 1.1 million men and women who served in the country's three armed services during the war. Until 1944, conscripts were not forced to serve overseas. Almost 60,000 agreed to change their status after they had enlisted, however, providing 10 percent of all of the army's wartime volunteers. Another 60,000 remained available to man countless defence posts and other establishments across Canada, thus releasing a similar number of volunteers to proceed to Europe. The bulk of that latter 60,000 were still in uniform in late 1944, when shortages of reinforcements led to a crisis over sending 16,000 of them overseas that almost tore apart the government of Prime Minister William Lyon Mackenzie King.[1]

The numbers raised by conscription are significant. Yet the direct effects of this massive wartime mobilization have largely been forgotten. Few historians have investigated the creation, administration, or impact of the training system that was set up under the NRMA, or the experiences of the hundreds of thousands of Canadians who were subjected to it. Instead, attention has focused on political aspects of conscription, partly due to the sheer significance of the issue during the Second World War, and partly due to the reliance of most historians on the records of Prime Minister King and his Cabinet colleagues to tell the story of the events. Early on, historians also came to concentrate on these aspects thanks to a sensational allegation reported by Bruce Hutchison in *Maclean's* in 1952. In an excerpt from an upcoming popular biography of King, Hutchison revealed for the first time the prime minister's claim that in 1944 he had been confronted with a "revolt of the generals" that had forced him to extend conscription to overseas service or face mass resignations by the army's senior leaders. According to King, by taking matters into their own hands in this manner the generals had threatened the very foundation of democracy in Canada. So he had yielded in order to preserve at least the outward appearance of civilian control.[2]

As a result of studying conscription from this perspective, a number of historians have come to be particularly critical of the army's role in wartime events. King's official biographer, R. MacGregor Dawson, was motivated by Hutchison's revelations to interview participants and prepare three advance chapters on the subject, which were later published separately after he died (although this meant he was unable to go back and perhaps reconsider his initial, more critical reactions). While dismissing the notion of an outright revolt, Dawson viewed developments from the point of view of King and other political leaders who had firmly opposed extending conscription to overseas service. He took the generals to task for the large, inflexible training organization they had built up in Canada during the Second World War, and for what he considered to be their open resistance to attempts to find alternatives to sending the conscripts overseas in 1944.[3] Later accounts by J.L. Granatstein and J.M. Hitsman relied on more thorough research in the papers of the various political figures who had been involved, but also ultimately blamed the army's commanders for a lack of foresight in building up a military force larger than could be maintained through voluntary service.[4] In 2001, Michael Stevenson investigated the actual machinery that had been created to mobilize civilian manpower below the political level. But given that he studied events almost entirely from the point of view of the key government agency that had to reconcile the competing needs for men between the military and other parts of Canada's war effort, he too tended to be critical of the army's constant demands.[5] Most recently, Richard Walker has been even more damning in his judgments of the senior generals who commanded the wartime army, suggesting that they knowingly misled and even coerced their civilian masters into accepting a force that was too large to be maintained throughout the war, without regard for the consequences.[6]

Even those authors who have explained the role of the army more sympathetically have tended to concentrate on its actions mainly because of their political implications with respect to conscription. In 1956, E.L.M. Burns, a former Canadian general and one of the architects of the army's wartime conscription machinery, produced a thorough study of how the army had used its human resources during the war, titled *Manpower in the Canadian Army*. In its pages, he suggested that political factors such as prewar neglect of military affairs by the politicians, their requirement that military leaders maintain two distinct administrative systems for conscripts and volunteers before 1944, and the wish for reasons of sovereignty to maintain a national reinforcement system completely independent of Britain's overseas (and for two separate theatres, after Canadian troops became engaged in both Italy and northwest Europe in 1943–44) had all helped cause waste and inefficiency in wartime mobilization.

As a result, even if it was not entirely their own fault, the army had used too many men, and by 1944 there were no alternatives to sending conscripts overseas.[7] In a somewhat similar vein, historians such as J.E. Rea and David Allan Wilson have argued that the army also grew to be larger than intended in those years because of the reluctance of the federal Cabinet to face having to reign in either it or various other aspects of the country's larger war effort.[8] In the most thorough account of the military aspects of the crisis to date, C.P. Stacey, the army's official historian, concluded in 1970 that senior officers had only acted properly and done their constitutional duty in late 1944 by trying to make their political superiors aware that the overseas army no longer had enough volunteers to sustain it in its present form.[9] But even Stacey's primary focus remained to explain the background to and the events of the crisis around the Cabinet table, rather than to examine in great detail developments at lower levels within the army itself.

This book goes below the political level to explore the actual role of the Canadian army in creating and administering compulsory military training during the Second World War, and particularly the influence of H.D.G. "Harry" Crerar, its overall commander when the program was introduced in 1940, and later its commander in northwest Europe in 1944–45. While conscripts were not compelled to serve overseas until late 1944, from the time the program was first created in 1940 many men changed their status voluntarily. Faced with a directive from civilian leaders to design a program to mobilize and train conscripts, but one that their political superiors were for the most part then satisfied to leave to the army to run as long as it did not later result in having to send conscripts overseas, Crerar and his subordinates allowed many of their own personal and – even more importantly – professional ambitions for the place of the army in Canada after the war to shape the result. In particular, in their desire to create a large, powerful army that could take a leading role in the fighting overseas (and therefore gain greater recognition among postwar Canadians), they deliberately organized the army's training system to encourage as many conscripts as possible to convert after the men had been placed in uniform. One consequence was that although for the early part of the war Crerar still tended at heart to be a conscriptionist, he and to a greater extent his fellow senior officers seem to have convinced themselves that they could maintain a larger volunteer force in Europe than had at first been thought possible, simply by calling out more conscripts for home defence whenever necessary. Based on that certainty, they then convinced their political superiors to authorize what became known at the time and later as the "big army" of five divisions and ancillary units that was eventually formed overseas. This study's review of these developments will provide a fuller answer than has been put forward by previous historians as to why military officials were prepared to push so hard for the "big army" during the first half of the war (and, even more importantly, why their political superiors were willing to accept it).

Another consequence of the way that conscription evolved after 1940 was that increasing pressures were placed on the conscripts to volunteer for overseas service. Ultimately, this led to allegations of verbal and even physical abuse. Using statistical records and other sources that have been unknown or ignored until now, this book explores the history of all 157,841 men who served as conscripts between 1940 and 1945 – their ethnic, linguistic, religious, and occupational backgrounds, their experiences of compulsory training, the ways that army officials attempted to convince them to volunteer once they were in uniform, and the responses of conscripts themselves to those pressures. By the middle of the war, the Canadian public knew them pejoratively as "zombies," after the undead movie monsters of the 1930s, who mindlessly obeyed their masters' commands without feeling or opposition. Nobody was quite sure where exactly the term originated.[10] But many people assumed that they were mostly French Canadian, or from other ethnic groups that did not share the dominant British Canadian beliefs of the time. Yet more than has been previously realized, these men tended to reflect the makeup of the country as a whole. And they had many reasons for refusing to volunteer. No historian has explored these aspects of conscription in detail until now.

By 1944, almost all of the country's easily available reserves of manpower had been exhausted, and only those men who had firmly resisted all attempts to make them volunteer seemed available as potential reinforcements. Suddenly, the army's leaders discovered that they might have to ask their political superiors to order conscripts overseas after all. The federal Cabinet agreed to do so, but only after weeks of acrimonious debate, the forced resignation of the federal defence minister, J.L. Ralston, and the voluntary exit of another powerful minister, C.G. Power.[11] Prime Minister King came to see the crisis as a betrayal by his military leaders, with negative consequences for the larger and more influential postwar army that H.D.G. Crerar had been hoping to build as a result of its wartime successes. The events of late 1944 are much more understandable, however, when we know how conscription actually operated below the political level, the characteristics of the conscripts themselves, and how all of this came together to affect events.

This study also provides considerable information about how Canada's entire wartime army was mobilized, and how hundreds of thousands of both conscripts and volunteers experienced military training and service during the war. The ability to raise so many additional soldiers through the NRMA, at a time when Canada was also greatly threatened generally, led to the creation of a domestic network of training camps and defences larger than anything Canadians have ever experienced on their own soil, before or since. The daily sight of hundreds of men in uniform in dozens of small communities across the country was a regular reminder of the war's huge scope and its potential human costs for all Canadians.[12] Beyond that, conscription itself became part of the collective experience of an even larger number of Canadians who were friends, parents, brothers, sisters, girlfriends, and spouses of men called out under the NRMA. At an even broader level, almost no Canadian male between the ages of eighteen and forty-five escaped being affected by some aspect of the military mobilization system during the war. Thus, the NRMA is a significant part of the history of Canada in its own right and should be better known.

Furthermore, this study highlights the degree to which at least some French Canadians participated in military activities, both in the training centres and among the larger public. As a result of the NRMA, large numbers of francophones entered the Canadian army, even if not all of them did so willingly. Senior officers were forced to deal with the situation by creating many new French Canadian training centres and military units and finding French-speaking officers to command them. Although the participation rate of French Canadians never came close to matching that of their English Canadian counterparts, National Defence Headquarters calculated in March 1944 that they made up 19.1 percent of the army's total strength, including conscripts (perhaps as many as 95,000 French-speaking volunteers alone served during the war as a whole, and 132,000 in the three services in total). This was a small proportion of Quebec's population compared to other provinces, but a considerable number in real terms.[13] And while opportunities for French Canadians to use their own language within the army remained limited beyond the unit level, they gained the ability to function in French to an extent greater than before, and English- and French-speaking soldiers themselves often worked closely together, getting to know each other better not only overseas but in numerous defence posts up and down the east and west coasts of North America (and even slightly beyond). These developments predated by more than two decades, and helped lay some of the groundwork for, the bilingual policies the federal government developed from the late 1960s onwards.[14] And while we have tended to focus on the statements and actions of the most vocal nationalist critics in describing Quebec's opposition towards conscription and the war,[15] many leading political and religious figures as well as press organs actually supported Canada's participation. They were able to distinguish between conscription for overseas service (which was still clearly opposed by a large majority of Quebec's French-speaking population) and conscription to help defend the soil of Canada, and they were aware that some Quebeckers might wish to play an even more willing role overseas as volunteers.[16] Yet this has all largely been forgotten, by both English- and French-language historians. It was certainly a surprise to me as an anglophone historian, when I began my own research on this subject in the mid-1990s, although since then a dedicated group of French-speaking authors has been attempting to revive the memory of this part of French Canada's war effort.[17] I hope my own work will add to that understanding.

One thing this book unfortunately is not, is a detailed study of the personal feelings and reactions of individual conscripts towards their time in uniform. While the sources I found in my research allowed me to reconstruct the character and experiences of the NRMA men, as a group, to a degree much greater than I first expected, my focus remained on administrative sources, to reconstruct the decision-making that took place regarding how such men would be used within the larger Canadian army. In addition, while in the course of my research I met a few individuals and families who were indirectly affected by compulsory military service in some manner during the war, the prevailingly negative public attitudes that were expressed towards conscripts in the 1940s have tended to make it difficult to locate people who experienced such service more directly, even today. But I do hope that this book will help spur a few among the shrinking number of remaining veterans who experienced conscription first-hand, to record their memories and make them available to archival depositories for the benefit of future historians.

Lastly, in carrying out this study I have been influenced from the beginning by the fact that every historian who writes about politics in the first half of the twentieth century has available to him or her the well-known personal diaries of Prime Minister King. First published in edited form between 1960 and 1970, they have since been made available directly to the public and today are fully available online.[18] In their detailed, comprehensive entries, they do provide a wealth of information about almost every aspect of Canada's Second World War effort. Yet, ultimately, they were produced by King himself, and as Tim Cook has recently noted, as part of King's process of using his diary to help bring himself to political decisions (or to justify his reasons for making them, after the fact), "he had an amazing capacity to deceive himself, or to make sense of the day by slighting others and putting himself in the best light."[19] For this reason, whenever possible in my own research I have tried to make greater use of other sources, such as the now mostly published accounts of behind-the-scenes events recorded by journalist Grant Dexter, and the minutes of the

Cabinet War Committee that oversaw most key decision-making from 1940 onwards. All of these have also been consulted by other historians, but perhaps not so deliberately as I have, as alternatives to the King diaries. I make no apologies that my goal is to describe the events surrounding conscription at the highest political levels from these alternative points of view rather than from King's, even while acknowledging that clearly he played one of the most important roles in (and almost always had the final word on) Canadian policy-making during the Second World War.

Overall, then, the goal of this book is to remind readers of the extent to which Canada, the Canadian army, and the political debates of the war were all shaped by the way the wartime compulsory training system was set up and functioned between 1940 and 1945. In doing so, I hope to make readers more aware of the degree to which conscription was a fact of life for every citizen in those years, and especially how it came to affect tens of thousands of people directly. While it has not been a part of our country's history since the Second World War, it is worth remembering that, for a considerable time during those years, conscription was of more than simply abstract academic interest for millions of Canadians.

Part 1: The Historical Legacy

The Zombie Psalm[1]

Mackenzie King is my Shepherd,
I shall not wander.
He maketh me not to wear the G.S. Badge.
He restoreth my vote.
He leadeth me along the paths of Canada for
his Party's sake.
Yea, though I move about from one camp to another
I fear no draft.
For Mackenzie King is with me.
His Government and his Cabinet they comfort me.
He prepareth a table before me
In the presence of my Active enemies.
He does not clip my hair too short.
My glass runneth over with Canadian beer,
Surely the Government will not alter this
Its policy at this late date
And I shall live in the confines of Canada forever.

AMEN

1
Conscription and Canadian History, 1627–1939

THE MANNER IN WHICH conscription was instituted after 1939 was shaped in many ways by the memory of what had occurred in the First World War, and even before. It was a response particularly to the attitudes of French Canadians towards conscription, and towards the Canadian army in general, as both evolved before 1914 and then were exacerbated by the European conflict that began in that year. Full-time professional troops had been provided only rarely by the metropolitan authorities for the first 150 years of French Canadian history (and almost never in large numbers); as a consequence, most French Canadians came to see the very real need to perform regular military service to help protect their homes, first against the neighbouring Iroquois, with whom they found themselves at war for much of the 1600s, and then against their English counterparts in the Thirteen Colonies to the south. As early as 1627, all male residents of the French settlement of Port Royal had been ordered to help provide for its defence, and the earliest records of a militia organization in Quebec date from 1636. By the early 1670s, a more formal system had been created, wherein all male citizens between sixteen and sixty were divided into separate units for each district, and directed to meet every one or two weeks to practise marksmanship and other basic military skills. The system was so widespread that the militia captains who commanded local units came to be relied on as part of the larger governing apparatus of the colony. And in times of war, thousands of men reported for duty, not only to fight but to perform any number of other vital functions, such as helping move supplies or guard lines of communication.[1] During the Seven Years' War in the late 1750s, so many men answered their calls that agricultural production was disrupted, and flour and other provisions that were normally produced locally had to be imported from France simply to allow the colony's military forces to keep fighting.[2]

Yet from the beginning, the distinction was clear that French Canadian militiamen were there mostly to help protect their own homes and families rather than to serve larger imperial interests. Complaints were received as early as the 1690s, when settlers were called out to perform military duties in peacetime in place of regular troops.[3] Immediately after the fall of New France in 1763, roughly three hundred volunteers from the administrative regions of Quebec City, Trois-Rivières, and Montreal served in the British campaign that helped end the Pontiac Rebellion of 1763–66, by Aboriginal groups who were resisting Britain's new dominance of eastern North America. But General James Murray had some trouble finding enough men to provide even his small share from the Quebec area who were ready to undertake such a distant expedition.[4] When the American Revolution broke out a decade later, it was not clear at first whether French Canadians would side with the British or the Americans. Hundreds turned out to fight on each side. When the British began planning a counterattack under General John Burgoyne that would result in his defeat at the Battle of Saratoga in October 1777, a new law was passed that formally revived the local militia organization from the French period, and included the return of compulsory service. French Canadians who were called out under its provisions were unhappy that they were expected to help invade the new United States rather than defend their homes, and as they crossed the frontier they began to desert in droves.[5] This was the first step in breaking down their allegiance to their by then lengthy military traditions.[6]

In spite of that experience, French Canadians remained willing to serve the British to help defend Canadian territory. They joined the Royal Canadian Volunteer Regiment, a provincial corps raised by the British for service only in North America, during the French and Napoleonic Wars after 1793, and the *Voltigeurs canadiens* under Lieutenant-Colonel Charles de Salabarry, a French Canadian career officer in the British regular army, in the lead-up to the War of 1812. Most militiamen also reported for duty when called out on the outbreak of the war that June, although in the Lachine area some rural units resisted because they did not want to have to leave their farms at the height of the agricultural season. Led by the *Voltigeurs*, French Canadian militiamen formed the bulk of the force that won the Battle of Chateauguay against an invading American army in October 1813.[7] As Allan Greer has argued, in the approach to the Rebellions of 1837–38 the militia was still such a large part of rural French Canadian society that Patriote supporters called on local militia captains, who tended to be elected by consensus by their men, to aid the cause. And hundreds of its members later fought on the Patriote side.[8]

In a broader sense, from the beginning of French settlement in North America the society that would later come to be centred within the province of Quebec also evolved to be different from the later English Canadian population. By the 1760s, New France was heavily influenced by its Roman Catholic faith, by a firm attachment to the land and rural values that seemed to have allowed its population to grow and flourish, and by a French language that distinguished it from the predominantly English-speaking European population of much of the rest of the continent. They were then left to survive largely on their own after Britain defeated France in North America in 1763, and were cut off even more from their former mother country by the outbreak of the French Revolution, largely thanks to revulsion at the revolutionaries' attacks on the Catholic Church there in the early 1790s. In contrast, the Church came to play an even greater spiritual and even political role in guiding French Canadian society over the years. Its leaders usually supported British and later federal Canadian authority at times when francophones seemed to be under threat in Canada, in order to preserve their own position as well as to avoid provoking attacks that might undermine the freedom of religion and other rights that French Canadians had won within the British Empire. By the end of the 1800s, the former French settlers felt little direct attachment to France, from which they were now many generations removed, in contrast to the way many English Canadians retained their more immediate ties to Britain as the new mother country that guided Canada's fortunes. Although industrialization and urbanization were already transforming Quebec society just like that of the rest of the country by the early 1900s, a significant proportion of French-speaking Canadians continued to live in the countryside. Demographically, French Canadian men and women continued to marry younger and to have more children, compared to the rest of Canada. During the First World War, this would mean that such men were either less able or less willing (or both) to leave their families to go off and fight in foreign lands, where they would most likely have to deal with not being able to speak French, as well as more difficult access to religious and other cultural supports.[9] Partly thanks to the influence of the Catholic Church, familiarity with military traditions remained alive in one form, cadet corps being supported as much or more strongly in Quebec than the rest of the country for the way that they helped to reinforce a trinity of healthy mind, body, and spirit. By 1914, 40,000 young men were enrolled in such corps across Canada and military training was beginning at the university level. A good proportion of both programs were offered in Quebec.[10]

Conscription had also been known to the early English-speaking settlers of Canada before the 1900s. But ironically, they had never accepted it quite so strongly. As James Wood has recently argued, English views towards maintaining armed forces in peacetime were shaped by the tradition of the navy, rather than the army, providing the bulwark of the country's defence. And while most average English-speaking citizens might not have thought consciously about it, their aversion towards maintaining a large peacetime military organization was also shaped by the negative memory of their country's Civil War, and especially the resulting seizure of power by the military under Oliver Cromwell in the mid-1600s.[11] English-speaking settlers in one part of what would later become Canada also experienced divided loyalties during the American Revolution, along the lines of those experienced within Quebec, in this case because the majority of the population in Nova Scotia had arrived very recently from New England and preferred not to have to help actively defend their colony against attack from their former neighbours.[12] And despite the myth that was created in English Canada in later years about their loyal service during the War of 1812, most men in the colony of Upper Canada ignored calls to turn out and fight in particular battles during the conflict, tending instead to report only after the guns had gone silent so that they could surrender to American commanders and legally avoid having to perform further military duty by claiming right of "parole."[13]

The result of these various trends was that by the 1850s in British North America, while conscription remained a theoretical obligation for all able-bodied men, political leaders had come to rely mostly on the imperial army to provide local defences, aided by domestic militias only when absolutely necessary. When Britain's regular troops were recalled in large numbers to fight in the Crimean War in Europe, members of the colonial government in what were by then the united Canadas decided to build on the growing enthusiasm of a number of citizens who had become dissatisfied with the current state of the militia to raise a semi-permanent force of 5,000 men in 1855. Weapons and other equipment were supplied at public expense, and members were paid to train for ten days a year (later six) in order to provide some greater readiness in the event of war. The policy was so popular that more units were soon authorized, whose members at first could not even be paid. Yet what became known as the Non-Permanent Active Militia (NPAM) was largely an English-speaking institution. Only about one-quarter of the units in Canada East, and one small company in Bytown (later Ottawa), Canada West, were French-speaking. Expanded before Confederation in response to increasing worries about the American buildup to the south during the Civil War there, and after 1867 to include forces that had been created in the separate colonies of New Brunswick and Nova Scotia in the same period, it came to number closer to 40,000 men.[14]

At the head of the post-Confederation militia was a francophone, George-Étienne Cartier, as Minister of Militia and Defence. And in the early years after 1867, he consciously tried to encourage both English- and French-speaking Canadians to participate. Quebec was organized into three military districts, two of which were to be staffed by French-speaking officers and to include French-speaking units.[15] Out of a total reported strength of 37,170 men across the country in 1868, 6,812 or 18.3 percent came from these two districts, and perhaps as many as 2,000 French Canadians were part of the third primarily

"English-speaking" one. Thus, a proportion of French Canadian men did remain committed to serving voluntarily in the military. The commanders of the two French-speaking districts even argued that more men would serve if it was made compulsory, as it had been under the old traditions, so that employers would not penalize those who wished to miss work to attend training.[16]

While the North-West Rebellion of 1885 was and remains a low point in Canada's relations with Aboriginal peoples, the response was organized by another francophone Minister of Militia and Defence, Adolphe Caron, and the fighting on the government side was carried out almost entirely by volunteers from the Canadian militia. Among them were the French-speaking 65th *Carabiniers Mont-Royal* and the 9th *Voltigeurs de Québec*. But due to worries on the part of the British officer assigned to command the militia, Frederick Middleton, that they would be required to face the French-speaking *métis* in battle, he assigned the two units only secondary roles. These developments, along with the animosities that arose between English and French Canadians over whether to execute Louis Riel for treason afterwards, further soured the latter's views towards participating in larger Canadian military affairs.[17]

The NPAM declined everywhere during a time of extremely rigid budgets from the 1870s to the 1890s. Rural units suffered the most, as their once-a-year summer training camps were cancelled as an economy measure, and since a larger proportion of French Canadian units were rural, they suffered worst of all. Urban units remained popular among both English and French Canadians. In Montreal, as many as 2,000 civilian spectators regularly attended the evening training periods of the *Voltigeurs*, and crowds at the *Carabiniers*' annual public inspections reached as high as 50,000.[18] But increasing attempts to make the militia less political and more professional as a whole, also made it even more British in character thanks to reliance on the current mother country to provide various officers, training standards, and other models to guide its evolution, as well as the increasing strength of imperial sentiment among English Canadians generally by the late 1800s.[19] Among the most frequently cited examples of the militia commanders' insensitivity to the desires of French Canadians was their refusal to authorize an attempt to revive a battalion in Montreal by permitting it to wear *Zouave* uniforms to link it to recent Catholic traditions in Europe, because doing so would have strayed too far from British traditions. From the time of its founding in 1876, the Royal Military College of Canada (RMC) required cadets to function entirely in English, and to pursue heavily mathematics-based studies rather than the more traditional liberal arts that were at the core of most French Canadian educational programs. The goal of enhancing professionalism was furthered by the creation after 1871 of what came to be known as the Permanent Force, whose individual units were to serve as year-round schools for the NPAM. The first, an artillery battery created in Quebec City when the last British regular troops left Canada in 1871, contained a sizable number of francophones, and a French-speaking infantry headquarters was formed at St-Jean after 1883. But the latter remained very small, and in 1880 the artillery battery was exchanged with its counterpart in the anglophone centre of Kingston, Ontario. In the words of historian Desmond Morton: "The bilingual character of the unit was lost within a few years."[20]

Canada's involvement in the South African War from 1899 to 1902 brought differences between English- and French-speaking Canadians further into the open. Small but vocal groups of critics emerged in English Canada among farmers, labour groups, German and Irish Canadians (who respectively identified ethnically with the Dutch Boers, or against the British due to ongoing sectarian conflicts in the British Isles), and individual religious leaders and pacifist groups.[21] Not all French Canadians opposed the war, and careful efforts were made to try to ensure that they were represented in the first contingent that sailed for South Africa in October 1899. A total of six contingents and 7,368 Canadian volunteers were eventually raised to serve there. But many French Canadians also identified with the Boers, given that they were another linguistic minority surrounded by and facing pressure from a larger British majority. From their perspective, the conflict was also far from Canada's shores and was being fought to further British imperial interests rather than direct Canadian ones. Ultimately, French Canadians made up only 5.4 percent of the first contingent and under 3 percent of all Canadian recruits.[22]

The differences between English and French Canadians were reflected in the Cabinet of Prime Minister Wilfrid Laurier, the first francophone to hold the post after Confederation. One of his overriding goals throughout his career was to preserve national unity by trying to find a middle ground that could allow English and French Canadians to live in compromise.[23] In the case of the Boer War, he managed to hammer out an agreement that the first contingent would be raised, equipped, and officered by Canadians, but would come under British control as soon as it arrived in South Africa, to make it clear that he was not setting a precedent that Canadians would automatically support future imperial adventures.[24] Even then, one of Laurier's protegés, Liberal MP Henri Bourassa, resigned his seat in protest against what he saw as a precedent (in fact if not in theory) as well as against British treatment of the Boers generally. He was re-elected by acclamation, making him a rising star among nationalists in Quebec, who were also growing concerned about other ways in which English Canadians seemed to be pushing aside the rights of French Canadians in battles over the preservation of French outside the province. Bourassa and other nationalists did not necessarily speak for all or even a majority of francophones in Quebec. But as a result of events in 1899, he began to attract support among other French Canadian elites, who saw him as standing up for their community against threats especially to their language of education in various parts of Canada.[25] For a time, Laurier's efforts to promote compromise helped keep larger divisions from appearing. They also helped him to stay in power for over fifteen years – still today the longest uninterrupted period of rule by any Canadian prime minister.

Laurier's downfall was finally brought about in part by another debate over Canadian defence policy, in 1911. Thanks to technological changes, as well as the rise of several countries as political and economic rivals by the early twentieth century, British governments found themselves increasingly pressed to maintain the naval dominance the Empire had enjoyed for the previous century. In 1909, a short-term panic led to fears that Germany would take the lead in building modern battleships. In an attempt to find a compromise once again, Laurier decided to create a separate and distinct Canadian naval service that would be controlled by the Canadian government in times of peace but could be placed under command of the Royal Navy in times of war. Bourassa and other nationalist figures within Quebec again challenged him, arguing that this would simply make it easier to place Canadian sailors in the hands of the British to serve the latter's interests. As was sometimes his habit, Bourassa allowed his rhetoric to take him beyond what was realistically likely, and argued that even conscription would probably become necessary to maintain the strength of the navy given that it would be subject to constant use by the British. Thus, by the early 1900s, at least among Bourassa and his followers, conscription had come to be seen as a negative force to compel French Canadians to serve interests beyond their own homeland. For his part, Conservative leader Robert Borden initially supported creating a separate naval force. But under pressure from French and English Canadian wings within his own party that were more divided between extremes than was the case among the Liberals, he eventually came to a somewhat more awkward solution. He opposed the existing naval plan as either going too far or not far enough for his supporters, depending on to whom he was addressing his particular arguments, and he also promised to provide an immediate cash payment to Britain to help them build more battleships now. When a wide-ranging free trade deal with the United States also materialized unexpectedly in 1911, Laurier called an early election, but then found himself facing a rising chorus of business people who opposed the deal in English Canada. Borden attacked Laurier on this front outside Quebec, while inside the province, nationalist-leaning Conservatives led by F.D. Monk cooperated openly with Bourassa to campaign against Laurier's navy. Laurier still won the most seats in Quebec, but with a reduced majority. And Borden won the election. With his English Canadian seats, he did not need support from his French Canadian MPs in order to remain in power, and he began to consider their advice less and less often. After further consultations with the British, in 1912 he decided to present a bill to Parliament to provide his cash payment, relying on closure for the first time in the history of the Canadian House of Commons to end the lengthy debate it engendered. But at the end of May 1913, the Liberal-dominated Senate sent the bill back, and ultimately nothing was accomplished. The consequences could not have been foreseen at the time, but over the next few years Borden would be keenly affected by the lack of major voices within his party to help him understand French Canada's concerns during the First World War.[26] And in the meantime, English Canadian opinion towards military affairs had gone in the opposite direction, towards supporting a more militant version of British imperialism, and a very small but influential and vocal group of intellectuals and other public figures even began to call for universal training, both to improve Canada's defence preparedness and for its perceived health and other benefits.[27]

When Britain went to war in August 1914, Canada was also automatically at war. Both Laurier and Bourassa famously agreed that Canada should take an active role in the conflict. So did Catholic leaders and most other organs of public opinion in Quebec. But Bourassa was careful to make clear that he saw the war as justified more for the dispassionate reason that Britain and France had to maintain the balance of power compared to Germany in Europe, and he argued that Canada should not participate beyond its own rational capacity to contribute.[28] At first, it seemed that the principle of voluntary as opposed to compulsory service would allow the country to play a role in the war to the limits of even its most ardent supporters. Within days, Borden's Cabinet agreed to send a force of 25,000 volunteers to Europe. Thanks to the mistrust of professional military officers in favour of the part-time militia by its minister, Sam Hughes, as well as what he saw as the need to get Canadians overseas as quickly as possible generally, he dismissed the existing mobilization plans, which had provided for an orderly call-up of units from the various military districts across the country. Instead, he sent a series of personal telegrams directly to commanders across the country, almost all of whom were English Canadian, and instructed them to collect suitable volunteers and bring them directly to a new camp that was to be built at Valcartier, Quebec. Eight weeks later, 30,621 Canadians were sailing for England, a justifiable accomplishment at the time but one that left what would become the Canadian Expeditionary Force (CEF) to have to work out a number of difficulties after they arrived in England.[29]

More significantly, while a considerable number of French Canadians (1,245) were part of the first contingent of volunteers to proceed overseas in the fall of 1914, all were submerged within larger English-speaking units. This suggested that at least some were ready to serve – approximately 15,000 did so as volunteers in the army throughout the war, 5,000 in other British and Allied forces, and 15,000 as conscripts overseas, or in total roughly 11 percent of the 318,705 Canadian-born men who served within the CEF, and 5.6 percent of the entire strength of 619,636 men in the CEF, including British-born citizens.[30] It also showed the spirit of cooperation with which lower-level commanders had responded to the confusion into which Hughes threw mobilization, in that smaller groups of French-speaking soldiers were welcomed into the entirely new, composite, numbered infantry battalions and engineering, artillery, and other units that were formed as small and disparate groups of volunteers poured in from various cities and regions. Anonymous-sounding numbered units would become the model for organizing the entire CEF for the rest of the war. As it became obvious that the fighting would last longer than people had initially expected, in September the Borden government decided to double its contribution by raising a second contingent. By December 1914 they were planning for a third. In Sam Hughes's world, there was no understanding that French Canadians as a group might not automatically support a war outside North America as ardently as English Canadians, and only after a large delegation of influential Quebeckers led by Dr. Arthur Mignault waited on Borden in Ottawa was the 22nd Battalion finally authorized specifically as a unit for French-speaking soldiers as part of the second contingent.[31] Over the next year, further waves of Canadian troops were raised and proceeded overseas, and the government increased its authorized totals of Canadian volunteers that it promised to maintain in uniform to 150,000 in July 1915, and 250,000 that November. Finally, on January 1, 1916, without even consulting his full Cabinet, Borden announced a grandiose target of 500,000 men (out of a total Canadian population of about eight million at the time). While the reasons for his actions are not entirely clear, at that point recruiting still seemed to be going well. It was also a way to try to help inspire further efforts. In addition, historians have suggested that Borden had begun to realize the lack of influence Canada was having in shaping British direction of the war effort, and that he saw the new number as a significant enough increase in its commitments to justify such influence.[32]

By the fall of 1916 a Canadian Corps of four divisions was serving in France, and a fifth division was forming in England, along with a number of separate

Canadian formations in other roles. Gradually, career officers took control of mobilization and other operations within Canada. Courses provided by more experienced British military authorities, not to mention the large number of British staff officers who were assigned directly to the Canadian Corps to help guide it for most of the war, helped make the CEF the equal of any professional army on any side by 1918.[33] By 1917, Canadian generals Richard Turner and Arthur Currie had come to command the country's forces in England and France, respectively, thus directly guiding both their training and their operations in the field. At the highest level, in June 1918 Prime Minister Borden deliberately sought out Currie to provide independent military advice when dealing with British political leaders over the conduct of the war.[34] Yet despite prodigious efforts by individuals in local communities across Canada, who managed to maintain patriotic enthusiasm until well into 1916 (and who ultimately did find at least an overall total of upwards of 500,000 men for the army), by early 1917 the flow of volunteers had fallen off considerably. In addition, the Canadian economy, which had been idle in 1914, now needed more men to produce food, munitions, and other materials after having expanded to support the war. And the long lists of casualties from France had given Canadians a fuller sense of the true costs of volunteering. This had been one problem with Borden's and Hughes's whole understanding of the war: both men seem to have ignored the fact that after completed units were sent overseas, men might actually be injured or killed in the fighting and need to be replaced. This meant that many more than 500,000 volunteers would be necessary to maintain a force of that size for any length of time.[35] While several further French Canadian battalions were authorized to recruit in Canada, only one or two were able to reach full strength, due to problems of competition and duplication of effort that plagued recruiting across the country after 1915, as well as the lack of a more open acceptance of French-language contributions earlier in the war. None of the new battalions got farther than England before they had to be broken up to find enough reinforcements just to keep the 22nd Battalion at strength.[36]

By then, another primary reason why recruiting had fallen off among French Canadians was that discord had begun to appear more broadly between the two main language groups. English Canadians began to note with increasing insistence that their numbers of volunteers were larger than those of French Canadians. Not only had the latter been alienated by the frustrations of the recruiting system but, as we have seen, they viewed participation in British wars differently from English Canadians. Furthermore, the bulk of French Canadians still lived in rural areas, where enlistment rates tended to be lower across the country due to the complex needs of agriculture (and especially its large demands on male family members) as well as to wartime publicity campaigns that encouraged farmers to increase production for the war effort. And Quebeckers did marry earlier and have children at a younger age than elsewhere, which meant that fewer of them could leave their homes as easily to go off and serve. According to figures that were calculated for Parliament at the height of wartime debates in Canada in 1917, Quebec had far fewer single men between twenty and forty-five – the likeliest group from which to be able to find volunteers – with a total of 143,540, compared to Ontario at 243,050. These figures were 22.2 percent and 33.6 percent, respectively, of all single men in the country in that age group. In comparison, each province's overall share of the national population (including men and women) was 27.8 percent and 35.1 percent.[37] And just 51.4 percent of the entire CEF was Canadian-born, suggesting that recruiting numbers outside Quebec were inflated by recent immigrants with stronger ties to Europe, and especially to Britain (38.3 percent).[38] Feelings between the two groups were also aggravated by the revival of old animosities over the language of schooling outside Quebec, and specifically by Regulation 17, which limited the use of French in Roman Catholic education in Ontario.[39] At the outbreak of the war, the rush to volunteer had seemed so positive that Borden had stated publicly that conscription would never be required.[40] Throughout 1916 and into 1917, federal leaders did everything else they could to find men, including creating a National Service Board to try to gain a better sense of how the expanding economy was affecting enlistment. The members of the Board advocated a mandatory national registration of manpower, which began in January 1917, but only after Cabinet had overruled them and made it voluntary. An abortive attempt was also made to create a Canadian Defence Force in the spring of 1917, comprised of volunteers who would serve only in Canada, so that others providing internal security could be released to go overseas. The army's overall commander as Chief of the General Staff (CGS) in Ottawa, Major-General Willoughby Gwatkin, suggested calling out the militia to meet this need, a use of conscription that might have been more acceptable since it was still technically a part of Canadian law and would clearly be limited to home defence. In a later memorandum, he even noted that it might help encourage some of such men to volunteer to serve overseas once they were in uniform. But instead the Cabinet relied on the voluntary Canadian Defence Force, which ultimately raised less than 200 men out of a planned 50,000. In early April the neighbouring United States entered the war, immediately instituting conscription. In mid-May, Borden returned from a trip to England and France, where he had seen first-hand the horrors of the war while visiting Canadian soldiers in military hospitals and at the front, and been told both by British leaders and by his own Canadian generals that even more men would be needed to win the conflict. After a brief consultation with his Cabinet, he reversed himself and publicly declared his government's support for conscription.[41]

Much as they do when discussing the Second World War, historians have come to focus mostly on the political aspects of how conscription was instituted in 1917–18. Certainly, the events were dramatic.[42] From the moment he announced his policy of conscription, Borden began trying to form a political coalition with the Liberal opposition. Laurier ultimately refused to participate, fearing that beyond his personal abhorrence as a traditional liberal at overriding the individual rights of Canadians in that way, conscription was clearly directed at French Canadians, and would alienate them from the Liberal Party and drive them into the arms of Bourassa, who Laurier feared might come to have an even greater influence and thus help divide English and French Canadians even further in the future.[43] Borden's government was old, had suffered from a number of scandals related to other aspects of Canada's mobilization during the first half of the war, and now seemed to be trying to use conscription to avoid having to face Canadians in an election that politicians had agreed in February 1916 to delay beyond the constitutional maximum of five years due to the fighting but that Laurier was less and less willing to continue to support. Nevertheless, Borden was eventually able to convince most other English-speaking national and provincial Liberal leaders to join him. He was aided in this goal by two blatantly political measures: the Military Voters Act, which created a system for collecting votes from serving soldiers overseas but seemed to give Conservative organizers considerable latitude to assign those votes to any constituency they wished in order to counteract Liberal support in particular ridings; and the Wartime Elections Act, which removed the right to vote from any immigrant who had been born in or whose mother tongue was that of an enemy country, and who had been naturalized as a Canadian resident after 1902 (most of whom tended to vote Liberal). At the same time, it granted the vote to all women who were the wives, widows, mothers, sisters, or daughters of serving soldiers.[44] The election that followed quickly became a national referendum on conscription, and saw some of the nastiest vitriol ever recorded in a Canadian campaign, with Borden's new Union Government increasingly targeting Henri Bourassa and Quebec as the cause of almost all of the country's ills during the war. The Unionists won a decisive victory, taking 153 out of 235 seats in the House of Commons. But the popular vote was much closer, and Liberals who had remained loyal to Laurier were elected in sixty-two out of sixty-five seats in Quebec. As a result, for at least a generation afterwards the Conservatives became the party of conscription there.

Just as would be the case during the Second World War, however, there was much more to conscription than simply its direct political impacts. In early August 1917, the Cartierville summer home of Lord Atholstan (Hugh Graham), the publisher of the *Montreal Star*, was dynamited due to his vocal support for the policy. By then, troops passing through Quebec City to sail overseas were being booed and pelted with rocks, ice, and rotten vegetables. Riots broke out in Montreal when the Military Service Act (MSA) that authorized conscription was formally enacted at the end of August, with shots fired into the air and windows broken. In Shawinigan a few days later, shops were looted and the local recruiting officer run out of town. Across the province, one man died and seven others were wounded in such incidents. The Dominion Police, meanwhile, were busy searching for the rest of the 350 pounds of explosives that had been stolen from a quarry at the beginning of August and used in the Cartierville bombing, as well as miscellaneous rifles that were said to be missing from

RAIN MONTREAL, THURSDAY, AUGUST 9, 1917

SCENE OF THE CARTIERVILLE DYNAMITE OUTRAGE

The dynamite was evidently placed under the corner of the house in the foreground. The force of the explosion was downward and inward. A large hole was torn through the lower foundations and the rooms above were badly shattered.

Figure 4 Newspaper clipping from the *Montreal Daily Star*, illustrating the damage suffered by the home of Lord Atholstan (Hugh Graham). *Source:* LAC, e-011157760.

various local cadet corps. Eventually, twelve men were arrested and tried for a list of further targets they claimed to have been planning to attack. More extreme speakers were calling for open rebellion. Nationalist Tancrède Marsil was quoted as saying that the people of Quebec would prefer to see "two or three thousand men killed in the streets" than the same number forced overseas, and labour activist Gédèon Martel proclaimed that "if they come to shoot us we will be the first to do the shooting." During the election itself, most Unionist candidates dared not even try to speak in most of the province. The enforcement of the MSA sparked even more serious rioting in Quebec City over the Easter weekend of 1918, when a man was arrested for being unable to produce his certificate proving exemption from military training, and crowds assembled and attacked the police station to which he had been taken. The rioting escalated from there, lasting for five days, killing at least four civilians, wounding 150 soldiers and townspeople, and causing $300,000 of damage. It only ended after the federal Cabinet ordered in hundreds of troops from other parts of the country (many of whom were recently enrolled English Canadian conscripts). In addition Henri Bourassa, higher Catholic clergymen and political officials all appealed for people to end the violence and respect authority. Signalling the depth of alienation felt by at least some French Canadians, Joseph-Napoléon Francoeur introduced a motion in the Quebec legislature in January 1918: "That this House is of [the] opinion that the Province of Quebec would be disposed to accept the breaking of the Confederation pact of 1867 if, in the other Provinces, it is believed she is an obstacle to the Union, progress and development of Canada." While he withdrew it after several members (including the premier, Lomer Gouin) rose to defend Confederation, more alarmist Canadians could be excused for thinking that the country itself seemed to be in danger of coming apart by early 1918.[45] And the trends seemed even more potentially threatening, just months after popular uprisings had led to the collapse of the tsarist government during the Russian Revolution.[46]

Moreover, Quebec was not the only place where divisions over related issues came into the open. As recruiting got more desperate in the still very German Canadian city of Berlin, Ontario, in 1916, pro- and anti-German accusations flew, and soldiers physically assaulted Lutheran clergyman C.R. Tappert for making statements defending local Germans. Two referenda were held that year that narrowly resulted in the city being renamed Kitchener, after the British war minister, Lord Kitchener, who died in the midst of the events when a ship on which he was a passenger struck a German mine. During the federal election of 1917, several thousand people clashed in the streets on the day of a visit from Robert Borden, and at his campaign rally that evening he was shouted down by the same crowd, which seemed especially upset about how conscription would impact the riding's rural residents.[47] Over several days in August 1918, mobs of returned soldiers attacked non-British ethnic groups in Toronto out of anger at the latter's supposedly having stayed behind and taken their jobs while they had been serving overseas. The violence only ended when five hundred troops were brought in from Camp Niagara and Mayor Tommy Church threatened to read the Riot Act.[48] In early 1919, returned men disrupted meetings by political radicals in several western cities, and in Winnipeg the attacks escalated into two days of rioting against similar ethnic groups.[49]

Among particular occupational groups, furthermore, farmers across Canada were incensed in late 1917 that conscription would take them and their sons away from agricultural production. At the high point of the election on December 2, the Union Government's new militia minister, Major-General Sydney Mewburn (Sam Hughes had finally been removed from office in late 1916) made a public statement on behalf of the Cabinet, promising a blanket exemption for farmers in order to retain their votes. But those exemptions were cancelled a few months afterwards, due to new worries over manpower overseas, after the German army launched a final attempt to win the war on the Western Front in March 1918. Five thousand farmers, mostly from Ontario and Quebec, descended on Ottawa in early May to make their anger known. Conscription was not the only issue about which rural groups were upset: the war had accelerated urbanization across the country, and rural communities had felt threatened by their resulting loss of social as well as political influence since well before 1914. The imposition of compulsory service by urban politicians in the face of rural opposition was seen as the final straw, and over the next few months and years, farmers expressed their resentment at the ballot box, winning control of provincial governments in Ontario, Alberta, and Manitoba between 1919 and 1922 and making strong showings in New Brunswick and Nova Scotia. At the national level, they won enough seats to form the official Opposition in the federal election of 1921. Internal debates over the exact part they should play in the political system precluded them from acting in that role, and by the end of the decade, Prime Minister King had largely succeeded in coaxing them into his revived Liberal Party.[50]

Also affected by conscription were industrial workers, and women. For the former, the war brought acceleration of the prewar trend of dilution of skilled labour in industry, in order to aid wartime production. Inflation greatly outstripped wage increases, and a series of increasingly stringent government controls culminated in September 1918 with the outlawing of the right to strike. Then, just as male labourers and their families were facing all of these pressures most strongly in late 1917 and early 1918, they found themselves in danger of being forcibly removed from their jobs and livelihoods by conscription. Workers in western Canada protested, sometimes violently, and large numbers openly evaded the MSA – on Vancouver Island, labour leader Albert "Ginger" Goodwin even died in mysterious circumstances after he was shot by a Dominion Police officer, allegedly for trying to escape after being apprehended but more likely in retaliation for his labour activism. Working-class anger was demonstrated in a wave of unrest across the country after the fighting ended, the best-remembered example being the Winnipeg General Strike of May and June 1919.[51]

For women, the war tends to be remembered by Canadians as a more positive experience, since they gained the vote, found jobs of their own replacing men in the factories, and seemed to win greater control over their lives generally. Yet as historians who have studied the topic in greater detail remind us, many women had already worked before the war, most of the other changes that took place after 1914 had already been well under way before then, and the conflict merely increased the pressures and demands placed on women as developments such as conscription came to divide society generally. In addition, 3,141 military nurses saw the costs of war first-hand (2,504 of them served overseas, and 46 died), and more than 2,000 women played somewhat similar roles in Voluntary Aid Detachments on the home front (at least 500 of them in military hospitals in Britain). Hundreds of thousands more women spent the war years worrying over the return of husbands, fathers, sons, or brothers who had left to fight.[52]

About the workings of the Military Service Act itself, and its impacts on the men who were placed in uniform after 1917, even less is known. In October, men were ordered to complete another national registration, this time compulsorily, so that the people in the Department of Justice who were assigned to administer the MSA would know exactly how many were available. When the first group of single men aged twenty to thirty-four was directed to begin reporting for potential service in November, 83 percent or more applied for exemptions in every province of Canada, on the basis of one or more of the very broad grounds permitted under the MSA. Ultimately, of the 401,882 men across the country who were expected to present themselves as potential recruits, only 25,253 did so without requesting exemptions of some kind (18,028 of whom ended up in uniform). Of the remainder, another 81,028 eventually had their exemptions refused or overturned, and a further 65,610 men aged twenty to twenty-two were called out after the farmers' exemptions were cancelled in March 1918, for a total of 146,638. Out of that number, 27,631 men refused to report for training throughout the operation of the MSA, and 24,139 remained at large at the end of the war. Of them, 18,827 or 68.1 percent were from Quebec (40.8 percent of all of the 46,104 men who were called from that province under the MSA – the next closest default rate was Nova Scotia, at 16.7 percent, Ontario was in the middle of the pack at 9.3 percent, and the overall default rate for the country was 19.4 percent). In the end, 86,144 men were put in uniform by the MSA, and another 19,644 volunteered for other CEF units and 7,673 for other countries' forces (for example, for the Royal Air Force training program that was then in operation in Canada). This means that the MSA provided 105,788 men for the CEF and 113,461 in total.[53] (For a detailed breakdown of the operation of the MSA, see Table 1.)

For many years, historians argued that delays in getting men into uniform caused by the complicated exemption process made conscription a failure in the First World War, since only 47,509 made it to England and 24,132 to France before the war ended. But more recently, we have come to recognize that these same numbers provided the Canadian Corps with a good portion of the men necessary to maintain it at full strength through some of the harshest fighting, in the last several months leading up to the armistice.[54] They also provided 1,653 out of 4,210 Canadian soldiers who were sent to Siberia in 1918–19 as part of an Allied attempt to combat the Bolsheviks who had seized power there, and thus bring Russia back into the war.[55] Unfortunately, aside from a single government report that was produced at the end of the war, and that provides most of the statistical information given above, historians have not investigated in detail how conscription was administered during the First World War, and how it affected the lives of individual Canadians. This is no doubt at least partly because of the political significance of the issue, again as was the case after the Second World War. But it is also because a few years after the war the man who had acted as the central appeal judge under the MSA, Justice Lyman Duff of the Supreme Court of Canada, deliberately destroyed the records of the almost 1,600 local and regional tribunals that had dealt with exemption requests. As he explained his reasoning in later years, "he could not bear the thought of having the conscription records placed anywhere where the public could reach them. The papers of the local tribunals and appeal bodies in Quebec were full of hatred and bitterness and would have been a living menace to national unity." According to Duff, in Quebec, French-speaking Canadians had been granted blanket exemptions, while almost every English-speaking request was rejected.[56] Two regional appeal judges also reportedly simply refused to hear the cases referred to them, effectively exempting all of their appellants, although it is not clear whether one or both of those judges were actually located in Quebec.[57]

Table 1

The operation of the Military Service Act, 1917–18

Province	Total population N	% ↓	Total registered[a] N	% ↓	Requested exemptions N	% ←	Did not request exemptions N	% ←	Number medically unfit	Reported voluntarily	Ordered to report	Total obtained	Total made available[b] N	% ↓
PEI	93,728	1.3	4,501	1.1	4,231	94.0	270	6.0	123	54	93	147	1,739	1.0
NS	492,338	6.8	25,616	6.4	23,556	92.0	2,060	8.0	843	521	696	1,217	11,122	6.2
NB	351,889	4.9	16,902	4.2	15,553	92.0	1,349	8.0	496	193	660	853	9,071	5.0
Quebec	2,005,776	27.8	115,602	28.8	113,291	98.0	2,311	2.0	423	1,065	823	1,888	55,814	31.0
Ontario	2,527,292	35.1	124,965	31.1	116,092	92.9	8,873	7.1	1,157	4,007	3,709	7,716	55,145	30.6
Manitoba	461,394	6.4	22,515	5.6	20,124	89.4	2,391	10.6	885	596	910	1,506	12,591	7.0
Sask.	492,432	6.8	45,536	11.3	43,318	95.1	2,218	4.9	740	374	1,104	1,478	14,863	8.3
Alberta	374,295	5.2	28,076	7.0	25,389	90.4	2,687	9.6	1,085	539	1,063	1,602	9,871	5.5
BC	392,480	5.4	18,169	4.5	15,075	83.0	3,094	17.0	1,181	763	1,150	1,913	9,717	5.4
Yukon/NWT	15,019	0.2	[N/A]		[N/A]		[N/A]		–	–	–	–	[N/A]	
Totals	*7,206,643*	*100.0*	*401,882*	*100.0*	*376,629*	*93.7*	*25,253*	*6.3*	*6,933*	*8,112*	*10,208*	*18,320*	*179,933*	*100.0*
												[18,028[c]]		

179,933 – 26,225[d] = *153,708*
– 16,108[e] = *137,600*
– 24,139[f] = *113,461*
– 27,317[g] = *86,144 men directly conscripted as part of MSA*

Notes:

a Number of eligible men (20 years old or over) as determined by compulsory national registration held October 13 to November 10, 1917 (H.A.C. Machin, *Report of the Director of the Military Service Branch* (Ottawa: King's Printer, 1919), 42.

b Total for this column includes all men whose claims were eventually rejected by local tribunals and/or on appeal (aggregate total of 49,140), 20–22-year-olds for whom exemptions were cancelled March 1918 and who were ordered to report or did so voluntarily (65,610), people whose exemptions were later investigated and reversed on appeal by military authorities, for medical or other reasons (31,888), men who never requested exemptions and were immediately processed (listed above, in Table – 18,028), 19-year-olds who were required to register in 1917, not liable to report yet, but did so voluntarily (3,272), and lastly, those men who did not obey the registration order but were later discovered and added to the government's lists of men liable for training (i.e., draft evaders, or described in Machin's *Report* as "Group I defaulters" – 11,995). Several of these numbers are given differently in separate places within the *Report*, but the ones given here seem to be the most accurate based on a reading of the various pages.

c To reach 179,933 in final column, Machin's *Report* uses the number of 18,028 men obtained, rather than 18,320 that it gives in its earlier pages (actually, 18,220 in *Report*, due to incorrect Saskatchewan figures noted below).

d Men who were subject to call but had not yet been sent notices to report for training as of November 11, 1918.

e Men discharged at some point after having been placed in uniform, due to lowering of medical category (because civilian doctors had incorrectly placed men in higher categories, changes after enlisted, etc.).

f "Group III defaulters" (people who were actually sent notices to report for training but did not do so) who remained unapprehended at end of war.

g Men who after registering either volunteered directly for a CEF unit (19,644), or in military forces outside the CEF (British, American by reciprocal agreement [see Machin, *Report*, 68], etc. – 7,673) before they were ordered to report for training under the MSA. These numbers appear to be included within the various figures listed in note "b," above, but are not ever specifically listed under those headings in the *Report*.

Source: M.C. Urquhart and K.A.H. Buckley, eds., *Historical Statistics of Canada* (Toronto: Macmillan, 1965), series A2-14; Machin, 42, 44, 72, 74, 117. Unfortunately, the tables in Machin's *Report* contain a number of typographical errors, and/or numbers that have been changed without explanation between one section and another. By careful reading, I have managed to correct for these. In particular, the total in the exemption requests column is incorrectly given as 379,629 rather than 376,629 in the *Report*, and the numbers in this Table for Saskatchewan under "Ordered to Report" and "Obtained" are listed incorrectly in the *Report* as 1,004 and 1,378. Because the figures from which the *Report* was compiled were by military district, those for Yukon and Northwest Territories appear to be merged within provincial numbers. Lastly, the percentages for total national population do not add up to exactly 100%, due to rounding of decimals.

Tantalizing hints appear in other sources, of English Canadian tribunals conversely refusing to grant almost every request even among apparently legitimate farmers on the prairies.[58]

More recently, a few records have been unearthed that provide us with slightly greater insight into how the appeal system affected Canadians. In one unpublished paper, Molly Ungar explored the documents of a single tribunal from downtown Montreal, which happen to have been preserved in the files of the army's representative on the body, Émile Vaillancourt. They suggest that in that one predominantly English-speaking district at least, there was little sign of discrimination, since exemptions were granted widely to both groups.[59] Through a diligent reading of local newspapers in Toronto, Ian Miller has been able to provide some understanding of how the tribunals operated in that city, finding that like their prairie counterparts they rejected exemptions with increasing rigidity.[60] Amy Shaw has partly reconstructed the experiences of conscientious objectors in front of tribunals across the country.[61] And Patrick Dennis has finally taken on the task of trying to piece together the experiences of the conscripts who actually served in uniform during the war.[62]

Clearly, conscription came to have a widespread influence on Canadians during the First World War. And it was due to such experiences, and their accompanying political implications, that civilian leaders such as Mackenzie King were anxious to prevent the return of such a deeply harmful policy after 1918. A pioneering student of industrial relations, and another of Laurier's protegés, King was recruited into the Department of Labour in 1900 and rose to become its deputy minister. In 1908, he entered politics and within a few months became labour minister. Defeated in the general election of 1911, he came to work for John D. Rockefeller, Jr., advising him especially in the months following one of the United States' most infamous cases of industrial violence, when a clash between state militiamen and striking coal miners in one of Rockefeller's companies in Ludlow, Colorado, led to the deaths of a number of men, women, and children in early 1914. King privately supported conscription in 1917, but only if it was applied to "all essential war services" and not just to finding soldiers. And ultimately, the perspective that he had absorbed from Laurier, that the highest priority must be to preserve national unity, led him to run as an anticonscriptionist Liberal in North York. He lost, although in a relatively competitive contest. He was narrowly chosen as the Liberal Party's new leader after the Laurier's death in 1919, partly thanks to how his wartime loyalty and especially his actions in 1917 were perceived by the party's French Canadian delegates, and he held power as prime minister for most of the period from 1921 to 1930, at least partly as a result of the strength with which French Canadians voted for him as a bloc in Quebec.[63] In the early postwar years, he steered Canada carefully through the two Imperial Conferences of 1923 and 1926 that gave the country its full independence in the world, and that had come out of wartime developments under Robert Borden. He especially worried that English Canadians would not understand that he wished to sever only the country's most direct legal and constitutional ties to the British Commonwealth, but not its historical and emotional ones. And conversely, he worked to ensure that Canada would not be drawn into external disputes as a consequence of those same sorts of ties – especially during the Chanak crisis between Britain and Turkey in 1922 – to avoid raising fears among French Canadians that the events of the First World War would be repeated. In a country that was exhausted both by the financial and by the emotional exertions of that war, and where the prevailing view seemed to be that nobody could ever again be willing to fight a future conflict on such a scale, he also cut back heavily on the military services. The absence of any obvious external threat to Canada for most of the 1920s made it difficult to justify any other course.[64]

Unfortunately, the rise of dictatorial regimes in Italy, Japan, and Germany, and then their increasingly bellicose actions from the early 1930s onwards, made war begin to appear much more likely again. Privately, King acknowledged that the country would probably be drawn in once more. But he chose to tread more carefully in public, to try to help Canadians remain united in such an event. His refusal to take a stand frustrated not only some of his fellow Canadians but also British leaders who were looking for some sign of the Dominion's intentions.[65] He did see the need to begin trying to prepare the country militarily for such a conflict, and he began a rearmament program after 1936 that cost him some political capital. He made sure that the program focused on improving Canada's own defences, by relying mainly on ships and aircraft. He also made it abundantly clear in public statements that no commitment of any kind to Europe was being contemplated in advance, so that if war did come, hopefully the country would be able to avoid the high casualties as well as the accompanying political pressures that had led to conscription during the First World War.[66]

By September 1938, at the time of the Munich crisis, the world seemed once more to be on the brink of war. Even many critics were beginning to realize that it might not be possible to stop Hitler in any other way. In March 1939, further German aggression in Czechoslovakia increased the pressure on King, and he determined to make a clear public statement of his position. The new leader of the Conservative Party, Robert Manion, stole a step on him (while at the same time showing that at least he and some of his members had attempted to learn from their party's First World War policies towards French Canada) by becoming the first national leader to state publicly that while he felt that Canada should take part in another war in Europe, he would not rely on conscription to do so. King responded a few days later, with an even more explicit promise that "so long as this government may be in power, no such measure will be enacted."[67] He was followed by Ernest Lapointe, who since the 1920s had been widely seen as King's Quebec lieutenant in the Cabinet, and who emphasized the promise that much further.[68] As a result, French Canadians apparently reconciled themselves to the idea of war, but only if in return the government upheld what seemed to be a firm pledge to never revive conscription for overseas service during the coming conflict.

Thus, almost up to the moment that the Second World War began, memories of compulsion during the First World War remained a key influence on developments. After 1939, every political decision related to manpower would be framed around trying to avoid what conscription had done to Canada during the earlier conflict. It was in that atmosphere that not only the politicians, but also the generals whose duty it would be to impose a limited form of conscription after 1940, would have to work. And Canada's history up to the 1930s also played a major role in shaping the views of the generals, as well as the ways they approached many issues surrounding civil–military relations. From their point of view, the small size of the NPAM and later the Permanent Force in the late 1800s had made military service as unattractive to potential career officers as it had been to many soldiers, and attempts to promote higher military standards on the part of a string of British officers who were seconded to Canada during the late 1800s to command those forces mostly instead just led to conflict with the civilian authorities, who remained paramount in making defence policy.[69] The influence of professional officers weakened even further when Sam Hughes refused to listen to their advice on mobilization and other matters at the beginning of the First World War. Most of Canada's wartime soldiers still viewed themselves as "civilians in uniform," who would serve only for the duration of the conflict, just as militiamen in the past had done. But they and the rest of the Canadian public soon learned the costs of not accepting professional standards. By 1918, the country's generals had reason to hope that at least some Canadians now understood that a volunteer militia would not be sufficient, generally, or allow the loss of life to be minimized, more specifically, if it ever became necessary again for Canada to participate in such a conflict. They also had reason to hope that they would have some say in proferring advice to their political superiors on such matters.[70]

Even more significantly, and in much the same way as for Canada's civilian leaders, the First World War was a formative experience for most of the key military commanders who would come to build the army in the Second World War. H.D.G. Crerar, for example, who would figure so prominently in later developments, had attended RMC before 1914 but then left to become a civilian engineer. He went overseas with the first contingent as the second in command of his local part-time artillery unit. He then held a series of increasingly senior command and staff positions within that branch over the next four years, before deciding to stay on after 1918.[71] Ken Stuart, who succeeded Crerar as CGS in late 1941, and who later ran the army's Second World War headquarters in London, was also a prewar graduate of RMC. He rose to lead the 7th Battalion, Canadian Engineers, through the campaigns of the last Hundred Days from August to November 1918.[72] E.L.M. Burns, one of the authors mentioned at the beginning of this book, helped organize the training plan for conscripts in 1940–41 before going on to command I Canadian Corps in Italy for most of 1944. He entered RMC just as the First World War broke out in 1914, left at the end of his first year to become a junior signals officer overseas, and by 1918 was the youngest staff captain in the Canadian Expeditionary Force at the age of twenty-one.[73] His superior officer at that time was the acting commander of the 12th Canadian Infantry Brigade, J.L. Ralston, who would go on to become Minister of National Defence in the late 1920s and again for most of the Second World War. Ralston had joined the 85th (Nova Scotia) Battalion with no previous military experience in 1915, but quickly became its adjutant and later its commanding officer, earning a distinguished record for his conduct under fire (as did all of the men mentioned here). While he did not blindly accede to the army's wishes on all matters during the Second World War, his own earlier time in uniform no doubt helped shape his tendency to defer to the army's leaders when making military policy for much of that conflict.[74]

Nevertheless, when the First World War ended, almost all of Canada's political leaders and most of its public returned to prewar patterns of civil–military relations. For officers such as Crerar, Stuart, and Burns, these were frustrating years, during which they struggled to preserve the skills and professionalism that Canadians had won at such cost on the battlefield. Stuart found an outlet from 1929 onwards by editing the *Canadian Defence Quarterly*, an interwar publication that did its best to promote high-level intellectual debate and reflection among army officers.[75] Burns wrote a number of articles for the *CDQ*, one of which sparked the most significant exchange of the interwar period in 1938, with Guy Simonds, who would also go on to command Canadians at the most senior levels during the Second World War. In addition, Burns secretly wrote articles for H.L. Mencken's literary journal in the United States, the *American Mercury*, as well as other short stories, plays, and a published novel.[76]

In its training, and especially how it prepared officers for senior command, throughout the interwar period the Canadian army continued to be shaped to a large degree by British models. Most training manuals and other materials were supplied directly by the War Office in London, and at certain points in their careers, officers were permitted and sometimes even expected to attend schools in Britain. From the mid-1920s onwards, British officials revived a prewar tradition of allowing Canadians to participate in the very exclusive Staff College courses offered at Camberley in England and Quetta in India, to prepare candidates from around the Commonwealth for higher-level postings. One or two of the most promising Canadian officers were also permitted to attend the Imperial Defence College in London each year. There, military personnel mingled with senior politicians, to promote greater cooperation between military and civilian leaders and thus help both groups gain a greater understanding of the complexities of making defence policy at that level. Crerar, Stuart, Burns, and most of the Canadian army's key Second World War commanders all attended Staff College in the interwar period, and Crerar and Burns were among those who studied at the Imperial Defence College.[77] For two years in the mid-1920s, Crerar also gained important experience as "General Staff Officer 2" in the Directorate of Military Operations in London – a significant position within the British army's own headquarters system and one of a number of similar positions that were also open to Canadians through regular interchanges between the two militaries in the interwar years.[78] Conversely, despite the events of the First World War, militia service remained popular among a small number of French Canadians, who made up an average of 6 to 7 percent of the force in the interwar years. And several of the army's senior officers came to support preserving the 22nd Battalion as one of its three Permanent Force infantry regiments shortly after the war. But only a handful of francophones were among the dozens of Canadian officers who attended the British staff colleges between 1925 and 1939.[79]

In addition, as the chief assistant to and later himself the Director of Military Operations and Intelligence for most of the early 1930s, Crerar was one of the central figures involved in drafting the very plans that would guide the army's mobilization during the Second World War – ones that his superiors spent several years in the later 1930s struggling to convince civilian leaders to accept so that hopefully there would be no repeat of Sam Hughes's haphazard call for volunteers in 1914. By 1939, schemes existed to cover all major contingencies, and the militia had been reorganized to allow for the systematic raising of a total force of six infantry divisions and one cavalry division in the event of another major conflict. As Stephen Harris and Paul Dickson have noted, these plans clearly served as the blueprint for Crerar's later wartime expansion of the army in 1940–42. Yet they never received formal civilian approval, beyond tacit acknowledgment from the defence minister, Ian Mackenzie, in the years leading up to the Second World War. And no detailed demographic studies were conducted to confirm that sufficient manpower would be available to support the numbers contained in the plans.[80] Furthermore, Crerar was an ambitious man, both with respect to his own career and on behalf of the Canadian army as a whole, which he felt should be a larger and more respected part of Canadian society. Some of his Second World War behaviour makes it difficult to weigh his role in wartime events dispassionately, in particular considering that he spent months during the height of the crisis in Europe in 1940–41 lobbying J.L. Ralston to be promoted to lieutenant-general, arguing that as CGS he needed the rank to have his views properly considered in higher-level policy-making. And in 1942–43 he aided in a whispering campaign against his predecessor and mentor, Lieutenant-General A.G.L. McNaughton, that eventually removed him in favour of Crerar as the overall commander of the Canadian army in Europe.[81] But what drove both Crerar and contemporaries such as McNaughton even more strongly during the Second World War was the memory of the successes of the Canadian Corps on the Western Front in 1916–18, and a professional desire to match and even exceed that memory, in both size and accomplishments. Crerar also argued, for strategic reasons, that Canada needed to do everything it could to build up its forces beyond what had originally been intended, to help replace the large number of Allied divisions that were lost in the military collapse in western Europe in 1940, at a time when neither the Soviet Union nor the United States had yet to officially join the conflict, and which made Canada Britain's largest remaining ally from which to draw such resources. Lastly, through its achievements on the battlefield, Crerar hoped that the Canadian army would come to be seen (for a second time in a generation) as an important component of Canadian defence policy, one that needed to be maintained at a higher level of professionalism in peacetime, and to be listened to more fully when policy was made in the future. As his biographer Paul Dickson has put it: "In seeking to so advance his profession, Crerar was convinced that it was in the interests of Canada as a nation. Similarly, he perceived his own career advancement as a necessary step in his goal even while he recognized the obvious career and family benefits ... In fact, professional, national, career and personal motives were e[n]meshed and inseparable."[82]

All of these factors would come together after 1939. As a result of their own experiences during and after the First World War – and particularly the lack of attention that had continued to be paid to the Canadian army by civilian leaders after 1918 – generals such as Crerar were determined that this time

Figure 5 H.D.G. Crerar at Canadian Military Headquarters, London, England, as a lieutenant-general in the later years of the Second World War. *Source:* LAC, PA-116458.

around something more positive and permanent must come out of the conflict. At the same time, although Dickson argues that Crerar tended to see conscription as inevitable, as we shall see, his recognition of the importance of manpower to industry and other parts of the war effort as well as to the army in his submissions to the Cabinet War Committee suggest that he also understood that building a large overseas force would be even more likely if he could assure politicians that they would not again have to face maintaining it through compulsory service, for as long as possible during the war (if at all). When the fighting took a serious turn in 1940, and for their own reasons the politicians themselves introduced a new form of compulsory military training that summer, Crerar would see his opportunity to make his ambitions a reality by hopefully being able to have the best of both worlds.

In a larger sense, although the army's senior leadership did not in any way deliberately bring about the crisis of 1944, and although even more certainly they never intended to place the government of King in a position where he feared that they were attempting to take over civilian decision-making, their decisions and actions did come very much to shape how conscription was implemented in Canada between 1940 and 1945. That then came to shape the larger political developments. This all had major consequences, both for the compulsory training organization that was created under the authority of the National Resources Mobilization Act after 1940, and for the volunteer army that was built up overseas. Eventually the two would become distinct but inseparable, with fateful consequences for Crerar and his successors in command of the army, for the politicians who had come to believe in his assurances, and even arguably for the postwar army as a whole, which would emerge after 1945 with its many battlefield accomplishments tarnished once again by the memory of the more negative social and political implications of conscription as a major part of the country's wartime experience.

Part 2: The National Resources Mobilization Act and the Rise of the Big Army

The Song of the Seventh Platoon[1]

When the government decided we would have to train,
We found out that Hitler was the guy we had to blame;
So we take the thirty days just learning how to shoot,
So we won't be crushed by any Nazi boot.

Chorus –

We're the members of the Seventh,
We're the members of the Seventh,
We're the members of the Seventh –
The best of the bunch we are.

We are the Seventh Platoon, the best of all the bunch,
Even though the Corporals always keep us late for lunch:
We never falter when they yell to rise and shine,
But we wish they would take a jump into the salty brine.

Chorus –

We never talk at night, we never get the chance,
For if we do the corporals would all begin to prance:
When Corporal Frenchie yells "Come on and get to sleep!"
We never make a gol-darn-peep.

Chorus –

We like the thirty days, we think it's lots of fun,
But there are a lot of things we rather would have done;
When the time has come we may not want to go,
But we won't be sorry that we're leaving Corporal Lowe.

Chorus –

We were in the factory and we had a boss,
We thought he was a hard guy 'til we got ole Sargeant [sic] Ross,
Now he keeps on yelling from the dawn until the night,
"By the holy here (and there), you guys are sure a sight!"

Chorus –

Col. Keeler is the one we'll have to cultivate,
If we wish the passes that will keep us out quite late;
We won't be thinking of the fences any more,
But we'll use the gate as we should have done before.

Chorus –

2
Mobilizing Canada: The Creation of the Thirty-Day Training System, 1939–40

In September 1939, Canadians went to war against Germany for the second time in twenty-five years. Their political leaders entered the Second World War determined that conscription would not be the divisive issue that it had been in the earlier conflict. Canada now had the right to declare war on its own, and Prime Minister King was careful to make sure that Parliament met to express the will of its people. During the debate, he repeated the promise he had made in March that conscription would not be imposed for overseas service. This was reaffirmed when Quebec premier Maurice Duplessis called a snap election later that month, arguing that the federal government would use the war to force conscription and several other unpopular policies on the province. Quebec's three federal Cabinet ministers, Ernest Lapointe, Charles G. "Chubby" Power, and P.J.A. Cardin, all took an unprecedented part in the provincial election campaign, each declaring that he would never allow conscription to be imposed as long as he served in Ottawa. Moreover, all vowed to resign their posts immediately if Duplessis were re-elected. Thanks to this action, and their very active intervention in the election generally, Duplessis was soundly defeated. This removed a serious barrier to wartime relations between Quebec City and Ottawa. But the result was interpreted on both sides as a further cementing of the federal leaders' prewar vows to forgo conscription in return for French Canadian support for the war effort. As C.G. Power later put it, the promise was "looked upon by us, and I think by the great majority of the people of Quebec, as a sort of understanding or pact between them and the people of the other provinces. The pact was very frequently alluded to in after years." In the words of nationalist André Laurendeau: "A Parliament bound by a promise – that was what the French-Canadian people remembered."[1]

In spite of these apparent promises, within ten months compulsory military service was a reality. On June 21, 1940, the National Resources Mobilization Act (NRMA) became law, providing the federal government with the authority to impose conscription. Service was explicitly limited to Canadian territory, and at first the NRMA was seen as only a short-term measure, in response to the desperate Allied situation that had developed in Europe that spring. It still did not seem to presage the huge political and social divisions that had been sparked in the First World War. In fact, conscription attracted little significant opposition throughout the first year of its existence.

Yet during that same period the foundations were laid for a program that would come to be a much more permanent and far-reaching part of the country's war effort, and that would eventually help make conscription as potentially volatile an issue as it had been during the First World War. The story of the first year of the NRMA was one of uncertainty and confusion, followed by increasing rationalization as military planners fitted it more fully into their broader mobilization schemes. By early 1941, conscription had begun to take on the form it would retain for most of the war, and one that would have an important impact both on the country's political affairs and on the thousands of individuals who would be compelled to serve as conscripts from then on.

Historians have come to see the first few months of the Second World War as a time when Canadians devoted less than their full attention to the conflict. Throughout the winter of 1939–40, federal policy was guided by the principle of "limited liability," or the production of food, raw materials, and industrial goods rather than large armies for overseas service. King championed these policies as a way to minimize the likelihood of costly drains on manpower as had occurred during the First World War, and the resulting need to impose conscription. But it is much easier to see these policies as limited looking back in hindsight than it was at the time. In the early months, the country already seemed to be contributing to the war effort to the best of its ability, and perhaps even beyond. The armies of France and Britain, as well as the entire Atlantic Ocean, stood between Canada and any realistic threat to its security, and the economy was still recovering from the Great Depression of the 1930s, an event that had left deep psychological wounds on the country. That this policy would benefit Canada's own economy was considered only proper. It would also help expand the country's industrial capacity so that it could later contribute even more fully to the war effort. At the same time, the policy promised to permit federal politicians to increase the size of the country's military, slowly but steadily, so that it could field larger wartime forces in a controlled and manageable way should they later become necessary overseas.

The military contributions that Canada did make in 1939–40 were likewise arranged with a view to reducing the threat of conscription. In the first days of the conflict, the army was permitted to recruit two volunteer divisions, as per its prewar plans, but only one of these was earmarked to go overseas.[2] The Royal Canadian Navy (RCN) concentrated on acquiring, fitting out, and manning suitable government and civilian ships to augment its coastal defence forces. It also implemented the first convoys of the war. Over the next few months, Cabinet authorized the building of some ninety new minesweepers and (especially) Flower-class corvettes, a number of them for British use but the majority for the RCN so that it could gradually increase its coastal defence and convoy activities, while close to doubling its prewar strength from 3,000 to about 5,500.[3] But the country's major military effort was soon identified as the British Commonwealth Air Training Plan (BCATP), an extension of a very limited scheme to train pilots and air crews in Canada that had been negotiated earlier in 1939. When British authorities proposed expanding the BCATP that October to include large numbers of personnel from the entire Commonwealth, this provided a welcome opportunity to use Canada's wide-open spaces and distance from enemy borders to contribute to the war effort, while keeping thousands of Canadians at home to operate the program, as it was intended that the Royal Canadian Air Force (RCAF) would provide most of the personnel to run it. The BCATP would also allow the country to focus its military contributions on the air war overseas, as Canadians completed their training in the BCATP and units were eventually built up in Great Britain, since casualties were expected to be considerably lower there than among the large ground formations of 1914–18. It is even conceivable that the army's 1st Canadian Division might not have been permitted to sail for England when it did in December 1939, had the British suggested the BCATP a few days earlier in September, given that the latter would require huge amounts of men and resources; as part of the agreement, King insisted that the British government publicly acknowledge it as the most important way in which Canada would contribute to the war militarily. As it was, the final agreement was signed on the same day as soldiers of the 1st Division began arriving overseas, and by the end of the year the army had almost 60,000 men on duty in what was known as the "Canadian Active Service Force," enlisted for service anywhere during the war. By the end of March 1940, the RCAF had gone from a little over 4,000 men to over 10,000 and was in the final stages of preparing to put the BCATP into operation. Its total strength, including personnel on home defence service and overseas duty, was eventually expected to grow to nearly 45,000.[4]

The government's last prewar budget for the entire Department of National Defence (1939–40) had been $60,000,000 (a roughly fourfold increase from its low point in 1932–33). In the fall, Cabinet agreed to raise that figure to just over $300,000,000, but only after strong efforts were made to keep it at that. Considering that for the first three years the BCATP alone was expected to cost over $287,000,000, clearly that program was a major national undertaking at that point in the war. And Canada's military spending, generally, was only "limited" in comparison to what we now know was to come in the years after 1939.[5] In the industrial sphere, meanwhile, the British government of Neville

Chamberlain also struggled to restrain spending. Orders for industrial products were much lower than Canadian leaders had hoped, and at the negotiating table that winter the British and Canadians drove hard bargains during seemingly interminable discussions over bulk purchases of wheat, bacon, and other products.[6]

The Conservative Party did press the federal government to make greater military commitments to the war effort; despite this, conscription also failed to attract much political interest after the end of the Quebec election in the fall of 1939. When Ontario premier Mitchell Hepburn passed a motion in his province's legislature in January 1940 in which he accused the federal government of not doing enough to prosecute the war, King seized upon this as an excuse to call a federal election, which was due soon but had been difficult to justify in the tense international atmosphere of 1938–39, and even more so after the country went to war. Ignoring the protests of some of his members, who wanted to campaign for outright conscription, Conservative leader Robert Manion called only for a "National Government" uniting leaders from all parties, for which some business leaders had been attempting to whip up support since before the war. But in the words of J.L. Granatstein: "The phoney war, as it then was, was not rousing the people against the government, and most seemed satisfied with King's 'limited liability' policies." In addition, National Government still reminded too many people of the Union Government of the First World War. Manion would later recall that everywhere he went during the election, the first request he received from Conservative candidates was to repeat his promises that there would be no compulsory service. King was returned to power in March 1940 with the largest majority to that point in Canadian history. Manion resigned as Conservative leader soon after and was replaced by R.B. Hanson.[7]

Furthermore, after the Quebec provincial election of September 1939, French Canadians especially seemed much less troubled by matters related to the war compared to 1914–18. This time the Canadian army was permitted to conduct a more orderly mobilization, which included plans for French-speaking units. The former 22nd Battalion, since June 1921 known as the *Royal 22e Régiment*, proceeded overseas as part of 1st Canadian Division. The French-speaking *Régiment de Maisonneuve* was proud to be the first militia unit of either language called out for active service to reach full strength, on September 20. The *Fusiliers Mont-Royal* reached the same goal two weeks later. Montreal's *La Presse*, which catered to a broad readership, regularly published photographs of troops in training and stories highlighting the backgrounds and experiences of individual volunteers. A few hundred French Canadians also volunteered for the RCN and the RCAF, even though throughout the Second World War the first was an entirely English-speaking institution, and the second largely the same, especially in the early days. There was even hope of forming an entire French-speaking 5th Brigade in 2nd Division. Unfortunately, the decision to send only one division overseas in September 1939 threw off the army's planning, as the *Royal 22e Régiment* had originally been intended to be part of that brigade. Then, in the spring of 1940 the *Fusiliers Mont-Royal* had to be removed and rushed to Iceland. And because the number of French-speaking officers in the prewar militia had still been very small overall, not enough of them could be found for its headquarters when it was eventually established in England. Its francophone commander, Brigadier P.-E. Leclerc, eventually recommended that the project be shelved.[8]

The army's mobilization remained limited in other ways in the fall of 1939. Shortages of uniforms and other basic equipment hindered the ability to accept volunteers, and by mid-October recruiting had been suspended for units other than 1st Division, so that it could complete its organization and proceed to England. Over that first winter, recruiting, training, and even the selection of officers were left to individual regiments, although having learned from the First World War, officials did set up depots in each military district to act as ongoing recruiting centres, so that future losses could be replenished from more anonymous but also more efficient pools of reinforcements. Plans to begin concentrating all new recruits in training centres where lessons and procedures could be standardized rather than in individual units were put off until January 1940. As Yves Tremblay has argued, the result was that training was haphazard, and focused on parade square drill or on (sometimes) obsolete First World War tactics. Recruiting resumed across the country in January and was hastened when the Cabinet agreed that the 2nd Division would also eventually proceed to England, a decision encouraged by the prime minister largely because it would forestall attacks at the beginning of the federal election campaign that the Liberals were not doing enough to support the war effort.[9]

But then came the series of rapid German advances during the spring of 1940. In April, its forces invaded Denmark and Norway, capturing the first almost immediately, and Norway after strong resistance in early June. By that time, Hitler had extended his reach to France, Belgium, Luxembourg, and the Netherlands, beginning on May 10. By early June, France was all but defeated, and the bulk of the British army had barely escaped destruction at the French port of Dunkirk. Italy declared war on the Allies on June 10. Suddenly, Canada ranked as Britain's most powerful ally, and it seemed that almost every sacrifice would be necessary to help defend the British Isles themselves. Over the next few weeks, Cabinet authorized shipping all of Canada's available stocks of weapons and supplies to Great Britain, and industrial production greatly expanded in response to now more desperate British munitions orders. In late May, King announced plans to speed up sending 2nd Canadian Division overseas, along with additional forestry and railway troops and a corps headquarters to command Canadian forces in the field. Two more divisions would be mobilized to take over home defence duties in North America. Canadian units replaced British garrisons in Iceland, Newfoundland, and the West Indies, and the RCAF took on a much greater share of responsibility for the BCATP, and accelerated its planned buildup to meet the changed situation overseas.[10] In addition, it rushed its only fully equipped fighter squadron to England, whose men spent the early autumn helping defend the approaches to London in the later days of the Battle of Britain.[11] The RCN also sent all four of its currently available destroyers on the east coast across the Atlantic. The capture of most of western Europe would allow German U-boats to extend their operations, and orders were tendered for further corvettes and minesweepers to augment the RCN's strength for escorting convoys. In September, British prime minister Winston Churchill concluded an agreement with US president Franklin D. Roosevelt to acquire fifty older First World War era destroyers, and the RCN took on responsibility for manning six of them (and later a seventh).[12]

The National Resources Mobilization Act was conceived and passed in this atmosphere, in mid-June 1940. Unfortunately, given the rush of those weeks, few records have survived that would allow us to answer several questions about the reasoning behind it. Most of our knowledge of the early developments is based on the records of Prime Minister King, who clearly was the central figure guiding its evolution. He modelled the NRMA directly on a similar measure in Britain, the Emergency Powers (Defence) Act of May 22, 1940. In Britain, compulsory military service was already in place, and the new law simply extended the British government's powers (primarily to direct industrial manpower).[13] In Canada, the government could theoretically do virtually anything it wanted already simply by passing an Order-in-Council under the War Measures Act (WMA), which had been enacted at the beginning of the First World War and then put back into force by proclamation on September 1, 1939.[14] Much less detailed and technical than the WMA, the NRMA consisted of a preamble and six brief sections, only two of which formed its core (the full text of the NRMA is reproduced in the Appendix). The preamble laid the groundwork, indicating that because "a special emergency has arisen and the national safety of Canada has become endangered," it was "therefore, expedient to confer upon the Governor in Council special emergency powers to permit of the mobilization of all of the effective resources of the nation, both human and material, for the purpose of the defence and security of Canada." Section 2 then repeated some of the wording of the War Measures Act (although it added a more specific reference to persons, services, and property), in granting the federal government the power to

> do and authorize such acts and things, and make from time to time such orders and regulations, requiring persons to place themselves, their services and their property at the disposal of His Majesty in the right of Canada, as may be deemed necessary or expedient for securing the public safety, the defence of Canada, the maintenance of public order, or the efficient prosecution of the war, or for maintaining supplies or services essential to the life of the community.

Section 3 then did nothing more than explicitly limit any powers that might be exercised to impose military service through Section 2, to "Canada and the territorial waters thereof."[15]

According to E.L.M. Burns, at the time an army officer, but who would later write about these events, the broader powers of Section 2 were merely window dressing to hide the true purpose of the NRMA, which was to authorize conscription for home defence.[16] In his diary, King stressed his own worries about its implications for that,[17] and certainly the NRMA came to be identified very quickly with compulsory service alone. But a close reading of the developments of the time suggests that King originally intended it to do more. The crisis of May and June had brought new pressure to bear from a number of individuals and organizations to expand Canada's war effort. This included numerous demands to conscript wealth and industry as well as manpower.[18] King actually drafted the NRMA following a visit from R.B. Hanson, who in Hanson's words requested that he pass "legislation putting at the disposition of the State all the manpower and material resources of the nation."[19] The Cabinet War Committee (CWC), a small inner circle of senior ministers that had been established in the fall of 1939 to decide the government's war policies, also focused on broader aspects of the NRMA in its deliberations. Several members favoured using it to impose controls over industrial workers and incomes in addition to military conscription.[20] Furthermore, as J.W. Pickersgill has noted, King was genuinely shocked by the speed of German advances in the spring of 1940, and feared that almost any measure might be necessary to help keep Britain in the war, as the first line of defence for Canada itself. He also wished to prevent panic and stabilize public opinion. The NRMA was designed to do this by setting out explicit powers that the government possessed but had not yet exercised under the existing War Measures Act.[21] It thus served to remind and educate Canadians about those powers, while emphasizing the new and dangerous situation that was behind choosing to exercise them at this precise moment. Compared to the WMA, which merely justified the powers because a state of war existed, the NRMA went beyond this by emphasizing the higher purpose for which the King government intended to exercise them, and the limitations it was placing on itself in doing so. As the prime minister put it while recording his discussion with Hanson, "the plan now was to steady matters a bit with wider power under the War Measures Act and under the Constitution, providing for a general levy to call out all the people we need for national service." But he was also keeping in mind other future actions that might be taken under its authority.[22] All in all, the NRMA sent a strong signal of the government's leadership in the current crisis, while differentiating its actions from those of the Borden government of 1914–18. During the debate on the NRMA in the House of Commons, King also emphasized the psychological aims of the new bill, stating repeatedly that it was meant to do more than simply conscript manpower. These comments were echoed by several members of the opposition parties.[23]

In essence, then, the new NRMA was a compromise that gave the government any conceivable power it might need in the dark days of June 1940, while making it clear that it would not go so far as to impose conscription for overseas service. Indeed, many of the measures envisioned at the time were eventually brought into effect during the war, including higher levels of taxation and a detailed system of controls over wages, prices, and industrial manpower. Having decided to introduce a limited form of compulsory military service for political reasons, however, the government then left it to the army to work out the details of creating and administering the new training system, and of finding the manpower and other resources to operate it. As a result, the compulsory military training program that emerged over the next few months would come to be based much more on the needs of the army than on those of the politicians, and thus set the stage for problems that would become increasingly visible as the war went on. It also began the creation of two essentially separate armies for the country, one of which could be used for service anywhere while the other was limited to home defence. This was a typical policy for King, whose first instinct when faced with a divisive issue was usually to try to keep as many options open as possible, for as long as possible, in the hope that either the problem would eventually solve itself, or at the very least conditions would become more favourable so that a decision could later be made that would alienate the smallest number of people. In this case, it almost worked for the duration of the war. For now, especially, nobody knew exactly what was to come, and it seemed that the prime minister had managed to overcome a potentially very serious threat to national unity in the spring and summer of 1940.

ONE SIGN THAT KING had read public opinion well in putting forward the NRMA was the reaction in Quebec to it and to other developments. The events of May and June were just as shocking to French Canadians as they were to English Canadians given that they still maintained a number of cultural ties to France. During the first discussion in the CWC about what became the NRMA, on June 17, King was "somewhat surprised" when he heard C.G. Power, the fluently bilingual Cabinet minister who represented the majority French-speaking riding of Quebec South and who had a particular sensitivity to French Canadian concerns,

> come out strongly demanding that we should have a measure that would enable us to call out every man in Canada for military training and for the defence of Canada ... I found that they had been talking matters over among themselves and that Lapointe was agreeable to this as long as it was for the defence of Canada and that it was to be likewise and equally levied upon [all] youth.[24]

La Presse also indicated its acceptance when the NRMA was announced, emphasizing the threat that existed to Canada in its editorials and news stories. Premier Adélard Godbout pledged his government's support in carrying out the compulsory national registration that would be the first step in putting the new measures into operation. And when Camillien Houde, the populist mayor of Montreal, chose to declare publicly at the beginning of August that he would refuse to obey the registration, "All present" at a meeting of King's Cabinet agreed to take the drastic step of interning him rather than openly charging him and trying him in court for breaking the law, mainly to prevent him from being able to draw any further attention to his stance through a public trial. Supporters of the prime minister's actions included P.J.A. Cardin and Ernest Lapointe, his other two key Cabinet ministers from Quebec. Indeed, it was Lapointe, as justice minister, who signed the order to detain Houde. Despite King's worries that the action might cause "riots and serious difficulties throughout the Province of Quebec," there was little overt reaction. This was at least partly because press censorship had been imposed, and most newspapers likely watched what they said. But *La Presse* leaned clearly against Houde, quoting statements from third parties saying that he would have been better off using less radical means, and noting in an editorial that the registration had been legitimately decreed by the federal Parliament and thus people should submit to it fully and loyally. In some ways, *Le Devoir*, the former newspaper of Henri Bourassa and still the leading nationalist organ in Quebec, went further, openly criticizing Houde for behaving so foolishly.[25] Thus, French Canadians as a whole might not have been happy to see conscription in effect, but they seem to have at least accepted its being used within the limitation of home defence, given recent developments in the war.

As for the history of the NRMA itself, the first need that arose after it was passed in June 1940 was, as in the First World War, to take stock of the actual reserves of manpower and other resources that were available to the government. King announced the new national registration at the same time as he introduced the NRMA in the House of Commons. Formal regulations for it were approved in early July, and a Department of National War Services was established to oversee it. That department would be responsible for administering civilian aspects of the NRMA afterwards, including deciding which men would be called out for military training and notifying them of their duty to report, as well as coordinating the country's other voluntary contributions to the war effort. From August 19 to 21, eight million Canadians between the ages of sixteen and forty-five reported to polling stations across the country to fill out and return cards stating their age, marital status, occupation, and other data. These cards became the foundation for the increasingly complex mobilization of society that took place over the next few years. Under the terms of the NRMA, any man who married after July 15, 1940, was legally considered to be single for the duration of the war. Regulations also provided for the ongoing registration of adolescents as they turned sixteen by requiring them to fill out cards at their local post office.[26]

Meanwhile, the army's planners had begun organizing for the beginning of compulsory training. At first, considerable confusion existed as a result of the death of the defence minister, Norman Rogers, in an airplane crash on June 10.[27] King had chosen Rogers for the post in place of his prewar minister, Ian Mackenzie, in mid-September 1939, partly because Mackenzie had gotten into trouble over his control of the department generally (and in particular a public controversy in 1938 related to acquiring Bren light machine guns), and partly because King discovered on the outbreak of the war that as we have seen Mackenzie had permitted his generals to prepare plans for an overseas expeditionary force in advance, even though the prime minister had opposed doing so in the late 1930s. King considered Rogers better able to resist the increased role that the military would inevitably play in wartime policy-making.[28] In contrast, Rogers's new successor, J.L. Ralston, would come to be seen as much more supportive of the army's wishes over the next few years.[29] Although King's decision to shift Ralston from the finance to the defence portfolio seemed natural in the dark days of June 1940, it may also have been pushed on him somewhat by a lack of other clear candidates for the position. Ralston did not officially leave the Department of Finance until July 5, and in the interim, the army's planners were left without a firm sense of the government's wishes regarding compulsory military training. In the circumstances, it is hardly surprising that those planners would come to play an even more important role in defining the new organization than might otherwise have been the case.

The other factor that shaped the organization of the new training system was that at the same time as senior officials within National Defence Headquarters (NDHQ) were trying to get it up and running, they faced an even higher priority: expanding what was now the separate overseas army in response to the crisis in Europe. In the wake of that crisis, over 30,000 men volunteered in June alone, and the same again in July, partly to fill the new 3rd and 4th Divisions, into which men were again enlisted directly rather than first going through unified training centres. But after July, district induction depots were given responsibility for all future recruiting. By the summer of 1940, sixteen centralized camps had been created for training all future recruits, including seven for infantry (five for rifle and two for machine gun units), two specialized small arms training centres, and one each for armoured, artillery, signals, engineer, service, ordnance, and medical personnel. All featured longer and more rigorous periods of training to attempt to prepare men for actual combat overseas, and seemed as if they would be entirely disrupted if they now had to be merged with a new training program for NRMA recruits.[30] They also had to have priority in terms of finding equipment and other resources to support them, as well as to fit out the new 3rd and 4th Divisions and eight other infantry units that were activated in July 1940 for home defence purposes.

In the absence of Ralston, the first reference to the government's plans for training under the NRMA was made by C.G. Power, as Acting Minister of National Defence, during the debate on the act in the House of Commons in June. At that point, he could say little more than that: "Every ablebodied [*sic*] man in Canada will be given an opportunity of training in the use of arms ... so as to be prepared for the active defence of this dominion." The training would be entrusted to units of the Non-Permanent Active Militia (NPAM), and each man would be called out either for "a continuous period of three months or for a lesser time." Faced with the government's sudden decision to begin compulsory training, Power's military staff originally thought in terms of eight weeks, which was the minimum they considered necessary to teach basic skills to raw troops. A joint memorandum written a few days after his speech by the Deputy CGS, the Judge Advocate General, and the Director of Military Training indicates that they considered having conscripts live at home and train part-time in the armouries of local militia units, or using such facilities to house and train conscripts full-time, much as had been done over the previous winter for overseas volunteers. But they rejected those options as too costly and impractical, since far higher numbers of instructors would be required to provide the training, and the limited equipment that was available after accounting for other, higher-priority needs would be spread far too thinly. Furthermore, the experiences of the past winter had shown how difficult it was to maintain coherence and discipline when training was handled by individual units. Instead, they agreed on a larger and more centrally located system of camps, which would be purpose-built across the country specifically to train the new conscripts.[31] By July 10, J.L. Ralston, who had by then taken over as defence minister, was speaking publicly of the training being "probably six weeks" (or thirty days, not including weekends, the same as the yearly total for most militia units), and stating that "probably the first quota will be called up within two months."[32] By the time planning got under way in earnest in August, the thirty days had been compressed to one month, including the weekends.

What increased the focus and intensity of the planning between July and August was the arrival of Major-General H.D.G. Crerar to take the reins at NDHQ. One of Ralston's first acts as minister was to recall Crerar, who was serving as Senior Officer at Canadian Military Headquarters in London (the senior non-battlefield position in the Canadian army overseas; in the later years of the war it would be renamed Chief of Staff), and appoint him CGS in Ottawa.[33] Crerar's appointment marked a new stage in organizing both the NRMA and the larger war effort on an efficient basis. But for the moment, his major concern was merely to get the compulsory military training program up and running. As he reported later to Major-General A.G.L. McNaughton, his interwar mentor and now the commander of the Canadian Corps overseas,

> On my arrival I found the Government happily committed to compulsory training and, indeed, service but with a very superficial scheme for training and utilizing the man-power so called up. It was too late to change the basis of the training scheme which had already been announced but I made it plain that the best we could hope for after six weeks training of the individual (incidentally, with practically no weapons to train with), was to make these men "military minded." I also stressed to the Minister that this scheme must be regarded as purely an interim measure and that in the course of the next few months the Government would need to face the entire problem of the future organization of military service for Canada.[34]

Under Crerar's direction, the Department of National Defence had its more specific training plans ready by mid-August. All available staff and equipment would be consolidated into thirty-nine new training centres, which would be built in small but relatively easily accessible communities across the country. Thirty thousand men between the ages of twenty-one and twenty-four would be called out for training every four to six weeks. They would be treated as civilians until they arrived in the camps, where they would be formally enrolled in the army; thereafter, they would remain under military authority until they were formally discharged again when they left the centres. The men would be posted to nearby militia battalions, officially to continue their training but more importantly so that they could be kept track of in case they were needed again in the future. In practice, they would return to civilian life. At first, the plan was not expected to be permanent. It would last for roughly one year, after which all eligible male citizens were expected to have received their training.[35]

The rest of the summer saw a flurry of activity as the army scrambled to prepare for the new scheme. Commanders for the centres were selected and notified to report for duty as early as the last week of July, and immediately left for refresher training as well as other new courses to upgrade their skills. Further senior officers and instructors were chosen throughout August. In early September the complete staffs were gathered together in special camps in each of the country's eleven military districts, for another month's training before taking over their individual centres.[36] In selecting these staffs, NDHQ relied heavily on Canada's existing militia organization. In fact, without the contributions of the NPAM it is unlikely that the compulsory military training system could have been established in 1940. It provided many militia members with a way to contribute to the war regardless of the limitations of age or physical status, and most proved to be eager and conscientious officers and non-commissioned officers (NCOs). Lieutenant-Colonel Eugène Nantel, for example, the first commander of No. 44 Canadian Militia Training Centre (CMTC) in St-Jérôme, Quebec (this title for the camps was later changed to Canadian Army (Basic) Training Centre, or CA(B)TC, as a result of the developments of early 1941 discussed later in this chapter), had served in the 22nd Battalion during the First World War, where he was twice wounded, and then in the Canadian force sent to Siberia in 1918–19, before rising to command the *Régiment de Châteauguay* in the interwar period. When the new compulsory training program was announced, he was serving as Director of Auxiliary Services in Military District No. 4 (Montreal).[37] Another officer had lost a hand in the First World War, but apparently continued to serve usefully within the militia in the interwar years.[38] At least two men seem to have been accepted and trained as conscripts in the early camps despite having similar disabilities.[39] At the same time, younger members gained the opportunity to participate in the war at a time when the supply of volunteers still far outstripped the pace of the army's expansion in England. For example, Howard Ripstein joined the staff of the Huntingdon training centre as an underage NCO, until he reached the age at which he could be sent overseas.[40]

Personnel also came from a number of other sources, including former British units and the Veterans Home Guard (later the Veterans Guard of Canada), a body that was created in the summer of 1940 to permit over-age veterans of the First World War to serve by guarding vital defence points, internment camps for enemy aliens, and prisoner-of-war camps across the country. The Canadian Officers' Training Corps, the arm of the NPAM in Canada's universities, provided further officers, some of whom were professors and others still students. The most notable was Captain G.F.G. Stanley, a well known military historian and professor at Mount Allison University, who later served in the wartime Army Historical Section in London, before going on to a distinguished postwar civilian career.[41] These sources were still barely sufficient to meet the demand for qualified personnel. In the words of the war diarist for the training centre in Farnham, Quebec (the often anonymous military officer assigned to keep a daily record of various activities in every unit): "Difficulty was encountered in securing N.C.O's. who would make good instructors. Very few available except younger men who only had a few weeks experience in a NPAM summer camp, or had a course of instruction in gas or S[mall].A[rms].T[raining]."[42] In some cases, junior NCOs were selected directly from neighbouring militia units as they held their annual summer camps alongside those of the training centre staffs.[43] But by the time the compulsory military training centres opened in early October, most centres had managed to find enough men to fulfill their requirements.

At the same time as the staffs of the training centres were preparing for their new duties, construction crews were hard at work building the facilities which would soon house the thousands of new conscripts. Training centres were designed to accommodate recruits in groups of 250, 500, 750, or 1,000, divided into one, two, three, or four special training companies, along with an additional 75 to 200 staff.[44] Twenty-one out of the 39 centres contained the full four companies; most of these served the more populated areas of Quebec, Ontario, and the four western provinces (see Figure 1). Those centres in parts of the country where the population was less concentrated, such as Nova Scotia, New Brunswick, western Quebec, the Eastern Townships, eastern Ontario, and Fort William near the western end of Lake Superior (today part of Thunder Bay), each numbered either 500 or 750. Five 250-man camps were established in places where the population was even smaller but still considerable enough (or remote enough) to require separate sites (Charlottetown, Prince Edward Island; Edmundston, New Brunswick; Chicoutimi and Lac-Mégantic, Quebec; and Grande Prairie, Alberta).[45] In places like Grande Prairie, camps were located at regional railway junctions to make it easier for men from outlying areas to reach them, and they sometimes had to change their training schedules to accommodate the railways.[46] In some cases, army planners used existing buildings, such as Fort William, where engineers renovated a vacant factory owned by the Steel Company of Canada to serve as offices, living quarters, and training areas. In Charlottetown, officials leased a local luxury hotel and converted it into a barracks.[47] Several camps were built on community fairground or exhibition sites, where some accommodations and other facilities were already available, along with areas for outdoor training.

Still, most of the centres had to be created from the ground up. In all, over 1,150 buildings were erected across the country in a matter of weeks.[48] Crews were often hard at work finishing barrack huts and other buildings even as the first recruits arrived to commence their training on October 9, since lumber and other supplies were not available in many locations before the middle of September.[49] In Portage la Prairie, Manitoba, and Grande Prairie, Alberta, men ate in nearby restaurants at government expense for the first few days, until kitchens and dining halls in the camps could be completed, and in Peterborough, Ontario, trainees spent their first night sleeping on the floors of their huts as their beds had not yet arrived.[50] In many cases, training staffs pitched in to help finish buildings and outfit them just before the first trainees began to use them. Several drill halls were not yet complete when the camps opened, and in some cases they were not ready until January 1941, leaving two successive groups of men to have to do much of their training outdoors in the depths of the Canadian winter. In a few cases, recruits spent physical training periods shovelling snow or tramping it down on outdoor parade squares so that training could continue.[51] In many centres, it was weeks before camp hospitals, rifle ranges, and other buildings were fully operational.

Provisions were also made to conduct training in both official languages. Nine of the fourteen camps in Quebec were organized to carry out all instruction in French, and another three made provisions for men of both languages to train at the same time, in separate French- or English-speaking companies. The centres in North Bay and Cornwall, Ontario, and Edmundston, New Brunswick, were organized so that bilingual instructors could train some men in either language (one company's worth in each of the two Ontario camps, and 150 out of the total of 250 men in Edmundston). One of Saskatchewan's two centres, Dundurn, reported sufficient officers and NCOs on hand to do the same, although it was not officially listed as accepting French-language recruits. And

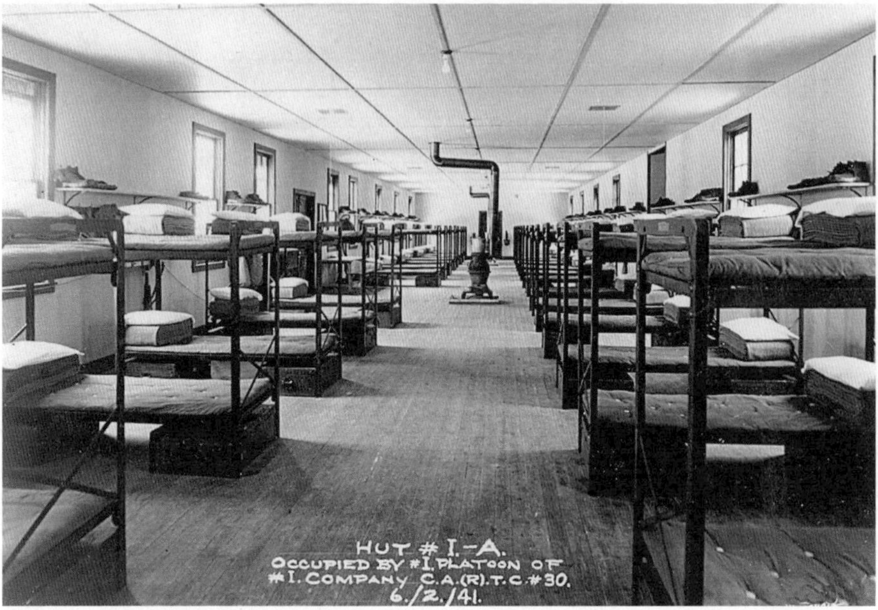

Figure 6 Interior of a typical NRMA barrack hut, Brockville, Ontario, February 1941. *Source:* LAC, C-143820.

according to Jean Pariseau and Serge Bernier, the same thing happened in Fredericton, New Brunswick, although in that case, G.F.G. Stanley (who besides being a historian was a bilingual Albertan) actually found himself needing to organize training for some of the province's Acadian population.[52] Altogether, out of the total of 29,750 places organized for individual trainees across the country by September 1940, 6,600 (or 22.2 percent, all in Quebec) were solely French-speaking, and another 650 (2.2 percent, all in Ontario and New Brunswick) were bilingual.[53] In comparison, according to the 1941 census, 17.2 percent of all male Canadians across the country were French-speaking and 14.2 percent were bilingual, and French-speaking and bilingual men from Quebec alone made up a slightly smaller proportion of 15.9 percent and 8.9 percent, respectively, of the total national male population.[54] When it became clear that the number of English-speaking conscripts in the first class of trainees to be called up in the Montreal area would fall short of what had been expected, local staffs were reorganized in a few weeks, with remarkably little disruption, so that Huntingdon could also become French-speaking. By the start of training for the second group of conscripts, Sherbrooke too had gone from bilingual to French-only, bringing the totals to eleven French-speaking and two bilingual camps in Quebec. The number of bilingual spots in Cornwall was raised by 100, bringing the total number of unilingual French ones to 7,950 or 26.9 percent, and bilingual to 750 or 2.5 percent, out of a new total of 29,600 overall.[55] These arrangements suggest once again the large and important contributions made to the NRMA by many French-speaking militiamen and army officials, so that the camps could be set up and operate in this manner in 1940.[56]

When selecting sites for the training centres, planners clearly wanted to distribute them efficiently in relation to the country's main population centres. But in the case of major cities such as Toronto and Montreal, they were often located in smaller towns slightly farther away than might have seemed logical simply for reasons of efficiency. Another, more important motive seems to have been to place them in smaller local communities that had not yet experienced the war on a large scale, and thus provide nearby populations with an opportunity to support and feel more directly part of it. It also did not hurt to spread the government's military funds around, to benefit many towns that had not yet seen any stimulus from wartime mobilization.[57]

Civilians in these communities contributed to the success of the camps in many ways. One of the most interesting cases occurred when J.L. Ralston sent a telegram to the mayors of all towns and cities involved in the new program in mid-September, asking for aid in supplying musical bands for training and entertainment purposes. Most replies were favourable, and several towns and cities promised to provide musicians or instruments. Some respondents raised questions of travel, pay, and the amount of time that could be devoted to such activities by civilian band members. But most went on to express sentiments along the lines of those of Gérard Lacourcière, the mayor of Lac-Mégantic, Quebec, who wrote: "We are glad to offer this contribution. We gather from your message that you want those boys to feel that there is somebody who is interested in them and in what they are undertaking to do, and shall do our utmost to meet your desires."[58] In Red Deer, Alberta, the city donated a set of instruments that had originally been purchased by the trustees of a local CEF unit after the First World War, providing a direct link between its contributions to the two conflicts.[59]

In many districts, the announcement that a training centre would be built nearby was significant local news and received considerable coverage in regional newspapers. In early August, for example, the *Camrose Canadian* trumpeted the announcement that the city was being considered for a camp, and continued to report on every development over the next two months.[60] At the same time, not everyone seems to have fully understood the purpose of the camps. In mid-July, H.C. Nixon, the Provincial Secretary of Ontario and a key figure in the Hepburn government, apparently had in mind the defence department's unemployment relief camps which had attempted to help alleviate conditions during the Great Depression when he wrote to J.G. Gardiner, newly appointed as Minister of National War Services in addition to being the agriculture minister, to request that married men of thirty-five or even forty years of age be included in the first group of conscripts so that the province could "purge" itself of unemployed men who were still drawing government relief payments.[61]

In mid-August, representatives from four of the country's major service organizations – the Canadian Legion, the Knights of Columbus, the Salvation Army, and the Young Men's Christian Association (YMCA) – met with officials in Ottawa to arrange to provide "Canteen" or "Recreation" huts in each camp.[62] Responsibilities were divided among the four, and soon citizens in almost every city and town where a training centre was located were raising money and collecting books, magazines, writing supplies, radios, games, and furniture for the use of the men. By early December, according to its war diary, the Knights of Columbus Hut at No. 71 CMTC in Edmundston, New Brunswick, boasted a piano, a violin, a movie projector, Ping-Pong tables, "and divers[e] other forms of entertainment."[63] In Kitchener, Ontario, citizens organized a camp library that contained over five hundred books and magazines, along with "all local weekly and daily newspapers represented by our trainees."[64] In Fort William, the city library opened a part-time branch in the local training centre, and a "Summary" of events of the first month of training prepared by an anonymous author reported that its personnel had commented on the "kindly and welcome manner" with which they had been received generally by the citizens there.[65]

Public interest in the training centres continued over the next few weeks. In Woodstock, Ontario, 5,000 civilians lined the streets for a civic ceremony to welcome the military staff when they arrived to take charge of the camp. Similar scenes were played out in St-Jérôme and Joliette, Quebec.[66] The Department of National Defence ordered district commanders to cooperate as much as possible with reporters wishing to visit the camps, particularly for the arrival of the first group of trainees on Wednesday, October 9, and newspapers in several communities printed lengthy stories about the occasion. In Kitchener, the director of the centre's new YMCA canteen hosted a live broadcast on a local radio station, interviewing men as they arrived. And in Rimouski and Cornwall, the first day was recorded by the "Associated Screen News" and "March of Time" newsreel organizations.[67] In Quebec, camps were blessed by the local Roman Catholic clergy, including the Bishops of Chicoutimi and Valleyfield, as well as by Cardinal Jean-Marie-Rodrigue Villeneuve, the head of the Church in the province, who made a tour of several centres around Quebec City.[68] This provided not only religious but also significant political support for the undertaking, particularly given that as a young man in 1917 the Cardinal had opposed conscription as a terrible scourge on French Canadians.[69] And Villeneuve went further. He supported the creation of a "day of prayer for victory and peace" on February 9, 1941, during which the text of that prayer was read in every church in Quebec. He and Ernest Lapointe presided over the main ceremony in Montreal, which was broadcast on Radio-Canada and the BBC and even in parts of the United States and South America.[70] This support no doubt was somewhat defensive in intent, to show English Canadians that Quebeckers were behind the war and in particular to alleviate the threat of serious divisions of the sort that had developed in the First World War. But it also suggests that Villeneuve and other leaders perhaps had somewhat more hope about the direction the Second World War was taking so far.[71] The participation of French Canadians from the broader community in events at the various training centres indicates that if they did not support the war effort outright, they were at least curious to know more, since the facilities were a new phenomenon for most of them, just as they were for people across the country. The first Sunday of the training period saw hundreds and even thousands of civilians visit centres in every province, for the first of many weekly visitor's days over the next few months. And prominent local and national figures continued to make other visits to see and support the training.

Once the initial confusion of examining, documenting, inoculating, clothing, and equipping trainees and finding sleeping quarters for their first night was over, it was time to begin the work for which the centres had been created. In describing the training carried out in the early NRMA camps, historians such as J.L. Granatstein and J.M. Hitsman have stressed the degree to which the centres were designed simply to accustom recruits to the army, and show them that military service could be enjoyable.[72] Indeed, local newspapers and even some of the units themselves emphasized the same.[73] At the national level, R.B. Hanson criticized the Liberal government in August for not providing a more extensive program of training, charging that its plans were motivated by political rather than military concerns. And in October, the Toronto magazine *Saturday Night* labelled the training a "tragic joke" that would produce men "who can just manage to form threes and shoulder arms if not barked at too ferociously." The *Canadian Forum* did point out that those newspapers that were criticizing the plan the most strongly were also the ones that had been most critical of the King government generally over the past few months.[74] But compared to the separate camps that were at the same time attempting to prepare men for potential combat overseas, they certainly did not measure up, as there was no real collective training beyond the company level. Nevertheless, the army's planners did try to prepare recruits for future military service on some level, given the constraints within which they were forced to operate in 1940. Condensed within the four-week syllabus was the same basic military knowledge that any militiaman would be expected to have acquired after a year or more of training, and that knowledge was being disseminated all at once rather than over the year, so that recruits could consolidate and build immediately on their knowledge with each lesson. As one war diary summarized the program, the trainees were expected to achieve the level of physical fitness, understanding of drill, and combat skills required of an infantrymen at the section level.[75] To that end, the thirty days of training were divided into 220 periods, lasting forty-five minutes each (with an accompanying fifteen-minute break in each case), as follows:

Drill (general, and carrying small arms)	- 48 periods
Marching	- 25 periods
Physical training	- 24 periods
Small arms training, including:	- 51 periods
- general use of rifle (26 periods)	
- use of bayonet (12 periods)	
- use of rifle for anti-aircraft fire (7 periods)	
- live firing on indoor range (6 periods)	
Tactics (fieldcraft, scouting and patrol work, trench digging, laying barbed wire, and road blocks)	- 35 periods
Protection against gas	- 20 periods
Demonstrations by selected squads	- 3 periods
Military education (lectures on discipline, regimental histories of various units to which men were to be posted after training, general infantry organization and characteristics of arms)	- 6 periods
Spare periods (pay parades, barrack inspections, etc.)	- 8 periods[76]

Most camps scheduled compulsory sports programs on Wednesday nights or Saturday afternoons as part of their physical training. But on other evenings, the men were left on their own. On Sundays, there were church parades in the morning (usually compulsory) and visits to the camps by relatives and friends in the afternoon. In the memory of Lucien Côté, from the village of Sayabec in the Gaspé, who had just turned twenty-three and attended the first camp in Rimouski in November 1940, his training gave him more confidence and maturity and thus "made him a man" ("plus «homme»"). And when he was later called out to complete four months of training (see next chapter), he felt that his earlier experience had given him a head start over his fellow trainees. This

Figure 7 Slightly distracted thirty-day trainees attempt to view a lecture while the Minister of National Defence, J.L. Ralston, looks on, during a visit to Cornwall, Ontario, October 22, 1940. *Source:* LAC, e-010994310.

was essentially what the army's planners had been aiming for with the early thirty-day program. Côté would go on to serve as a volunteer in the *Royal 22e Régiment* in Italy in 1943–45, and in the postwar army from 1948 to 1963.

As Côté remembered it, the staffs of the training centres were also very dedicated and hard working and took their jobs seriously.[77] Despite many officers and instructors being First World War veterans, they do not seem to have clung to their experiences of the previous conflict, and instead tried to provide a level of training that reflected the knowledge available to the Canadian army in 1940–41. In January 1941, for example, when the staff at one centre were shown a film on tanks produced in 1924, they quickly dismissed it as "obsolete and of little value" (although the fact that they were being shown such a film suggests a judgment of its own as to what was considered fit to be distributed as training material in 1940).[78] Some local commanders invited squads from nearby centres where training was being conducted for overseas volunteers, to demonstrate advanced weaponry that was not included in the NRMA syllabus, such as heavy machine guns, anti-tank rifles, and even armoured cars.[79] By the end of each training period, recruits were expected to be able to endure lengthy route marches of several kilometres, and had experienced detailed tactical schemes that incorporated the various elements learned during training. These sometimes included complicated night manoeuvres, or cooperation with aircraft from local RCAF bases. In Woodstock, Ontario, the camp's staff tried to make such an exercise more realistic by adding smoke generators and bags of flour dropped from cooperating aircraft, while in Red Deer, Alberta, they arranged to have a Trans-Canada airliner fly low overhead during a regularly scheduled flight and used fireworks to simulate anti-aircraft fire. To its war diarist, at least, the results "proved to be very realistic."[80] At a Montreal-area camp, men participated in a night exercise that tested their ability to use stealth and concealment to approach a group of sentries without being detected. "The only platoon to succeed," the centre reported, was one "[in] which 82% of the men were Italians [i.e., Italian Canadians]. Imagine Herr Hitler's wrath if he only knew."[81] Although the war diarist who recorded this comment was making light of the number of Italian Canadians in his training centre (Sorel, Quebec), Italian-speaking conscripts did make up a higher proportion of NRMA men as a whole, compared to their proportion of the larger population, as did those speaking German (see Table 6 in Chapter 5). Given that Italy was at war with Canada, that fascism had had some adherents among Italian Canadians before 1935 (when Benito Mussolini's invasion of Ethiopia began to call his exact motives for advocating fascism into question), that several hundred Italian Canadians had been interned just a few months earlier after Italy formally declared war, and that others had been rounded up and taken in for questioning, it is perhaps not surprising that some members of this ethnic group might have felt less interested in volunteering for the Allied war effort, especially at that particular moment in time. The high concentration in the Sorel centre was also probably at least partly due to the fact that Italian Canadians were mostly located in large numbers only in Toronto and Montreal in the 1940s, and thus more men may have been subject to being sent there in the first place.[82]

The training accomplished in the thirty-day program over the winter of 1940–41 is even more notable when one considers the shortages of equipment with which most had to deal. Recruits were issued with Ross rifles, the First World War Canadian-designed and -produced weapon that had been removed from service in 1916 after a series of controversies over its suitability for the battlefield. They were sufficient for elementary training, however, and more importantly they were the only weapons available in large numbers in 1940. They were supplemented with American-designed Springfield rifles and with special models of the British Lee-Enfield, both of which had been manufactured in the United States during the First World War. Some arrived still in the original cases into which they had been packed in 1917.[83] Reports from several camps commented on faulty or mismatched bayonets, sights, and even bolts that arrived with their rifles, a legacy of their First World War service. Shortages of other items were reported, such as barbed wire, gas and anti-aircraft training equipment, uniforms, and blankets.[84] When machine guns were added to the syllabus in March 1941, most centres had to make do with First World War–era Lewis guns for another year until they could finally replace them with modern Bren guns produced in Canada.[85] As they had done in supplying staffs for the training centres, local NPAM units again provided vital assistance in meeting these shortages by temporarily lending weapons and other equipment from their own meagre stocks.

A number of other minor problems came to light as the thirty-day training centres went into operation. In Prince Edward Island, planners suddenly discovered that no local infantry unit existed to which the men could be posted after they completed their training. As a result, they became troopers in a local cavalry regiment. Similar arrangements were made to post trainees in Temiskaming, Quebec, to a nearby pioneer unit.[86] Conscientious objectors were required to undergo training but were permitted to substitute work in camp hospitals and store rooms, and other administrative duties, for weapons training. As Major-General Crerar reported to J.L. Ralston in March 1941: "In many cases such recruits subsequently volunteered to follow the complete training programme and several have even volunteered and been accepted for the Active Army."[87] The more rigorous objectors were formally but unassumingly placed under arrest in the camps' guard rooms while their colleagues completed their training, and then returned home with everyone else at the end of the thirty days.[88] After April 1941, when compulsory service was extended to the duration of the war (see next chapter), provisions were made to allow them to carry out alternative service outside the army. Unfortunately, it was up to officials in the Department of National War Services (later the Department of Labour) to decide the status of objectors, and some claims were rejected. This led to at least one case where several Jehovah's Witnesses, who were unable to claim status as conscientious objectors because their sect was then considered illegal by the government, were subjected to the harsh discipline of a formal military detention barracks, apparently for the duration of the war.[89] In contrast, in late 1941 two conscientious objectors in Camrose, Alberta, not only agreed to serve in the army after a few days of official detention in their camp, but one of them was eventually awarded the rank of lance corporal for the high quality of his conduct during his training.[90] According to Thomas Socknat, a total of 12,600 men claimed conscientious objector status under the NRMA during the war. Of that number, 768 later chose to enlist, while the majority carried out various forms of alternative service.[91]

ACCORDING TO THE contemporary records of the Department of National War Services, during the first three training periods a total of 94,771 men were ordered to report for compulsory training across the country; 90,336 (95.3 percent) reported in response to the calls. Another 7,335 were released after reporting, mostly for medical reasons, leaving 82,981 men who completed the program and joined the rolls of the Canadian militia.[92] This represented more than a 75 percent increase over its paper strength of 107,219 men in August 1940 – a number that had itself more than doubled from 47,343 a month earlier, likely due to men seeking to avoid the stigma of training under the NRMA by instead joining the militia (or who simply preferred to perform their service part-time by that route).[93] On the whole, the early thirty-day camps ran smoothly, and the results of the training lived up to the expectations of at least the staffs who were conducting it. One commanding officer labelled his men the equal of soldiers in the NPAM, adding that some of his junior officers even considered the NRMA recruits to be superior to average militiamen.[94] When four local militia commanders came to Woodstock, Ontario, to view the men assigned to join their units after the training, they reportedly "expressed astonishment and pleasure at the progress shown by the Personnel undergoing training."[95] In early 1941, Major-General Crerar also gave his approval to the program, again comparing it favourably to the work of the country's part-time militia units.[96] As Lieutenant-Colonel D. Carmichael noted at the end of the third thirty-day training period at his training centre in Brockville, Ontario, in addition to the trainees his staff could also "now be considered to be very good. They are very keen to excel in their work. Although they find the training hours daily, [*sic*] somewhat long they realize that the thirty day training period is rather short in which to reach the desired standard and they work hard to get results."[97] Comments on the energies and skills of the staffs of the training centres could be repeated from numerous war diaries and other reports from this period. Still, commanders were ready to criticize the lack of competence of their staffs when necessary, or to point out areas where training could be improved for future recruits, again showing their devotion to their new duties.[98]

Despite being compelled to undergo training, and the intensity of the work itself, the recruits in the thirty-day training centres seem to have enjoyed their experiences. Although the evidence is clearly biased, many commanding officers and war diarists commented on the enthusiasm shown by the conscripts towards their work.[99] And based on stories by reporters who were obviously allowed into the camps in the hope that they would produce favourable copy, local newspapers echoed the praise. Yet there is no evidence that the men who spoke to reporters were compelled to make any of the statements they did. As the *Camrose Canadian* reported at the end of the first training period, the trainees there "were pretty proud of their accomplishments" and happy with their instructors.[100] The *Peterborough Examiner* recounted the experiences of four local recruits whom the reporter tracked down after they had finished their training, under the title "Trainees Opposed To Camp Life Change Opinions As Time Passes." All four of the men interviewed – Neil Blewett of Young's Town, Robert Dixon of Buckhorn, and George Brown and Floyd Abrams from Peterborough – had complaints about having had to adjust to army life during the first day or two of the camp, the monotony of the food, and not being allowed to spend longer away from the training centre in their evening hours. But they also acknowledged that parts of the work had been interesting. In addition: "The thirty days has done us the world of good in health and it also puts all men on the same standing; in other words one man, no matter what his position on equal basis with each other."[101] As one anonymous trainee in Grande Prairie, Alberta was quoted as saying: "It has been a glorious, inexpensive 30 days holiday," while French-speaking recruits Roland Dumont and Marcel Naud from the then-separate cities of Rouyn and Noranda, and Aimé Godbout and Jean-Baptiste Gauthier from Montreal, all also treated their experience in the St-Jérôme centre lightly, Dumont noting simply that his girlfriend was missing him while he was away, and Gauthier stating that he had liked the young ladies of that town better than the training.[102]

In Quebec, in fact, in the words of one often-quoted study from Military District No. 5, which included Quebec City and other eastern parts of the province, the results of the training were "almost unexpectedly successful." According to the reports of individual camps from which the study was compiled, they "may not have taught much of the technical science of modern warfare, but [they] have laid the beginnings of a foundation of public service, and knocked a lot of mischievious [*sic*] nonsense out of the minds of the young men of the district." In addition, the author of the survey noted, local cities and towns had done a great deal to ensure the success of the training centres, and citizens were so friendly (and treated soldiers to drinks in local bars so often) that it was apparently becoming a danger "which might lead to the extraction of information by enemy agents." While the writer may have been getting carried away, his comments do seem to reflect the tenor of the reports on which the study was based.[103] Pierre Vennat notes that other than complaints about the food in the Huntingdon training centre (a complaint that authorities announced would be immediately investigated), francophone recruits in the Montreal area generally

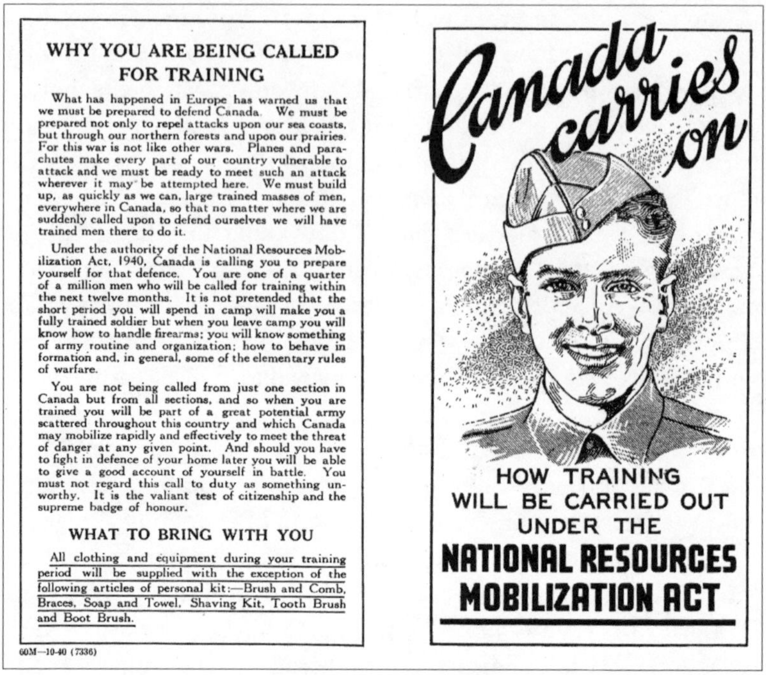

WHY YOU ARE BEING CALLED FOR TRAINING

What has happened in Europe has warned us that we must be prepared to defend Canada. We must be prepared not only to repel attacks upon our sea coasts, but through our northern forests and upon our prairies. For this war is not like other wars. Planes and parachutes make every part of our country vulnerable to attack and we must be ready to meet such an attack wherever it may be attempted here. We must build up, as quickly as we can, large trained masses of men, everywhere in Canada, so that no matter where we are suddenly called upon to defend ourselves we will have trained men there to do it.

Under the authority of the National Resources Mobilization Act, 1940, Canada is calling you to prepare yourself for that defence. You are one of a quarter of a million men who will be called for training within the next twelve months. It is not pretended that the short period you will spend in camp will make you a fully trained soldier but when you leave camp you will know how to handle firearms; you will know something of army routine and organization; how to behave in formation and, in general, some of the elementary rules of warfare.

You are not being called from just one section in Canada but from all sections, and so when you are trained you will be part of a great potential army scattered throughout this country and which Canada may mobilize rapidly and effectively to meet the threat of danger at any given point. And should you have to fight in defence of your home later you will be able to give a good account of yourself in battle. You must not regard this call to duty as something unworthy. It is the valiant test of citizenship and the supreme badge of honour.

WHAT TO BRING WITH YOU

All clothing and equipment during your training period will be supplied with the exception of the following articles of personal kit:—Brush and Comb, Braces, Soap and Towel, Shaving Kit, Tooth Brush and Boot Brush.

60M—10-40 (7336)

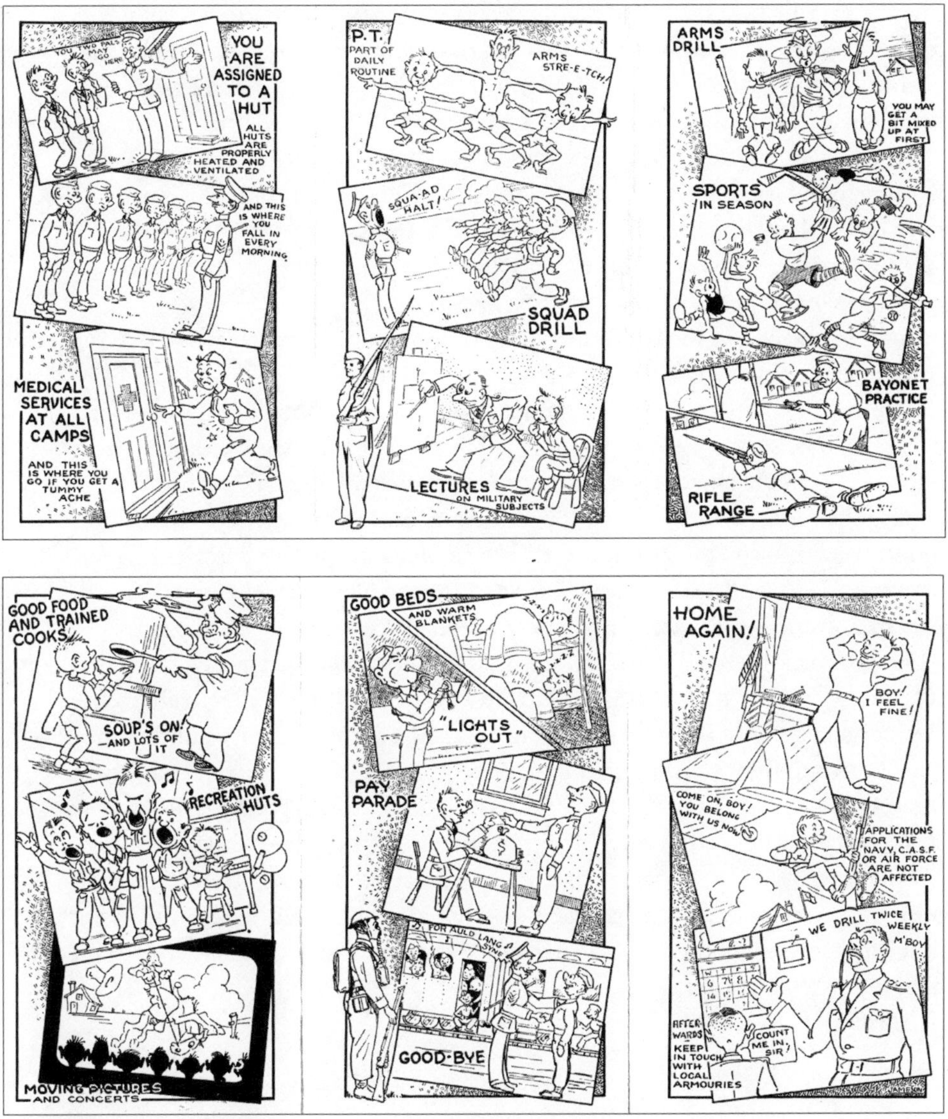

Figure 8 The above pamphlet was prepared for distribution to recruits in the early thirty-day training centres, and suggests the degree to which authorities tended to emphasize the variety of activities and the more enjoyable aspects that the experience would include. *Source:* LAC, e-0111577 and e-011157757_s1.

saw the training positively, and many even indicated their intention to volunteer for active service afterwards.[104] A year later, well after compulsory training had been extended to the duration of the war, according to the Liberal Party's political organizer for the Quebec City area it was still being well received there. As he put it, "many of the farm lads who were called up and who left their homes in tears, found camp life very enjoyable and their English-speaking compatriots fine chaps. They have been good advertisers for military service. Many of these lads were pretty wayward at home, and the influence of military training in the eyes of the parish priests, has been very good."[105]

Thus, by the end of the third thirty-day training period in February 1941, the compulsory military training program was well established. It had provoked relatively little public opposition, and at the same time it had garnered a high degree of local support. Commanders had worked to make the training as thorough and realistic as possible for the men, and even taken advantage of local conditions to make unique additions to the training syllabus. Over the winter months, recruits in Fort William, Ontario, carried out special exercises in manoeuvre and camouflage in the snow, and centres in Newmarket and in Vernon, British Columbia, added ski instruction for small groups of qualified trainees.[106] Although these men may not have lived up to the standards required for Allied soldiers overseas, the Canadian army had responded quite effectively to the government's political requirements in 1940 by creating a short but comprehensive program of training that introduced thousands of conscripts to life in the military and that instilled in them the duty be prepared to defend their country in case of need. At the same time, the program did not disrupt the flow of volunteers who were going through the separate training stream that had been set up to build up the parallel non-NRMA army in Canada and Britain, that was itself just about to begin growing larger and larger in its demands on manpower over the next several months.

3
Enshrining the NRMA: Compulsory Military Service, 1940–41

By the time the new thirty-day training program was up and running under the authority of the NRMA, a number of developments were taking place that would soon change the entire way in which it fit into the larger planning of the Canadian army. The major influence behind this change was Major-General H.D.G. Crerar, who was anxious to rationalize the army's various functions. As he reported to a friend as early as September 1940, "I have taken every opportunity to point out to the Minister that this present scheme of compulsory training and service must be considered as an interim arrangement for in fact it solves none of our military problems and introduces several new and complicated ones."[1] Crerar repeated these sentiments in a public speech in October, in which he argued that the length of training had been limited only by the shortages of weapons and equipment available in 1940. As he also noted, "the short training period [had] enabled a larger number of young Canadians to gain a proper conception of their national obligations within a given time." And while Canada still needed to build up larger forces to help Britain match the strength of Germany for the future, what it required even more was to make its army mechanized and base it on tactics similar to those of the German army, in order to match that country on the battlefield. That would mean more reliance on machines and less on sheer numbers of men, and thus the pace of calling up the latter should be coordinated more rationally with the corresponding expansion of industrial capacity to outfit and equip them. Taken together, his comments did not necessarily imply a smaller army in total. But they did suggest that industry also needed to be considered in calculations of how Canada's manpower would be divided up, and perhaps even that simply using conscription to attempt to build the largest army possible would be counterproductive.[2] He was considerably more forthright about that aspect of the current thirty-day compulsory training program in private. According to journalist Grant Dexter, the parliamentary correspondent for the *Winnipeg Free Press* and a close confidant of several Ottawa insiders, Crerar described it as "very costly and completely useless" and noted that the government's attempts to follow the dual policies of conscription for home defence and voluntary service overseas were "mutually destructive and in combination they must hamstring our industrial effort."[3]

Over the next few months, Crerar would turn the compulsory military training program into a much more integral part of the overall army. In the process, he also seems to have come to see it as a way not just to meet the original 1940 directive from the army's political superiors to provide training for home defence, but to meet some of his own wishes for the army itself. In particular, it soon became apparent that once trainees had discovered what life in uniform was all about, large numbers were quite willing to consider volunteering for overseas service. And even those who were not willing to volunteer could serve usefully on more permanent home defence duties, so that other men could be freed up to proceed overseas. While rationalizing the training system in early 1941, Crerar and some of his staff organized it so that they could take advantage of both notions. He also added the possibilities offered by the NRMA to other arguments that he had begun marshalling to try to convince the Cabinet War Committee (CWC) that the country could maintain larger overseas ground forces than had previously been thought possible. Thanks to further events both inside and outside Canada in the summer of 1941, he succeeded in that goal, and apparently it encouraged him to begin thinking that even more might be possible. Thus, it was the first step in what would become a much larger expansion in the overseas army, and one that the NRMA would play a key role in shaping.

By the time Crerar made the comments noted above about the thirty-day training system's lack of efficiency, he had already begun putting forward his solution to the problem. In early September he submitted a comprehensive and thoughtful memorandum to his minister, J.L. Ralston, that began by noting that the army would still need to expand as much as possible over the next few months to replace some of the many French and other divisions that had been lost to the Allies in 1940. He estimated that if Canada exerted its maximum effort, it could raise and maintain five to seven divisions overseas – a figure very close to what he and other officers had used for mobilization planning in the 1930s. At the same time, men would be needed to replace the volunteers who went overseas, and for this Crerar advocated relying on the NRMA. Since the current training system divided the resources of the army between the NRMA and overseas service, the logical answer was to combine the two schemes. This would result in a four-month training program for both groups; in Crerar's view, the minimum length of time necessary to produce fully trained modern soldiers. Conveniently, it would also reduce the disruption caused to industry by the current compulsory training plan, by calling out only one-quarter of the present number of men each month. It would also prevent large numbers of volunteer militiamen from being drawn from their civilian jobs to man local defences on long-term duty. In this way, the country could continue to expand its industrial contributions to the war effort even as it built up its forces in England. At no time, Crerar added, would there be any need to rely on conscription for overseas service. In a final note that betrayed his postwar ambitions for the army, Crerar added that reorganizing it would allow Canada to create a "proper" military force that would free the country from continued dependence on Britain and the United States by making it fully capable of looking after its own defence needs after the war.[4] Clearly, he had learned well from his experiences as part of the interwar Canadian army, for he framed his arguments in a manner designed to be greatly appealing to political leaders such as Prime Minister King, who had similar objectives.

Crerar soon followed this memorandum with a more formal written statement of his "Canadian Army Programme for 1941." Among his recommendations were plans to send the army's 3rd and 4th Divisions overseas by the summer of 1941, along with one independent tank brigade. Units would be mobilized to create two new divisions in Canada to replace the departing formations, as well as a full armoured division, which would proceed overseas at a later date. To avoid having to duplicate the army's resources by maintaining two separate training streams, he called on the government to merge the two systems to create a new "Active" army, which would consist of all volunteers who had enlisted to serve outside Canada, and a "Reserve" made up of the current militia force and men called out for training under the NRMA. The training centres themselves would also be merged, and most of the NRMA camps would become basic training centres, where all Canadian soldiers would receive their first two months of training. Existing volunteer facilities would be transformed into advanced training centres, where men would spend another two months learning the skills of the particular part of the army in which they were expected to serve. The two groups would be known as "A" and "R" recruits and would train side by side in the same centres. Very conveniently, once again, the number of "R" recruits trained in 1941 would be just sufficient to replace the number of volunteers sent overseas during the same period. In his plans, Crerar also continued to stress the need to provide for the expansion of industry as well as manpower.[5]

Ralston presented Crerar's recommendations to the CWC on October 1. From the start, they sparked lengthy debates. King's reluctance to expand the army soon became clear, and he quickly supported the Minister of National Defence for Naval Services, Angus L. Macdonald, when the latter recommended deciding among the priorities of the army, the navy, and the air force (all of which were expected to grow significantly over the coming year) before approving the army's plans. King agreed, and the CWC agreed to call for the RCN and RCAF to present their own plans before any final decisions were made. Crerar and his naval and air force counterparts appeared before the CWC twice over the next ten days. Like Crerar, Rear-Admiral Percy Nelles hoped to create a more substantial and professional force for after the war. He argued that to meet both wartime and postwar needs, the government should authorize a program to purchase two Tribal-class destroyers a year over several years from Britain, and even consider acquiring a few battle cruisers. A.L. Macdonald won King's support for this by emphasizing that approving larger programs for the navy and air force would help show that the government was maintaining a balanced effort, rather than focusing solely on building up the army, as in the First World War.[6] Aside from the existing plans for the BCATP in Canada, which would eventually also advance the goal of building up its air forces overseas, the main "ask" from Air Vice-Marshal Lloyd S. Breadner, the Chief of the Air Staff, was that plans to expand coastal defence forces be completed that had been put off during the crisis earlier in the year. King also ultimately supported that recommendation.[7] Meanwhile, Crerar reduced his own expectations, asking only that one further division be established overseas by mid-1941. The CWC then postponed further debate while J.L. Ilsley, the finance minister, considered the budgetary ramifications of the three services' plans. By late October, Ralston was pressing his colleagues for an early decision on the new training arrangements so that detailed planning could begin as soon as possible. The result was another discussion on October 23, during which members questioned whether conscripts should be given an opportunity to volunteer for service in the RCN or RCAF, or released to jobs in wartime industries, at the end of the first thirty days of the new, longer compulsory training. Clearly, this was another way to emphasize those three wartime uses of manpower as equal or greater in priority to serving in the army. But by the end of the month, the CWC had approved Crerar's general proposals, and planning began to combine the two training systems.[8]

Unfortunately, no manpower decision was ever that simple, even this early in the war. In late November, Crerar presented his formal scheme for the new training program to the CWC. The meeting provided another occasion for King to state his opposition to increasing the country's ground forces before final decisions had been made about the other two services. Crerar was asked to prepare another version of his plan, one that would allow conscripts to transfer more easily to industry or to the other armed forces while undergoing training. He and his staff had resisted such changes, since it would mean forfeiting all the time and effort spent training men up to that point. By mid-December, however, a revised plan was ready for the CWC. This time, the decision was deferred until the return of Ralston, who was visiting England, accompanied by Crerar, to ascertain first-hand the military needs of the British for the coming year.[9] Discussion resumed on January 8, 1941, on the basis of a telegram from Ralston in London in which he called for urgent approval of Crerar's army program.[10] But once again the debate was deferred; the other members of the CWC wanted Ralston to return and explain the changes directly. Only in late January was the final decision made to approve both the army plan and the new training program on which it would be founded. In addition, tentative procedures were approved to allow NRMA recruits to transfer voluntarily to the RCAF or the RCN after their first two months of basic training. Employers would also be allowed to request the withdrawal of essential employees at that time. The plans of the RCAF and RCN were then approved without substantial reductions, the army program having been the key point on which most of the CWC's members had focused their attention during the discussions. Even the prime minister had increasingly come around to Crerar's plan "as the only one that had any real military value to it."[11]

The result was a substantial victory for Crerar. Despite their obvious concerns, he had managed to convince the prime minister and other Cabinet ministers that it was necessary to increase the army overseas, and that the country would be able to maintain that army through voluntary service. The new plan called for 3rd Canadian Infantry Division and a full armoured division to arrive in Britain by the end of 1941, along with sufficient men to complete the army's corps headquarters overseas. Even if King and others had wanted to challenge the program more strongly, they had few grounds upon which they could have done so in early 1941, especially given the strength and coherence with which Crerar had advanced his arguments.

For Crerar, the change marked the culmination of his plans to reorganize the army in Canada. As he wrote in an often-quoted letter to A.G.L. McNaughton in May 1941:

> The decision to retain the "trainees" in the Service for an indefinite period after they have finished their four months in the Training Centres has been well received. I believe that a high proportion of these 21-year olds will volunteer for overseas and those which do not will be introduced into Coast Defence and Internal Security Battalions. All these rather represent several bites at the cherry – the cherry being conscription for service anywhere. On the other hand, this progressive process is educating the public to what may well be the inevitable and I believe that if this comes to pass, the final stage will be taken with a minimum of fuss by all concerned. In the meantime, and certainly for the balance of this year, we are assured of all the man-power we require either as reinforcements or for new units in overseas formations.[12]

Combined with Crerar's public statement in October 1940, and the arguments he had used with Ralston and the CWC to rationalize his changes since then, his reference here to conscription being "inevitable" is not necessarily hypocritical. Rather, he was arguably pushing for what he considered to be Canada's best interests, which were to build up as large an army as possible for overseas. At the same time, he understood his government's position well enough to try to help keep it from having to make an all-or-nothing decision between conscription and such an army. And if, as he suggested both here and in his earlier speech, the current program was also helping educate Canadians that military service was not so horrible and that they had a duty to serve their country, then even if it did gradually come to be extended it might not be as much of an issue. Tellingly, although it is not recorded in the official CWC minutes, even King may have agreed with such sentiments to a certain point. As he recorded approvingly in his own diary as the four-month plan was being authorized on January 28: "Ralston expressed the hope that this system might be continued after the war. Lapointe agreed with him. In other words, all seemed to feel that a period of military training for every citizen is a good thing."[13] One way or another, in the meantime the result would be to make the NRMA a much more significant part of the broader structure of the Canadian army over the next four years, with implications that would come to be increasingly clear, both to the country's political leaders and to the thousands of conscripts who entered the new four-month training centres after March 1941.

How the two factors had started to come together – of trying to meet the government's political objective of avoiding conscription for overseas service, while at the same time allowing Crerar to build up the largest possible army in Europe – is suggested particularly by the CWC members' demands that conscripts be permitted to transfer to the RCAF and RCN when Crerar was arguing before them for his new training program in early 1941. As soon as the first thirty-day training centres had opened in October 1940, many camps had begun reporting large numbers of NRMA trainees who were volunteering for overseas service in all three armed forces. In Charlottetown, for example, three hundred out of five hundred trainees reportedly became members of various active service forces during the first two training classes, while in Fort William, Ontario, as many as 80 percent were said to have been ready to volunteer after the first thirty-day period, if only the army had had the necessary facilities ready to receive them within the camps. Several other centres reported that 45 to 50 percent of men were making similar promises.[14] In Military District No. 5 (Quebec City), authorities even included a question on the enrolment form used in the camps that asked men in what part of the army they would be willing to serve if they were later called to active duty – although one has to wonder at the wisdom of including such a question on forms in a mostly French-speaking region where people might already have been more than a little suspicious of the thirty-day training (and some men did in fact react that way).[15] Nevertheless, many centres across the country recorded a small but steady flow of men leaving during each early thirty-day training period to join one of the three armed services, and several commanders made formal efforts to encourage men to volunteer, through lectures and other efforts. In several cases, officers from active service units and even the RCAF attended the centres themselves to recruit.[16] In others, commanders noted the number of men spontaneously deciding to volunteer after experiencing life in the camps, and called for the army to prepare proper machinery to encourage such actions among future groups of trainees.[17] Facing a shortage of trained tradesmen for its overseas forces in the fall of 1940, authorities in Ottawa also combed the compulsory centres for men willing to volunteer for those duties.[18]

By the end of the first training period, 11.6 percent of NRMA men had reportedly been willing to consider joining the RCAF and 3.5 percent the RCN, overall, while 5 percent had declared that they were planning to take jobs in war industry. And 8 percent of all men in the second training class were said to have stated their readiness to serve anywhere within the army.[19] In January 1941, Crerar reported to Ralston that the same figures for all conscripts in the first two training classes together were 15 percent in favour of the RCN or RCAF, and 10 percent the army.[20] By the time provisions for such transfers had been presented to the CWC in December 1940 as part of the new four-month training program, his staff were projecting that as many as 2,000 to 2,500 men from each future group of 8,000 called out for training could be expected to volunteer for the RCN or RCAF or to work in war industry, and others for overseas service in the army.[21] All of this provided another powerful motive for Crerar to merge the two training programs in 1941. Shortly after the first four-month class reported in March, he was also recommending that conscripts be retained in service for the duration of the war rather than returned to civilian life after completing their training. That change was authorized in mid-April, and trainees were informed of their new status.[22]

NDHQ kept careful track of the reactions of recruits to the news and directed training centres to do the same. Although the evidence is again biased, most of the men seem to have expected the change, and accepted it with little overt reaction either way.[23] As the commander of the Chicoutimi camp summarized the situation: "The men affected took the news ... philosophically. There was no enthusiasm shown but neither were there any recriminations or other untoward incident." Discipline among the new "A" recruits actually seemed to be worse than that of the "R" men, he added, because the former were an older and more mixed group, and "the declaration of policy of the Minister of National Defence has [not] noticiably [*sic*] affected the usually satisfactory behaviour of the 'R' recruits." But he did add that the attitude of the broader public in Chicoutimi seemed to be "one of resigned submission to the inevitable."[24] In the words of a similar report from the adjutant of the Newmarket, Ontario, training centre: "The consensus of opinion is that the men themselves expected this to happen ... There was no mass enthusiasm or cheering but just philosophical and cheerful acceptance of the order." As he added, the men had had questions such as "'are we going to be in a position where we will have to accept epithets such as 'conscripts'['], or ... 'Can we still volunteer for service in the Canadian Active Army.'"[25] Among the broader public, as Granatstein and Hitsman note, "reaction to the extension of service for the NRMA conscripts was generally favourable in the press, English-language newspapers seeing this as a long overdue step," although some Opposition MPs criticized the policy for not going further.[26] And an unsigned summary of major newspapers from across the country produced by a member of the prime minister's staff found that English-speaking ones ranged from that view, towards seeing the policy as a good balance between the needs of industry and the overseas forces and between English and French Canadian views on conscription. On the French-language side, the author of the summary noted that *Le Devoir* assumed it was just another step towards extending conscription further, while the Liberal newspaper *Le Soleil* along with *Le Droit* of Ottawa both supported it, on the understanding that it was designed to provide as much aid as possible to Britain without having to send conscripts overseas.[27]

Even more than that, there is plenty of evidence that the organizers of the new training system had seen its potential to encourage even more "R" recruits to volunteer for overseas service. As early as July 1940, the Adjutant-General (the chief officer responsible for managing manpower in the army), Major-General B.W. Browne, had noted the likelihood that conscripts might volunteer for overseas service once they began their compulsory training under the earlier thirty-day system.[28] According to journalist Grant Dexter, these views were shared by the Master-General of the Ordnance (the chief officer responsible for acquiring weapons and munitions), Victor Sifton, the former publisher of the *Winnipeg Free Press*. He had joined the Department of National Defence in December 1940 at the request of J.L. Ralston, and thus had Ralston's ear, and had apparently discussed the notion openly with Ralston, Crerar, and Browne.[29] One way or the other, by March 1941 Browne was writing to Crerar to report that voluntary recruiting numbers were beginning to fall below requirements in several military districts. "I feel that not enough attention has been paid previously to the Reserve Army," he added, "which is our natural source of recruits. I have advocated all along basing our military effort in reinforcement requirements on the Reserve Army, and I am convinced that this course is the best to pursue."[30] By July he was drawing district commanders' attention to "the excellent recruiting results" that resulted from parading "A" and "R" recruits together publicly in the training centres from the time they arrived, in order to call for volunteers:

> It has been found that the Active Army personnel present encourage the first volunteers from the "R" recruits, with the result that more "R" recruits step forward to offer their services ... It is suggested that this method be adopted generally, in all Training Centres, as "R" recruits, whose hold on civilian life has already broken and whose change of status from Home Defence to Active Army involves no financial or other problems, should prove to be a rich source of recruits for the Active Army.[31]

A month later, commanders were reminded that another class of "R" recruits was about to finish its training and that they would automatically be posted to home defence units if they did not volunteer for active service. Browne's letter directed that this "be clearly explained to them beyond any possibility of doubt and that every encouragement be given to them to enlist in the Active Army."[32] The following month, he reported that the number of "R" men volunteering for active service in each training centre had ranged from zero to 78 percent among the first group of recruits to complete the new program. The average for all basic training centres was 20 percent, while another 16 percent had volunteered while undergoing advanced training. Clearly, Browne's enthusiasm was rooted in the experiences of the training centres themselves: as we will see in Chapter 6, several of them were reporting that 90 to 100 percent of their NRMA personnel were "going active" in the summer of 1941. As he concluded, "It appears from the general results that this rich potential source of recruits is by no means being fully tapped. It is felt that a substantial increase over the percentages mentioned above could be obtained if organized and energetic methods were adopted in encouraging 'R' recruits to join the Active Army, Navy or Air Force." His solution to achieve this was to order reports from the commanders of every training centre, describing the methods used to convince men to volunteer.[33] As the replies were received, he and his staff began preparing a more formal set of instructions to govern such activities.

These instructions, released in November 1941, relied heavily on the recommendations of the local training centres. Commanding officers were told to hold special parades when men first arrived in basic training, to stress the need for volunteers and to ask for "converts" from among NRMA recruits. They were also directed to mix together "A" and "R" men in training units, and to hold open competitions "between Platoons and Companies to see who can reach 100% active first." Trainees were to be bombarded with posters and other appeals to their sense of duty. Even chaplains were asked to aid the effort through their sermons. In addition, commanders were given permission to award special leaves to any platoon that went 100 percent active. Junior officers and NCOs received similar instructions, and company commanders and their superiors were directed to meet with each man individually, after all other methods had had an opportunity to work. "A friendly, informal personal talk in which the recruit finds himself able to ventilate his personal circumstances and views to a sympathetic senior Officer," the document noted, "is often the first occasion on which he realizes he is regarded as more than a cog in the machine." Above all, the plan stressed the "importance of continuous effort to achieve the desired results." Browne did end his directions, however, by adding explicitly that the "coercion of 'R' recruits to go Active is strictly prohibited."[34]

Such methods would lead to allegations that NRMA men were being systematically compelled to volunteer as the war went on. Even more importantly, reliance on the NRMA to supply "volunteers" for overseas service would come to influence Crerar's broader goal, which was to create an even larger volunteer army overseas in 1942 and 1943. Yet in the meantime, conscription had gone from being explicitly repudiated by the current Liberal government in 1939, to being instituted as an emergency measure in 1940, and now accepted and integrated into the army's planning for the duration of the war. Although both King and Lapointe had been careful to promise that they were opposed only to conscription for overseas service when they had spoken against it publicly in March and again in September 1939, developments in the war and especially the collapse of western Europe in 1940 had altered both the military and the political situation in Canada. Crerar had exploited this by arguing that the country needed to make a much larger contribution to the war. By 1941 he had achieved his twin goals of convincing the government to begin expanding its ground forces overseas, and reorganizing the training system at home so that it focused on supporting operations overseas, whether an individual soldier was a conscript or a volunteer.

After early 1941, meanwhile, the result at the military level was that the thirty-nine training centres from the NRMA training program were merged with the sixteen existing camps for overseas reinforcements. Most of the former thirty-day camps continued their work, but now, as newly renamed basic training centres, where they taught a standard syllabus to all men for their first two months of training that was literally titled "Common to All Arms." All trainees then went on to the closest advanced training centre for the particular corps or other part of the army they would be joining after completing their training, where they took a second, two-month "Special to the Arm" syllabus that focused on the specific skills expected of infantrymen, artillerymen, signallers, engineers, armoured troopers, members of the ordnance corps, medics, or men in the army service corps. Most of these new advanced camps were the former training centres for volunteers. Although the system evolved further as the war went on, in the early days after the reorganization seven infantry training centres ended up being spread out across the country from Aldershot, Nova Scotia, to Calgary, Alberta. There were also four artillery centres, two in Petawawa, Ontario, and the others in Brandon and Shilo, Manitoba. Engineering, service corps, specialized machine gun, and small arms training were each provided at two schools, one in eastern and one in western Canada. The armoured corps had two centres, both at Camp Borden in Ontario. The rest had one training centre each, although these were also spread somewhat around the country. Camp Borden was the single largest training location (as it remains in today's Canadian Forces), with the two armoured corps centres, two infantry centres, and the service corps centre for eastern Canada. Lastly, a completely new, special centre was established in Eastern Passage (near Halifax), Nova Scotia, to teach the men required for the numerous coast defence and anti-aircraft artillery units now being created on the east and west coasts as the production of both guns and soldiers caught up to the demands generated by the crisis of the previous summer (for the locations of all basic and advanced training centres as of April 1941, see Figure 2).[35] According to then-Colonel E.L.M. Burns, who was involved in planning this new training system as an assistant to Major-General Crerar, forcing men to learn all parts of a common syllabus in the basic training centres rather than separating them out into their individual corps for more specialized training from the beginning was actually less efficient. But a shortage of experienced instructors meant that they had to be concentrated within the more specialized advanced training centres instead of being parcelled out among all camps. Only after the army stopped constantly expanding its total numbers in 1943, and the focus became on training just the regular stream of reinforcements needed to keep existing units up to strength overseas, would the opportunity arise once again to begin trying to rationalize training operations within Canada.[36]

In Quebec, while information about the provisions made to train specific numbers of men in French or English is more difficult to piece together than it was for the thirty-day centres, a total of eleven basic training camps carried over under the new plan (one of which, Lac-Mégantic, was changed in August to a Junior Leaders' School for non-commissioned officers below the rank of sergeant). Seven of these were French-only, and another three were mostly French but as in the earlier days had some spots devoted to training separate groups of men in English.[37] Including advanced infantry training centres at Valcartier and Farnham, and one for machine guns at Trois-Rivières, there were fourteen basic and advanced centres in Quebec out of fifty-four across the country (the former thirty-day training centre in St-Hyacinthe also apparently became a School of Administration, but only for a short time). Given that the machine gun centre trained men only in English, and the two infantry centres in both languages, this means that only half the camps in the province now operated solely in French, although the proportion of French-speaking spaces available to individual men was certainly larger (and the training system still probably had an upper limit of about 20 percent of spaces available to francophones across the country). For francophones who might wish to serve in their own language within the military (or had no choice but to serve, under the NRMA), there were also few options other than the infantry.[38]

Given that fewer basic training centres were required than under the previous NRMA system, some of the former thirty-day camps were transformed into new advanced training centres. These included Farnham in Quebec and Brandon in Manitoba, both mentioned above, as well as Long Branch, Ontario (the Canadian Small Arms Training Centre for eastern Canada), Dundurn, Saskatchewan (the machine gun training centre for western Canada), and Red Deer, Alberta (the Royal Canadian Army Service Corps training centre for western Canada). Like St-Hyacinthe in Quebec, Woodstock's centre in Ontario was converted into a more specialized "Driving and Maintenance School." Brockville, Ontario, and Gordon Head, British Columbia, became new officer training centres, to ensure that all junior officers entering the army would now receive standardized training too. Only Valcartier, Quebec, among the former thirty-day training centres, was closed, no doubt partly because the same army base housed one of the former overseas infantry training centres, which carried over as a new advanced training centre. Altogether, twenty-nine of the original thirty-nine camps were preserved as basic training centres. The only major new elements added to their syllabus were machine guns and anti-tank rifles,[39] both of which had already been taught on a voluntary basis in some earlier cases.

In the following months, the new four-month training program also came to be tied much more closely to the broader issue of providing reinforcements both for Canada and for overseas, as the army's planners came to grasp the NRMA's potential for meeting its manpower needs. In fact, the first development that helped bring commanders to see the value of the NRMA as a source of reinforcements for the Canadian army came just after the reorganized basic

Figure 9 No. 131 Canadian Army (Basic) Training Centre, Camrose, Alberta, June 1941. *Source:* LAC, C-145119.

training centres went into operation in March and April 1941. In early May, the federal government announced its first official recruiting drive of the war, a campaign that would seek more than 30,000 volunteers from among the civilian population. In describing the 1941 recruiting campaign, commentators at the time and later historians have emphasized the shortage of potential volunteers that it seemed to reveal at even this early stage in the war, and the slow response of Canadians to it.[40] Yet the drive should more accurately be seen as the logical result of Crerar's first expansionary "Canadian Army Programme" for 1941, which the CWC had authorized earlier that spring. As numerous units began to be mobilized to make up the new formations that would be added to the force, it was only natural that the army's need for men would grow, and the recruiting campaign was designed more to take advantage of what was still at that point a relatively untapped reserve of manpower in the country to provide a short-term influx of volunteers to fill that need, rather than to meet shortages in existing overseas units.[41]

The recruiting campaign was even more directly a result of the evolution of arrangements for compulsory training under the NRMA in the same period. The idea for it actually emerged on April 23, on the same day that J.L. Ralston came before the CWC to present Major-General Crerar's request to extend the length of service under the NRMA to the duration of the war. When Ralston pointed out that the extension was needed in order to meet the requirements of the new army program by releasing volunteers from home defence duties, because he was worried about finding enough volunteers in the short term from the general public to meet all of the army's new needs, Prime Minister King suggested that the CWC organize a formal recruiting drive at the same time so that the army would not have to rely solely on the NRMA to accomplish everything. Over the next few weeks, plans for the drive were finalized, and the campaign was officially approved by the CWC on May 9.[42] Two days later, Ralston announced its commencement to the Canadian public.[43]

Although the 1941 recruiting drive began slowly, the army did eventually reach and then exceed its targets. A number of methods were used to encourage men to volunteer. These included public relations drives shaped by expert advisers; broadcasts and speeches by Ralston, Ernest Lapointe, and other government ministers; and a speaking tour of western Canada by King in late June. In the end, roughly 48,000 men came forward during the campaign, of whom 34,625 were accepted and placed in uniform. Another 12,000 Canadians joined the RCAF in the same period, and 3,500 the RCN, bringing the total number of volunteers found during the drive to more than 60,000.[44] Civilian recruiting would be conducted on a much more systematic and continuous basis for the rest of the war.

Another way in which the NRMA was involved in the 1941 recruiting drive was through the participation of the army's training organization itself. As the central focus of the war effort in many communities, and in some cases the only military installations for miles around, the army's newly reorganized basic training centres played particularly significant roles in finding civilian volunteers. Several camps doubled as local recruiting depots, to take in and process men from towns and cities across their regions.[45] Especially in Quebec, where recruiters were less hopeful about finding recruits, a succession of entries in the various centres' war diaries suggest that they were an even more coordinated part of the campaign.[46] Across the country, men in the camps organized military displays and parades and participated in civilian rallies designed to stimulate public interest.[47] Efforts to find volunteers also sometimes merged with other activities, such as the 1941 Victory Loan campaign, which was going on at the same time and occasioned further parades and rallies in individual training centres.[48] In Quebec, the lieutenant-governor, Eugène Fiset, who was a former medical officer, army general, and Deputy Minister (DM) of National Defence (and a veteran of South Africa), along with future Governor-General Georges Vanier (soon to be promoted to command Military District No. 5 in Quebec

City), the current DM for the army, Henri DesRosiers, the commander of the Montreal military district, Brigadier Édouard de Bellefeuille Panet, and Premier Adélard Godbout all joined the nationalist *Association catholique de la jeunesse canadienne-française* in La Fontaine Park on May 24 to celebrate the military heroes of New France, as part of a tradition popularized in the interwar years by nationalist Quebec historian Lionel Groulx. In mid-June (and in a description that in some ways almost sounds a little too similar to the Nazi rallies of the 1930s), 16,000 people attended a night-time ceremony in McGill University's Percival Molson Stadium to welcome a special "Victory Torch" that was making its way across the country. Illuminated by the flames of five hundred individual torches, and led by Montreal mayor Adhémar Raynault, they recited a mass oath to remain at the side of Britain until victory and peace were secured. Considering that McGill was an English-language institution and that a large proportion of the local population was English Canadian, the crowd likely included more anglophones than francophones. But *La Presse* also reported favourably on it, which suggests the degree to which people on both sides were following the recruiting campaign.[49]

Of the many activities carried out by the training centres themselves in an effort to further the campaign's objectives, one of the largest and most popular was Army Day. It was held on the last Saturday of June 1941, in every training centre and on every other base across the country, and drew thousands of visitors. Every centre provided displays of physical training and military drill for the occasion, along with rifle shooting and the use of other weapons, tactical exercises, leisure activities, life in the barracks, and even the types of food served to the men. Army Day that Saturday was followed by special church parades in each training centre the following morning, to which the public was again invited.[50] The weekend's activities were so successful that they were repeated two weeks later in most Montreal-area camps,[51] and nationally in 1942 as part of an even larger Army Week program.[52] As the 1941 campaign wrapped up in early July, a "Call to Arms" proclamation was distributed to thousands of towns and cities across Canada. The training centres and other military units provided honour guards for dozens of processions and other ceremonies that accompanied the proclamation's reading in nearby communities.[53] Other efforts to recruit civilian volunteers continued after the end of the formal campaign in July.[54] As they headed home to celebrate Christmas in late 1941, trainees were promised an extra day of leave (up to a maximum of three) for each new civilian they persuaded to volunteer while they were there.[55] In early 1942, an Army Train crossed the country with fifteen cars full of military displays, once more with the support of many training centres and other military units along the way.[56]

GRANDE DEMONSTRATION
d'Une Colonne Motorisée
AU CAMP CARILLON DE ST-JEROME

ARRIVEE
Mercredi le 23 juillet à 5 heures p. m.

Arrivée de la colonne motorisée à la jonction des routes Montréal-St-Jérôme et St-Jérôme-St-Lin.

100 unités mécanisées - Canon 4.5 pces - Une boutique mobile - Porte-troupes - Chars d'assauts miniatures - Cuisine mobiles - Cantine des Chevaliers de Colomb - Porte mitrailleuses Bren, etc.

DEFILÉ

Grande parade à travers les rues de la ville.
Rue St-Georges jusque chez L. C. Taillon, rue Labelle jusqu'au Bureau de Poste. Salut militaire aux autorités de la ville, puis rue Labelle jusqu'à jonction Labelle et St-Georges, descente de la rue St-Georges jusqu'à rue Nantel, rue Fournier à Palais, Palais à Melançon, Melançon à Parent, Parent à St-Georges, St-Georges jusqu'au Camp.

Programme de la Soirée à 8 heures
Centre d'entrainement illuminé :: Camp ouvert au public

Exercices de drill --- Canons et mitrailleuses en action --- Attaques simulées avec tanks, artillerie et infanterie --- Grenade à mains --- Fusées incendiaires, etc...

Venez visiter le camp en foule avec vos amis à cette occasion
Entrée gratuite sur le terrain.

La Cie de Publication de Saint-Jérôme, Ltée, Saint-Jérôme, P. Q.

Figure 10 Poster announcing the arrival of a motorized column of army vehicles that toured several training centres in the Montreal area, including St-Jérôme, in July 1941. *Source:* LAC, e-011157754.

Although the official recruiting campaign proved to be quite successful in 1941, returns were sparse in certain areas, and especially in the Montreal region, which fell short of its share of the national recruiting quota. War diaries for Montreal-area training centres confirm these results, noting that in many cases local populations turned out in large numbers for recruiting rallies but that few men were willing to come forward to volunteer.[57] Thus, there was a clear dichotomy between merely showing interest in what was an unusual spectacle in many communities, and actually enlisting when the time came. It may even possibly suggest the beginning of a hardening of attitudes more generally within Quebec, against both conscription and the broader war effort, as the demands for both grew more insistent during 1941. That the staffs of the training centres put so much effort into encouraging recruiting everywhere, however, and that some men still chose to volunteer for general service, reminds us of the dangers of generalizing about the opinions and actions of any given group during the war. In fact, Montreal was not the only military district across the country to fall short of its recruiting quota. Military Districts No. 3 (eastern Ontario) and 11 (British Columbia) also failed to reach their assigned totals. At the same time, the more francophone of the two districts in Quebec (No. 5) considerably exceeded its goals during the campaign, suggesting once again that reactions were more complex than simply all French Canadians disliking the army or the war, or all English Canadians wishing to rush forward immediately and volunteer.[58]

The large numbers of volunteers found by the training centres in May and June 1941 did not come wholly from the communities outside their gates, either. At least 1,300 came directly from the centres themselves, and possibly as many as 2,600. Another 400 to 1,350 were accepted into the RCAF or RCN.[59] Throughout the summer of 1941, war diaries recorded an almost constant stream of "R" recruits converting to active service in individual training centres, and a similar stream of recruiting officers visiting the camps looking for men for their particular units and formations. At times, it seemed as if the only reason for establishing the training centres had been for their recruiting benefits. They played host to representatives from seemingly every arm and corps of the Canadian army, as well as monthly visits from the RCAF and less frequent ones from the RCN.[60] In most cases, the results were satisfactory, although in at least one centre a representative from the Royal Canadian Corps of Signals probably did not impress potential recruits when he managed to start a small fire while attempting to demonstrate the operation of a radio set.[61] Throughout 1941, a total of 7,868 NRMA men converted to general service – over 7 percent of all of the army's volunteers for the year. An additional 3,725 went to the RCAF, and 376 to the RCN, for a final total of almost 12,000 volunteers found in 1941 thanks directly to the NRMA.[62]

As the above figures suggest, among the many outside recruiting officers who visited the training centres in 1941, those from the RCAF were the most welcome. Between the RCAF and the RCN, by far the largest number of NRMA recruits went to the former that year, and recruiting in the training centres by both services proved to be so successful that it was ended in May 1942 in order to prevent them from constantly being able to lure away the army's best-educated and thus most desirable recruits.[63] Most of the 1,357 NRMA recruits who transferred to the RCAF for the rest of the war presumably already had been on waiting lists for the junior service but were only processed after they were also called up for army training.[64] The irony is that 1941 was also the year when the BCATP began to produce pilots and aircrew in large numbers for overseas service, the majority of whom went on to Bomber Command, the strategic bombing arm of Britain's RAF. It turned out to be one of the most intensively engaged and costly combat formations of the Second World War (experts calculated shortly after the conflict ended that its personnel had had only about a 25 percent chance of completing their first tour of thirty missions without being killed, wounded, or shot down and captured by the enemy).[65] Many of the NRMA men, along with other active service recruits who also chose to transfer from the army to the RCAF in 1941, probably found themselves facing even harsher conditions in the air war overseas in later years than they might have found if they had remained in the army.

Along with recruits undergoing training, thousands of personnel on the staffs of the training centres were affected by the increased emphasis on recruiting for overseas service in the summer of 1941. When the centres were first organized in the fall of 1940, most militiamen who were called out to work in them were paid at the same rates as other volunteers, but were not made liable for overseas service. In mid-1941, they were asked to change their status so that they could be moved more easily among various camps, and rotated with personnel who had begun returning from Britain to instruct recruits on the most up-to-date tactics being used there. In most cases, all or nearly all of the camps' staffs volunteered for general service, and some also went on to join the RCAF or RCN in the same way as their trainees. The Peterborough, Ontario, training centre attracted considerable attention when its administrative and training staff joined one of its classes of NRMA recruits in early July to make the entire camp officially 100 percent active, just as the government's official recruiting campaign came to an end.[66] In the French-speaking centre in Sorel, Quebec, all of the officers and sergeants volunteered for active service after a talk by their commander, Colonel G.D. Massue.[67] Not all staff members chose to volunteer in every training centre. But once again, that trend was noticeable not only in Quebec.[68]

All of these developments set the stage for planners to take the first step in expanding the overseas army further in mid-1941. In early June, Major-General Crerar appeared before the CWC to urge that 3rd Canadian Division now be sent overseas, as had been envisioned in his army program for 1941. At the same time, he recommended that a new unit be formed in Canada to replace the 3rd Division – a political requirement more than a military one for Canadian authorities. The new 6th Division was made necessary by defence plans between Canada and the United States that had recently been completed by the Permanent Joint Board on Defence, which had itself been created following a meeting between Prime Minister King and President Roosevelt in Ogdensburg, New York, in August 1940.[69] Under these arrangements, the Canadian government agreed to maintain at least two divisions on home defence duties at all times, mainly at the insistence of the Americans, although for the most part strategic planners in Canada agreed with the assessments of their counterparts. Most of the infantry battalions needed to form the new division had already been mobilized for internal security duties, Crerar informed the CWC, and all that needed to be done was to authorize the remaining units and bring them up to full strength. Since the division would remain in Canada, "R" recruits could be used to fill out the new formation, under the arrangements made in April to extend the length of their service. Perhaps too conveniently, the first large numbers of these men were just about to begin passing out of the advanced training centres, thus becoming available for this use. Thanks to the success of the 1941 recruiting campaign, and the assurances offered by developments in the NRMA training system over the past few months, there seemed to be more than enough men to provide for the expansion of units both at home and overseas in the summer of 1941, and to keep them at full strength.[70]

Still, Crerar's recommendations provoked considerable discussion before the CWC permitted him to proceed. King especially worried that even the current request would result in a force that was too large to maintain without eventually having to send conscripts overseas. Ernest Lapointe as well as the mines and resources minister, T.A. Crerar (no relation to H.D.G. Crerar), both suggested that the three armed forces were too focused on building up more men just for the sake of having more men.[71] Along with King and Lapointe (who had been a rising Liberal MP at the time), T.A. Crerar had directly experienced the events of 1917, in his case as one of the non-Conservatives recruited into the Union Government. But that experience had made him generally opposed to conscription now; he saw it as too likely to stir up the same divisions once again.[72] As had been the case earlier in the year, however, the arguments put forward by H.D.G. Crerar were difficult to refute, especially considering the current favourable situation with respect to manpower. And although the request was clearly calculated to increase the size of the Canadian army, from the point of view of the CWC in the summer of 1941 it also may have offered a way to set limits on its future expansion. Because legally, no conscript could be sent outside Canada against his will at that time, by approving the new formation on the terms stated by Crerar the CWC could ensure that "A" and "R" recruits became so mixed together that it would be more difficult for Crerar to later argue that it, too, should go overseas – at least not without inciting a very public debate that would not have been in the interests of either side at that point in the war. In fact, during the summer of 1941 Crerar was facing not only the traditional suspicions of the military held by Canadian politicians, but also relatively strong criticism from the *Globe and Mail* and other newspapers, which questioned his newly organized training program, arguing that these men should instead be called up and trained by local militia units, an idea that harkened back to the procedures of the First World War.[73]

Another factor in the discussions was the broader military and political developments of that summer: in April, Germany conquered Yugoslavia and Greece in a campaign that ended with the capture of Crete in May. In both of the latter two places, significant Commonwealth forces had once again directly faced and been defeated by the German army, suggesting that the British still needed as much military support as possible overseas. Then, on June 22, in the midst of both the recruiting drive in Canada and the debate over the 6th Division, Germany invaded the Soviet Union. In hindsight, we have come to see this event as a turning point in the war in favour of the Allies, in that it shifted the massive resources of the Soviet Union into the war on their side. More immediately, it began to cause huge losses to the German army. But in the early days the Soviet army seemed to be collapsing, and by the end of the year their position still seemed precarious.[74] At the same time, Canadian troops who had been on the front lines of Britain's defence in the summer of 1940 now appeared to be sitting out these and other key battles, which seemed to have moved on to other places, and for the Commonwealth armies especially to North Africa. Some more prominent Conservatives in Canada, such as MP Herbert Bruce, were becoming more and more openly critical of government policy, supported by newspapers such as the *Toronto Telegram*, the *Globe and Mail*, and the *Montreal Gazette*.[75] King's senior ministers were beginning to feel the pressure, and on May 20, as they discussed the apparent lack of enthusiasm among Canadians in the initial days of the army's recruiting campaign, Ralston noted that it was more difficult to show them how much the men were needed when the troops were not in action overseas. Despite King's quite justified comment about how questionable it was for Cabinet to be deliberating sending troops into harm's way for other than military reasons, Ralston was supported by C.G. Power, who suggested seeing whether an infantry brigade could play a role in Egypt. Power was backed up in that suggestion by T.A. Crerar, and J.G. Gardiner "agreed that the public were demanding that there should be some action on the part of Canadians." Significantly, all three men were against overseas conscription but, given the current situation, were apparently willing to support greater action that could increase the likelihood of it down the road. The CWC decided to send a written statement to the British government, something that King said he had already stressed in conversation with its High Commissioner in Ottawa, Malcolm MacDonald, in that the Canadian government was prepared to send its troops wherever the British felt they might best contribute. Having agreed to send a telegram to Winston Churchill along these lines, King drafted it, but for whatever reason, he then filed it and never sent it.[76] But all of these issues were clearly on the minds of the CWC members as they debated the proposal to complete the 6th Division in June and July.

As a result of all of these factors, Crerar's recommendation was approved at the end of July. The CWC formally committed Canada to maintain a total of four divisions overseas (1st, 2nd, and 3rd Canadian Infantry Divisions, along with one independent tank brigade and 5th Canadian Armoured Division, which was still being organized but was due to go overseas before the end of the year). Two further home defence formations would remain in the country (4th and 6th Canadian Infantry Divisions). For now, the latter would consist of only its three main infantry brigade groups, without the other supporting arms and service units that would normally accompany a division in the field. They would serve as defensive reserves that could be called upon in case of emergency in eastern, central, and western Canada. Before the CWC came to that conclusion, a significant exchange took place between King and Ralston, who for reasons that will be discussed further in Chapter 4 was already beginning to hint at further potential expansion, suggesting that it might be possible to send the 4th Division overseas for a total of five, and replace it with a 7th Division for the defence of Canada. King indicated explicitly that he could support the decision only if it could be guaranteed not to result in conscription for overseas service, and Ralston replied that "he did not wish to be regarded as accepting, in advance, the principle that our participation would be limited by what could be done by means of voluntary enlistment." King's answer to that was that he "would resign rather than support such a measure." Yet at the end of the discussion, King and the rest of the CWC still agreed to formalize the creation of the 6th Division.[77]

As for Crerar, at this point he does seem to have still had conscription in mind. As he wrote to a friend as the 6th Division was being debated in mid-July, using the German invasion of Greece as an example, the military's professional opinions and the requirements of national policy sometimes conflicted, and even in hindsight he agreed with Churchill's decision to send some resources to Greece in the interests of public opinion, despite the worries of British military advisers, even though the defeat would most likely do harm to Britain's military capacity down the road. As Crerar concluded his letter:

> As regards our Canadian man-power problem I would refer you to last week's Saturday Night in which paper there was expressed a realization that this country had, by gradual steps, proceeded very far in adopting what amounts to conscription for overseas service. As the majority of the young men now called up for compulsory training and compulsory service for home defence under the N.R.M.

> Act and now in the Advanced Training Centres are actually volunteering for service overseas, it might be said that a form of popular referendum is now being taken and that popular feeling is in favour of unrestricted national service. Certainly, if these favourable results continue to show themselves for another couple of months, it should make the Government's job an easier one should it decide to take the step which many believe should be adopted now.[78]

Considering that Crerar never did push that far throughout 1941, and combined with his comments about deferring to civilian authority above, this at first perhaps damning-sounding letter does not necessarily mean he was trying to force the government to accept conscription as soon as possible, regardless of the consequences. Instead, increasingly that possibility seems to have receded as the NRMA proved to be a more and more useful resource from which to find the men to help build up his desired military force overseas, while at the same time enabling him to abide by his government's policy that conscription would not be extended that far. As he had put it to E.L.M. Burns earlier that year, in writing about how he had managed to gain permission to reopen recruiting to complete the 4th Division in May, "I expect a good many of these volunteers will be obtained from the 21-year old trainees who are now in the Army for an indefinite period and many of whom will prefer to serve overseas if they are to serve at all."[79] As has already been noted, that same month Victor Sifton was stating privately that the NRMA should be used to maintain the strength of the army's volunteers overseas (even though he in fact strongly disagreed with Crerar's plans to increase the overall size of the force). Even Ralston referred to the idea of relying on the NRMA to provide future volunteers when he spoke at a press conference in mid-July, announcing the end of the government's spring recruiting campaign. He pointed specifically to two basic training centres where 100 percent of "R" recruits had recently gone active, noting that in the future "this would be a very valuable source of recruiting."[80]

Thus, from Crerar's point of view, the strategic situation remained much the same, and Canada needed to continue building up its forces as strongly as possible to aid the British overseas. Under the arrangements made for the NRMA by mid-1941, it seemed quite possible to find all the men who were needed in the near future, either directly by recruiting civilians into the army, or alternatively by simply increasing the flow of those called up under the NRMA. The possibility remained that at some point in the future conscription might still be necessary to support a larger Canadian army overseas. But it was beginning to seem less and less likely under the new arrangements made for the NRMA that that day would ever come. One difficulty that seems to have begun to creep into Crerar's calculations, was that although he had seen much combat himself in the First World War, neither he nor any of the other current senior Canadian generals had actually had to deal with the complexities of supplying manpower of the right types, in the right places, and at the right times, at this level in a time of war. And the Canadian army had not yet seen combat in the Second World War on a scale that would remind its leaders how complex the task really was. As we will see below, he still seemed to be thinking in terms of the exact numbers needed to build up Canadian formations overseas, and then a specific figure for reinforcements that would be needed afterwards based on the size of those formations, and then extrapolating from the first two figures the maximum that could be maintained if everything went exactly right, rather than what might happen if things went wrong and those precise calculations were thrown off (as would occur in 1944). In the meantime, with the approval of the 6th Division compulsory military training became an even more integral part of his existing plans for the volunteer Canadian army – plans that would be taken that much further by Crerar himself, and then his successor as CGS, Lieutenant-General Ken Stuart, over the second half of 1941 and the early months of 1942.

4
Creating the "Big Army": Conscription and Army Expansion, 1941–43

BETWEEN 1941 AND 1943, the Canadian army expanded to its largest size of the Second World War. By 1943, Canada had created an entire field army overseas, numbering three infantry divisions (roughly 18,000 troops each, depending on the exact time in the war[1]), two armoured divisions (each somewhat smaller in numbers of personnel), and two independent tank brigades, along with two corps headquarters, an overall army field headquarters, and the tens of thousands of additional troops needed to continuously supply and otherwise maintain these units. At the same time, the country's domestic defence forces increased dramatically in response to the continued deterioration of the war effort in both Europe and the Pacific during 1941 and 1942. Dozens of independent artillery and anti-aircraft units were established on both coasts, and the better part of three further infantry divisions were mobilized, bringing the total number of divisions formally maintained by the country to eight. At its peak in March 1944, the Canadian army totalled almost half a million men and women (495,804, of whom 242,463 were overseas). The RCAF reached its maximum size at the end of 1943 (206,350, including 46,272 overseas), while the RCN was still expanding, with 71,549 personnel by January 1944, and only topping out at 92,441 in January 1945 (although for the RCN it was less easy to separate out people serving "overseas").[2] This does not include the large additional number of men and women who needed to be taken into the services continuously to keep them up to strength over time, as people were discharged for medical or other reasons, and increasingly as Canadians began to lose their lives in all three services. This ultimately brought the final total of citizens who wore a uniform in one of the three armed forces during the war to roughly 1.1 million (including the 157,841 who were enlisted as conscripts, and 49,941 women). And that number did not include countless more men and women who had wished to serve but were screened out at some point as unsuitable.

All of this was accomplished at the same time that war industry was booming (according to C.P. Stacey, it peaked at a similar total of 1.1 million workers at the end of 1943)[3] – and all from an overall Canadian population of 11,506,655 according to the 1941 census. The latter figure included 5,900,536 men, who remained the dominant group from which the Canadian military drew throughout the Second World War. The total number of men who were between fourteen and forty-seven years of age (the main range from which men were likely to be found for military service throughout the war, who were still forty-five or under in 1939, or who reached the age of eighteen by 1945), was 3,017,460. And the number who were between those ages and single, and thus the easiest to recruit, was (by an educated guess, using the existing census figures) 1,732,546.[4] The total of almost 1.1 million men who served in uniform during the war is approximately 36.5 percent and 63.5 percent, respectively, of the two figures given here for manpower available to serve. Put another way, of the 1,816,868 men who were actually in the classes liable for service under the NRMA on the day the fighting ended in northwest Europe, May 7, 1945, 769,764 (42.4 percent) were in the armed forces.[5] Thus, the numbers of Canadians who served during the war, compared to the human resources available, were huge no matter how one looks at them.

A large factor in the demands made on manpower from 1942 onwards was the "big army," a term coined in 1941 by journalist Grant Dexter to describe the army of five divisions and ancillary units that was eventually created overseas.[6] The question for historians ever since has been why the CWC accepted the plan for this big army in December 1941 and January 1942, despite the considerable acrimony that arose over the issue at the time, and in the face of serious doubts that it would be possible to maintain such a force throughout the war without extending conscription to overseas service. The NRMA was one key factor that shaped the actions of both generals and politicians. Thanks to the way it was operating to help find "converts" from among its recruits by late 1941, over the next two years most of the army's major decision-makers came to see (or at least, they thought they did) that if the number of civilian volunteers ever began to fall short of requirements, the NRMA could still be used to maintain the strength of units in Europe even without actually having to send conscripts there. For H.D.G. Crerar, in particular, this provided an opportunity to build the larger, more powerful, professional army that he hoped would both allow Canada to play the strongest role possible in helping the Allies win the war, and as a consequence increase acceptance of that army within Canada in the peacetime years afterwards. For Prime Minister King and other Cabinet ministers, it offered the promise (or in the case of J.L. Ralston, the hope) that the army could be expanded to meet public demands for greater forces overseas after 1941, without having to rely on extending conscription to overseas service. The result, by early 1942, was approval for Crerar's plans – a decision that set in train the exact developments that some ministers had feared during these debates.

One major problem with all of this was that just as these plans were being debated by the CWC, another front was opening up – the war on the Pacific coast. The politicians still authorized the big army. And for a while afterwards,

Crerar and his successor as CGS, Lieutenant-General Ken Stuart, seemed to have been remarkably prescient: the training system they had created allowed them to expand the Canadian army at home in response to a number of further demands being put on them by their political superiors to expand the defences on the west coast, while at the same time maintaining the flow of volunteers to fill out the big army overseas. But although they had foreseen a military threat to the west coast, and factored it into their calculations in putting the big army forward in 1941, they could not have foreseen just how many new demands would be put on them afterwards, particularly by the prime minister, King (ironically, in an apparent bid to keep more men at home, so that conscription for overseas service would be less likely). As a result, the manpower that had been expected to last for much longer was already coming to a limit by late 1943. And while the generals deserve some of the blame for calling for such a large army in 1941–42, it is worth remembering that ultimately Crerar and Stuart were not the only people at fault for this development.

Before these debates even began, for the remainder of 1941 the NRMA played a key role in expanding the existing home defence army in Canada. It should be noted in recalling that expansion that not all men who were conscripted went on to serve as infantry soldiers. In presenting Crerar's request to the CWC in April, to extend service under the NRMA to the duration of the war, Ralston had noted that what were needed most were artillerymen to fill the ranks of the many coast defence units that had been planned as far back as the late 1930s, but were only now being formed as modern arms and equipment began to flow out of Canadian factories.[7] He repeated these arguments in his speech inaugurating the government's recruiting campaign in May, adding that only 10 percent of all volunteers needed by the army at that time were intended to be infantrymen.[8] By the late summer of 1941, a few "R" recruits had also begun to trickle back to various training centres, to take up positions such as batmen, clerks, cooks, and even instructors, so that some of the general service volunteers on the staffs could move on to other duties.[9] As the months went by, the trickle turned into a steady flow into various home defence units across the country.[10] By October 1941, the total strength of such forces had risen to 147,149 officers and other ranks, of whom 13,974 (9.5 percent) were NRMA recruits, or "Members (HD [Home Defence])," as those who had completed their training and been assigned to specific home defence units came to be referred to officially from 1941 onwards. At the start of February 1942, 1,586 (15.6 percent) of the 10,140 men in the still-forming 6th Division were conscripts, while NRMA men made up 3,075 (21.3 percent) of the further 14,431 personnel who were serving on coast defence and anti-aircraft duties across the country.[11]

As 1941 went on, the attention of both the army's planners and their political superiors began to be drawn even more towards the vital issue of manpower. As early as July 1941, when the CWC was still considering Crerar's request to mobilize a sixth division, he had started to lay the groundwork for an even larger force overseas. In this task he was inadvertently aided by Ralston, who in late May asked the Adjutant-General to review the implications for the army of a recent study on manpower produced by the Department of Munitions and Supply. Browne's study reflected the optimism of his source, portraying the manpower situation very positively with respect to the army. According to the figures, Browne stated, the country had enough manpower to create at least two more divisions for overseas service, in addition to the four that were then authorized; more importantly, it would be able to keep such a larger force up to strength for more than six years. If the government instead used some of those extra reinforcements to build up more divisions, as many as ten could be mobilized and maintained for over four years, even after taking into account the additional needs of the air force and navy. Browne's report was very brief and offered few details about how he had calculated his estimates of manpower needs. And despite their scale, he called his figures conservative. Weighing in on the debate, Crerar suggested that the casualty numbers estimated by Browne were likely too high and that this would give the army even more of a margin for error if it went ahead with plans for further forces.[12] The result was that by the end of July, as noted in the previous chapter, Ralston had raised the possibility in the CWC of sending the 4th Division to England and replacing it with a seventh division in Canada.

Browne's study also appears to be the source of a more critical version of the army's expansion plans reported by Grant Dexter, following a private conversation with Victor Sifton early in June. As Dexter put it,

> Victor says that there is a plot to double the size of the army. The plotters are McNaughton and Crerar with Price Montague [the Senior Officer at Canadian Military Headquarters in London] as a consenting party. Both staffs of course are in it (McNaughton's and Crerar's). These people want 2 corps of 3 divisions each plus one armoured division and 1 tank brigade, each.[13]

In another memo later that summer, Dexter also recorded his conversation with

> Prof. Goforth, formerly of McGill, now a major on the general staff. I was astounded to find him fairly sizzling with the plan for 8 divisions – 4 armoured, 4 infantry. He was quite communicative, indicating that the plan has been very widely discussed by the general staff. The plan, he said, came from McNaughton

> and the British war office and represented what Canada was believed able to do. ... The politicians, he intimated, were under steady pressure and would cave in sooner or later. Already a great deal of the 8 division establishment was approved and in existence, without the politicians knowing what was being done. Thus the army training establishment was of 8 division calibre and so on. It would be very wasteful indeed, not to fill out the programme now.

As Dexter later added, "Ralston knows all about this. He has *no* [emphasis in original] confidence in the general staff but is at a loss to know how to handle Crerar. He cannot fire him unless he has a successor in view, which he hasn't."[14]

There is little evidence in the private writings of various generals in the summer of 1941 to indicate that they were working to quite so deliberate a plan, or scheming in such a well-coordinated way. But Crerar was clearly thinking in terms of at least one additional overseas division at the time, and the further possible implications for him and his colleagues. As he suggested in August to Lieutenant-General A.G.L. McNaughton, "This would result in too large a Corps, but have you ever considered the pros and cons of a Canadian Army comprising 2 Corps each of 2 Divisions and an Armoured Division? I fully admit that this is a pretty ambitious proposal because the necessary increase in Corps, etc., troops will be fairly heavy. At the same time, I do not think that the picture is an impossible one."[15] Taking into account further formations in Canada, the result would be a total force of seven divisions, the same one again as that projected by the army during the 1930s. Yet those earlier plans had not taken into account the need to simultaneously maintain the huge efforts of the RCAF and RCN in the Second World War, or the massive demands caused by the expansion of industrial output.

Links between prewar plans and Crerar's wartime program are confirmed by one further memorandum that he forwarded to Ralston in September 1941, shortly before submitting his own official "Army Programme" for 1942–43, which laid out his plans to bring the army to five divisions overseas and two in Canada. It was written by Brigadier Maurice Pope, the Assistant CGS, and another of the army's rising stars who had taken advantage of various British staff and Imperial Defence College training opportunities in the interwar years. As Crerar's deputy in the Directorate of Military Operations and Intelligence during the 1930s, Pope had helped carry out the militia's interwar restructuring. And he had been born in Quebec and raised as a bilingual Catholic, and would later openly oppose extending conscription to overseas service in the fall of 1944. At the same time, he felt throughout the war that "our one great problem was to build up, and to maintain, our Army overseas," and thus for him apparently the two goals did not have to be contradictory.[16] His current report referred explicitly to the interwar defence scheme, which was "based on the carefully thought-out presumption that so far as could then be foreseen, the maximum strength of a Canadian Army which might be maintained in the field, in a war of long duration, would not exceed six divisions, [and] a cavalry division, together with the necessary complement of non-divisional units." The Non-Permanent Active Militia had been reorganized in the late 1930s to ensure that the proper infrastructure was in place to mobilize seven wartime divisions. These units had then been mobilized in more or less that order as the army expanded after 1939. The government's passing of the NRMA had changed the situation, Pope suggested, not so much by providing a justification for the army to increase its forces in Europe by sending conscripts overseas, as by allowing it to begin using them to replace volunteers in Canada so that all of its commitments could be maintained, both at home and overseas, for the foreseeable future under the present policy.[17]

Pope's memorandum had actually been written to deal with another issue that had been raised by the combining of the overseas mobilization plans with the NRMA after April 1941: as he noted, as more and more long-term "R" recruits were becoming available for service, the army was beginning to run out of units into which to put the roughly 1,500 per month who were exiting the training centres. After the reorganizations of the 1930s, and now having raised six divisions and other home defence battalions, it had few militia regiments left that could serve as the nucleus around which to mobilize further active service units. One possible solution was to create entirely new units, but Pope argued against this alternative as both wasteful and inefficient. The real problem, he noted, was that only a few home defence formations had been officially designated to receive NRMA men, mainly for political reasons since most of them had been recruited from volunteers in their local communities, and still hoped to proceed overseas together rather than be broken up and go as anonymous reinforcements. The arrival of even a few "R" recruits would signal the end of such hopes (a problem that caused Ralston's good friend Allan Magee, whom he had brought into the Department of National Defence in 1940 to act as one of his key civilian advisers, to write to Ralston a few days later arguing for the option that Pope had rejected).[18] In forwarding Pope's report to Ralston, Major-General Crerar noted that there was little hope of any of these units ever going overseas, and agreed with Pope that the army should now be permitted to begin filling them with NRMA men, and withdrawing the volunteers to send overseas.[19] Thus, Pope's memorandum suggests that Crerar genuinely saw his upcoming "Army Programme" as the end of its expansion overseas, since under the government's existing policy no further units could be sent there once they had been filled out with NRMA recruits. At the same time, clearly he seemed to be assuming that conscription would remain limited to home defence in the future, and from now on he would simply rely on it to help supplement the flow of volunteers to overseas units by releasing those men who were already in uniform in Canada.

All of these efforts culminated in Crerar's formal army program for 1942–43, which was submitted to Ralston in mid-November 1941, following another trip to England by both men to consult with their British counterparts as to how the Canadian army could best continue to contribute to the larger war effort. In his formal presentation to the CWC, Crerar noted that the strategic situation had improved in Canada over the past few months, as the United States came closer to being fully involved in the war. But the provision of additional divisions remained a priority overseas, to help defend the British Isles and to release British divisions to fight in North Africa, the last land theatre where Commonwealth forces remained in direct contact with the enemy. These factors, Crerar suggested, along with the possibility of continuing to use the NRMA to release volunteers for overseas service, meant that the country's forces in Britain could and should be expanded further. This could be done by sending 4th Canadian Infantry Division to Europe, after converting it into an armoured division to meet British requests for further mechanized units. A second independent tank brigade would also be required to support existing infantry divisions overseas, along with a second corps headquarters to command the 4th and 5th Armoured Divisions in battle. Under the new program, no further formations would actually need to be created in Canada, since the 4th Division would remain there until at least early 1942. After that, the 6th Division would be sufficient to meet the country's needs. Should the situation deteriorate (but only in that case), it could be met by mobilizing a 7th Division made up predominately of recruits from the NRMA – a convenient source of men that would allow the army to maintain its overseas expansion while at the same time putting the NRMA to the exact military use for which it had ostensibly been introduced in 1940.[20] With the submission of this new program, Crerar turned over his post as CGS to Major-General (Lieutenant-General after November) Ken Stuart, the former Vice-CGS, who had been hand-picked by Crerar as his replacement. Crerar then left to take up a field command in England as General Officer Commanding, 2nd Canadian Division.[21]

In the meantime, between June and November the CWC had finally begun investigating the remaining manpower potential of the country. In June (in a sign of how large and complex the management of the war effort was becoming) the CWC had created a National Labour Supply Council to advise on matters related to war industry. That had led to an Inter-Departmental Committee on Labour Co-ordination, which in turn begat a Labour Supply Investigation Committee (LSIC), whose task was to make a detailed assessment of how manpower was currently being used, and what was still available. In October, the LSIC delivered a roughly two-hundred-page report that was considerably more critical of the country's available reserves of manpower than was the army. Its estimate of the maximum number of men who might be freed from various sectors of the economy for the armed forces, without too negatively impeding the country's capacity to also produce food and material, was 609,000 men between the ages of seventeen and forty. And that figure was achievable only if much more rigorous measures were taken to free them up. Even if more men from Quebec were placed in uniform, there would not be enough French-speaking officers to command them (a legacy of the pre-1939 lack of attention to francophone needs within the military). To find enough men to maintain eight army divisions would completely empty the Maritimes and British Columbia and push the prairies to their limit as well. On the civilian side, enough resources could be found to meet estimated needs only by curtailing non-essential production and adding another 421,000 women to the 140,000 who had already moved into the workforce since August 1940 (according to the 1941 census, the total number of women over fourteen working at that time was 832,840; this compared to 638,000 in August 1939).[22] Many of those 421,000 lived in areas remote from industrial centres, and the government would also have to overcome prevailing attitudes towards women in the workplace that made it more difficult to recruit them for such tasks. Men, too, were not distributed efficiently across the country, and they would need to be encouraged to move from less important to more important wartime industries.[23]

At the same time as the LSIC's report was being presented to the CWC, Lieutenant-General Stuart forwarded a new report to Ralston that provided details of the Adjutant-General's plans for finding manpower to support the 1942–43 army program, as well as schedules for filling out specific formations. Browne forecast that, based on experience with the first three classes of "R" recruits trained under the four-month program, 20 percent of each new group would volunteer for the army in the future, 20 percent would go to the RCAF or RCN or be discharged for various reasons before being formally enrolled as NRMA men (this was before the rules were changed to prevent such transfers), and the remaining 60 percent would stay in uniform as conscripts. "If 5,000 'R' recruits are requisitioned each month," he concluded, "it is therefore assumed ... that 1,000 of each such requisitions [*sic*] will enlist into the Active Army." Stuart himself estimated that another 1,000 volunteers would be released from home defence duties by conscripts each month, thus providing a total of roughly

2,000 out of the figure of 7,500 per month that the army would need in order to meet its expanded plans overseas.[24]

By this time, furthermore, the RCAF's and the RCN's requests were becoming larger and larger. By the end of 1941, the BCATP was just beginning to churn out graduates in large numbers. Leaving aside the complicated question of whether RCAF personnel proceeding overseas would end up attached to RAF squadrons or specifically RCAF ones (about which Canada's official historians have already provided detailed accounts),[25] at the end of 1941 the RCAF was still expecting to take in another 96,818 men over the following eighteen months (to March 31, 1943), compared to the army's plans for an added 104,000.[26] The bombing campaign especially was still ramping up overseas, and it would eventually become the RCAF's largest single contribution to the war. Besides this, the RCN needed to man all of the ships that by then were coming down the slips in large numbers – and this was before the Battle of the Atlantic intensified more than expected, so that it would demand even more resources in 1942–43. Over the course of 1941, the RCN's authorized establishment had risen from 15,000 to 28,000, and for the upcoming CWC discussions it was requesting another 13,000 to March 1943 (its strength would actually be 48,000 by the start of 1943, and as noted earlier, it only reached its peak at over 90,000 in January 1945). By early 1943, it expected to have fifteen destroyers, forty-eight minesweepers, and one hundred corvettes manned and in operation.[27]

The CWC finally began discussing the specifics of the army program in the first days of December. C.D. Howe and T.A. Crerar both quickly pointed to the problems the army would face in meeting all of its new commitments, when added to the drain caused by the country's efforts to simultaneously maintain two other large armed services, as well as industrial output.[28] From the beginning, King also wanted to be certain that the army's plans would not require the extension of conscription. In response to Ralston's indication once again that he could not make such a guarantee, although his goal was to "try his utmost to get the men without conscription," the prime minister "told him that I felt conscription would split the country from coast to coast; create a wound in its side that would never be healed."[29] According to the version of the same meeting recorded in the CWC minutes, King raised the more specific issue of whether the army could guarantee that 5,500 volunteers could be found from the public every month (the number on which the army program was based, after deducting the expected 1,000 volunteers per month from among NRMA recruits).[30] At that point, the NRMA became particularly significant in the debates. The following day, as King's own diary entry emphasizes, he raised the same concerns.[31] Stuart and Browne were brought into the room to defend the army's plans, and he confronted them directly:

> Could the Army staff give any assurance that their proposed programme could be carried out by the voluntary method; further, was this programme being presented as an effective maximum Army contribution on Canada's part, or would it be subject to increase later on? ... The Chief of the General Staff replied that, in his opinion, the programme proposed could be carried out on the voluntary system and it had been prepared solely on that basis ... In a recent memorandum to the Minister he had expressed the view that the programme represented the "visible ceiling." Its adoption would constitute an excellent, well-balanced and adequate contribution by the Canadian Army in the European theatre.[32]

As Granatstein and Hitsman have commented in their history of conscription in Canada, "from this moment King's eventual support for the army program was guaranteed."[33] But even more importantly from the point of view of the ties between the larger army program and the NRMA, Browne's response when King asked him the same question right afterwards was to state explicitly that the NRMA men already in uniform would allow "the diversion of maximum numbers of active service personnel from home defence units"; thus, the army would not have to rely solely on the recruitment of new volunteers from the public to find the whole 5,500 each month. Alluding to the broader powers of the NRMA to direct human resources that had been put in place when it was established in 1940, and clearly aware of the more recent debates surrounding the LSIC report, both Browne and Stuart also "agreed that the extension of the National Resources Mobilization Act, to provide for national selective service within Canada would assist recruiting." Presumably, this was because it would begin rationalizing industry and freeing up additional men to volunteer. Beyond even that was the unspoken but clearly implicit reliance on the NRMA to encourage further men to volunteer after they had been placed in training. As King himself had recorded privately in advance of the meeting that day, while setting down his thoughts so that he could be sure not to lose track of his larger concerns once the discussion began: "It must be remembered that conscription for service in Canada, means providing men properly trained for service overseas who may wish to enlist voluntarily."[34]

Aside from these specific connections, there was also the broader context. As King noted in his diary just before describing the above events, "I liked General Stuart's complete frankness and also felt quite impressed by his personality. Indeed I feel every confidence in him." As he added later:

> I confess these statements from the Chief of Staff [*sic*] and the Adjutant General impressed me very much and helped to meet the difficulty that has been the only real one which presents itself, namely that of resorting to conscription to get [the]

> numbers required ... Generals Stuart and Brown[e] have made a real impression on me by their personality and attitudes and I feel a great confidence in them as administrators.[35]

To try to explain the above events, Richard Walker has gone so far as to suggest that Stuart was behaving "disingeniously."[36] But as J.L. Granatstein has noted, Stuart had been born and raised in Quebec (Trois-Rivières), and in another conversation with the prime minister a few weeks later, Stuart "expressed great bitterness at the way the Great War experience had caused disunity."[37] As we will see, the lengths to which he went to avoid having to ask the government to impose conscription in 1944 also suggest that he was firmly committed to maintaining the policy. What seems at least a little more possible, then, is that Stuart in fact had such confidence because he and his predecessor Crerar knew, first, that they had achieved their ultimate goal and really did not intend to have the army grow any further than this overseas, and second, that thanks to the NRMA a system was now in place that seemed to give them a way to achieve that aim, hopefully without ever having to rely on conscription beyond the borders of Canada itself.

Although Crerar's army program for 1942 was not officially approved at this meeting, it was never again subjected to such lengthy or detailed discussion. When Stuart met with journalist Grant Dexter a month later, he seemed quite satisfied: "I asked him if a Canadian army of two corps plus two tank brigades was absolutely all the general staff wanted in this war. He said – absolutely all. This he said is the kind of an army a soldier dreams of commanding, hard-hitting, beautifully balanced, incredibly powerful."[38] Stuart's sentiments probably would have been mirrored by Crerar, who had laid most of the groundwork for the force and who was now overseas ready to command some of the same divisions. A few months later, partly thanks to the combined arguments of McNaughton and Crerar overseas, the CWC consented to add an army field headquarters to the country's forces in England, to command the two corps, five divisions, and additional support units that had already been established. Such a step seemed only logical once everything else had been authorized. And it was difficult to avoid, if the government wished its forces to fight together on the battlefield.[39]

Even more importantly, the result of these deliberations was the establishment of the "big army" that would fight for Canada in Europe from 1943 to 1945. As Granatstein and Hitsman have summarized the outcome of the debate,

> a crucial decision had been taken and Canada was now committed to maintaining a large army, possibly one larger than the country could support. Given the

> enormous scope of the industrial and agricultural effort, an army of five divisions plus the thousands of ancillary troops, as well as a very large air force and a substantial navy would be exceedingly difficult to maintain. In retrospect, it is clear that the conscription crisis of 1944 became almost a certainty with this decision.[40]

These conclusions are obvious enough in hindsight. But when the big army was being planned, its architect Crerar could not have foreseen just how much the war would be transformed with Japan's entry into the war only a few weeks later. Even then, as was his duty, he had considered the general possibility of an expansion in requirements for home defence, and he clearly relied on the NRMA to meet such dangers. If his political masters were really serious in their public statements that compulsory military service was intended to provide for such needs, then it was only logical and natural that he do so.[41] At the same time, Crerar had organized the compulsory military training system to ensure that even if it was never needed to defend against a direct attack on Canada, it could be used as efficiently as possible to support the army's existing efforts in Europe. This policy made sense from a military point of view but was less clearly the intention of his political superiors. The difficulty would arise when the country suddenly needed to try to do both things at once after December 1941, and on a scale for which few people could have been expected to be fully prepared.

On December 7, 1941, a new and highly significant threat to the Allied war effort appeared when Japan launched its surprise attack on the US naval base at Pearl Harbor. Over the next several hours and days, attacks followed on Guam and Wake islands, the Philippines, Hong Kong, Malaya, and Burma. Ultimately, the entry of the US into the war as a result of these attacks would prove to be another turning point in the conflict. Yet for the next several months, success seemed to follow success for the Japanese forces. In early May and early June, the Americans finally began to turn the tide at the battles of the Coral Sea and Midway. But by that time, Japan's conquests stretched from the Dutch East Indies across the Pacific to Attu and Kiska, the two westernmost of the Aleutian Islands that were part of Alaska.[42] On June 20, a Japanese vessel even directly attacked Canadian territory for the first and last time in the war, when a submarine shelled a remote lighthouse on Vancouver Island.[43]

As it turned out, Canada would not play a large role in the Pacific. However, Hong Kong marked the first major combat action for the country's troops. Two units, the Winnipeg Grenadiers and the Royal Rifles of Canada (an anglophone unit based in Quebec City but recruited from various parts of the province, and that included 30 to 40 percent francophones from the Gaspé), were lost when the garrison surrendered on Christmas Day, after a short but sharp battle.[44] At home, these defeats, along with Japan's entry into the war, added a new sense of immediacy to plans for home defence. They also led to new calls for conscription to be extended to overseas service. In November 1941, Arthur Meighen had succeeded R.B. Hanson as leader of the Conservative Party. As the author of the Military Service Act in the First World War, King's nemesis for much of the 1920s, an earlier leader of the Conservatives, and still a staunch conscriptionist, Meighen was now expected to make it a political issue once again.[45]

While these events were going on, the Liberal government was still grappling with the army program for 1942–43 and its manpower implications. In early December, a special Cabinet Manpower Committee was formed to begin considering ways to transfer men from jobs of lesser importance to positions in war industry or the armed forces.[46] As members came to focus more and more on the political consequences of these various developments, the broader discussions moved from the CWC to the larger Cabinet. In particular, Ralston began to harden his stance, refusing to commit to maintaining the proposed big army overseas while continuing to promise that conscripts would never have to be used to support it, given that he could not be certain what future directions the war might take. He argued more and more strongly that the government should actually remove the limits it had imposed on conscription, as a sign of its awareness of the new seriousness of the war. At times, the arguments became highly acrimonious, and this led to major rifts between individual ministers. In addition, Ernest Lapointe had died of a heart attack on November 26, and King was now even more concerned to honour Lapointe's past views on conscription. After a brief search, King recruited Louis St. Laurent, a well-regarded corporate lawyer in Quebec, to take over Lapointe's former position as lead voice for the province within the Cabinet. But St. Laurent was not involved in the discussions, as he had yet to enter Parliament. He would be confirmed as an MP as part of four by-elections that King called for February 9, 1942. One of the other four was in York South, where Arthur Meighen would also be attempting to re-enter the House of Commons.[47]

King's answer to these various concerns turned out to be to hold a national plebiscite, to ask Canadians to release the government from its unwritten pledge of 1940 against conscription for overseas service. The idea had been suggested more than once during the earlier discussions on manpower and the army program, and not just by the prime minister: according to him, on December 3, even Ralston suggested that if conscription did later turn out to be necessary to maintain the army, the government could implement the decision and then face the people either in a confidence vote in the House of Commons or directly in a referendum.[48] But King now decided to make such a request of the people first, before changing the policy. His use of the word plebiscite in place of referendum was also deliberate, for it suggested a non-binding vote simply to allow the public to express its opinion to the government.[49] And it did not hurt that it would immediately undermine Meighen's key argument that the government was not doing enough to prosecute the war effort, especially with respect to extending conscription. If nothing else, as in 1940 it was a way for the King to delay until the situation became clearer. In this case, there was always the chance that the population would vote either all yes or all no, with no division between Quebec and the rest of the country, and one way or the other that would settle the issue. The vote, to be held on April 27, was announced in the Speech from the Throne that began a new session of the House of Commons in January 1942. The question, as finalized, followed King's often somewhat convoluted but always very careful style: "Are you in favour of releasing the government from any obligation arising out of any past commitments restricting the methods of raising men for military service?"[50]

The first result of the plebiscite announcement was felt by Meighen, in that it did weaken his attacks on the King government over conscription. Although an unwritten tradition suggested that he should not run opposed, the Co-operative Commonwealth Federation (CCF) – the social democratic party that had emerged out of the Great Depression in the early 1930s – was finding increasing support from Canadians as the war went on, and it decided to challenge Meighen. It ran a popular local candidate, Joseph Noseworthy, and attacked Meighen as a representative of the country's old moneyed interests, while emphasizing new promises of postwar social policies. Meighen lost.[51]

In Quebec, the plebiscite did not go so well. There, as André Laurendeau has noted, for him and fellow nationalists the plebiscite was the true crisis over conscription, and the final decision to send men overseas that came in late 1944 was inevitable after April 1942. Furthermore, King's federal government was asking the entire country to release it from its pledge, knowing what the feelings of most English Canadians would likely be, even though in Laurendeau's view the pledge had originally been made only to Quebec.[52] He helped bring together a loose coalition of opposition groups under the umbrella of the *Ligue pour la défense du Canada*, including agricultural, working-class, and labour representatives and the newspaper *Le Devoir*. They were denied access to the government's airwaves and were opposed by Catholic leaders and most mainstream newspapers, which as a whole continued to support the war. But the no side began to see a groundswell of support. On the yes side, meanwhile, the

Figure 11 Handbill distributed by the *Ligue pour la défense du Canada* during the 1942 plebiscite. *Source:* LAC, e-011157753.

federal government's campaign was lacklustre – perhaps not surprisingly, given that the prime minister was so worried personally about the implications of extending conscription. Most of his French-speaking backbench MPs declined to campaign, leaving it to the few Cabinet ministers from Quebec, who were forced to take on the role in the absence of Lapointe. The final result made divisions between Quebec and the rest of the country more rather than less apparent. Nationally, 64 percent of the population voted for the change, while 73 percent of Quebeckers voted against it (and 85 percent of French-speaking Quebeckers).[53] Interestingly, based on a public reading of the events rather than what was going on behind the scenes in Ottawa, Pierre Vennat has suggested that had the yes side focused its argument more clearly on the need to trust and support King, so that the future decision about when to use conscription would remain firmly in his hands (and had Lapointe still been alive to back up the position), it might have had more success. But moderate Quebeckers had as much difficulty trying to puzzle out King's exact public stance on the issue as other Canadians.[54]

The outcome led to weeks of further debate within the Cabinet. Sensing that the plebiscite might simply be a way for King and other Cabinet ministers to put off having to acknowledge that conscription might prove to be necessary at some future point, Ralston pressed during the campaign for a decision as to exactly what would be done in the event that the country voted yes.[55] Cabinet later reached a compromise of sorts, agreeing to repeal Section 3 of the NRMA, but to not actually extend conscription to overseas service until it became "necessary" to do so. Even then, the prime minister's preference was to recall Parliament in that event and request formal authority to alter the government's previous policies. This decision had supposedly just been approved by the plebiscite, however, and Ralston and other ministers feared that such a process would only spark a renewal of the debates that were currently taking place within the Cabinet, and further delays as the changes were then debated in the House of Commons. Their worries came remarkably close to what actually happened in 1944 and probably accurately reflected the hopes of King and some of the other Cabinet ministers in 1942.[56] Ralston considered resigning more than once, and finally submitted a formal letter in early July. But King refused to accept it.[57] In the end, in the event that conscription became "necessary," the Cabinet agreed in advance to just pass an Order-in-Council and then recall the House of Commons for a brief vote of confidence on the measure before it was implemented, with a limit of two days for any debate. Section 3 of the NRMA was then finally repealed through Bill 80, which passed into law in early August 1942. In King's famous words during his speech on the second reading of the bill, his policy would be "not necessarily conscription, but conscription if necessary" (a statement that was later reversed to become the one better-known to history).[58] The repeal of Section 3 was followed shortly thereafter by the resignation in protest of P.J.A. Cardin, the senior French Canadian minister in the Cabinet after the death of Ernest Lapointe, over what he felt was the breaking of the government's 1939 pledge to Quebec. But King managed to avoid further defections, and with this step came the end of what has come to be known by historians as the "first conscription crisis."[59]

Despite the significance of the first conscription crisis at the political level, in practice it changed very little with respect to administering the NRMA. What was more important during this period was that the organization that had been built up over the past two years enabled the army to respond easily to the vastly increased calls for home defence that emerged after Pearl Harbor. In fact, as panic gripped the west coast, the country's defence forces greatly expanded. But in spite of the severe implications of these developments for the army's future manpower needs, the expansion came not out of pressure from the generals but from their political masters, and particularly the prime minister. Almost as soon as the extent of the Japanese attacks was known in early December, King was raising the question of whether the army program for 1942 should go ahead or whether the country might be better to focus on increasing its own defences, a policy that would also clearly help divert attention away from the idea of extending conscription to overseas service by showing the need for such forces at home. Yet as all three service chiefs noted, there was still little chance of a direct attack on Canadian territory in any form larger than a temporary raid, an undertaking that even if it were to take place, from a military point of view would be intended by the enemy to do just what King was suggesting and divert Canadian and American attention away from Europe, the theatre the Allies had agreed as early as the summer of 1940 would be their first concern even in the event of a Japanese attack in the Pacific. As a result, Lieutenant-General Stuart recommended against making any change to the army's previous plans for expansion in England.[60]

On the west coast itself, the RCMP and the RCN showed similar calm, arresting thirty-eight Japanese Canadians who were now enemy aliens and impounding 1,200 fishing boats in the days immediately after Pearl Harbor, in the remote event that enemy agents might use them to aid an attack on Canada. But with the fall of Hong Kong and the surrender of the Canadians there on December 25, calls grew in British Columbia for the entire Japanese Canadian community to be interned due to fears of fifth columnists. Local military commanders from all three services began to reflect the same worries, pointing to the danger of potential large-scale attacks or even an invasion attempt. As the war went more and more badly in the Pacific in January 1942, the *Vancouver Sun*, Vancouver City Council, and various MPs from British Columbia began to call more urgently for attention to the west coast's outward defences as well. All of this registered with King, and while it would have hugely negative implications for Japanese Canadians over the next few years, it also made him begin to question the strategic assessments of his military advisers, who had repeatedly argued that the country's current defence arrangements were more than adequate.[61] The three service chiefs were again summoned to appear before the CWC, where they repeated their previous opinions, noting that there was little danger of a direct attack on North America larger than a nuisance raid. As Stuart pointed out, even American planners had recently confirmed that the Allies' first priority should be Europe, reversing their own earlier preferences.[62] In an emergency, Canada still had the unmobilized members of its part-time reserve army to rely on, in addition to thousands of staff and other personnel in training centres and military camps across the country, enough of whom were sufficiently well-trained and well-equipped to be rapidly concentrated into another division of troops if it proved necessary for them to fight in the field.[63]

Nevertheless, King continued to press for further consideration of the issue. His motives for advocating such changes were also more personal. According to Grant Dexter, King saw recent Japanese successes as a sign that his military experts were unable to properly judge strategic matters, and consequently the prime minister was trying to use the situation to reduce their influence in Cabinet. As King reportedly stated, "the true ambition of our general staff was to build up an army in Britain not particularly for the defence of Britain but to be the spearhead of the attack on Germany" – a view that was accurate, but that betrayed a degree of confusion over why the army had been established there in the first place. In Dexter's words, "King egged Brucie [Hutchison – then also a journalist in Ottawa] and me on to keep banging away at the generals. He had done nothing to quiet the row on the Pacific Coast for more defence. He hoped it would continue."[64] During the CWC meeting of March 6, which A.G.L. McNaughton was attending while on a visit to Canada, King asked McNaughton to confirm that the defence of British Columbia should be receiving greater attention from Canada's three military services. But McNaughton supported the views of Stuart and the other service advisers, arguing that the focus should continue to be on Europe. Before the general left to return to England, the two men had another private conversation, during which McNaughton again recommended against attempting to defend against attack from everywhere, noting that a single "mobile force of considerable size" would be preferable, that could be centrally located to respond to any threat, precisely as the defence chiefs were recommending. Yet at another CWC meeting the next day, King emphasized an opposite interpretation of McNaughton's comments, saying that McNaughton now "recognized the need of taking measures to allay public apprehension as a result of reverses in the Pacific. In this connection, he had expressed the view that a large mobile force should be established on the west coast."[65]

In response to continued pressure from King and the CWC, both the RCAF and the army brought forward plans to increase their home defence forces. Much like the army, the RCAF ended up expanding beyond what its own experts felt to be necessary, largely driven by public opinion and political pressures. At its peak, the RCAF reached a strength of thirty-six home defence squadrons, although as a fully volunteer organization, in later years it could draw down its strength and transfer excess personnel to Europe more easily than the army (and which it did once the threat to North America had again diminished).[66] In the army's case, Stuart turned to Crerar's earlier projections and recommended that the government complete the mobilization of the 6th Division as a field formation by adding the necessary headquarters and other administrative units, and raise the main brigade groups necessary for a 7th Division, to replace the 4th Division by keeping two full divisions in Canada after the latter went overseas later in the year. In addition, Ralston told the CWC during these discussions that the army would increase the size of its independent defence formations in individual localities in British Columbia, and "longer range plans would probably call for an 8th Division."[67] Two days later, he returned to the CWC to request formal permission to complete the 7th Division and mobilize the three main brigade groups for the 8th Division, which "would be stationed across the country to provide additional defensive strength."[68] By June, Stuart was also requesting the formation of the 8th Division's command headquarters, to help exercise control over the numerous widely scattered units that were being added to the west coast defences.[69]

The next step for Stuart and the rest of the army's leadership was to find the men to fill out all of these new formations. Over the next few months, some twenty new infantry battalions were mobilized and brought up to strength, along with dozens of communications, logistics, artillery, and headquarters units, all for the 7th and 8th Divisions, and further infantry, artillery, and anti-aircraft formations for separate coast defence duties. In May 1942, the requirements for coast defence anti-aircraft units alone were estimated at sixty separate batteries of guns (thirty-nine on the east coast and twenty-one on the west, or about 6,000 men). The 8th Division was so short of qualified officers and NCOs that units were authorized to recruit them directly from among university students with only partial training in the Canadian Officers' Training Corps, and even by directly commissioning suitable civilian businessmen.[70] Another eleven basic training centres were hurriedly established in early 1942 to meet the new training requirements, and for a while "R" recruits were actually posted directly to operational units after completing their first two months of training.[71] In some cases, they went straight to units from the depots where they were first inducted into the army. As the anonymous author of a later report on the creation of anti-aircraft defences on the Pacific coast described the situation: "Often the unit's issue of Bofors guns arrived practically simultaneously with substantial incoming drafts of untrained 'R' recruits, and all would be plunged immediately into an operational role."[72] In two cases, the results were particularly ironic: in early January 1942, the Winnipeg Grenadiers and the Royal Rifles of Canada, the two infantry battalions that had been lost at Hong Kong, were reconstituted in an effort to improve recruiting and boost morale. Instead, both units had to be brought up to strength using large numbers of "R" recruits taken from training centres in Quebec, Ontario, Manitoba, and Alberta. They totalled over half the normal wartime strength of the two battalions.[73]

Nevertheless, NRMA men provided the resources needed to mobilize numerous infantry, artillery, and anti-aircraft regiments. In July 1942, officials even established No. 1 Armoured Train in British Columbia, a specially designed and built armour-plated engine and railway cars, which carried several artillery and anti-aircraft guns and a company of infantry. It made regular trips over the single rail line linking Prince Rupert and Terrace, starting at the end of that month. It ran twice a day at first, then once a day, and later once per week until September 1943 – an indication of the scale on which the west coast had been mobilized, as well as the difficulty (and wastefulness, in terms of manpower and other resources) of attempting to protect every part of such a large, unsettled region.[74] When Major-General George Pearkes arrived in September 1942 to become General Officer Commanding-in-Chief of the newly created Pacific Command, which would exercise control over all of these units, he was taken aback by the level of defensive preparations, given that he had just left commanding 1st Canadian Division in England, where the level of immediate threat had been considered much greater but had not occasioned nearly so much activity.[75] The rapid mobilization and concentration of units on the west coast also set off a new wave of defence construction, and crews worked feverishly throughout 1942 to complete permanent barracks and other facilities for dozens of new units, some of which still spent most of the winter of 1942–43 under canvas.[76]

The extent to which Canada came to be mobilized for war also increased in other ways during this period. In early 1942 the reserve army, which was made up of those soldiers on the old militia model who had jobs in civilian life but were still willing to give up part of their free time to train, was extensively reorganized and given a serious operational role: to act as a second line of defence for the country in the event of a direct attack. Since late 1940, when Crerar had reorganized the army, the reserve's primary role had been to provide reinforcements for active units.[77] As the number of volunteers who could easily leave civilian society began to decline in the summer of 1941, Crerar began searching for other functions, finally settling on what he considered "the quite limited but respectably reasonable responsibilities of 'Home Guard' and 'Aid to the Civil Power.'"[78] With the events of December 1941 and afterwards, the first of these roles suddenly became much more important, and reserve units were formed into twelve brigade groups across the country, which theoretically could be mobilized quickly to fight as field formations should it become necessary. Although service remained part-time, training was made much longer and more thorough, and efforts were made to equip units as much as possible to wartime standards. For the scheme to work, they also needed to be kept at wartime strengths in personnel, and in April 1942 a major drive was launched to find enough men to bring every unit up to its full establishment.[79] According to one memorandum, in March 1942 the total strength of the reserve army was 132,959 officers and men, including 16,835 former thirty-day NRMA recruits who had apparently not yet been recalled for their full four-month training, and another 46,464 who were listed as "supernumerary to establishment" and were due to be called up for further compulsory training in the near future. By January 1944, the reserve army was listed as 88,357 all ranks, although no figures are available to indicate whether any NRMA men remained within it.[80]

Some individual reserve units made very visible contributions to the war. Authorities in British Columbia organized 115 companies of "Pacific Coast Militia Rangers" in the summer of 1942 (a total of over 14,000 men), to augment the defences of more remote areas along the coast. At their peak in 1943 they numbered 137 companies and 15,000 volunteers.[81] In Quebec, the *Fusiliers du St. Laurent* raised a 2nd and a 3rd Battalion of their regiment, 2,500 men in all, to guard the Gaspé area after German submarines entered the St. Lawrence River in the same period.[82] These forces enabled army commanders to respond to public concerns without having to dissipate other resources.

Meanwhile, the CWC was still wrestling with the implications of the big army and the combined overall needs of the army, the RCAF, the RCN, and wartime industry. At the end of January 1942, the Cabinet Manpower Committee reported on ways to increase the number of men in wartime industry and the armed forces, and the CWC began to consider various controls on civilian manpower.[83] The main causes of disagreement were the degree to which the measures should focus on finding men for industry, agriculture, or the armed forces, and to which such measures should be compulsory. The result was that the CWC attempted to do everything, and at the end of March a National Selective Service (NSS) organization officially came into existence, with responsibilities divided between the Departments of National War Services and Labour. At its head was Elliot Little, an industrialist who was among the civilians who had come to Ottawa during the war, in his case to direct the Wartime Bureau of Technical Personnel. To administer the scheme, NSS representatives would be attached to offices of the Unemployment Insurance Commission, which had been set up in 1940 as part of King's introduction of that program across the country. In July the commission itself was folded into the Department of Labour.[84] As the months went on, and the demand for manpower of all types increased, more debate followed, with ministers repeatedly failing to reach any final decision on the exact priorities to assign to NSS. In March, a list of non-essential occupations was created by Order-in-Council, in which no physically fit man between seventeen and forty-five was officially allowed to be employed. In May and September, new national registrations were held to identify all unemployed males, and then all women between twenty and twenty-four. By June, no person could be given a job without an NSS permit showing that he or she was not needed more urgently elsewhere, and after September no employee could be fired from or leave a position without written notice. All advertising of work was made illegal except by NSS. In the same month, Elliot Little recommended that some non-essential industries and even sectors of the economy be completely shut down and that female workers be drawn on more fully, in order to meet the continuing need for resources for the army, navy, air force, and military production. But, warned by a competing report that had been requested from Donald Gordon, the head of the Wartime Prices and Trade Board, and which contended that the result would be widespread shortages, rationing, and standardization of products, King and other Cabinet ministers demurred. With his own position undermined, Little resigned in November. The CWC did give some new powers to his successor, Arthur MacNamara, who was the former head of the Unemployment Commission and an associate deputy minister in the Department of Labour. As Michael Stevenson has noted, MacNamara was "the living embodiment of the concept of gradualness," and for the rest of the war he would strongly resist requests from Ralston and some of his own officials that NSS exercise its powers more forcefully than it was already doing.[85] This set the stage for further clashes over manpower in the future.

As the armed forces and industry expanded, and the number of men available for these roles began to decline, women began to play an increasingly significant part in the war effort. In October 1943, the number working in paid employment peaked at 1,075,000. Another 750,000 were estimated to be contributing to the operation of family farms.[86] In mid-1941 the Canadian Women's Auxiliary Air Force (later the RCAF Women's Division) and the Canadian Women's Army Corps (CWAC) came into existence, followed a year later by the Women's Royal Canadian Naval Service, adding to the smaller numbers of women who had already been participating in the services as nursing sisters and in other medical roles, like in the First World War. Over the rest of the Second World War, 21,624 women served in the CWAC, performing duties ranging from traditional "women's jobs" such as cooks, clerks, or waitresses, to non-traditional ones such as drivers, mechanics, and wireless operators. As Ruth Roach Pierson has noted, the CWAC came to be authorized largely because the women who joined it were seen within the Department of National Defence as a resource that could be used to free up male volunteers to serve overseas, much like the NRMA. And the decision to create the CWAC evolved over the same period of 1940–41 as policies related to the NRMA, in the face of the same concerns about finding enough men for the army's expansion. Rather than hiring civilian women who would have seen such work merely as employment, placing them in uniform gave the army the ability to control exactly where, when, and how women served, as well as to educate them in the specific jargon and procedures used within the military.[87] Small numbers of such women began arriving in training centres in mid-1942.

One last development took place in 1942–43 that reveals the extent to which the country's defence forces had expanded by then, both numerically and in the scope of their service. The repeal of Section 3 of the NRMA in August 1942 resulted in a number of successive extensions of the definitions of where conscripts could be ordered to serve. Even before Japan's entry into the war in December 1941, Brigadier Pope and Lieutenant-General Stuart had begun exploring the possibility of extending service to include areas such as Newfoundland, which could be viewed as directly vital to national security and where the likelihood of attack was not much greater than on Canadian soil. If this could be done, then further general service soldiers could be released from North America for duties overseas.[88] The first official extension came as Bill 80 was being debated in Parliament, when small numbers were ordered to the United States as part of their routine duties in mid-May.[89] As events in the Pacific went from bad to worse, Canadian airmen and then ground troops were sent as far as Alaska to help defend US territory. The first major amendment to the NRMA came a month after Bill 80 passed into law, when two anti-aircraft batteries were sent to Annette Island on the Alaskan panhandle just north of Prince Rupert and the Queen Charlotte Islands (today Haida Gwaii), to protect RCAF aircraft there.[90] In a matter of days, service under the NRMA was extended to include Newfoundland and Labrador, and by August 1943 authorities had passed a blanket Order-in-Council permitting NRMA recruits to be sent there as well as to the United States, Bermuda, the Bahamas, Jamaica, and British Guiana (in other words, to every place in the Western Hemisphere where Canadian troops were currently serving).[91]

In August 1943, a sizable number of NRMA men even saw action on a combat basis. On August 15 and 16, 1943, more than 5,000 Canadian soldiers of the combined Canadian–American First Special Service Force and 13th Canadian Infantry Brigade joined roughly 30,000 Americans in landings on Kiska, in the Aleutian Islands, to retake it from the Japanese. The event was notable for two reasons: it marked the first time that Canadian troops had ever taken part in a field operation under US higher command, and the first use of NRMA soldiers in a combat role in the war. The campaign had grown out of closer ties between Canadian and American commanders that had developed in the earlier years of the conflict, with the need to coordinate various defence measures in North America, particularly on the west coast. There, Major-General Pearkes had formed a strong working relationship with Lieutenant-General John L. DeWitt, his American counterpart, and in April 1943 Pearkes suggested that DeWitt consider including Canadians in planned US operations in the Aleutians. The idea made its way to Ottawa through the US military, which contacted the CGS, Stuart, via Maurice Pope, who was by then serving as chairman of the Canadian Joint Staff Mission in Washington. By the time Stuart took the idea to his minister, Ralston, it had already been worked out in most of its essentials, and the CWC was not happy to be presented with this fait accompli. But Pearkes, Stuart, and a few other officials strongly supported the plan, noting that it would further Canadian–American relations, improve the training, morale, and public exposure of the country's home defence forces, and especially give conscripts an opportunity to take an active role in defending the continent, dispelling some of the public animosity that had begun to grow towards them. The CWC agreed to permit Canadian forces to participate in the attack, but with a number of reservations that were designed to prevent any repeat of the criticisms about untrained and poorly equipped troops being sent to fight in the Pacific that had followed the loss of the Winnipeg Grenadiers and the Royal Rifles of Canada at Hong Kong.[92]

Asked to contribute a force similar to a US "Regimental Combat Team" (roughly a brigade), Pearkes assigned 13th Canadian Infantry Brigade from the 6th Division, the most senior brigade in his command, to act as the headquarters for the operation. Infantry battalions and other units were chosen from throughout Pacific Command, to ensure that only the strongest and best-trained were sent. Among those selected were the reconstituted Winnipeg Grenadiers, the Canadian Fusiliers from London, Ontario, and the Rocky Mountain Rangers from British Columbia. A fourth infantry battalion, the *Régiment de Hull*, was added to the normal three of a Canadian infantry brigade to carry out the duties of combat engineer troops that were usually part of a US regimental combat team. Its role would be to defend the landing beaches from possible enemy counterattacks and to bring up supplies for the three lead battalions, a task for which the brigade commander later noted its men were "highly praised by all concerned" during the operation.[93] With the addition of the *Régiment de Hull*, as well as other support units, the brigade also conveniently included elements from all parts of the country.[94] That summer, Canadian soldiers turned in their British-pattern equipment for US tools, helmets, Arctic clothing, and other supplies – again for the first time in the country's history – keeping only their British-style battledress and personal weapons. Special Orders-in-Council were passed to ensure that NRMA soldiers could be sent to the Aleutians and to allow Canadian soldiers to come under the command of American officers. Both were implemented in a series of stages as the CWC assured itself that every possible step was being taken to guarantee the force's readiness.[95]

Figure 12 The scene at the former central Japanese base on Kiska following the Canadian-American landings. *Source:* LAC, C-144117.

Figure 13 A member of the 13th Brigade's Intelligence Section poses for a picture on Kiska, illustrating his British-pattern battledress but mostly American-issue helmet and other equipment. *Source:* LAC, C-144120.

Ultimately, to the embarrassment of many people (although undoubtedly the relief of most of the men participating in the attack), the force arrived on Kiska only to find that the Japanese garrison had abandoned the island three weeks earlier. In retrospect, a number of signs of this might have been detected. But at the time, commanders were preoccupied by the apparent lessons of recent combat in the Pacific, where Japanese forces had refused to concede territory and had repeatedly fought to the last man. Preparations for the campaign had been taken especially seriously after the capture of neighbouring Attu required a month of hard fighting in May, resulting in casualties of roughly one-third of the attacking force and the deaths of almost the entire Japanese garrison of 2,500 men.[96] The Japanese fleet that evacuated Kiska had been spotted but was assumed to be bringing reinforcements to the island, which already had at least twice as many defenders as Attu. When activity ceased on Kiska in early August, it seemed only that the garrison had left its main headquarters to move into prepared defences in the hills, which would make the fighting even tougher. Fog and bad weather then combined to make it difficult to confirm or deny their presence.[97] The attack was not completely bloodless; a number of men accidentally fired at each other in the fog, or set off Japanese booby traps, land mines, or other munitions. The casualties included four Canadian dead: Lieutenant S. Vessey of the Rocky Mountain Rangers, Private P. Poshtar of the Winnipeg Grenadiers, and Privates G. Boisclair and G. Desjardins of the *Régiment de Hull.* Judging by the comments of the 13th Brigade's war diarist shortly after the landings, it was just as well that the force had not faced the Japanese as "every hill, more especially every high ridge, was alive with Jap positions and dummy positions. This would have been a terrific fight."[98]

WITH THE END OF THE KISKA landings came the end of the almost continual expansion of the Canadian army that had been going on for the past two years. By the beginning of July 1943, it numbered 478,053, out of which 69,389 were NRMA recruits or members (HD). Thus, 14.5 percent of the entire full-time army was made up of conscripts. Of these, 9,613 were serving outside Canada, and 3,129 (around one-third) of those were on Kiska. One-quarter of the total of 264,084 men and women who served on Canadian soil were conscripts (66,260 men), and the proportions performing direct operational duties were much higher: 8,419 NRMA men in 6th Canadian Division (70.7 percent out of 11,902), 6,903 in the 7th (68.8 percent out of 10,027), and 5,945 in the 8th (72.4 percent out of 8,215). Over 80 percent (82.9 percent, or 2,998) of the 3,617 men of 21st Canadian Infantry Brigade Group, which was then posted independently in Valcartier, Quebec, were NRMA recruits, as were almost half (15,435, or 49.4 percent) of the remaining 31,232 personnel carrying out other operational duties in Atlantic Command, Pacific Command, and miscellaneous coast and internal defence units.[99] Canada had managed to raise a total ground force equating to almost nine divisions, and one that was now proving itself capable of sending combat troops to two major theatres of war in Europe and the Pacific simultaneously. The country had been extensively mobilized in other ways by 1943, and was now maintaining three huge armed services while also making economic contributions out of all proportion to its size. All of this would earn Canada a respected position among the world's major powers after the war.

Yet this was exactly the situation that many members of the Cabinet and the CWC had feared in 1940 and 1941. By August 1943, the Canadian army had grown far beyond what had been foreseen at the beginning of the war, partly due to the influence of the senior generals who had been responsible for shaping its character in those years, but partly also due to the events of the war itself. After December 7, 1941, with the big army still dominating the CWC's discussions, King had been as prepared as his generals to press for expanding the Canadian military. Not only that, but despite the merging of the volunteer and NRMA training systems in early 1941, the Canadian army clearly continued to be divided (mentally and administratively, if not physically) into two separate forces, one for service anywhere and one only for Canada. As the war continued this would make it more and more difficult to streamline the organization, in spite of increasing attempts. The zombie army was there to stay for the duration.

As we have seen, the NRMA also allowed H.D.G. Crerar and his successors to argue for expanding the army throughout 1941 and 1942, and not necessarily because they disagreed with their political masters regarding conscription for overseas service, although they never pretended that such a large force might not come to require such support at some point. But they do at least genuinely seem to have believed by late 1941 that the army could be maintained without having to resort to that (or at least that, just as their political masters hoped, they would be able to get by for as long as possible without needing to do so), thanks to the successful way in which compulsory military service had come to function within Canada. The NRMA also enabled Crerar's successor, Ken Stuart, to respond to huge new demands following the outbreak of war in the Pacific in late 1941, without disrupting the army's existing plans for overseas expansion, which were still officially viewed by the politicians and the generals alike as one of the country's primary wartime contributions. The NRMA may even have helped encourage some of Stuart's political superiors to believe that the army could keep expanding in this period without having to face some of the tough questions that were beginning to be raised about wartime manpower resources generally.

Unfortunately, these decisions ended up creating a force that did prove to be larger than the army could maintain indefinitely, especially given the combined pressures of competition from the country's two other armed services, the needs of civilian industry, and rising casualties in Italy and later in northwest Europe throughout 1943 and 1944. Military planners had not foreseen any of this on quite the scale they would eventually face. The main difficulty would come if the rigid and complex structure that had been built up to maintain the army by taking advantage of the NRMA ever began to break down, thus ending the constant stream of reinforcements that the planners now counted on to build up and maintain the country's overseas forces. By August 1943, some of the problems that would begin to cause this breakdown were becoming apparent. Over the next few months they would become more and more obvious, and would cause even the army's leaders to begin questioning their ability to maintain such large forces overseas. In the meantime, as we will see in Part 3 of this book, by 1943 the willingness of NRMA recruits to become active service volunteers had begun to decline under the weight of the many pressures they came to face to do so. The results of both trends were fewer and fewer volunteers, and ultimately a second and even more serious conscription crisis in the fall of 1944.

Part 3:
Canadian Conscripts and Their Experiences during the War

A Trainees [sic] Lament[1]

They dragged me into the Army
I didn't want to go,
But one day, I got a letter,
And I didn't dare say no.

They took me off to a Training Camp,
Where there's lots of drill to do,
And they walked, worked, and drilled me,
Till I was black and blue.

For four months they kept me a prisoner,
With only small respite,
And many times if I had the nerve,
I should have taken flight.

At last the months were over,
My time was nearly done,
And I would be going home,
To have my nights of fun.

But the Sergeant said "No never"
"It's home defence for you,
And if you're needed overseas,
There's nothing you can do.["]

So they sent me off to an outpost,
To guard our great Domain
With an old Mark II Ross rifle,
Out in the mud and rain.

If I ever get back my freedom,
No more will I remain
A happy and free young man,
Cause they might take me again.

I'll get me a wife,
No matter old or young,
As long as I can get along with her,
And still have lots of fun.

5
Canada's Zombies, Part 1: A Statistical Portrait

UNTIL NOW, LITTLE HAS been known about the makeup of the tens of thousands of Canadians who served as conscripts during the Second World War. In October 1944, when the federal Cabinet faced the issue of sending them overseas, francophone members resented the idea that all conscripts were "shirkers" from French Canada. In the words of Louis St. Laurent, who had by then begun to take on more fully Ernest Lapointe's previous role as King's Quebec lieutenant, "the fact was that these men were composed of one-third French Canadians, one-third of English Canadians, and one-third of people who had more or less recently come to the country from Europe."[1] A few months earlier, Brigadier W.H.S. Macklin, the commander of 13th Canadian Infantry Brigade in British Columbia, had offered a similar view that has come to be one of the most widely reproduced comments on the NRMA. Macklin first pointed to the large number of French Canadian conscripts serving in his command. But as he then added:

> As regards the English-speaking NRMA soldiers ... The great majority are of non-British origin – German, Italian, and Slavic nationalities of origin probably predominating. Moreover most of them come from farms. They are of deplorably low education, know almost nothing of Canadian or British History and in fact are typical European peasants, with a passionate attachment for the land. A good many of them speak their native tongues much more fluently than they speak English and amongst them the ancient racial grudges and prejudices of Europe still persist.[2]

Putting aside the general attitudes towards ethnic minorities revealed by these comments, like many observers Macklin was clearly looking to explain the lack of willingness of the "zombies" to volunteer for overseas service by pointing to the degree to which they were cut off from mainstream English Canadian society and its ideals in one way or another. Presumably, the most important of these ideals was their support for the war effort overseas.

Only in recent years have statistics on the NRMA turned up among the unaccessioned records of the Department of National Defence (DND) held by Library and Archives Canada. Those records make it possible to test such conclusions in greater detail. The tables on the following pages are based on information that was provided by each conscript himself at the time he began his military service. That information was then later compiled and tabulated by army officials.[3] As these numbers indicate, the NRMA men largely reflected the society from which they were drawn. In many ways, including their ethnic and geographical origins, languages spoken, religious convictions, and even the occupations they had pursued before being called up for military training, NRMA recruits more closely mirrored the population at large than has previously been suggested. Before examining more fully the statistical information on which these conclusions are based, it should be noted that the number of men listed as NRMA in these statistical records differs slightly from final postwar totals, apparently due to duplication of records. But this error should not be large enough to invalidate the conclusions drawn here.[4]

Not surprisingly for an organization that required men to report for training by age groups, the first piece of information collected by DND from each conscript was their date of birth. Table 2 lists this information by the year in which each man was born and the year he was called out for training. This is the greatest level of detail to which these statistics were later tabulated. But by reading the table diagonally, downwards and to the right, we can tell within a few months the ages of NRMA recruits at the time they entered compulsory service. As the information in Table 2 indicates, almost one-third of all conscripts were approximately twenty-one or twenty-two years old when called out for training, and nearly three-quarters were between eighteen and twenty-five. This conclusion is not surprising, since, as in the First World War, men in these age groups tended to be the most fit for military service. And in the early years of the NRMA's operation, all men called out were young and single and thus the least likely to have long-term jobs or other ties to keep them from being required for training. At the same time, close to 10 percent of all wartime NRMA recruits were over the age of thirty, a fact that reminds us that military service was not just an occupation for the young. Indeed, as we will see in Chapter 7, the groups liable for compulsory training were gradually expanded during the war until they included all single men between eighteen-and-a-half and forty-three, as well as married men from eighteen-and-a-half to thirty-two.[5] Unfortunately, from the information available, it is not possible to calculate the exact numbers of single or married men within the ranks of the zombies. But anecdotal evidence, combined with the priority given to unmarried men early in the war, would suggest that the majority were likely single at the time they were called out. As young, single males, NRMA recruits clearly differed in many important ways from the typical Canadian in the country at large (only 207,579 or 3.5 percent of the 5,900,536 men in Canada counted by the census of 1941

Table 2

Approximate ages of NRMA recruits on enrolment

	Year of enrolment								
Year born	1941	1942	1943	1944	1945	N.S.[a]	Total	Age[b]	%
1899	–	1	–	–	–	–		–	–
1900	–	1	–	–	–	–		–	–
1901	1	9	8	–	–	–		–	–
1902	–	192	201	–	–	–		–	–
1903	–	245	267	1	–	–		–	–
1904	–	302	311	1	–	–	1	43	0.0
1905	1	360	312	4	–	–	9	42	0.0
1906	1	345	397	31	–	–	211	41	0.1
1907	–	479	437	55	3	–	461	40	0.3
1908	2	602	530	69	9	–	560	39	0.4
1909	3	851	536	105	9	–	648	38	0.4
1910	17	960	695	128	17	[1]	821	37	0.5
1911	6	1,202	683	136	21	–	861	36	0.5
1912	6	1,599	844	175	31	–	1,132	35	0.7
1913	5	2,158	1,117	957	89	–	1,287	34	0.8
1914	14	3,098	1,498	903	90	–	1,715	33	1.1
1915	137	4,449	1,607	763	65	–	1,910	32	1.2
1916	345	6,142	1,595	724	92	–	3,110	31	2.0
1917	1,092	8,254	1,974	509	83	[1]	3,690	30	2.3
1918	4,120	9,231	1,717	498	87	[2]	4,517	29	2.9
1919	14,684	6,308	1,439	450	70	–	5,517	28	3.5
1920	11,212	7,512	1,747	566	114	–	6,654	27	4.2
1921	246	7,221	2,945	734	129	–	8,821	26	5.6
1922	19	5,392	3,918	989	149	–	10,880	25	6.9
1923	4	2,880	4,677	1,234	194	[1]	12,457	24	7.9
1924	1	41	4,120	2,553	294	–	13,058	23	8.3
1925	2	8	650	4,998	480	–	26,324	22	16.7
1926	1	6	5	1,123	1,496	–	23,879	21	15.1
1927	2	5	–	3	5	–	13,348	20	8.4
1928	1	6	1	1	–	–	13,513	19	8.5
1929	3	5	1	–	–	–	1,823	18	1.2
–	–	–	–	–	–	–	51	12–17[c]	0.0
Not stated	75	640	77	–	1	5	798	–	0.5
Totals	*32,000*	*70,504*	*34,309*	*17,710*	*3,528*	*5*	*158,056*[d]		*100.0*

Notes:

a Enrolment year "Not Stated" in documents used to compile table.

b Ages estimated by comparing year of birth to year of enrolment.

c These age numbers reflect errors apparently made in transcribing original information for tabulation. The total number of errors identified in this table is 386, or 0.2% of all NRMA records.

d This figure differs slightly from official postwar totals of NRMA recruits due to the later elimination of 215 incorrect records.

were twenty-one or twenty-two, and 841,169 or 14.3 percent were between eighteen and twenty-five).[6] Yet in this respect they did not differ so much from the majority of volunteers who made up the active army in Canada and overseas: according to two sets of figures that were collected for that force in the late summer of 1942 and again at the beginning of 1943, men in their late teens to mid-twenties made up 50 to 60 percent of all volunteers, compared to closer to 75 percent of conscripts; the difference was made up by volunteers in their late thirties, or in their forties and over (a category that included no conscripts, given that the ages of liability for compulsory service never reached that high).[7]

Tables 3 and 4 provide further information about the NRMA men. Table 3 lists recruits by their place of residence at the time they entered the army, and Table 4 by place of birth. As these numbers show, the proportions of conscripts from most provinces were slightly lower than those for the population as a whole. This was so, especially in Ontario. Meanwhile, the number from Quebec was somewhat higher. The increase in figures for Quebec from year to year is particularly noticeable. Thus, there is some degree of truth to wartime assumptions that French Canadians made up a disproportionate number of NRMA recruits, especially as the conflict went on. Nevertheless, according to one report compiled by the army in November 1944, of the 60,000 men who remained in uniform as conscripts at that point in the war, by place of origin about 39 percent came from Quebec, 24 percent from Ontario, and 37 percent from the remaining provinces.[8] These proportions did not differ from those of the larger population as much as one might expect. Clearly, then, there were plenty of men in every province who were fit for military service but who did not wish to serve in the army overseas.

In fact, the number of conscripts from Quebec comes even closer to its share of the national population when one considers that unlike in the First World War, when a higher proportion of the province's young men had been married, by the 1940s it actually had the largest number of single men in both the 15–24 and 25–34 age groups. Thus, if conscription was being applied without discrimination, it should be expected to have applied more to Quebec for simple demographic reasons. According to the 1941 census, Quebec had a total of 304,420 single men between fifteen and twenty-four (30.6 percent of the 996,302 single men aged 15–24 in Canada, compared to Quebec's 29.0 percent of the total population), while Ontario, the province with the largest share of the national population at 32.9 percent, had 302,473 single men who were 15–24 (30.4 percent of all single men of that age). The numbers were similar for single men between twenty-five and thirty-four, at 111,916 for Quebec (30.4 percent of the total of 368,247 men in Canada in that category) and 111,083 for Ontario (30.2 percent).[9] While they did not use quite the same age categories to break up their

Table 3

NRMA recruits by place of residence on enrolment

	1941		1942		1943		1944		1945		NRMA		Canada[a]	
Province	*N*	%	*N*	%	*N*	%	*N*	%	*N*	%	*N*	%	*N*	%
PEI	248	0.8	596	0.8	52	0.2	21	0.1	2	0.0	919	0.6	95,047	0.8
Nova Scotia	1,539	4.8	2,870	4.1	1,214	3.5	608	3.4	23	0.7	6,255	4.0	577,962	5.0
New Brunswick	1,360	4.3	3,422	4.9	1,782	5.2	469	2.6	132	3.7	7,165	4.5	457,401	4.0
Quebec	9,940	31.1	23,270	33.0	11,678	34.0	8,307	47.0	2,207	62.6	55,402	35.1	3,331,882	29.0
Ontario	9,777	30.6	21,368	30.3	9,607	28.0	3,956	22.3	446	12.6	45,158	28.6	3,787,655	32.9
Manitoba	2,127	6.6	3,664	5.2	2,582	7.5	970	5.5	165	4.7	9,508	6.0	729,744	6.3
Saskatchewan	2,944	9.2	5,811	8.2	2,575	7.5	774	4.4	155	4.4	12,259	7.8	895,992	7.8
Alberta	2,442	7.6	4,188	5.9	2,161	6.3	1,390	7.8	294	8.3	10,475	6.6	796,169	7.0
British Columbia	1,621	5.1	5,310	7.5	2,657	7.7	1,212	6.8	1,103	3.0	10,903	6.9	817,861	7.1
Yukon/NWT	–	–	–	–	–	–	–	–	–	–	–	–	16,942	0.1
Newfoundland	–	–	3	0.0	–	–	–	–	–	–	3	0.0	–	–
USA	2	0.0	2	0.0	1	0.0	3	0.0	1	0.0	9	0.0	–	–
Totals	*32,000*	*100.0*	*70,504*	*100.0*	*34,309*	*100.0*	*17,710*	*100.0*	*3,528*	*100.0*	*158,056*	*100.0*	*11,506,655*	*100.0*[b]

Notes:

a Numbers in this column are from Urquhart and Buckley, eds., *Historical Statistics of Canada*, series A2–14.

b Some columns do not total exactly 100 percent, due to rounding of decimals.

Table 4

NRMA recruits by place of birth

Place of birth		NRMA *N*	NRMA %[a]	Canada[b] *N*	Canada[b] %[a]
Canadian	PEI	965	0.6	108,423	0.9
	Nova Scotia	6,348	4.0	568,797	4.9
	New Brunswick	7,393	4.7	463,127	4.0
	Quebec	54,100	34.2	3,155,549	27.4
	Ontario	36,772	23.3	3,123,810	27.1
	Manitoba	10,405	6.6	570,349	5.0
	Saskatchewan	15,145	9.6	667,832	5.8
	Alberta	9,064	5.7	479,098	4.2
	British Columbia	5,238	3.3	335,554	2.9
	Yukon/NWT	9	0.0	12,267	0.1
	Not Stated, but Canadian	–	–	3,002	0.0
	Total Canadian	*145,439*	*92.0*	*9,487,808*	*82.5*
British	Newfoundland	112	0.0	25,837	0.2
	England/Wales	1,649	1.0	635,221	5.5
	Scotland	870	0.6	234,824	2.0
	Ireland	344	0.2	86,126	0.7
	Australia	17	0.0	N/A	–
	Tasmania	1	0.0	N/A	–
	New Zealand	1	0.0	N/A	–
	Union of South Africa	5	0.0	N/A	–
	British Africa	4	0.0	N/A	–
	British Guiana	3	0.0	N/A	–
	British India	8	0.0	N/A	–
	Other British Countries	27	0.0	21,761	0.2
	Total British	*3,041*	*1.9*	*1,003,769*	*8.7*
	Total British Born	*148,480*	*93.9*	*10,491,577*	*91.2*
American	USA	1,899	1.2	312,473	2.7
	Mexico	2	0.0	N/A	–
	Brazil	3	0.0	N/A	–
	Cuba	2	0.0	N/A	–
	Equador	1	0.0	N/A	–
	Haiti	3	0.0	N/A	–
	Argentina	4	0.0	N/A	–
	Other South American	5	0.0	N/A	–
	Total American	*1,919*	*1.2*	*312,473*	*2.7*
European	Poland	2,091	1.3	155,400	1.4
	Russia	949	0.6	117,598	1.0

Place of birth		NRMA N	NRMA %[a]	Canada[b] N	Canada[b] %[a]
	Italy	653	0.4	40,432	0.4
	Czecho-Slovakia	593	0.4	25,564	0.2
	Hungary	578	0.4	31,813	0.3
	Germany	394	0.2	28,479	0.2
	Roumania	326	0.2	28,454	0.2
	Norway	273	0.2	26,914	0.2
	Sweden	221	0.1	27,160	0.2
	Austria	196	0.1	50,713	0.4
	Denmark	185	0.1	13,974	0.1
	Finland	163	0.1	24,387	0.2
	Holland	119	0.1	9,923	0.1
	Belgium	111	0.1	14,773	0.1
	Greece	81	0.1	N/A	–
	Lithuania	81	0.1	N/A	–
	France	40	0.0	13,795	0.1
	Switzerland	35	0.0	N/A	–
	Syria	30	0.0	N/A	–
	Bulgaria	15	0.0	N/A	–
	Latvia	14	0.0	N/A	–
	Turkey	12	0.0	N/A	–
	Estonia	10	0.0	N/A	–
	Iceland	6	0.0	N/A	–
	Albania	3	0.0	N/A	–
	Servia	2	0.0	17,416	0.2[c]
	Luxembourg	2	0.0	N/A	–
	Other	–	–	23,298	0.2
	Total European	*7,183*	*4.5*	*65,3705*	*5.7*
Asian	China	9	0.0	29,095	0.3
	Siberia	3	0.0	N/A	–
	Japan	2	0.0	9,462	0.1
	Other Asian	6	0.0	5,886	0.1
	Total Asian	*20*	*0.0*	*44,443*	*0.4*
Non-British African		2	0.0	N/A	–
Not stated		452	0.3	4,457	0.0
Grand totals		*158,056*	*100.0*	*11,506,655*	*100.0*

Notes:

a Some percentages are not exact, due to rounding of decimals.

b Numbers in this column are from Canada, Dominion Bureau of Statistics, *Eighth Census of Canada*, 1941 (Ottawa: King's Printer, 1950), vol. 1, table 23, 668–69.

c Census figures are for "Yugoslavia," the only numbers available.

numbers as in the census, figures prepared by the Department of National War Services from the national registration of 1940 (and which are the ones on which all mobilization was based for the NRMA) also confirm this trend, showing that the total number of single men between the ages of eighteen and thirty in Quebec was 258,411, and in Ontario 255,037.[10] Thanks to the report of the Labour Supply Investigation Committee, J.L. Ralston and other politicians were well aware of the equality in these statistics between Quebec and Ontario as early as December 1941. At that point, Ralston reportedly viewed conscription more as a way to put English-speaking men into uniform, since the army had insufficient personnel to train many more French-speaking recruits, even had more of them been called up.[11] In later years, however, as the number of men available for compulsory military service in all provinces began to run short, the excess in Quebec would have been the final reserve of men on which to draw. In addition, as French Canadians came to be targeted more and more openly by public opinion in English Canada, the efforts of officials to locate conscripts may have become more concentrated on Quebec for other reasons. One way or the other, the result was that the figures from year to year came to include larger numbers of Quebeckers than earlier in the war.

Another notable feature of the NRMA was the range of languages spoken by its recruits, as shown in Table 5. Since this information was collected from the conscripts themselves, and each man appears only once, apparently they gave the languages with which they were most familiar – in other words, their mother tongue(s).[12] As Table 5 shows, the proportions of NRMA recruits who spoke French, or both French and English, were relatively close to those for Canada as a whole. Even if the first language of all bilingual recruits is assumed to have been French, then no more than 40 percent of all conscripts were francophones during the war. In contrast, the volunteer army did not reflect the larger population nearly so closely. In June 1942 military authorities made a rough estimation that based on the French-language last names of volunteers who had enlisted solely in Military Districts Nos. 4 and 5 in Quebec, francophones made up 8.4 percent of all general service recruits (although this was still a not inconsiderable figure of 29,651 men overall, and 52.3 percent of all of the enlistments from those two districts).[13]

In addition, the number of men who spoke neither English nor French was noticeably higher than among the larger population. This was true especially for the western provinces, since thanks to the original statistics from Library and Archives Canada on which Table 5 is based we know the figures down to that level.[14] A large majority of Italian-speaking NRMA recruits came from Ontario and Quebec, most likely reflecting the Italian Canadian community's ties to the two major cities of Montreal and Toronto during this period.[15] As we

Table 5

Languages of NRMA recruits

Language	NRMA N	NRMA %	Canada[a] N	Canada[a] %	Canada[b] N	Canada[b] %
English	59,255	37.5	6,488,190	56.4	7,735,486	67.2
French	30,125	19.1	3,354,753	29.2	2,181,746	19.0
Both	33,143	21.0	–	–	1,474,009	12.8
Neither	–	–	–	–	115,414	1.0
German	6,470	4.1	322,228	2.8	–	–
Polish	3,766	2.4	128,711	1.1	–	–
Italian	3,033	1.9	80,260	0.7	–	–
Russian	1,038	0.7	52,431	0.5	–	–
Spanish	50	0.0	1,030	0.0	–	–
Chinese	38	0.0	33,500	0.3	–	–
Japanese	2	0.0	22,359	0.2	–	–
Other	19,310	12.2	1,021,546	8.9	–	–
Not stated	1,826	1.2	1,647	0.0	–	–
Totals	*158,056*	*100.0*	*11,506,655*	*100.0*	*11,506,655*	*100.0*

Notes:

a Numbers in this column are based on mother tongues as listed by census respondents, in F.H. Leacy, ed., *Historical Statistics of Canada*, 2nd ed. (Ottawa: Statistics Canada, 1983), series A185–237; and *Eighth Census of Canada*, 1941, vol. 1, table 45, 710.

b Numbers in this column are from *Eighth Census of Canada*, 1941, vol. 1, table 38, 700–1, which provides information only on ability to speak Canada's two official languages.

have already seen, as an ethnic group from a country with which Canada was at war, and considering their treatment following Italy's entry into the war in 1940, it may be less surprising that they made up a higher proportion of NRMA men than among the population at large (as also may have been true for German speakers, although the reason for the proportion of Polish-speaking conscripts being noticeably higher than among the general population is not as clear). More broadly, these results again seem to confirm at least some of the conclusions stated by Brigadier Macklin in his 1944 report, quoted at the beginning of this chapter. They are further confirmed by the army's figures for the 60,000 NRMA recruits who remained in service in November 1944, also mentioned above, which found that 28 percent were English-speaking, 20 percent French-speaking, and 23 percent bilingual, while a relatively large proportion of 25 percent were recorded as simply "of other races." The same report concluded that no more than 37 percent of all NRMA recruits were francophones, although it is not clear exactly how the army arrived at that figure.[16] But even after allowing for higher proportions of French Canadians and other ethnic minorities in the ranks of the NRMA, it is clear that the zombies included men from all parts of Canadian society.

Religion was another area where NRMA recruits reflected the population of Canada reasonably closely. As Table 6 indicates, the country was still overwhelmingly Christian in the 1940s, with over 90 percent of both NRMA recruits and Canadians as a whole professing their adherence to Christian faiths. More noticeable in this table is the contrast in the breakdown between Protestants and Roman Catholics for the NRMA, compared to the overall population of the country. It is not clear exactly why this was so. According to the more detailed statistics on which this table is based, which again are broken down by province, Quebeckers made up over half of all Roman Catholic conscripts, a number that is actually slightly less than their proportion of Roman Catholics in the national population. At the same time, the numbers of conscripts listed as Roman Catholic from New Brunswick, Ontario, Manitoba, and Saskatchewan were all higher than each province's percentage for the country as a whole, with Manitoba having the most significant discrepancy at 5.6 percent of Roman Catholic NRMA recruits compared to 2.9 percent of all Roman Catholics in the country.[17] Since Manitoba and New Brunswick both contained sizable minorities of French-speaking Canadians, it is possible that many Roman Catholic conscripts from these provinces were francophones. But like today, Canada in the 1940s also contained large numbers of Roman Catholics of other nationalities, such as Irish and Italian Canadians. Like Italian Canadians, Irish Catholics may have felt less willing to serve, given the past history of relations between their country and Great Britain, and particularly the bitter feelings aroused by Ireland's struggle for independence during and after the First World War. Although Ireland was still part of the Commonwealth in 1939, it took advantage of its new independence to declare neutrality, and questions about how to treat Irish nationals living in Canada (who were still considered British citizens under the NRMA) created a considerable amount of paperwork during the war.[18] Certainly, the high number of Catholic conscripts cannot explained away simply as the result of greater French Canadian opposition.

Furthermore, it is not clear how closely the number of conscripts of "Other" religions included in Table 6 mirrored Canada in general, since the army did not differentiate beyond the major denominations listed here. One notable aspect of Table 6 is the lack of any adherents of the Greek or Ukrainian Orthodox churches among NRMA recruits. Members of eastern branches of the Orthodox church were often mistakenly identified as "Roman Catholic" during this period, and this would appear to be the most likely explanation for the absence of separate figures for the NRMA, especially given that there are a few

Table 6

Religions of NRMA recruits

Religion		NRMA *N*	NRMA %	Canada[a] *N*	Canada[a] %
Protestant	United Church	20,268	12.8	2,208,658	19.2
	Methodist	813	0.5	N/A	–[b]
	Congregational	6	0.0	N/A	–[b]
	Anglican	13,991	8.9	1,754,368	15.2
	Lutheran	7,428	4.7	401,836	3.5
	Presbyterian	7,070	4.5	830,597	7.2
	Baptist	5,381	3.4	484,465	4.2
	Salvation Army	172	0.1	33,609	0.3
	Total Protestant	*55,129*	*34.9*	*5,713,533*	*49.7*
Roman Catholic		91,320	57.8	4,806,431	41.8
Jewish		3,479	2.2	168,585	1.5
Other	Other Protestant	–	–	231,688	2.0
	Greek/Ukrainian	–	–	325,793	2.8
	Other	6,709	4.2	243,466	2.1
	Total "Other"	*6,709*	*4.2*	*800,947*	*7.0*
Not stated		922	0.6	17,159	0.1
No religion		497	0.3	–	–
Totals		*158,056*	*100.0*	*11,506,655*	*100.0*[c]

Notes:

a Urquhart and Buckley, eds., *Historical Statistics of Canada*, series A114–132.

b Included in figures for United Church.

c Some columns do not total exactly 100 percent, due to rounding of decimals.

pieces of evidence in the war diaries of the various training centres that men of those faiths did serve. If this is so, it would bring the proportion of Roman Catholic conscripts down to slightly closer to that for Canada as a whole. In addition, of the 6,709 recruits listed as "Other" in the army's statistics, large numbers came from western Canada, in the same way as conscripts speaking languages other than English or French in Table 5.[19] Once again, these numbers would seem to confirm that more than a representative portion of conscripts were of "non-British" origins, and that presumably a majority came from the many well-known ethnic communities that had helped settle western Canada since before the turn of the century. This may have been even more noticeable to people at the time, considering that according to one set of statistics from August 1941, volunteers were heavily weighted in the opposite direction, with as many as 36 percent being Anglican, 14 percent Presbyterian, and only 22 percent Roman Catholic.[20] Unfortunately, no similar comparative figures have been located for later time periods.

The number of Jewish conscripts listed in Table 6 is also worth noting. According to the army's figures, 2.2 percent of NRMA recruits were Jewish, compared to 1.5 percent of the general population (and 0.6 percent of active service volunteers, at least early in the war, according to the statistics from August 1941 cited at the end of the preceding paragraph). By far the largest proportion of Jewish NRMA recruits came from Ontario (45.7 percent) and Quebec (40.4 percent), reflecting the large communities of Jewish Canadians living in Toronto and Montreal at the time. As Gerald Tulchinsky has noted, there are a number of possible explanations for the higher number of Jewish conscripts during the war: feelings of responsibility to care for families at home; a perhaps weaker sense of direct personal loyalty to the British Commonwealth as a result of not being fully integrated into the larger Canadian population; a tradition for many families from eastern Europe of antipathy towards the military (another factor that likely affected ethnic groups from other countries in that region discussed above, as well); and support for the Co-operative Commonwealth Federation among some left-wing members of the community and thus also the thread of pacifism that had run through the interwar CCF.[21] In addition, the Canadian army did not have a long tradition of openly accommodating Jewish recruits who wished to join voluntarily. Nor did the country have a strong record of objecting to anti-Semitism, which in some ways had become more open and virulent in the 1930s, both internationally and domestically.[22] But what is most noticeable about Jewish conscripts is that they were included in the NRMA's figures at all, and in numbers fairly close to their share of the national population. Clearly, they supported or objected to wartime military service in proportions at least roughly similar to those of other Canadians, and had as many reasons why they were not interested in serving in uniform.

While no information seems to have been collected from NRMA recruits as to their actual ethnicity (unless they happened to have been born outside Canada), it is also important to remember that not every citizen was accepted readily into uniform during the war, even under the compulsory provisions of the NRMA. One group that was prevented from serving their country in any capacity was Asian Canadians. In late September 1940, the CWC quietly decided to omit Chinese and Japanese Canadians from being called out for compulsory training. The directive came in response to a letter from Duff Pattullo, the premier of British Columbia, who objected to the fact that Asians who had served in the First World War had been able to use that to gain the right to vote under the province's racially restricted system after 1918, and feared that they might use the same argument after the current conflict.[23] In spite of these policies, a few Chinese and Japanese Canadians did find their way into the Canadian army as conscripts, and some chose to volunteer once they were in uniform, just as did other men conscripted under the NRMA, as the war diary of at least one basic training centre confirms: in December 1941, local newspaper stories noted the presence of five Asian Canadian "R" recruits in Camrose, Alberta, two of whom had recently decided to "go active." They included Private Shogi Yamauchi, the sole Japanese Canadian in the group.[24] Other Canadians who faced difficulty being accepted for service in the military included Sikhs and other peoples from the Indian subcontinent. Army officials did not completely object to accepting Sikhs, but they refused to do so unless the numbers were large enough to justify forming separate units, where unique requirements of food and dress could more easily be accommodated. Due to the small size of the Sikh population at the time, even compulsory service would have applied to only a few dozen men, and thus the restriction was not likely to be overturned.[25]

In contrast, in some ways the NRMA actually worked to the benefit of Canadians of African descent. At a time when they still faced many types of discrimination, the NRMA was one measure that treated them just like any other citizens. War diaries note the presence of African Canadians in specific training centres, although in doing so they tend to repeat some of the stereotypes and assumptions of their age. Recruits came to the diarists' attention for their prowess as entertainers or boxers, or simply for performing duties as capably as other soldiers, something that apparently surprised the observers. Newmarket's centre appears to have had an entirely African Canadian training company of over one hundred men in May 1941, while Huntingdon played host to "a large number of British West Indians," presumably from the Montreal area.[26] When a story broke in late 1943 that local military officials had asked the civilian director of mobilization in Manitoba not to call out African Canadians for compulsory service, officers in both Winnipeg and Ottawa acted quickly to deny that there was any such policy. No trace of the request could be found, and the civilian director was censured for proceeding solely on the basis of an apparently verbal request from his military counterpart. The Department of National Defence specifically took the opportunity to state that "Negroes were being called regularly the same as any of the classes of persons designated by Proclamation for the purposes of the Mobilization Regulations."[27]

One further group who were affected by the NRMA, but who in this case objected to their treatment as citizens like any other, was Canada's Aboriginal peoples. Their resistance to compulsory service was based not on their desire to avoid being in the military, given that 3,500 to 4,000 Status Indians and an unknown number of others had served in the First World War, despite being unofficially excluded by many recruiters in the early part of the conflict, and that at least another 3,000 would do so again in the Second.[28] For some among a group that had been deliberately separated from the rest of Canadian society under successive Indian Acts, however, and many of whom had never formally accepted Canada's sovereignty over their lives and territories in the first place, being compelled to bear arms in the interests of that same state was unacceptable. The Indian Act prevented Native peoples from exercising many of the rights and privileges that most other Canadians took for granted, unless they renounced their status and accepted citizenship as full British subjects. In particular, they were treated legally as wards of the state. Yet when the government decided they should serve in uniform, they were seen as adults and required to perform one of the key duties the state expected of a citizen in Western society. When the Department of Justice was asked to rule on the applicability of the NRMA in January 1941, its legal experts declared that all Aboriginal Canadians were liable. They stuck to their decision in the face of numerous protests throughout the war, even though it proved to be much more difficult to enforce the regulations at the local level. The only concession was that when conscription was extended to overseas service in 1944, the CWC agreed to honour agreements that had been made in past treaties, and not force those specific groups to serve in Europe.[29]

The last four tables presented here provide information on the occupational backgrounds of conscripts during the Second World War. Table 7 lists NRMA recruits by the industries in which they had worked before they entered military service, and Table 8 by the type of work they had performed. Tables 9 and 10 list the top twenty-five occupations among both NRMA recruits and the larger Canadian population. Unfortunately, the large number of unclassified conscripts in Table 7 makes it difficult to come to firm conclusions about the industries from which NRMA recruits were drawn. Still, the proportion in most industries is relatively close to that for all Canadians. The proportion from agricultural backgrounds is noticeably smaller than for the population as a whole. As in the First World War, farming was viewed as a vital wartime occupation, and thus farmers were once again encouraged to increase production as much as possible after 1939. Male family members also felt that they needed to remain on the land because of the strong demands farms made on manpower. And as we will see in Chapter 7, as part of the post-1940 mobilization machinery, they could in fact be exempted from call-up. As Tables 8 and 9 indicate, however, farming was still in the 1940s by far the largest occupation among both NRMA recruits

Table 7

NRMA recruits by industry group

Industry group		NRMA[a] *N*	NRMA[a] %[c]	Canada[b] *N*	Canada[b] %[c]
Agriculture		38,318	24.2	1,062,928	31.6
Extractive industries	Forestry	3,953	2.5	93,313	2.8
	Fishing and trapping	1,958	1.2	50,533	1.5
	Mining	3,540	2.2	92,456	2.7
	Total	*9,451*	*6.0*	*236,302*	*7.0*
Manufacturing	Food/beverages/tobacco	4,079	2.6	87,979	2.6
	Leather and rubber products	1,556	1.0	32,392	1.0
	Textiles/clothing	2,086	1.3	76,294	2.3
	Wood/paper/publishing	4,531	2.9	160,327	4.8
	Metal/machinery/ transport	15,265	9.7	309,763	9.2
	Chemical/petroleum/ minerals	833	0.5	51,670	1.5
	Other	6,834	4.3	16,672	0.5
	Total	*35,184*	*22.3*	*735,097*	*21.9*
Transportation	Railways	5,327	3.4	123,514	3.7
	Other	13,248	8.4	123,321	3.7
	Total	*18,575*	*11.8*	*246,835*	*7.3*
Construction industry		11,663	7.4	218,732	6.5
Retail and wholesale trade		6,928	4.4	384,046	11.4
Finance/insurance/real estate		731	0.5	61,311	1.8
Electrical and gas utilities		107	0.1	21,134	0.6
Service industries	Education	1,824	1.2	35,872	1.1
	Health and welfare	284	0.2	27,998	0.8
	Food and lodging	2,023	1.3	58,312	1.7
	Personal and recreational	3,999	2.5	59,955	1.8
	Government	896	0.6	111,634	3.3
	Other	2,085	1.3	61,886	1.8
	Total	*11,111*	*7.0*	*355,657*	*10.6*
Not stated/insufficient data		25,988	16.4[d]	41,069	1.2
Grand totals		*158,056*	*100.0*	*3,363,111*	*100.0*

Notes:

a NRMA recruits classified according to guidelines in Canada, Dominion Bureau of Statistics, *Classification of Industries and Services*, Seventh Census, 1931 (Ottawa: King's Printer, 1931), and *Classification of Industries*, Eighth Census, 1941 (Ottawa: King's Printer, 1941).

b Numbers of "gainfully occupied" males, from Leacy, ed., *Historical Statistics of Canada*, 2nd ed., series D8–85.

c Some percentages are not exact, due to rounding of decimals.

d Includes 19,511 unspecified recruits listed simply as "Labourers" or "Workers," and 5,110 as clerks or other general office workers.

Table 8

NRMA recruits by occupation

Occupational category	NRMA[a]	%	Canada[b]	%
Owners and managers	2,436	1.5	212,460	6.3
Professional occupations	3,570	2.3	150,379	4.5
Clerical and sales workers	14,705	9.3	308,342	9.2
Operatives	76,047	48.1	1,375,879	40.9
Farmers and farm workers	38,734	24.5	1,061,896	31.6
Labourers	21,950	13.9	254,155	7.6
Not stated/insufficient data	614	0.4	–	–
Grand totals	*158,056*	*100.0*	*3,363,111*	*100.0*[c]

Notes:

a NRMA recruits classified according to guidelines in Canada, Dominion Bureau of Statistics, *Classification of Occupations*, Eighth Census, 1941 (Ottawa: King's Printer, 1941).

b Includes only "gainfully occupied" males. Leacy, ed., *Historical Statistics of Canada*, 2nd ed., series D86–106.

c This column does not total exactly 100 percent, due to rounding of decimals.

and the population as a whole, despite the steadily increasing urbanization of the country.

Another notable feature of the economic backgrounds of NRMA recruits is the smaller proportion who came from professional, higher-paid, or self-employed occupations, or from "white-collar" positions such as retail and wholesale trade, finance, insurance, and real estate. In contrast, the number of conscripts listed as "Operatives" (factory workers) or "Labourers" in Table 8 is clearly greater than for the population at large. This variation in the types of work performed suggests a degree of bias in the operation of the NRMA, with military service falling more heavily on groups that ranked lower on the socio-economic ladder. This conclusion is not particularly surprising. Many men in occupations classed as "skilled" or "essential" were considered to be making just as important contributions to the war effort in their current trades and thus were not forced to report for compulsory military training. As we have seen, a large majority of conscripts were young, single men, who likely had not been in the workforce long enough to obtain more skilled or higher-paying jobs. People with lower incomes also may have had less power to challenge the decrees of the large civilian bureaucracy that was created to call out men for compulsory training during the war. Conversely, people with more educational opportunities may have found it easier to argue the case for their utility to the bureaucrats. Lastly, the statistics may be affected by the lingering effects of the Great Depression. As many historians have suggested, unemployed men were

Table 9

Top 25 occupations of NRMA recruits

Rank	As listed by NRMA[a]	*N*	%[b]	By census category[c]	*N*	%[b]
1	Farmers	31,986	20.2	Farmers and stock raisers	32,592	20.6
2	Labourers	19,482	12.3	Non-farm labourers	21,950	13.9
3	Truck Drivers	8,300	5.3	Truck drivers	8,300	5.3
4	Clerks	4,117	2.6	Office clerks	6,467	4.1
5	Machinists	4,054	2.6	Farm labour (all)	5,676	3.6
6	Mechanics	3,548	2.2	Mechanics and repairmen	5,234	3.3
7	Farm Labourers	3,178	2.0	Machinists (all)	4,133	2.6
8	Carpenters	2,532	1.6	Store salespersons	3,918	2.5
9	Other Miners	2,468	1.6	Lumbermen (all)	3,818	2.4
10	Apple Packers	2,157	1.4	Miners and millmen	3,245	2.1
11	Store Clerks	2,077	1.3	Carpenters (all)	2,659	1.7
12	Machine Operators	1,947	1.2	Machine operators	2,100	1.3
13	Fishermen	1,774	1.1	Welders (all)	2,088	1.3
14	Painters	1,669	1.1	Painters/glaziers	1,892	1.2
15	Butchers	1,629	1.0	Clothing/textiles	1,792	1.1
16	Electricians	1,528	1.0	Fishermen	1,774	1.1
17	Salesmen	1,436	0.9	Electricians (all)	1,673	1.1
18	Welders	1,388	0.9	Retail owners/managers	1,630	1.0
19	Shippers	1,343	0.8	Butchers	1,629	1.0
20	Students	1,185	0.7	Shipping clerks	1,610	1.0
21	Other Iron & [*sic*] Steel Workers	1,101	0.7	Woodworkers and turners	1,334	0.8
22	Woodsmen	1,071	0.7	Students (all)	1,197	0.8
23	Plumbers	909	0.6	Iron/steel workers	1,101	0.7
24	Loggers	886	0.6	Sheet metal workers and tinsmiths	988	0.6
25	Lumberman	877	0.6	Plumbers	909	0.6
Totals		*102,333*	*64.7*		*119,709*	*75.8*

Notes:

a This column ranks occupations by the individual titles under which they were listed in the original NRMA records.

b Percentage of all NRMA recruits enrolled during the war (158,056).

c Information in this column is arranged by grouping NRMA records according to definitions in *Classification of Occupations*, Eighth Census, 1941.

among the volunteers who flocked to join the overseas army in 1939, and in the early years of the NRMA's operation the country was still moving towards full employment. Thus, some men may even have welcomed being made part of the more compulsory NRMA, in an occupation that paid them for their service while guaranteeing that they would not be forced to go overseas. In any case,

Table 10

Top 25 male occupations in Canada, 1941

Rank	Occupational category	*N*	% of workforce[a]
1	Farmers and stockraisers	630,709	18.8
2	Farm labourers	431,102	12.8
3	Labourers (not farm, forest, fishing, or mining)	251,889	7.5
4	Office clerks	110,043	3.3
5	Owners, managers, dealers – retail	100,756	3.0
6	Carpenters	90,470	2.7
7	Truck drivers	81,304	2.4
8	Salespersons in stores	81,270	2.4
9	Lumbermen	74,000	2.2
10	Mechanics and repairmen	67,246	2.0
11	Miners and millmen	51,503	1.5
12	Operatives – metal products manufacturing	49,052	1.5
13	Machinists – metal	43,077	1.3
14	Painters, decorators, glaziers	39,058	1.2
15	Fishermen	33,273	1.0
16	Accountants and auditors	31,384	0.9
17	Owners and managers – manufacturing	30,633	0.9
18	Commercial travellers	29,882	0.9
19	Stationary enginemen	29,792	0.9
20	Operatives – clothing and textiles	25,640	0.8
21	Sectionmen and trackmen	24,422	0.7
22	Shipping clerks	23,044	0.7
23	Electricians and wiremen	22,121	0.7
24	Teachers – school	21,988	0.7
25	Guards and caretakers	20,815	0.6
Totals		*2,394,473*	*71.2*

Note:
a Percentage of "gainfully occupied males" (total: 3,363,111).
Source: Eighth Census of Canada, 1941, table 61, 772–73.

throughout the tables the same occupations dominate the lists for both the NRMA and the larger male population, as shown particularly by comparing Tables 9 and 10. In both cases, "Labourers" made up the second-largest group of men, behind those involved in farming, while other positions recur in both lists.

Taken together, the statistics presented here allow us to make several broad conclusions about the NRMA men as a group. Like Canadians in general, most conscripts had been born in Canada or other parts of the British Commonwealth and had lived in all parts of the country before being called up for military training. Most were young, and they came from almost every type of occupation, although they were most likely to have been farmers or other skilled or unskilled labourers in civilian life. There was a somewhat higher chance that they were French-speaking, or members of ethnic minorities, but not excessively so. It should be remembered that in using statistics to portray the NRMA, it is probably as difficult to define the "typical" conscript as it would have been to define the typical "Canadian" in the 1940s. As in most other ways, in this respect NRMA recruits largely reflected the diversity of the broader society from which they came.

6 Canada's Zombies, Part 2: Life in Uniform

Knowing who the "zombies" were, as a group, can only provide a partial understanding of Canada's conscripts during the Second World War. To fully comprehend their experiences, it is also necessary to consider how they spent their many months and years in uniform. Unfortunately, few conscripts have recorded their memories of wartime service for posterity. But a number of sources allow us to reconstruct their experiences in at least a general way. By law, every training centre and operational unit was required to preserve several aspects of their activities in their war diary, and we can use that information to re-create the experiences not just of NRMA recruits but of all soldiers who served in Canada during the war.[1] The responses of individuals and whole communities to compulsory military service can be traced through these records, as well as through other papers preserved by the Department of National Defence and those of the individual political figures involved in running the program. Using these sources, we can learn a great deal about what the typical conscript was likely to have done and seen during his years of service in Canada.

Both before and after the changes of March and April 1941, the lives of all men who found themselves in uniform were dominated by the military in a manner that most Canadians had never experienced in peacetime. Conscripts in particular probably found this unsettling, at the very least, since they had not been given any choice about enlisting. Almost all aspects of their lives were regulated, from the time they woke in the morning until they went to sleep at night. Men were told how to dress and how to behave. They were taught to accept the distinctive hierarchy of authority and discipline that accompanied army life. Even diets were regulated: meals were served at prescribed times, and recruits had to choose from a menu that was sometimes monotonous, if at least nutritious.[2]

In order to be accepted into the army, a soldier already had to be in excellent health – especially for the infantry, where men were required to meet the highest standards simply so that they could survive the many physical and mental hazards of the battlefield.[3] All recruits received free medical and dental care from the time they enlisted, and for many Canadians this was probably the first time they had ever enjoyed such full and routine access to health care. The large numbers of men brought together by the army also helps reveal the state of health of the Canadian population more broadly in the 1940s. Because of the large numbers of men congregating in training centres and other military camps, there were a number of outbreaks of diseases such as meningitis, scarlet fever, measles, and influenza. These sometimes led to several barracks or entire camps being placed in quarantine, and even a few deaths among trainees.[4] As these cases remind us, all of these illnesses were much more serious and prevalent in the 1940s than today.

From his first day of military service, every soldier spent the bulk of his time in training. For the NRMA men, as we have seen, there had been at least some focus on this in the first thirty-day centres. But once they were merged with the volunteer system in 1941, the work took on an even more serious tone for both "A" and "R" recruits. In basic training, the primary goal remained simply to prepare men for service generally. This included physical training and drill, familiarization with key weapons, and core tactics. In advanced training, the work became more hands-on. For example, recruits in infantry centres began to learn how to operate in increasingly larger units at the section, platoon, and company level, how to cooperate together on the battlefield using tactics such as fire and movement (one group using its weapons to suppress the activity of enemy troops, while another manoeuvred to outflank their position), and other aspects of fieldcraft to allow them to survive in the front lines.[5]

Probably because these activities were so much a part of the mens' everyday routine, however, beyond the general information noted above, training did not usually stand out for further comment by most of the war diarists who kept each centre's records. As E.L.M. Burns has noted, individuals often required more than the minimum four months' training, and impressionistic evidence from lists of names in the war diaries of men constantly entering and exiting the camps tends to confirm that not every person moved through his training in precisely that time. It was often interrupted by illness, family or compassionate issues, or men needing to repeat tests until they got things right. Even after men got past that point, volunteers proceeding overseas regularly needed to receive additional refresher training.[6] The issue of an apparent lack of proper preparation among infantry reinforcements overseas generated a great deal of complaint from some unit commanders in the second half of 1944. Denis Whitaker, the commanding officer of the Royal Hamilton Light Infantry in northwest Europe, would later charge not only that new arrivals had very little familiarity with many weapons, but that their general discipline was poor, and they lacked physical "toughness."[7] More recently, Andrew Brown has used a sample of eighty-nine men taken from personnel records of reinforcements who joined the 48th Highlanders, a unit in Italy whose skills were criticized openly in 1944, and found that they had already spent an average of two years in the army before arriving in the front lines. After completing their basic and advanced training, they had taken refresher training not only in England but again in most cases when they reached the Mediterranean. And even then, some deficiencies were still noted. Caroline D'Amours has carried out the same sort of study for the French-speaking *Régiment de la Chaudière* in northwest Europe and found broadly similar results. These and other Canadian military historians are beginning to explore the whole question more fully. Interestingly, twenty-two of the eighty-nine men in Brown's sample (24.7 percent), and fifty-eight of the 138 (42.0 percent) in D'Amours's, either had been conscripts at some point and converted to general service, or had volunteered from the general public when it became clear that they were about to be conscripted – a topic that will be discussed further in Chapter 7.[8] And for at least one junior officer on the basic training staff in Cornwall, William L. Beattie, even physical toughening as noted by Whitaker was far from overlooked. Beattie, in his forties and a First World War veteran, joined the local Stormont, Dundas and Glengarry Highlanders at the start of the Second World War, and then No. 31 Canadian Army (Basic) Training Centre, where he rose to be second-in-command and occasionally acting commander of one of its four training companies. In the words of Beattie's son, the training was taken very seriously. In particular, as the younger Beattie remembered it, the recruits were mostly "just kids," and his father saw his whole job as an instructor as "to get them toughened up" (although his father was not beyond taking pity on the odd young man who had an especially tough time, occasionally helping a trainee carry a rifle on route marches).[9]

Training and other compulsory activities were not the only elements in the lives of newly enlisted soldiers, either before or after the voluntary and compulsory systems were merged in 1941. Recruits were encouraged to participate in a variety of athletic events as part of their physical conditioning. Organized events often included track-and-field days or broader programs of "tabloid sports," a term that took in less formal activities such as relay races, three-legged races, wheelbarrow races, tug-of-war contests, and obstacle courses.[10] Training staffs and recruits also arranged more voluntary activities, and almost every imaginable sport could be found in one or more camps. Drill halls doubled as gymnasiums for basketball, volleyball, boxing, wrestling, tennis, badminton, weightlifting, and gymnastics.[11] Outdoor pursuits ranged from baseball, soccer, rugby, and "football" (apparently referring to the North American adaptation of rugby), to rowing, curling, and skiing.[12] Training centres created their own leagues, with teams organized by companies or platoons, or competed in nearby city or military leagues. Others participated in exhibitions against local high schools, universities, or other competitors.[13] In Nanaimo, British Columbia,

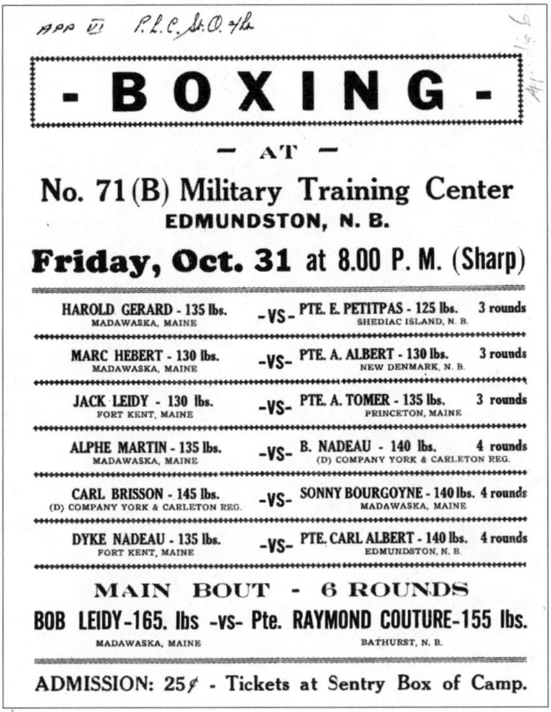

Figure 14 Poster announcing boxing match in No. 71 Canadian Army (Basic) Training Centre, Edmundston, New Brunswick, October 1941 *Source:* LAC, e-011157756.

men of 13th Canadian Infantry Brigade played an exhibition basketball game in January 1942 against the Harlem Globetrotters, before an audience of 1,200 of their fellow soldiers.[14] Many camps organized other competitions, especially boxing, which attracted much interest among both their own personnel and citizens of local communities.[15] In Lac-Mégantic, Quebec, for example, Gérard "K.O." Boisvert, a local amateur boxing champion, was called out as an "R" recruit and proceeded to win a further bout while carrying out his training.[16]

The sport that predominated in every training centre and army unit across the country was Canada's national winter pastime, hockey. Almost every centre built a skating rink, and military units formed teams that played at all competitive levels. By 1942, the workings of the compulsory military training system were beginning to have a very specific benefit for many centres and other operational units across the country, as from one training class to the next they might suddenly find themselves with star players from local civilian hockey teams in uniform as "R" recruits.[17] Players raided in this manner included semi-professionals from junior and senior farm teams connected to professional clubs.[18] Teams from Peterborough and Newmarket played in contests within the Ontario Hockey Association in 1942, and the former won the Senior B

Figure 15 Flyer announcing upcoming hockey game involving a team from No. 110 Canadian Militia Training Centre, Vernon, British Columbia, December 1940. *Source:* LAC, e-011157758.

Championship.[19] Cornwall's team became such a powerhouse that it beat the Montreal Canadiens in an exhibition game in October 1942. And in the spring of 1943 an army team from Victoria played for the Allan Cup, the symbol of senior hockey supremacy in Canada. They lost a close series to another army team from Ottawa, whose entire roster was made up of former National Hockey League players who were now serving in the armed forces.[20] In fact, the issue of professionals playing for the military became so problematic that in January 1944 the RCAF and the army both passed regulations barring their teams from participating in leagues that competed for either the Allan Cup or the Memorial Cup (for junior players).[21] Several training centres also arranged for recruits to attend local professional hockey games as spectators, especially in the early days of the thirty-day program in 1940.[22] In January 1941, conscripts in Long Branch, Ontario, were even marched several miles into Toronto to see a Maple Leafs game. The event took a tragic turn, however, when an automobile driven by one of the men from the camp struck the rest of the group as they marched home in the dark, resulting in one death and a number of other injuries.[23]

Aside from organized sports, soldiers in training centres and operational units had many other ways to fill their leisure time. What seemed an almost

Figure 16 Flyer for a concert organized by the Knights of Columbus for trainees in Joliette, Quebec, April 1941. *Source:* LAC, e-011157755.

endless round of local, regional, and even national shows and performers visited the camps.[24] Most concerts were presented by local voluntary organizations of various types, continuing the trend of strong support for the work of the training centres that countless cities and towns had established in the early days of the thirty-day program. In Woodstock, recruits were treated to plays provided by groups such as the "Dramatic Society of the Dundas Street United Church."[25] In Sorel, the "Calixa Lavallée Harmony," a group that apparently perpetuated the memory of the composer of "O Canada," did its part for the war effort, along with the town's local Women's Volunteer Reserve Corps, which presented a "Khaki Review" show for the men.[26]

Even more popular were the many dances that were held in every training centre and in most other army units across the country throughout the war. They were popular particularly because they were among the few occasions when women were permitted to enter military camps (aside from members of the CWAC, who at least officially were not permitted to fraternize with male soldiers). Civilian women were sometimes specifically recruited for dances by organizers and bused in to attend.[27] Again, community organizations played a vital role in arranging these functions, along with civilian recreation directors

Figure 17 Poster for winter carnival in Vernon, British Columbia, February 1942. *Source:* LAC, e-011157759.

in each camp, unit chaplains, and even the recruits themselves, who often formed orchestras to provide the music.[28] Many camps also arranged talent shows, "quiz shows," and other contests that tested the skills and abilities of the recruits. In the 1940s, radio was still in its infancy in many parts of Canada, and local stations were often happy to fill their programming schedules by broadcasting such activities, at the same time providing a wartime service to the community.[29] French-speaking recruits in North Bay created a weekly half-hour broadcast for the many francophone citizens of that region.[30] In Quebec, civilian workers from two stations toured various training centres at separate times in late 1940 and mid-1941, presenting a series of province-wide broadcasts.[31] Specific companies and platoons held their own informal social functions, such as "smokers," where men could gather for quieter conversation and camaraderie, bingo parties, and a variety of other activities.[32] Officers and NCOs had their own messes to which they could retreat for similar functions, as well as formal mess dinners held to mark significant dates on the military calendar, or for other reasons.[33]

Recruits also participated in a wide variety of events outside their gates. Most centres had some sort of pass system, and even from the earliest days in 1940 everyone received at least one weekend's leave to visit family and friends. Groups in nearby towns and cities organized civilian recreation centres where men could spend their leisure time.[34] In Orillia, Ontario, for example, the local Anglican church's "Maple Leaf Club" offered general recreational activities, and men could even bring in uniforms for help with sewing repairs, or join some of the more than two hundred local women who volunteered to act as hostesses at regular "dance nights" on Tuesdays and Thursdays.[35] Local churches and other community organizations invited smaller groups of staff and trainees to attend special dinners, teas, and other services, especially in more remote regions of the country where larger events were less frequent. Many were specifically tailored for men of the same ethnicity or religious faith, such as a dinner given for Ukrainian Canadian recruits in Fort William's local Ukrainian Hall.[36] At Christmas time, civilians opened their homes to personnel who were unable to visit their own families for the holidays, and many training centres held special holiday dinners and other ceremonies.[37] Recruits and staff members sometimes returned the favour, holding their own concerts and other demonstrations for the civilians of nearby towns and cities.[38]

For soldiers looking for other ways to spend their leisure time, a broad range of alternatives existed, especially in the early compulsory training centres. Recreation huts provided reading rooms, musical instruments, board games, cards, and a variety of other ways for men to keep occupied.[39] From the beginning of the compulsory military training program in October 1940, every centre was provided with a movie projector, along with a number of films, which were shown at least a few times in each training period, and sometimes as often as twice a week.[40] In Huntingdon, Quebec, a local theatre and an amusement company joined forces to donate a more substantial projection and sound system to the camp, along with a full-sized movie screen.[41] To see more current films, recruits could attend civilian theatres in their off-duty hours, some of which arranged for the entire personnel to attend free of charge at the start of each training period, or offered discounted rates at other times.[42] Several Quebec training centres provided a number of more productive opportunities for recruits to pass their time, including English or French classes, vocational training, and courses in mathematics, bookkeeping, typing, and shorthand.[43] A few camps even had their own amateur newspapers, which relied on recruits to provide material and usually contained a combination of brief reports on internal activities, schedules for upcoming events, and jokes of varying quality.[44]

Another area where conscripts were looked after, perhaps more than some of them might have wished, was religious services. Church parades were held for all Protestant and Roman Catholic recruits every Sunday, in drill halls, on parade squares, and in local churches across the country. Where numbers warranted, arrangements were made for separate services for Jewish Canadian recruits, although they were usually held on Sundays as part of the times already scheduled for such activities, rather than on Saturdays. The long-term nature of the compulsory training program in the Second World War actually seems to have brought about a change in the way the Canadian army dealt with Jewish Canadians. Most training camps and other units provided leaves for Jewish recruits whenever possible to honour specific holy days.[45] On at least two occasions, religious services in Huntingdon, Quebec, were led by Rabbi Gershon Levi, the chief Jewish chaplain for the Canadian army (and its only full-time Jewish chaplain, at that point in the war), who had been appointed to his post in March 1941. Howard Ripstein, who was a corporal on the training staff of the camp, later recalled Levi's visits, but did not think of them or of being Jewish as other than a minor aspect of his life in uniform. In one case, when he was told to find enough men to provide a "good crowd" for Levi, he simply walked into his barracks, pointed to his men, and said "You're Jewish."[46] At least one distinct service was also held specifically for Greek Orthodox personnel in Portage la Prairie, Manitoba.[47]

Every training centre and operational unit had at least one chaplain assigned to look after the religious needs of its personnel, although only larger ones with mixed groups of Protestants and Roman Catholics were permitted to retain chaplains of both faiths on a permanent basis. As a rule, the army provided one Protestant chaplain for every 1,000 troops within a particular military district, and one Catholic chaplain for every 500 men.[48] Mostly, there seems to have been no discrimination against the minority group, which was usually permitted to hold its own separate services within the camp or to attend ones in the outside communities where the training centres were located. Chaplains were also sometimes pressed into duty to lead services for men of other faiths. In one case, according to Gerald Tulchinsky, a Protestant chaplain had to be prevailed upon by a Jewish colleague in Ottawa to lead Rosh Hashanah and Yom Kippur services for Jewish recruits in remote Prince George, British Columbia. This man, Honorary Captain E.E. Brandt, apparently did so without incident, despite his own worries about his lack of knowledge of the faith.[49] Many camps established distinct chapels that served as interdenominational centres for worship, as well as focal points from which chaplains could carry out their many other roles in the Canadian army. These included providing personal and psychological counselling to recruits and helping arrange broader social activities. This was true especially in Quebec. Training centres in that province marked Catholic holidays with special ceremonies, and one chaplain from the basic training camp in Montmagny even undertook a tour of advanced training centres in

Ontario in the summer of 1941, to visit members of his flock who had gone on to complete their training there and to help ensure their adjustment to their new surroundings.[50]

Quite apart from the many organized social functions that were provided for NRMA recruits, a variety of less acceptable activities took place, over which commanding officers and community leaders could not exert nearly as much influence. One of the most common of these was drinking. All canteens in the early thirty-day training centres seem to have been "dry." Yet as one commanding officer reported in November 1940: "The majority of the recruits trained in our first course drank liquor in one form or another, frequenting the beer parlours in Vernon and adjacent towns & villages. At times they became a trifle noisy & boisterous, arriving back in camp somewhat 'under the weather.'" He went on to note that liquor bottles had been found in barracks rooms inside the training centre. His recommended solution was that a formal "wet" canteen be established where men could drink under more controlled conditions.[51] Trainees in Huntingdon, Quebec, were prohibited from entering a local restaurant after several men went absent without leave and were found drunk in a back room; as their commanding officer reported: "Further complaints were also received of girls being accosted outside the store."[52] In North Bay, Ontario, a "disturbance" that spilled into the streets and led to an entire evening of fighting and rowdiness was blamed on alcohol. In Edmundston, New Brunswick, similar problems provoked Reverend James R. Mutchmor, the joint secretary of the Board of Evangelism and Social Service of the United Church of Canada, to write to the local minister in protest. As E.W. Aitken wrote in reply: "This town is probably the wettest in the Province and the police tell me that to bring one to trial is like bucking up against the rock of Gibraltar." Still, he added, the situation was not due to the presence of the local training centre, but rather to the lack of local licensed establishments and controls on drinking in general.[53]

In actuality, drinking was one area where the Canadian army had a great deal of experience in balancing the desires of soldiers with the needs of military service. As Tim Cook has shown, during the First World War military authorities came to recognize the beneficial effects of alcohol for morale, for dealing with stress, and for other purposes, provided that it was used sparingly and under tightly regulated conditions.[54] Recognizing the advantages of bringing alcohol use under greater supervision, by the fall of 1941 officials had agreed to permit wet canteens in basic training centres across the country.[55] Yet alcohol remained a factor in disturbances, such as a brawl among men from the Highland Light Infantry that broke out on the streets of Quebec City in February 1941. In

May 1943, men of the Dufferin and Haldimand Rifles and the *Voltigeurs de Québec* became involved in a scuffle in Sussex Camp, Nova Scotia, that led to gunshots being fired and a few men wounded.[56]

Gambling was another activity that clearly existed in many training centres and operational units across the country, although as an illegal one it left very few traces in the records of these institutions. But the fact that most camps felt the need to prohibit such activities explicitly in the standing orders they issued to their men seems to suggest at least a fear of its presence. One of the few available accounts of life in training centres in Canada during the Second World War, Earle Birney's novel *Turvey*, alludes more than once to various games of chance among the men. Birney also refers several times to the yearning for female companionship that dominated the thoughts of many soldiers whenever they were permitted to leave camp, since they had so few opportunities to meet members of the opposite sex while on duty.[57] Given the surroundings, it would not be surprising if some recruits formed same-sex relationships during their time in the army as well. Unfortunately, because of the many social and legal proscriptions against publicly revealing such relationships in the 1940s, the war diaries of the centres make few to no specific comments.[58]

Along with drinking, gambling, and sex, a few recruits engaged in petty thievery and other, more serious criminal activities.[59] In Red Deer, Alberta, three men were caught stealing leftover food from the camp kitchen, including "a ten-pound pail of dripping [fat]," which apparently had considerable value as a source of glycerine from which to make explosives.[60] In Huntingdon, Quebec, an "R" recruit was arrested for stealing a car and using it to charge his colleagues for rides to nearby Montreal. Even jail did not enable him to escape compulsory service: he was convicted and transferred to a civilian facility to serve out his sentence, after which he was to be returned to complete his military training.[61] Another "R" recruit in the same camp was suspected of receiving $1,200 in money stolen from a bank in Outremont.[62] And an acting corporal on the staff of Vernon's early thirty-day training centre was arrested "on charges of indecency with recruits," although details about the event are sparse. In the end, he was not prosecuted due to lack of evidence.[63]

In a further form of illegality (as far as the army was concerned), both "A" and "R" recruits often failed to report back from leave at the appointed time. Such offences were usually minor, and they are part of any army. In the summer of 1941, the war diarist in Vernon noted that although at one point over seventy men were either absent without leave or in detention for the same offence, they had stayed away longer than permitted deliberately to visit with their families since they were about to move to another place for advanced training. All accepted punishment "with a smile."[64] But in Peterborough, Ontario, one "R" recruit chose not to return for more serious reasons. According to the camp's war diary, after going home on a weekend pass he "sent his uniform back with express prepaid. A letter in the mail from this man stated he was returning his uniform as he did not like the army."[65] Another NRMA recruit who was already being detained for other offences broke out of a cell and attempted to escape from his training centre.[66] Evidence from a few sources and the impressions given by various war diaries suggest that problems such as absences without leave and desertion were almost as numerous among volunteers as they were among conscripts. According to one of the few available sets of comparable statistics, the number of volunteers who deserted across the country between April 1942 and March 1943 was estimated to be 5,210, while the number of NRMA men was 3,720 – 9.5 percent of the total number of NRMA men then serving in Canada compared to 6.5 percent for the volunteers.[67] As was noted in Chapter 2, in the view of the Chicoutimi training centre's commanding officer the behaviour of active army recruits actually created more difficulty than that of "R" men.[68] In addition, there is no reason to suspect that any form of discrimination was practised against recruits of either type who were disciplined for such offences. In fact, commanders were explicitly reminded by army officials that all deserters were to be dealt with in the same way.[69] Other war diaries commented on the good behaviour shown by both groups, reminding us that during the war, hundreds of thousands of soldiers of both types passed through the training centres without incident.[70] The diarist in Sorel, Quebec, even noted the story of one trainee who found a purse lost by the wife of the town's mayor and took it upon himself to return it to her.[71]

Once "R" recruits had completed their work in the training centres, they were posted to operational units across the country, once more alongside volunteers. Most soldiers in home defence units found themselves assigned to isolated defence posts in British Columbia, eastern Quebec, and the Maritimes, and later Newfoundland and the Caribbean. As a result, fewer opportunities existed to hold concerts, dances, and other social activities, although citizens of nearby towns and cities did try to provide as many activities as possible for the men. Units in remote areas of British Columbia complained about the small number of movies available for viewing and how long it took to receive recently released features. As the war diarist for part of the 8th Division's headquarters in Prince George noted: "The quality of movies being shown to the troops is very poor and they are especially dissatisfied when they read of the American forces, even in more remote areas, getting the latest releases even in advance of the big-city houses."[72] For all soldiers, training remained the primary purpose of their existence, and they underwent a near-continuous round at the individual and unit levels, as well as larger exercises. For most conscripts as well as volunteer soldiers, boredom was probably their worst enemy.

The isolation experienced in these defence posts was that much worse for NRMA men whose first language was not English. Francophone recruits were numerous enough to form their own units and usually served together under commanders of similar backgrounds. By April 1942, the authorities in Ottawa listed eight infantry battalions, several independent companies of infantry protecting vital points, seven artillery and anti-aircraft batteries, and further engineer, field ambulance, and hospital units, all of which were French-speaking but many of which were required to serve in areas where there was very little knowledge of their language in the surrounding communities.[73] In one of the more extreme cases, as described by Donna Spalding, who grew up in Sydney, Nova Scotia (where soldiers were assigned to defend the steelworks), her family gradually formed a friendship with one man who was billeted in their home and whom she knew only by his nickname "Frenchy." At one point he broke down and shared his feelings with them, noting that he was "away from his family and his culture, and was living in a town that hated people like him." In the small community,

> He could not hide the fact that he was a so-called zombie, and he had no choice but to take the taunts thrown at him. When Frenchy and his co-workers went to local dances the so-called "nice girls" shunned them ... It was difficult to be despised and scorned everywhere he went. He felt that he was not welcome in Cape Breton, and this made him feel sad and very lonely.[74]

The public attitudes towards zombies alluded to above were not aimed solely at French Canadians during the war. And on the other hand, the presence of large numbers of well-trained French-speaking troops in Canada could have a positive side, such as in the aftermath of a sit-down strike at the Aluminum Company of Canada plant in Arvida, Quebec, in July 1941. Anger at the anglophone-dominated company and its president, R.E. Powell, at the English-speaking troops that the company eventually pressured the federal government to send to force an end to the shutdown, and at the Department of Labour's inability to provide a conciliator who spoke French to deal with the situation, was greatly eased when replacement French-speaking troops were brought in from Valcartier, for this showed that the army was not just another solidly anglophone institution lined up against the French-speaking workers.[75] When French Canadian troops served outside Quebec, Canadians on both sides of the language divide were also exposed to each other's cultures in ways that many had not experienced before. As one local newspaper noted, for example, while men from the *Régiment de Hull* serving in Nanaimo were "as far away from home as if they had crossed the Atlantic," they were becoming bilingual, at least partly "because of their friendly relations with the townspeople of Nanaimo who have been 'tres sympathetique.'"[76] *La Presse* later reported a similar story about the *Fusiliers de Sherbrooke*.[77] And Paul Brisson, a bilingual francophone who ended up in an artillery unit, spent what sounds like a more interesting time in uniform in Canada, first in an anti-aircraft battery as part of the general defences the army provided for the Alcan plant in Arvida, and then camped on the Plains of Abraham to help provide air defence for the first Quebec Conference between Winston Churchill and Franklin Roosevelt in August 1943. Brisson frankly admitted that he joined the artillery because after being called up at the age of twenty-nine in 1942, he had no particular problem with serving. Indeed, he was working in a munitions factory, where his employer offered to request an exemption on his behalf. But he refused it because, to paraphrase his account, he liked to travel and feared getting tied down too long in one place. He also decided that if he was going to join the army then he would make sure he was one of the large numbers of men who did not see the front line but only provided support to the units there. During the second political crisis over conscription in 1944, he was remustered into infantry and chose to volunteer before being forced overseas as a conscript. He found himself assigned as an instructor for other follow-on reinforcements in England, thanks to having taken a three-month course at the Long Branch small arms training centre near Toronto in 1943–44.[78]

In fact, on both military and political levels, throughout the war efforts were made to improve on Canada's performance towards its French-speaking citizens compared to the First World War. As the home defence organization was built up in 1941–42, the idea of forming a French-speaking brigade was revived, and the 15th and 21st Brigades were so designated (the 15th as part of the 7th Division, under the command of the same P.E. Leclerc who had commanded the 5th Brigade during the army's earlier attempt to make it French-speaking overseas). But these units received much less public attention than an overseas brigade might have, and within a year they were being scaled back in order to try to comb out volunteers of both languages for Europe. J.V. Allard, J.P.E. Bernatchez, and J.G. Gauvreau also rose to command brigades overseas. C.G. Power as Minister of National Defence for Air pressed for the creation of No. 425, "Alouette" Squadron, which went on to serve as part of the RCAF's contribution to Bomber Command. And at the Cabinet level, Ernest Lapointe promoted greater appointment of francophones in all three military services as well as in the government bureaucracy.[79]

Thus, there were some positive developments during the war. And once again the NRMA was the ultimate reason for many of these. Demands increased for French Canadian officers, and not just to serve in overseas units, since they were also needed to man large numbers of training centres and operational formations on Canadian soil. And while many of these units were usually unable to function in their first language when dealing with higher headquarters, at lower levels they did carry out training among their men in French. The need to deal with large numbers of French-speaking soldiers resulted in opportunities much greater than ever before for French Canadians to exist in a military organization where their language could at least have a chance to take root.

Furthermore, for senior officers in either language in the Canadian army, the war offered enhanced opportunities to practise their craft, and again not only overseas. By 1943, Canada's home defence forces had grown so large that several formations were successively rotated out of their defensive positions on the west coast so that they could participate in brigade-level exercises in Wainwright, Alberta, to learn how to work together better should they be called upon to repel an actual enemy attack.[80] These types of exercises had been non-existent in the interwar years, when Canada's Permanent Force had barely amounted to a single brigade's worth of troops, spread out across the country. Even in the First World War, few units of that size had been gathered together in Canada. The scale of these exercises remind us again of just how significantly the Canadian army was mobilized generally during the Second World War, as well.

By the end of the Second World War, every soldier who had served in Canada had been exposed to a variety of encounters and experiences. And despite their separate status as part of the home defence organization, for the "zombies" in particular life still went on in the training centres and operational units. But there was one way in which they differed unequivocally from their active service counterparts, and it would come to have a huge impact on their wartime experiences, as well as on the army itself. Until November 1944, conscripts could not be required to serve outside the Western Hemisphere, and the result was a gulf between NRMA men and volunteers that could never be bridged entirely. In addition, by March 1941 the Canadian army had been reorganized, with "A" and "R" recruits deliberately placed side by side in the new training centres, in the hope that as many of the latter as possible would volunteer. From the beginning the "R" recruits were clearly distinguished through variations in their uniforms and cap badges. Over the first few months of the new four-month training program in early 1941, some camps found their own ways to differentiate: only "A" recruits were permitted to wear the badges of the units and corps to which they were to be posted for later service, while "R" men were restricted to generic ones.[81] In late 1941, NDHQ introduced a more formal policy for all units, that prohibited NRMA recruits from wearing the "Canada" badges that were intended to help identify Canadian soldiers while they were serving with other forces overseas. A year later, after service for conscripts was extended beyond the precise borders of Canada and they also became entitled to wear those badges, the "General Service" badge was created for "A" recruits. Consisting of a small black circle with the letters "G.S." in red lettering, it was worn on the left forearm throughout the rest of the war to distinguish men who had volunteered for active service. The term itself soon came into general use to describe the volunteers, in contrast to "Member (HD)" for NRMA men.[82]

More importantly, over the next three years the additional "benefit" that the NRMA offered to the army by singling out "R" recruits as a source of volunteers was turned into a key aspect of the new training system, with consequences that would come to be very significant for many individuals. One of the best-known accounts of the implications of the new training system comes from Ralph Allen, a sportswriter who served briefly in the 30th ("Sportsmen's") Light Anti-Aircraft Battery, which was formed by Conn Smythe, the owner of the Toronto Maple Leafs, from among professional athletes in various sports as well as people with similar affiliations, such as Allen. Allen went on to become a war correspondent for the *Globe and Mail*, and afterwards he edited *Maclean's*. Despite being a volunteer, what he saw in his basic training in Brantford, Ontario, and during advanced training at Camp Petawawa, Ontario, clearly shaped his memory of the conflict negatively. As he put it while summarizing how the NRMA operated, in a popular history that he wrote two decades after the events:

> Inevitably and quickly the existence of two such armies side by side led to frictions and differences of the ugliest kind. In their training camps it was the habit – and in many cases the deliberate policy – to mix the R Men and A Men in fairly close ratios and hope that by moral pressure and sometimes by actual physical violence the A Men would help persuade the R Men to "go active" too. Between the two groups there were small distinctions in such things as cap badges and service ribbons and quite often larger ones in their treatment by their officers and non-commissioned officers. Officially there was no discrimination against the R Men and none has ever been officially admitted, but as an Active Service volunteer – who at that time shared the general prejudice against the R Men – the present writer can testify from his own experiences that there was. So can thousands of other ex-servicemen.[83]

Allen provided more detailed accounts in two novels, *Home Made Banners* (1946) and *The High White Forest* (1964). In both, he used the same fictional basic training centre as a setting through which to describe the pressures "R" men were subjected to. Those pressures included discrimination in the duties assigned to conscripts, and in granting leave; being subjected to ongoing lectures and interviews designed to encourage men to volunteer; and even emotional, verbal, and physical abuse on the part of other trainees. All of this was carried out with the implicit consent of superior officers and NCOs.[84] Conn Smythe added in his memoirs his own account of the same Brantford training centre that Allen had attended, describing a case where some of his NCOs subjected "R" recruits to a cold shower for more than two hours until the men agreed to volunteer.[85] And participants provided one or two further allegations in Barry Broadfoot's anonymous 1974 oral history collection, *Six War Years*. A former member of the training staff of the advanced artillery centre in Brandon described a case similar to Smythe's, where every morning in the middle of winter the staff made the "zombies" do their physical training at 6 a.m., in –20° Fahrenheit weather (almost –30° Celsius). As he put it, the measure "toughened 'em up, anyway, although I'm not sure it got any of them to go active service." As another former NRMA man stated: "You'll never know the harassment we underwent ... Would you believe ... That I was put in platoons, twenty-five men active service and myself the only Zombie, and they were told, and the n.c.o.'s were told, and the platoon commander was told, that I was fair game?"[86]

Until recently, it has not been possible to substantiate such charges any further. But a few records were kept by the army that do make clear that at least something was going on. Most of the evidence preserved was anonymous or came in roundabout ways from friends and relatives who wrote to the defence minister, which suggests there was a reluctance to use proper channels for fear of reprisal or due to frustrations with the normal procedures for registering complaints in the camps. But their essential truth is more than confirmed by many of the descriptions of the various techniques that are preserved in the war diaries of the training centres themselves, along with a few other first-hand accounts that have become available since the 1970s. Taken together, this evidence confirms Allen's and Broadfoot's basic claims and allows us to reconstruct some of the recruiting tactics that NRMA men faced.

From the beginning of their time in uniform, conscripts were explicitly reminded of the difference between them and other recruits, although most of the tactics that were used were not necessarily negative. In Kitchener, Ontario, for example, the centre's commanding officer held a parade for the first class of "A" and "R" recruits to arrive after the beginning of the new training program in March 1941, during which he noted that they would need to learn to work together and get along while they were there. As the war diarist chronicling the occasion added, "Recruits were left with no doubt as to what was expected of

Figure 18 Photo taken to publicize newly created volunteers, all of whom had converted from compulsory service over the previous few days in Huntingdon, Quebec, January 1942. *Source:* LAC, C-143821.

them."[87] In Newmarket, recruits were paraded to the camp's drill hall one Thursday afternoon in July 1941, led by the centre's pipe band, to hear patriotic talks from several officers. By the next day, 223 men had promised to go active, after which each of them was presented with a special pass entitling them to leave camp from then until the following Monday.[88] In North Bay, Brantford, Portage la Prairie, and Huntingdon, local newspapers followed the efforts of the training centres to encourage men to volunteer, publishing stories and in some cases photos featuring the new active service recruits.[89] In the case of Huntingdon, the town's newspaper noted one surge in recruiting a few days after the Japanese attacks on Pearl Harbor and Hong Kong in December 1941. But it was likely stimulated not just by larger events but also by the efforts of the camp's staff. As the centre's diarist had recorded a few days earlier, when the newest group of "R" recruits arrived in the camp, "over 150 men were received to-day and recruiting begun among them right away. To strike while the iron is hot is the intention."[90]

By many accounts, one of the training centres where staff worked the hardest to try to encourage "R" recruits to volunteer was Cornwall, under the command of Lieutenant-Colonel Rodolphe ("Rudy") Larose. One of the minority of French Canadian officers who had served in the First World War and then remained in the interwar militia, he had risen during that period to command the *Régiment de Hull*. By all accounts he was a dedicated soldier,[91] and like all of his fellow commanding officers in the Second World War training centres he tried to balance the conflicting goals of the army's policy towards NRMA soldiers. His camp's war diary faithfully recorded his efforts and those of other senior officers to gain volunteers, and particularly their personal appeals to "R" recruits as the first several classes arrived for training in the summer and fall of 1941. One of the best descriptions appeared in June 1941, and provides a very good example of the more positive forms that persuasion could take. In that case, almost a whole day was devoted to recruiting, beginning at the commanding officer's parade in the morning, where Larose's second-in-command, "Major Chambers ... made a stirring appeal to the R[eserve].F[orce]. recruits to join the A[ctive]. F[orce]." The result was 102 volunteers, who "were attested during the morning." That afternoon, Larose himself spoke to the men, at another "O.C.'s parade," gathering them around him in a hollow square so that he could better get and hold their attention. The result was an event that took on many of the undertones of an evangelical service. Larose spoke in both English and French, and called for converts to come forward. (This term, which again also had religious connotations, came to be applied to conscripts who changed their status in all training centres in contemporary documents.) This time, sixteen men responded. All of the day's 118 new recruits were then photographed for a feature story in the local newspaper, and in the evening they were piped into downtown Cornwall by the band of the Stormont, Dundas and Glengarry Highlanders, to see a free show at the Capitol Theatre, while carrying placards to make their deeds known to the townspeople.[92] Cornwall was not the only place where such techniques were used: fifty-four recruits were publicly acknowledged and praised for volunteering for active service in a similar manner in Rimouski, Quebec, in January 1942.[93] But more positive forms of appeal clearly worked for some of the men involved, and not every soldier volunteered simply because he was forced to do so.

At the same time, however, there were points where abuse could enter into the process. As Larose noted in reply to one complaint about the treatment of some of the NRMA men, after using the above methods and getting good results in January 1942 he had then offered a full weekend's leave to the last holdouts, twenty-five of whom went active immediately, and another twenty-five after a night in the barracks. As Larose's immediate superior noted in forwarding his comments to Ottawa, there was "no indication that abnormal procedure has been followed at the Training Centre concerned with a view to coercion of 'R' recruits."[94] But clearly, such techniques were designed to take advantage of peer pressure, as well as offers of more direct rewards such as permission to leave the camps for longer periods. When these efforts failed to convince the final recruits (at that point, 47 out of a total of over 1,000), more negative pressures began to be applied. The remaining recruits were assigned to all of the routine tasks of the camp, including cleaning, sentry duty, fire patrols, and kitchen fatigues. Still, in Larose's own words: "This Centre has nothing to hide as to its recruiting activities, and it is again pointed out that no pressure whatever is exerted on men to go active service."[95]

Unfortunately, even more serious claims about the procedures used in Cornwall were made in September 1941, when two men submitted formal affidavits alleging that, in the words of one man, they had enlisted for active service only after "all sorts of vexations, reprimands, [and] harsh punishments, all inflicted without any reason or right and solely with a view to putting pressure on me and to having me enlist against my will in the Active Force."[96] According to the second recruit, passes to leave camp had been routinely and openly denied to him, and he had only been permitted to travel home and visit his family "provided I would use my holiday to try and induce my wife to assent to my voluntary enlistment."[97] More importantly, two soldiers had reportedly threatened the first man, Private J.R. Miville, in front of twenty witnesses and two NCOs, and "upon the offer of these two soldiers to carry out their threats, all went out of the room and ... I was then beaten to the point of becoming unconscious and having to be taken to the Camp Military Hospital where I received medical attention for a whole day." Miville added that he had only gone active after the company commander and sergeant major both made it clear to him that such actions would continue unless he volunteered.[98]

The Cornwall case resulted in a formal court of inquiry. It had to be reinvestigated after the Adjutant-General rejected the first report for not treating the case seriously enough. The eye injury that caused Miville's hospitalization was never fully explained. Yet both men involved in the incident ended up retracting their statements.[99] Without more information, it is difficult to tell whether this was due to a lack of truthfulness in the claims, or pressures put on the men to drop them. Yet as Lieutenant-Colonel E.M. Ansell, the commanding officer in Chatham, explained a few months later in response to a similar complaint regarding his own training centre:

> occasionally strong methods are sometimes used by Active Service men in the same companies and platoons when officers and NCO's are not present. Active and Reserve recruits are placed in the same platoons for training, and it is the desire that these platoons become 100% Active. On the occasion of which, week-end leaves are granted to the whole platoon. Naturally when there are only one or two men left in a platoon who are still "R," they are bound to be a bit unpopular while they remain so. This sort of thing is of course discouraged as much as possible, but in spite of orders in this regard, incidents do occur.

Figure 19 J.L. Ralston during his visit to Cornwall on October 22, 1940, with Lieutenant-Colonel Rodolphe Larose standing behind and to his left. *Source:* LAC, e-010994311.

The complaint that led to this letter involved buttons being cut off a private's greatcoat and a rifle bolt being stolen and hidden – although the men responsible for the actions were eventually found and punished.[100]

The barracks excesses that recruits alleged in Cornwall and Chatham were not necessarily representative of the experiences of all men, either there or in other training centres. From Portage la Prairie, for example, we have copies of the actual talks given to the first class of new "A" and "R" recruits in 1941. There the commanding officer, Lieutenant-Colonel C.M. Ackland, chose to separate out the two groups only one time throughout their training, to speak to them as they arrived in the centre. He emphasized to each of them the number of sports and other activities that were provided for trainees, and he only explicitly referred to the situation once, when he told "A" recruits that the "R" men were mostly "young chaps from farms who haven't been around very much," and that they would be "quite anxious to join up in the Active Forces" if given a chance. They were "not by any means conscripts and we do not want that word or any similar word used in reference to them," he added, noting that "anything of this sort will be severely dealt with."[101] Yet to Burt Harper, who returned to Canada from England in 1942 as a member of the North Shore (New Brunswick) Regiment to pass on his experience to the trainees as an instructor, the Edmundston training centre went somewhat in the other direction. As he described the routine there, the recruits were fully mixed throughout their training, without difficulty. But roughly once a month, they would be lined up facing each other on the parade square. The band would play. An officer would make a speech "about service for the country, all of the good words about serving your country, and asking them or inviting them to come and sign up." Twenty or thirty men might respond, and be cheered, but "then [came] another spiel. A little more forceful this time and then maybe another ten would [convert] ... And then there would be a third and a fourth call ... And then the tone would change. 'What is the matter with you?' This type [of] thing. The regulars would be encouraged to boo them, hiss them. And then they would be told to come out. No one would."[102] Milan Bosnich (a Serbian Canadian, which reminds us of the mixed ethnic origins of some NRMA men) has described how his platoon commander used personal interviews to get to know his recruits, in the same Brantford camp referred to more negatively by Allen and Smythe above, to find the best appeals for each individual. And if they resisted, he notes, they would still receive veiled pressure from other general service men once word got around.[103]

Whether it was for more positive or more negative reasons, as the months went on several basic training centres reported phenomenal conversion rates among their recruits. In a number of training companies, 100 percent of men went active. In some cases, entire centres did so. Cornwall claimed rates of 100 percent of all "R" recruits in two successive months in the summer of 1941, and a year later all but one man volunteered from another group.[104] In Peterborough, 100 percent of conscripts volunteered in July 1941, while Newmarket and Kitchener reached 98 percent in July and September respectively. The latter two camps both exceeded 90 percent again in August and November 1941, and Charlottetown and Chatham each reported the same numbers that October, and November.[105] The staff in Peterborough were so successful at convincing "R" recruits to go active that 131 men from other training centres were transferred there in late October 1941, to encourage more to volunteer; within two hours of their arrival the camp had accumulated several new converts.[106] Many of these units recorded special leaves having been given to all companies that went 100 percent active, likely meaning that pressure had been put on some men by others to go along.[107] But clearly, once again, coercion alone cannot account for all of the successes. In the early days of the new four-month training program, it seems to have worked much as H.D.G. Crerar, B.W. Browne, and other Canadian generals had hoped, in that the men's ties to civilian life were cut, and now that they were in the army for the duration they felt they might as well volunteer. The war itself continued to go badly throughout mid-1941, and again in December with Japan's entry into the war, making the need for volunteers more obvious (this was why Milan Bosnich suggests that he eventually decided to volunteer[108]). On top of that, in the summer of 1941 the government's first major recruiting campaign was in high gear and the training centres were fully part of it. And as suggested by the experiences of "Frenchy" in Sydney, Nova Scotia, negative attitudes among the broader public may have helped convince some men to change their status. In the fictional case described by Ralph Allen in one of his two postwar novels, his main protagonist Haig Ballantyne decides to convert only after a woman with whom he is close begins to submit to public pressure and avoids discussing his status as a zombie in a conversation with him.[109] Roland Bernier, a real-life conscript from Quebec who was called up in December 1941, applied more fundamental reasoning: he volunteered because he calculated that he might actually be able to stay in Canada longer before he was sent overseas.[110]

Once NRMA men went on to advanced training, a new round of influences emerged to help convince them to volunteer. Only volunteers could choose which branch of the army they wished to join after basic training, and "R" recruits were reminded as they completed their first two months that unless they did that they would be put wherever the army needed them (most likely the infantry). As we have seen earlier, unilingual francophones had fewer options if they wanted to operate in their own language except to volunteer for or to remain conscripts in the infantry. But language barriers could work against them in even more negative ways. As one man from Quebec wrote to his father, in a French-language letter that was sent to the justice minister, Ernest Lapointe, in the summer of 1941 and then translated and forwarded to DND, during his basic training he had been told by the staff in Montmagny that he "might just as well" join an artillery battery that was then mobilizing, since otherwise he would have no choice about where he would serve when he left the camp. The work would be easier, and "they told us that it was merely a transfer and not an enlistment." The forms he had signed had been in English, so he had not been able to understand them.[111] In another case, men from St-Jérôme did not discover until they reached their advanced training centre in Petawawa that they had volunteered for active service in the Royal Canadian Engineers. As the commander of that military district, Brigadier F. Logie Armstrong, wrote in commenting on that case, the men now "regard Army matters with such suspicion that they were reluctant to sign the Pay Sheets."[112]

Language difficulties were by no means the only cause of such problems. In Lauzon, Quebec, several men were permitted to begin a course for tradesmen, and recruited to join the Royal Canadian Ordnance Corps afterwards, apparently without fully realizing that if they wished to do so they would have to go active. About one-third still did volunteer.[113] Probably the most bitter criticism of efforts to convince men to go active after basic training came from two anglophone authors, and was forwarded from the Prime Minister's Office to DND in July 1941. They were "indignant concerning the manner in which we were so rudely informed that our status as trainnees [*sic*] has been changed to sappers," and they cursed the prime minister in less than flattering (but also slightly confusing) terms as "you stupid blundering, imperialistic Mesphistophelean [*sic*]."[114]

For "R" recruits, pressures to enlist continued throughout advanced training. As another man reported in a letter that was intercepted by censors and that provides a good summary of the apparent experiences of many men in training centres across the country after 1941:

> The Commanding Officer has openly boasted that he intends to make it as tough as possible for those who do not intend to join ... Today we were given a chance to again signify what branch of the service we wished to entered [*sic*]. Those who did not volunteer were taken on a route march without equipment and also without our water bottles. This is in line with their policy of tough stuff ... I don't mind going away [to a home defence unit] but the thing that makes me so mad is the "Shit" that we will have to take between now and the time we are supposed to leave ... So far they have got about a third of the Company. I haven't done anything yet and I am at my wits end. God only know[s] how long the rest of the gang can hold out.[115]

The man's camp and company commanders both denied the claims when the letter was forwarded to them for comment.[116] Yet complaints and reports about the pressures experienced by NRMA recruits continued over the next three years. There were never enough specific accusations to follow up on, and they were routinely denied or downplayed by local commanders.[117] But clearly something was going on.

Once recruits were posted to home defence units, the pressures acting to encourage them to volunteer were less obvious. Isolation and the lack of entertainment and other activities undoubtedly exerted their own influences. One anonymous interviewee in Broadfoot's book, for example, remembered Terrace, British Columbia, as "a small, quiet hick town with two or three hundred people and a Liquor Commission and a movie theatre and a few stores, and this is where they dumped thousands of troops."[118] For the men of 13th Canadian Infantry Brigade, the Aleutian Island of Kiska was arguably the worst of all such postings, after the excitement of their rigorous training and the landings themselves wore off in late August 1943.[119] From the time they arrived, they discovered the vagaries of the local weather (earlier, their war diarist had described the area as a "land that only an Alaskan Tourist Guide book could depict as inviting)."[120] One of the soldiers' first activities was to dig pits approximately one metre deep into the surface tundra, so that their tents and other buildings could be anchored in solid permafrost, as well as to "winterize" them by sheltering them at least a small amount from the island's constant wind. Moisture still found its way into every corner when it rained, however, and the noise as the wind pulled at their canvas sides was "unbelievable."[121] In late October, one of the brigade's units reported that "one Marquee and six tents had just become air borne and 'when last seen were heading for Amchitka.'"[122] Several times in December and January 1943–44, parties of shovellers had to clear snow from doorways just so that men could leave their tents. And before the last Canadians left the island in early January three US servicemen had lost their lives – in one case after losing his way in a snowstorm while walking only 50 metres from his unit's mess hall to his tent after a Christmas celebration on December 25, and in another when a roof collapsed on two men from the weight of snow in early January.[123] Besides undergoing further training to keep them busy, the men created a small newspaper in cooperation with the Americans, and could access a local radio station created by US personnel, as well as the American "P.X." (Post Exchange) shop to purchase items such as cigarettes and candy. Special prepackaged recreational kits containing radios, gramophones, plastic flutes, sports equipment, and reading material were also provided for each unit.[124] And just before they left Kiska, the 13th Brigade's commanders took advantage of the men's presence on the barren island to put on a display of brigade-level combined arms in a live-firing exercise, on a scale that would have been much more difficult to achieve in its normal training areas in British Columbia.[125]

From 1941 to 1944, on Kiska and elsewhere, conscripts and volunteers served side by side on home defence duties. During their years of service, NRMA recruits came to play a larger and larger role in the country's home defence forces. As the proportion of NRMA members increased, it also became more and more difficult to distinguish between the two groups. They even had the right to become NCOs, and in those ranks theoretically they could exercise command over general service soldiers.[126] Army commanders discouraged such developments at first, and most NRMA NCOs were assigned to more mundane duties and administrative tasks. But given the proportions to which they were part of

Figure 20 The 13th Brigade's camp on Kiska, looking to the west across the island, with its tents dug down to the permafrost to anchor them and protect against the wind. *Source:* LAC, C-144121.

many units by 1944, at least some began to exercise command over fellow conscripts. The one other advantage that NRMA men had over their general service counterparts was that they could obtain leaves and take courses to upgrade their skills more easily, once they were posted to specific units, since there was no threat of being called away at the last minute to join a draft of overseas reinforcements. Lucien Côté, for example, who was referred to in Chapter 2 and was called up in 1940 for his thirty-day training and then in February 1941 to complete his four months and stayed in uniform afterwards, remembers taking a ski course at Lac Saint-Joseph near Valcartier, an ambulance course in Quebec City, a physical conditioning course in Long Branch, Ontario, one on three-inch mortars in Halifax, and a commando course at Lac-Mégantic, in addition to two general ones on instructional methods in Rimouski.[127]

In the meantime the service of NRMA men continued, as did the pressures they faced to volunteer. In 1946, three commanding officers from the various training centres and two from NRMA infantry battalions were gazetted as Officers in the Order of the British Empire for their work in convincing "R" recruits to go active.[128] And certainly there is plenty of evidence that some mistreatment of conscripts took place along the way. Yet in considering this question, the evidence from the early thirty-day training centres should be remembered, when often men had been pleasantly surprised to discover that army life was not as onerous as they believed and volunteered relatively willingly. There is no evidence that that did not continue to be the case for new recruits as the months and years went on, and it would not be any more realistic to assume that all recruits were treated poorly during their training than to ignore the opportunities for abuse that were inherent in the compulsory military training system as it came to exist in Canada during the Second World War.

One last major question that surrounds the men who served as conscripts during the war is why exactly they were so reluctant to volunteer for overseas service. Many of them spent months or even years continuing to refuse to do so even after they had donned a uniform. As the war went on and the army's need for men became more and more pressing, its leaders began to look for answers. But they soon discovered that, once again, just as for any group of Canadians these men's motivations were complex and difficult to define. Many people seemed to think they knew why the "zombies" would not volunteer: in the view of Brigadier W.H.S. Macklin, the author of the report quoted at the beginning of the previous chapter, one major reason was that a high proportion were French-speaking or otherwise non-British and thus did not identify as openly with Canada's war effort. As we have also seen above, he was not entirely accurate when he attempted to define who the conscripts were. And while by 1944 the ranks of the zombies did contain a larger proportion of French-speaking conscripts and men from other non-British backgrounds than among the national population, as we have seen throughout this book it is not surprising that larger numbers of French Canadians failed to identify with the war effort as fully as English-speaking Canadians. As an anonymous summary of the feelings of French-speaking NRMA personnel in the *Régiment de Hull* described their feelings in the spring of 1944, they tended to resist volunteering not necessarily to avoid serving in the army, but because participation in overseas wars had come to be seen as something forced on them by English Canadians rather than as a free choice on their part.[129]

Some of Macklin's other conclusions also have some hints of truth, such as when he identified many NRMA men as being tied to farming. Considering the conflicting statements that emanated from the Canadian government about the priority of agricultural production compared to military service during the war, it would not have been surprising if many people in rural areas felt quite justified in wanting to remain at home. Ultimately, the same thing was true for workers from any industry, who might have felt as if just when the economy was finally turning around after the Great Depression, they were now being prevented from trying to earn good money to allow them to care for their families.[130] In his report on the zombies, Macklin noted complaints from NRMA men about policies regarding leave for employment in essential industries that contradicted government claims that overseas service was the most important contribution that one could make to the war effort. As he put it in one blunt statement, "I am convinced that thousands of NRMA soldiers will resolutely decline to enlist as long as the prospect of farm or other leave is dangled before them like a carrot before a donkey."[131]

Among Macklin's conclusions, the most important and also most controversial was that many NRMA men refused to go active because of their broader opposition to the government's conscription policies. According to the summary of feelings in the *Régiment de Hull* mentioned above, which Macklin forwarded to authorities along with his own in May 1944:

> A large percentage of the NRMA. [*sic*] personnel are perfectly willing to serve their country anywhere but are firm in the stand that they should be ordered officially to go overseas ... A number are determined never to sign active in protest against the repeated attempts to have them sign, against the taunts and jibes suffered over the years from Active personnel and the public who classified them as "Zombies," "Westypoofs," "Conscripts," "Women's Home Companions," "Panty-waists," "Poltroons," "The Lily Livered" and other unmentionables.[132]

These arguments were echoed by a number of other officers in Macklin's brigade, with respect to both English- and French-speaking conscripts. And the notion that conscripts were refusing to volunteer because they hoped by holding out to force the government to order all men who were currently in uniform to serve overseas became so widespread during the war that it almost seems to have become received wisdom among military authorities, who clearly were not impartial on the subject.

In studying such events, we tend to forget that the people involved were human beings. And in fact, many conscripts had very personal reasons why they were not willing to volunteer. As one man described his situation when he was asked why he would not do so: "I have not definitely made up my mind about going active. The reason I haven't gone active is that my father is sickly and alone on the farm and I can get Harvest Leave to help him. After I get harvest leave I am going to consider the matter further."[133] In another case, a municipal politician wrote to J.L. Ralston on behalf of a Scottish Canadian widow in Alberta, whose only son had been called out for training and could not get harvest leave to return and help her work the family farm. In contrast to some of the popular conceptions about the racial character of the NRMA, the author complained that "If the boy had a German name ... he would be released at once." On further investigation, it turned out that the real problem was that he wished to remain in the army, and apparently was not volunteering simply because he still felt a certain sense of duty not to abandon his mother or the family farm completely.[134] A.G.L. McNaughton preserved boxes of files from his time as defence minister at the end of the war, a considerable proportion of which include letters from various families, in some cases almost pleading for their sons to be released, even at the height of the crisis over reinforcements in late 1944 and early 1945, so that they could help aged or ailing parents care for farms or other businesses.[135] And Wray Gardiner, who served in the RCAF during the war but one of whose best friends was conscripted, has suggested that given that his friend was an only son who had been born to his parents late in life, they just could not bear to lose him if anything happened to him overseas. The son appears to have managed to keep from being called up until September 1943, at the age of twenty-one, but then actually volunteered for the artillery and simply did not share the information with his family. He managed to remain in Canada on various home defence duties until August 1944, when he was remustered and later sent overseas as an infantry reinforcement. He died on his first day in the line during the Battle of the Hochwald Forest in March 1945.[136] The son of William Beattie, mentioned above in connection with the Cornwall training centre, also remembers one local businessman who did not want to lose an only son, and discretely (but unsuccessfully) attempted to gain Beattie's aid to keep his son out of harm's way.[137]

One more piece of evidence exists that provides a slightly more scientific picture of the views of at least one small group of conscripts, and in the process tends to confirm several of the broader conclusions noted above. In May 1944, 114 NRMA personnel were interviewed in southwestern Ontario to find out why they would not go active, and the results were recorded in detail. Well over half the men interviewed cited personal reasons. While in some cases recruits gave more than one answer, at least twenty-one emphasized particularly that they needed to stay in Canada to help ailing parents, or to support their families in other ways (many to maintain farms). Another twelve said they could not enlist due to resistance from parents or spouses (seven of these recruits were under twenty years of age). A further seventeen declared that they had either tried to volunteer and been rejected by one of the services, or felt that their health was too poor to withstand intensive training. Eighteen would not give any specific answer, and seven more either refused to talk or simply said that they would not go active for any reason. Sixteen indicated that they disliked the army or wished to enlist in an area other than infantry, the only arm where volunteers were being accepted by mid-1944 (in a number of cases, interviewers highlighted the immigrant origins of particular recruits, and four were described as anti-Canadian in some of their attitudes). When faced with the thought of seeing combat, one man was described as "very emotional, breaks out crying, and freely admits that he has not the intestinal forfitude [*sic*]." Seven men, meanwhile, suggested that they were annoyed that they had been forced into uniform while other people were still able to earn good money in civilian jobs. And six gave explanations that implied that they objected to the government's policies related to conscription – and in at least two of those cases, that they were consciously attempting to pressure the country's leaders to send conscripts overseas by refusing to volunteer – sentiments that confirm the suggestions noted by Brigadier Macklin above, but that also indicate how few men made this claim when they were actually forced to consider their reasons for not volunteering. Of the last ten conscripts, four were described as having one, two, or even three brothers already serving as volunteers in various Canadian forces (and thus presumably their families did not want to risk having all of their male sons killed in the war).[138] In the end, another three did decide to go active, two agreed to reconsider, and the last was an American who was willing to enlist as long as it did not affect his citizenship. In addition, three of the men already listed above stated that they planned to volunteer as soon as they could get family problems put in order in Canada, and two more were willing to try doing the same. Interestingly, of a larger total of 143 NRMA men for whom information was collected as background for these interviews, eighty-seven (60.8 percent) were single and fifty-four (37.8 percent) married (thirty-four with one or more children), while the status of two men was not recorded. Eighty-one (56.6 percent) were Roman Catholic, fifty-three (37.1 percent) Protestant, six (4.2 percent) listed as either Greek Catholic or Greek Orthodox, and three (2.1 percent) Jewish – figures that are very close to those given in Chapter 5 for the NRMA as a whole. At the same time, 115 (80.4 percent) out of the 143 men were Canadian-born – a proportion lower than provided earlier. Significantly, only fifty-three (37.1 percent) of the personnel surveyed came from families where both parents had been born in Canada.[139]

Explanations such as these are worth emphasizing, for they remind us that every individual soldier who served in the war faced similar emotions and deliberations, which often involved such mundane concerns as the needs of families or friends, or pressures from parents or spouses not to enlist. They also illustrate the complexity of trying to understand why so many men chose not to volunteer for overseas service, and remained firm in their convictions despite months or even years of pressures intended to convince them otherwise. The men the Canadian public came to refer to as "zombies" were also more complicated in other ways than the traditional picture we have come to have of them, and even among French Canadians there are reasons why fewer may have wished to volunteer during the war, and more may have ended up as conscripts. The zombies were just a fraction of the much larger number of Canadians who experienced the various training centres across the country during the war and served in far-flung defence posts on the east and west coasts, and beyond, and even in potential combat conditions on Kiska. Yet as the war continued, the attitudes of those conscripts who had managed to resist the many pressures put on them to volunteer during their weeks, months, and sometimes years of service began to harden more and more. Probably the most ominious fact that comes out of the interviews that were conducted in May 1944 was that by that point only six (5.3 percent) out of the entire 114 men were willing to go active or consider doing so immediately. It was a sign of how events were moving in the country as a whole, less than four weeks before the greatest armada in history was due to set sail from Britain to begin the invasion of France on June 6, 1944.

Part 4:
The Fall of the Big Army

Seventy Thousand Zombies[1]

Seventy thousand Zombies, isn't it a farce?
Seventy thousand Zombies, sitting on their – – – –
Eating up th[e] rations, Morning, Noon and Night,
Squatting here in Canada, while others go to fight[.]

Seventy thousand Zombies, hear the buzzards sing,
Here's our thanks to you Quebec, and old Mackenzie King
Never mind our Comrades, let them be the goats
As long as politicians protect their slimy Votes.

Seventy thousand Zombies refuse to play the game
God, our fair Dominion must hang its head in shame
Recruits are badly needed, you hear the urgent shout
But seventy thousand Zombies, reply "WE'RE STAYING OUT."

7

"No stone ... unturned": The Failure of Conscription and the Big Army, 1943–44

By mid-1943, the "big army" advocated by Harry Crerar, Ken Stuart, and other Canadian generals in the early years of the Second World War had become a reality. It numbered five divisions in Europe, along with all of the additional troops and formations necessary to accompany a force that large. After December 1941, it had also expanded at home. Almost as soon as this huge army had been created, however, planners began to dismantle some of it. Faced with rising casualties after Canadian troops became involved in combat in Sicily, and then the Italian mainland, after July 1943, they began to call more and more insistently on the resources available to them in Canada, first to supply the men necessary to fill out the last elements of the big army overseas, and then to keep it at strength as casualties began to take a rising toll.

By 1943 the army had become a huge operation, and as seems to be popularly accepted as a truth about large bureaucratic organizations of any type, it would prove to have been much easier to build up the big army before 1943 than it would be to reduce it back down later on. During the "second conscription crisis" of November 1944, several federal Cabinet ministers were shocked to discover that 120,000 general service soldiers remained in Canada, and another 90,000 in England. As R.M. Dawson wrote in 1961: "Any layman (and this, according to rumour, includes more than one Cabinet member of the time) simply cannot believe the statement that it was impossible to secure 15,000 men from a pool of 210,000, or, properly excluding those in the training stream, a pool of between 165,000 and 170,000."[1] As E.L.M. Burns and C.P. Stacey later pointed out in defending the army against such charges, the problem in November 1944 was not a shortage of all soldiers overseas, but more specifically a lack of infantry, the men who faced some of the harshest conditions in combat and bore some of the largest burdens in terms of casualties. They also had to be in the highest physical condition because of the hazards and stresses they faced, and roughly half of the volunteers who remained behind in Canada were too young, too old, or of too low a physical status to serve overseas. Another one-third were already in the training stream and due to be shipped overseas, and thus already calculated as part of the reinforcement figures. The rest were in headquarters, administrative, or support roles, where they might eventually have been freed up for duty in Europe. But at the time, the fear was that all current reinforcements would be exhausted within a few weeks, and there did not seem to be enough time to ferret such men out of the larger administrative organization.[2] In a broader sense, as J.L. Granatstein and J.M. Hitsman have noted, the problem was the big army itself. Its creation required huge numbers of men, as well as many other units to maintain and support it in the field.[3] This was even more true for a country the size of Canada, which could not as easily take advantage of economies of scale in building up its forces. The unexpected expansion of the country's home defence formations after the beginning of the Pacific war in 1941 also led the big army to drain the country of its reserves of manpower more quickly than planners had expected, even before the Allied invasions of Italy in July-September 1943 and of Normandy in June 1944 added two major combat theatres in Europe.

Yet none of the earlier historians of the 1944 crisis have delved deeply into the workings of the NRMA, to explain exactly how the army's commanders felt so certain there were no more suitable infantrymen left in Canada by 1944, despite the huge overall numbers that still appeared on their strength returns. By 1943, J.L. Ralston and his military advisers were well aware of the pressure the army was putting on the country's manpower and were doing their utmost to avoid having to face its implications. With the successful landing of Canadian troops on Kiska in August 1943, their focus turned almost immediately to reducing the army's home defence forces in an effort to remove as many general service men as possible for service overseas. And by early 1944, they had gone a long way towards weeding out all of the suitable reserves of manpower within Canada, despite the incredulity that was shown by politicians at the time and by some historians in later years at the number of volunteers who still remained in service.

In addition, throughout 1943 and into 1944, Ralston and several of his subordinates began to call more and more on National Selective Service to locate every last possible potential volunteer in civilian society. After late 1942, the age groups and classes of men called out for service steadily expanded. By 1943 and 1944, Ralston was embroiled in a number of disputes with his colleagues in the CWC that showed the seriousness of the situation, and particularly the difficulty of finding men from any other source to fill the needs of the big army. In early 1944 the army turned back to the only men it had left as a source of potential reinforcements, its conscripts under the NRMA, and a deliberate recruiting campaign was undertaken among the country's home defence forces in April and May 1944, in one more effort to persuade as many as possible of the remaining men to volunteer for overseas service. With the mixed results of that campaign came confirmation of the worst fears of officers in Canada. By mid-1944 it seemed clear to them, at least, that they had found almost every useful potential volunteer for overseas service from that source. As a result, the notion became firmly entrenched in the minds of some of the army's key commanders that should any further unexpected event take place to increase their need for reinforcements overseas, there would be few other places to turn but the thousands of Canadians who remained in uniform as conscripts.

As we have seen, none of the key generals involved in planning the country's home defence forces had ever felt nearly as much threat of a direct attack on Canada after December 1941 as their civilian counterparts. By August 1943 the landings on Kiska had made even that possibility much more remote. As early as March, Lieutenant-General Stuart was writing to Ralston to suggest that the army begin scaling back its home defence forces, consolidating units, and where possible replacing male soldiers with civilians or women from the CWAC, thus releasing general service men to go overseas, as had originally been planned before the Japanese attack on Pearl Harbor. This, Stuart reported, could free up as many as 44,000 general service personnel for Europe.[4] That July, five infantry battalions were disbanded, four of which were the third battalions of regiments that already had a first battalion serving overseas and a second one on active duty in Canada. In the same month five more infantry battalions, made up largely of volunteers, were withdrawn from home defence formations, and their general service men sent overseas, along with three Royal Canadian Artillery field regiments, one reconnaissance regiment, and a field company of the Royal Canadian Engineers, bringing the total number of cuts to 15,000 officers and men.[5] In addition, now that the training system no longer needed to serve a continuously expanding army, it was reorganized and consolidated in August. Under the new "Link Training Plan," men would choose their specialty before entering basic training, and in all corps except infantry, armoured, and medical they would do all of their training in the same location, rather than separately for basic and advanced. For the other three corps, the basic training centres remained but were "linked" to particular advanced centres, so that men in a specific corps would stay together throughout their time as trainees. This allowed Stuart to close thirteen basic training centres and reduce others in size.[6]

At the end of August, Stuart submitted a more formal memorandum to his minister, recommending that the entire 7th and 8th Divisions be disbanded, that coast defence units be reduced, and that the remaining units of the 6th Division be formed into three relatively independent brigade groups, which would remain in British Columbia as mobile reserves in the event of a deterioration in the war in the Pacific. The changes were carried out in October, and the new brigade groups were organized based on the structure used by the 13th

Brigade for Kiska, with four infantry battalions instead of the normal three. Atlantic Command's forces were reduced to a single "Training Brigade Group," which was created out of units taken from the former 7th Division and headquartered in Debert, Nova Scotia, to provide final refresher training for reinforcements of all arms before they proceeded overseas.[7]

Across the country, at least ten further infantry battalions were disbanded as a result of the cuts of October 1943, while other formations such as static artillery and anti-aircraft units were simply ordered to make do with 5 to 20 percent fewer men. Altogether, the cuts were expected to reduce the strengths of home defence forces by another 21,000 , allowing volunteers released from these duties to be sent directly to Europe, while "Members (HD)" moved on to other units to take the place of further volunteers. Infantry units were told to reduce their general service personnel to "a cadre of eighty key men per battalion."[8] Unfortunately, some of the savings proved illusory, as most formations had never managed to reach their full authorized strengths since being created in 1942 – a fact that Stuart made clear to the CWC when the reductions were being made.[9] But they lessened the need to continue to try to meet these larger requirements, and they did release another 14,000 men over the next few months for service overseas, for a total of close to 30,000. They also removed several headquarters units and other costly administrative formations, thus making Canada's remaining home defence forces that much more lean and efficient. But the cuts of 1943 were the first sign that both the army and the government recognized that the country could no longer afford to maintain such expansive home defence forces, at least not without significant military and political consequences.

A number of other signs began to emerge by late 1943 that the country was reaching the limits of its resources under current manpower policies. As calls for men had grown in all parts of the country during 1942 and 1943, conflicts had emerged over how many should go into industry, the army, or the other armed forces, and which should have priority. Concurrently, planners began to realize that the compulsory training system would not be able to live up to the demands that both they and their political superiors had tacitly assumed could be placed upon it when they had authorized the creation of the big army in 1941–42. Steadily increasing amounts of time and resources came to be devoted to finding decreasing numbers of NRMA recruits, and this in turn led to decreasing numbers of conscripts volunteering as they were called up and entered training.

Even in the midst of the CWC's lengthy debates over National Selective Service in 1942, signs had emerged that the number of men available for the army were, in the words of the Minister of National War Services J.T. Thorson, "far

Figure 21 Officers' mess, Cornwall basic training centre, Christmas 1943. *Source:* Courtesy of Stormont, Dundas and Glengarry Historical Society, Cornwall.

less than that indicated by statistical estimates." As Thorson (who had taken over as minister for that department from J.G. Gardiner in June 1941) told the CWC in mid-1942, the classes of men liable for compulsory military training now included all single men between twenty and forty years old. Among the younger men ostensibly added to the rolls by reducing the minimum age from twenty-one to twenty, large numbers could be expected to have already enlisted voluntarily, a fact that could not be confirmed until call-up notices had actually been mailed to prospective NRMA recruits. As older and older age groups were called up, and as calls were extended in the future to married men, the returns would be smaller and smaller due to lower numbers of candidates who could meet the army's physical standards. Moreover, many older men worked in essential industries. Already, Thorson noted, "it was necessary to send out as many as nine notices to obtain one man. Army requisitions for July, August and September could probably be met, but the [current] manpower pool available for the Army would, by then, be substantially exhausted."[10]

One remedy for this situation was to begin reducing the numbers of men employed in less essential industries, an idea that had been a major consideration behind the creation of NSS and then the widening of its powers throughout 1942. As the year went on, the number of potential recruits reporting for each new compulsory military training period began to fall increasingly short of the army's requirements, and J.L. Ralston began to press more firmly for NSS officials to put these new powers into practice, as well as to continue expanding the classes of men liable for training under the NRMA, despite the lower returns that could be expected. In particular, he urged that compulsory military service be extended to include married men. In response to opponents who argued that each of these actions would take workers away from essential industries and disrupt the continued expansion of wartime production, Ralston pointed out that the army needed only the most physically capable recruits, and that those who left employment ought to be able to be replaced by less fit men transferred from other industries. Unfortunately, the same indecision that had plagued the larger debates on creating NSS in 1942 also shaped the CWC's responses to this issue, and not until early December did members finally agree to extend compulsory training to all single men over the age of nineteen, and all married men between twenty and twenty-five. The larger debates over priorities continued into the new year.[11]

By early 1943, the proportion of NRMA recruits who were being accepted as suitable for compulsory military training compared to the numbers requested from the Department of Labour (which was, after the changes of September 1942, now responsible for calling out men) was falling to what the army considered dangerously low levels. According to its figures, the number of men entering the training centres had plummeted from over 90 percent of those requested of civilian officials on a regular basis up to mid-1942, to 30 percent or less over much of the period since then. This meant not only that fewer men were available from which to find volunteers in each training period but that some of the resources of the centres themselves were being wasted, in that instructors and other staffs still had to be in the camps whether they were operating below capacity or not. Notably, when the figures were calculated by military districts, since the beginning of the four-month program the area around Quebec City had come lowest in its proportions, with an average rate of 57.6 percent of men called for training ending up in military service, although Military District No. 3 (Kingston and eastern Ontario) was a close second at 59.9 percent. Montreal came fifth out of the eleven districts, with an average of 78.6 percent of calls for men being met, a respectable showing, especially considering that it had the country's highest concentration of industry, and compared to the Toronto area's lower rate of 66.7 percent. Military District No. 6 (Nova Scotia and Prince Edward Island) had the highest reporting rate at 88.0 percent.[12]

In addition to the widening gap between calls for men and the enrolment of NRMA recruits in early 1943, advisers at NDHQ began to worry privately about the attitudes revealed by NSS officials in a series of "Interpretive Letters" that the latter began to distribute to its regional mobilization boards, which assessed requests for postponement of training in a manner somewhat similar to but at a higher level than the tribunal system that had operated during the First World War. The letters had the commendable goal of ensuring greater uniformity in the policies used to call out men across the country. But as the Vice Adjutant-General, Brigadier A.E. Nash, wrote after viewing the first three directives, "the tone of all these letters so far seems to me to indicate a definite leaning towards industry and agriculture and against the Army."[13] He and other military representatives objected especially to "Interpretive Letter No. 1," which outlined policies for postponing military service for farm workers. It defined such workers very broadly, and recommended that boards accept requests for postponement without even asking individuals to provide evidence of their status, a procedure that made it difficult to question any claim. One of the most objectionable examples of these kinds of attitudes was a flyer NSS distributed publicly in April 1944. As it stated: "Mobilization Boards are giving postponement of military training to farm workers of military age ... Practically no applications are refused."[14]

Surprisingly, these directions drew more criticism from the military representatives on the local mobilization boards in rural provinces such as Saskatchewan, where one might have expected them to be more tolerant of requests for agricultural postponement, than in others where fewer people were involved in agriculture, again much as had been the case in the First World War. The change brought protests from one member of the NSS's board in Saskatchewan, who wrote to J.G. Gardiner, the province's representative in the federal Cabinet, to note the opposition that the new policy would spark from families that had already lost sons and husbands to voluntary service or the NRMA and now apparently had to watch others being exempted. If the new directions continued in effect, he added, almost everyone in Saskatchewan might request postponements on the basis of some connection to agriculture, and "it will be absolutely impossible to supply the manpower calls made by the Department of Militia and Defense [*sic*]."[15]

Along with these difficulties, Nash complained in February 1943 that several senior officials at NSS seemed to have no problem with the number of conscripts reporting to training centres falling short of that requested by the army, since numbers of civilian volunteers had been higher than expected in recent months, in their view making up the difference. In one case, Humphrey Mitchell, the labour minister and thus the man responsible for administering NSS after it was transferred from the Department of National War Services in September 1942, even forwarded an internal memorandum to Ralston stating just that.[16] "If voluntary enlistments suddenly take a dip and National Selective Service is counting on continued good results from voluntary recruiting," Nash noted, perhaps hinting at his own fears for the future, "then the combined results may seriously suffer."[17] To be fair, voluntary recruiting of men off the street did seem to be going well through 1942 and into 1943, running at roughly 10,000 or more every month from April to December 1942, with a peak of 14,741 in August. But that number fell to 7,472 in December, rose back up to 12,218 in January 1943, and then declined again in every month afterwards, down to 4,981 that July.[18] Nash and other people within NDHQ also acknowledged several times that their NSS counterparts seemed to be trying to cooperate with the army's demands. In addition, for NSS officials faced with conflicting demands for manpower from several directions, the situation probably did not seem nearly as serious as it did to the army, which had only its own needs to fill. Furthermore, NSS workers were hard-pressed owing to the extra burden created by both the transfer of their manpower functions to the Department of Labour in the fall of 1942, and changes made by the army in early 1943 that toughened physical standards for accepting men as NRMA recruits. This last development had actually resulted from the standards having temporarily been lowered for the previous few months, in hopes of being able to reclaim some men to useful service from lower medical categories. But the experiment did not produce adequate results, thereby again increasing the difficulties that both sets of officials faced in trying to find enough men to meet the army's needs.[19]

Still, from the army's point of view, the increasing difficulty in finding men qualified to be placed in uniform was problematic. Between the number of unplanned units that had had to be brought up to strength to man the country's home defence forces after December 1941, and the degree to which commanders had come to rely on the NRMA to provide both conscripts for home defence units and volunteers for overseas service, the army would need more potential recruits in the future, not fewer, in order to complete its program overseas.[20] Ralston was so disturbed by the various trends that he began what would turn out to be a lengthy correspondence with Mitchell. He understood NSS's difficulties in meeting the army's needs, Ralston wrote in April 1943, but greater efforts had to be made to keep up the flow of men. He suggested a number of steps that were not really his to demand of another minister, revealing the degree of strain to which the situation had brought the two men by then. NSS officials should create extra mobilization boards to deal with calling up men if the work was too heavy. New classes should be called out for training, this time by further extending the age of married men currently liable for service. Mitchell's own experts had strongly resisted that idea, as it was again expected to be disruptive to industry, and in their view unnecessary to meet the army's requirements, which they were confident would eventually be addressed. "Whether or not that may be so if spread over a long period of time," Ralston argued, his needs were urgent, and the current approach was "not panning out on [the] basis of the adjusted monthly requirements which we arranged with you."[21]

Ralston wrote once more to Mitchell, two days later, this time to protest Interpretive Letter No. 1 and its impact on rural manpower. "It would be different if the requisitions for men were being filled but week by week they are falling behind," he noted, "and the Army needs men."[22] At the end of the month, he took his concerns to the CWC, an action that provoked criticism of NSS's operations from several other ministers and launched debates about strengthening it that went on throughout the summer, both in the CWC and in the larger Cabinet. For the first time, other ministers seem to have begun to sense the need for tougher measures to compel civilians to move from less essential to more essential industries, and Ralston successfully argued for further extensions in the age groups and categories of men liable for training. Another result was a series of changes to NSS itself in August 1943, designed to strengthen the administration of civilian manpower regulations. At the same time, the CWC authorized a number of measures intended to push employees more firmly to transfer to work of greater importance to the war effort or be liable for military training.[23]

Unfortunately, the new measures were not much more successful than previous ones. NSS officials continued to disagree over priorities generally, and how far to enforce civilian mobilization regulations more specifically, and numbers continued to fall short of the army's needs. After the situation had deteriorated further over the winter of 1943–44, Ralston wrote once more to Mitchell in March, pressing even more firmly for NSS to meet the army's manpower requirements. Mitchell's only reply was to describe once again the difficulties faced by NSS. As he noted, in order to find 34,000 recruits for the army over the past six months, NSS personnel had had to issue call-up notices for almost 185,000 men, a situation that could only get worse as the age groups liable for compulsory training were expanded over the rest of the year. The result did not satisfy Ralston, who replied with his most forceful statement yet: "You say that 'No stone has been left unturned to meet the demand.' I of course, have to accept that, but can I suggest that there are some stones that, while they may have been turned, have, perhaps not been turned all the way over, under which there will be found quite a number of prospective recruits."[24] But aside from increasing the tensions between Ralston and Mitchell, the letter produced results no different from before. As Granatstein and Hitsman have aptly put it, "the country had effectively reached the bottom of the manpower barrel."[25]

As frustrating as it was for Ralston and his senior officers, of course, they had to rely on the civilian NSS organization to find their "R" recruits, because as Prime Minister King had provided for when the NRMA was created in 1940, the entire human resources of the country now had to be allocated for wartime purposes. As a result, NSS was left to try to balance the various civilian and military demands. And the army was not the only military organization that was still making demands in 1943. In retrospect, the peak of the Battle of the Atlantic came only that May, and the RCN was still growing to meet this and other commitments. The BCATP had been renewed and expanded in June 1942 to provide even more aircrew..[26] And the RCAF had stood up No. 6 Group as part of Bomber Command on January 1, 1943.[27] Ultimately, divisions in Cabinet and the CWC between advocates of the various military forces, and industrial expansion and output, made it difficult to come to a clear decision on priorities despite King's desire to focus on the air force and navy at the beginning of the war. Yet most historians seem to blame the army alone for causing the manpower difficulties of 1943–45, by asking for too much. By mid-1943 it was becoming clear that the BCATP was producing far more men than it or the other Commonwealth air forces needed overseas, and that November it began to be scaled back, much like the army was then doing.[28] Allan English has defended the RCAF's high demands for manpower generally, rightly pointing out that it had been difficult in 1941 and 1942 to predict the Allies' exact needs for 1944, that its manpower priorities were decided by policies made in Britain rather than in Canada, that until it was certain that men were not needed overseas it could not take the chance on winding down its training system, and that the RCAF had needed to draw on larger numbers than it actually required in order to find enough men of high enough standards to complete the training.[29] But the army faced many of the same difficulties. In 1941, as it was being built up, nobody knew that even more forces might not be needed. In late 1944, as Britain and the United States were cannibalizing their own divisions to find enough men to continue fighting, they implicitly relied on First Canadian Army to bear the weight of a certain amount of the fighting so that they could accomplish their own reductions. As a junior ally whose political leaders have been criticized for seeming to want to play as small a role as possible in higher decision-making earlier in the war, by that point Canada could do little to protest or to make reductions of its own.[30] Nothwithstanding that the infantry has sometimes been viewed as a dumping ground for the least educated or skilled potential soldiers,[31] in order to survive the rigours of the battlefield infantrymen also needed to be of a very high physical and mental standard, thus making it more difficult to find suitable recruits. Furthermore, in 1943 (and partly thanks to what in hindsight turned out to be ill-conceived pressure from Ralston, against the wishes of his senior military commander overseas, McNaughton), the CWC agreed to ask the British to include a Canadian division and ultimately the full I Canadian Corps in the Italian campaign that began in Sicily that July, because by then it was becoming clear that an attack would not be made on the mainland of northwest Europe for another year. Even King responded to rising feeling in Cabinet that the army should be "doing something" at that time, especially given that its only major actions up to then had resulted in losses of large numbers of men dead and taken prisoner, first at Hong Kong in December 1941 and then at Dieppe in France in August 1942. As a consequence of a political decision, an extension of forces to the Mediterranean was put in motion that would add that many more burdens to the Canadian army overseas in terms of administrative duplication – and, far more importantly, losses in battle.[32]

At the same time as the debates discussed above were going on between Ralston and Mitchell, several other pieces of evidence were emerging that help explain why Ralston was so adamant about increasing the calls for conscripts, as well as yet another way that the NRMA worked to help find volunteers for all three armed services during the Second World War. In November 1943, planners conducted a study that confirmed an assumption that had been evident in many of the CWC's discussions about the NRMA. Out of almost 200,000 volunteers who were surveyed, all of whom had entered the army directly from civilian life, 37 percent reported that they had done so at some point after receiving their first notice to report for medical examination under the compulsory mobilization regulations but before presenting themselves for induction.[33] As Mitchell had noted during his earlier exchanges with Ralston, even many workers in essential industries only received postponements from training because their employers applied on their behalf, and they then often ended up volunteering shortly afterwards, thanks to a combination of peer pressure and the need to apply for exemption having led them to realize that they were needed overseas: "In one company reporting recently from Toronto, nine of the first ten men listed as key workers for whom postponements was [*sic*] requested became volunteers in a period of six or eight months."[34] According to Hugh McVicar, a civilian bookkeeper who found himself in the infantry in March 1944, receiving his call-up notice was very much what made him decide to volunteer instead: "At age 30, with a wife and two children to support, I didn't really think I'd get called up. But never mind that. I'm here. I certainly don't expect to make much difference to our overall war effort, but I'll do my bit ... I just don't want to feel, afterward, that I could have done more but didn't."[35] In a similar vein, for Maurice Prud'homme and Raymond Meloche, as it began to seem that they might be subject to conscription with the plebscite of 1942, they both decided they might as well volunteer before the NRMA was applied to them, Prud'homme joining the army and Meloche the navy.[36] If the above proportion of 37 percent held true for the entire army, then it is possible that the NRMA was responsible for helping nudge more than 200,000 of the total of 572,318 men and women who volunteered for general service in the army directly from civilian society throughout the war to take that step, in addition to the 58,434 men who converted to general service at some point after formally being enrolled as conscripts under the NRMA. Thus, over 40 percent of all men who served as volunteers in the Canadian army during the war may have been induced to do so either directly or indirectly through the workings of the NRMA.[37] In unguarded moments during the war, Ralston and other federal Cabinet ministers revealed that they were relying on such effects, and Mitchell even publicly acknowledged that it was "common knowledge" at a routine press conference in April 1944.[38]

Another factor that brought Ralston into conflict with his colleagues in the CWC was the issue of leave policies for soldiers to work in civilian jobs. As manpower resources shrank throughout 1942 and 1943, some ministers began calling for Ralston to release larger numbers of troops in order to address shortages in specific industries. As early as 1940, Ralston had responded to requests to provide for agricultural leave by having his officers draft regulations allowing men to return home indefinitely if their families were engaged in farming.[39] By March 1942, soldiers could request to be released from service for up to six months to work in war industries and other seasonal and essential occupations.[40] Leading the charge for further measures was C.D. Howe, who was responsible for industrial mobilization as Minister of Munitions and Supply. Debate centred on several key primary industries, that had some of the harshest working conditions in Canada and that were losing men steadily to other, better-paying wartime jobs. They also needed the most fit, healthy men, the same ones the army most desired. In March 1943, Howe drew attention to further labour shortages in industries that he felt were critical for wartime production, and as a result Ralston expanded the army's existing leave policies so that men could be released temporarily for spring and fall agricultural work, as well as for logging in British Columbia.[41] At Howe's behest, in May the CWC declared a state of national emergency in deep coal mining, even though during the interdepartmental discussions that led up to it, Brigadier Nash of the Adjutant-General's branch argued that Howe could produce no actual statistics that supported his claims of need.[42] In September came shortages of nickel and other base metal miners. Yet when Nash looked more deeply at the situation, he noted that only the International Nickel Company was experiencing shortages and that it was more likely due to the harsh way that INCO treated its workers. The other base metal companies were losing men to other better-paying jobs rather than simply to the attractions of enlistment in the army, as was usually assumed to be the cause in most of these cases. In Nash's view, this was something that could be better addressed by more rigorous reliance on the existing civilian manpower regulations.[43] That December, once more at Howe's request, 1,900 men of the Canadian Forestry Corps returned home from cutting trees in aid of the war effort in Britain.[44] Before the war was over, further small numbers of men had been assigned while in uniform to help maintain tracks for the national railways, and to form two port companies totalling more than 650 men to help load war material onto ships.[45] Ralston resisted such developments, arguing that the army could not be expected to meet industry's needs simply because other civilian mobilization regulations were not being applied more firmly. Concessions would only encourage employers in other industrial sectors to make similar demands, discourage direct recruiting for the army, and encourage the idea that military service was not the most important way that men could contribute to the war effort. But as the debates went on it became more and more clear that the majority of the CWC were prepared to treat industry more leniently than the army.[46]

The needs of various industries continued to be debated over the winter of 1943–44.[47] Meanwhile, a few thousand more men were drawn off that the army desperately needed to meet its own manpower requirements. By mid-1943, at least 3,000 NRMA soldiers had been temporarily excused from compulsory service, with even higher numbers being released for agricultural reasons during the spring and fall. By late September 1944, more than 13,000 men had been released on leaves of various types, and in November, after conscription exploded back onto the political scene, they still totalled almost 9,000.[48] This ensured that it would be even more difficult to convince many conscripts to volunteer for overseas service, given that the new measures offered them the opportunity to have the best of both worlds, by fulfilling their obligation to serve their country without leaving Canada, while also working in very lucrative jobs in wartime industries.

Another development during this period that again shows how badly men were needed for the NRMA was the government's decision to widen the classes liable for training to include people who were not even Canadian citizens. This issue had been raised as early as late 1941.[49] But for diplomatic and legal reasons, extending the NRMA required a series of complicated reciprocal agreements and other arrangements with various Commonwealth countries, the United States, and the governments-in-exile of several European countries, who were currently recruiting and training forces from among their own nationals in Canada with the permission of the Canadian government.[50] Changes were also made to naturalization and immigration laws for men from neutral countries, who under international law could not be compelled to serve in the forces of a belligerent. When called up, they would now have to either formally declare their intention to become Canadian citizens, and then undergo training, or identify themselves as neutrals. If they chose the second option, they were permanently barred from becoming permanent Canadian residents and threatened with deportation at the end of the war. Army leaders even agreed to accept aliens from countries with which Canada was currently at war, for both compulsory and voluntary service, as long as the recruits declared their intention of becoming Canadian residents in the same way as neutrals, and passed a security check by the RCMP.[51]

These changes added 35,000 more men to the lists of potential NRMA recruits, from late 1942 onwards.[52] As the statistics provided in Chapter 5 of this study show (Table 4), the final number of men enlisted under the NRMA who were born outside Canada was over 12,500, a not inconsiderable number, although it is not clear how many were already naturalized Canadian residents before 1942 and thus previously subject to the NRMA. Still, the new results were again comparatively small when set against the amount of time and effort that had gone into achieving them. This was yet another sign of the decreasing numbers of men available by 1943.

One last trend that revealed even more clearly the need for men for the army, and the great reluctance on the part of some Canadians to serve under the NRMA, was the increasingly strong effort that was made to locate deserters and defaulters after 1943. From the beginning of compulsory training in 1940, at least a few men had failed to report, and the Department of National War Services had developed policies for dealing with such cases.[53] But as manpower resources declined during 1942 and the number of delinquents began to rise, Ralston began pressing Cabinet colleagues J.T. Thorson and Louis St. Laurent (who was responsible for the RCMP as Minister of Justice) for more thorough efforts to apprehend and prosecute such offenders.[54]

Unfortunately, when it came to enforcing NRMA regulations, authorities were faced with a number of difficulties, as well as with a whole series of ways that could be used to delay or avoid military service. Before the government could even be aware of a man's eligibility for call-up, he had to have made it known that he was available by filling out his card during the national registration of 1940 – a step that relied on the traditionally law-abiding habits of Canadians. After the registration, every man received a certificate as proof of his status, which under the policies brought in after the creation of NSS had to be presented before he could legally work in most jobs. Yet employers could "look the other way," especially as manpower became more and more scarce after 1942. Some men also altered or borrowed certificates themselves, or even ordered official duplicates for friends who did not possess them by reporting their own as lost or stolen.[55] As the war went on, a number of cases emerged of certificates being forged, or sold on the black market. Other records were also forged, such as certificates of rejection or postponement from compulsory military service, or discharge from the armed forces for medical or other reasons.[56] As Michael Stevenson describes the most spectacular case of the war, the Divisional Registrar responsible for guiding NSS mobilization operations in the Montreal area was arrested along with two other men in April 1941 for selling deferment certificates to members of the city's Syrian Canadian community.[57]

Even after a man had complied fully with all registration requirements, there were a number of ways he could avoid service, both legal and illegal. Although procedures changed slightly over time, as it came to be formalized by the middle of the war the first step in the actual mobilization process was the receipt of a notice to report for medical examination, which usually arrived by registered mail a few weeks before authorities planned to have the man begin training. Prospective recruits were required to visit a civilian doctor of their choice and undergo an examination, under directions provided by the army. Anyone who did not meet its physical standards was categorized as unwanted and thus exempt from compulsory service. Officials soon realized that some doctors tended to be more lenient than others, and by 1942 special boards had been created to review questionable cases.[58] More than one civilian doctor and even some military personnel were also implicated in accepting bribes for deliberately placing men in lower medical categories than they should have been.[59] Others accepted money even when they already knew that a man was never likely to be called.[60] And local mobilization officials reported attempts being made to bribe them to alter such records in their district offices.[61]

The next stage in becoming an NRMA recruit was the actual call for training, which again arrived by registered mail. Any man who felt that his services were more vital to the war effort in agriculture or industry could apply for postponement. Many people requested such consideration, which resulted in still more time and paperwork being spent dealing with each case. Postponements of compulsory military training for all reasons totalled 246,133 on January 31, 1943, and 246,938 on May 31, 1944. By the time the war in Europe ended on May 7, 1945, 280,926 men either currently had their training postponed or were in the process of applying for postponement, while another 25,004 had been exempted as members of various police forces, the clergy, or other specific categories. This adds up to 305,930, or 16.8 percent of the total of 1,816,868 men who were in the age groups and classes by that time liable for training. For the war as a whole, officials processed 746,478 requests for postponements and granted 664,525 (although some of these were for extensions rather than new requests).[62]

If a man did not want to break the law, technically there was one more step he could take to avoid reporting for training before he was actually considered a delinquent. Knowing what registered letters addressed to them from the Department of National War Services (later NSS) likely meant, many men simply refused to accept them. Police officers then had to attempt to deliver the notices in person to legally establish that the addressees had rejected them – another costly and time-consuming task.[63] Mobilization officials came to depend on the voluntary cooperation of local and provincial police forces to carry out such duties, despite early difficulties in Ontario and Quebec, both of which objected to the extra burden the work would place on their officers. Ontario eventually agreed to cooperate, but Quebec refused, and several letters from Ernest Lapointe to Quebec's attorney general asking for aid went unanswered in late 1940 and early 1941. Officials finally agreed informally to help prosecute offenders in provincial courts on behalf of the federal government, if men were apprehended by the RCMP. But throughout the war they refused to participate actively in enforcing the NRMA. This decision was probably motivated by the generally higher level of distaste for the NRMA in Quebec, as well as by Premier Adélard Godbout's need to distance his government from its federal Liberal counterpart, which as we have seen had helped so openly to get him elected in 1939, but which had then introduced the relatively unpopular policy into the province in 1940 and extended it in 1941 and again after the plebiscite of 1942.[64] Officials were so frustrated by men refusing to accept notices even when delivered by police officers that they submitted recommendations to the Department of Justice more than once that such actions be made automatically illegal. Experts resisted doing so, noting that it would introduce the principle of assuming in advance that someone was going to commit an illegal act (refusing to report for their training), and then proceeding to prosecute them without waiting to be certain that that was what actually occurred.[65]

Large numbers of notices also went undelivered during the war, often for simpler reasons, such as men moving from their homes and not notifying the

Figure 22 (facing page, top to bottom) Samples of the various forms used to mobilize recruits for compulsory training in the early years of the war: notice to report for medical examination; notice to report for medical re-examination; notice of postponement of military training; notice to report for military training. *Source:* LAC, e-011157761 to e-011157764.

HAND THIS NOTICE TO THE EXAMINING PHYSICIAN

EXAMINING PHYSICIAN WILL PLEASE ATTACH THIS NOTICE TO THE MEDICAL EXAMINATION AND CERTIFICATE FORM COMPLETED FOR THIS MAN AND TO BE SENT TO THE DIVISIONAL REGISTRAR.

From: Divisional Registrar,
Administrative Division "A",
National War Services,
Carling Block,
London, Ont.

DEPARTMENT OF NATIONAL WAR SERVICES
National Resources Mobilization Act, 1940
National War Services Regulations, 1940 (Recruits)

NOTICE OF CALL
Serial Number
Re A

Date Issued:

BY PROCLAMATION OF HIS EXCELLENCY THE GOVERNOR GENERAL

TO

SPECIMEN

NOTE:—This department will pay the examining physician but no other cost in connection with your medical examination.

You have been called out to undergo military training and, in accordance with the National War Services Regulations, 1940, (Recruits), are hereby notified to present yourself for medical examination, within three clear days, to any one of the nearest **duly appointed** examining physicians in this Administrative Division. If you are found fit, you will be notified to report for military training at a time and place which will be indicated to you. If necessary, a warrant for transportation will be forwarded with the notice to report for training.

HAND THIS NOTICE TO THE MEDICAL REVISION BOARD

"NOTICE—MEDICAL RE-EXAMINATION"

From: Divisional Registrar,
Administrative Division "F",
National War Services,
Post Office, Upper Town,
Quebec City, P.Q.

DEPARTMENT OF NATIONAL WAR SERVICES
(National Resources Mobilization Act, 1940)
(National War Services Regulations, 1940 (Recruits) (Consolidation 1941))

NOTICE OF CALL
Serial Number
Re

Date issued:

In accordance with Section 12 (4) of the National War Services Regulations, 1940 (Recruits) (Consolidation 1941) you are hereby notified to present yourself for medical re-examination by a National War Services medical revision board at the time and place indicated hereunder. If you are found fit for military training, you may expect to be notified by your Divisional Registrar to report at a military training centre to perform military

TO

SPECIMEN

training as prescribed by Proclamation of the Governor in Council. The Department will pay the fees of the members of the board but no other cost in connection with your medical re-examination.

Report to........ On........ At........

From: Divisional Registrar,
Administrative Division "N",
National War Services,
Court House,
Edmonton, Alta.

DEPARTMENT OF NATIONAL WAR SERVICES
(National Resources Mobilization Act, 1940)
(National War Services Regulations, 1940 (Recruits) (Consolidation 1941))

"Notice—Medical Examination" serial number to be inserted here:

Date issued:........

After due consideration, your application for the postponement of your period of military training has been .... by the Board of this Administrative Division.

TO

SPECIMEN

Your period of military training, therefore, is postponed until .... Unless further representations are received from you **at least one full month** before the expiration of your postponement, you may expect, if medically fit, to be called for the period of military training immediately following the expiration of your postponement. It is important that you quote the serial number appearing in the upper right hand corner of this postponement order in any communication addressed to the Divisional Registrar. Any change of address must be notified **forthwith** to the Divisional Registrar. Under National War Services Regulations, 1940 (Recruits) (Consolidation 1941) heavy penalties are provided for failure to notify such change of address to the Divisional Registrar.

NATIONAL WAR SERVICES REGULATIONS, 1940 (RECRUITS) (CONSOLIDATION 1941) DO NOT PROVIDE FOR ANY EXEMPTION. THIS POSTPONEMENT IS TEMPORARY AND MAY BE REVOKED AT ANY TIME, WHEN IT MUST BE RETURNED AS MAY BE DIRECTED. THIS POSTPONEMENT ORDER MUST BE RETURNED TO THE DIVISIONAL REGISTRAR WHEN APPLYING FOR A FURTHER POSTPONEMENT. NO APPLICATION FOR A FURTHER POSTPONEMENT WILL BE CONSIDERED UNLESS THIS POSTPONEMENT ORDER IS IN THE HANDS OF THE DIVISIONAL REGISTRAR.

NPO

(Notice—Military Training)

DEPARTMENT OF NATIONAL WAR SERVICES
(National Resources Mobilization Act, 1940)
From: The Divisional Registrar,
Administrative Division "N"
Court House,
Edmonton, Alta. (Date issued):

NOTICE OF CALL
Serial Number used on "Notice—Medical Examination" to be inserted here

BY PROCLAMATION OF HIS EXCELLENCY THE GOVERNOR GENERAL

You have been called out to undergo military training and, in accordance with National War Services Regulations, 1940 (Recruits) have been medically examined and found fit for training. Therefore, you are hereby notified to report, within three clear days, to the Officer Commanding, Military

TO

SPECIMEN

Training Centre at........
Transport Warrant No. .... is enclosed herewith.
(Note: If transportation is not required, Divisional Registrar will strike out.)

National Registrar of their new addresses. As early as 1942, NSS authorities began checking names against lists from DND of men who had volunteered for the army, to eliminate obviously irrelevant cases from its files, and in 1943 private companies were hired to help do some of that work.[66] But in a number of cases the actions of such men proved to be more deliberate.[67] And even after they had officially received their notices to report for military training, many did disobey the orders (and often fled the area), thus officially becoming defaulters. Others left the army after they had been fully inducted, becoming deserters. The need to investigate each man individually and confirm that he was a defaulter, and often to return him to the jurisdiction where he had committed the offence to be prosecuted, added yet more tasks to the already heavy workload of RCMP officers and NSS officials. For the four months from March to June 1943, for example, the RCMP opened 19,384 new cases for investigation under NRMA regulations, and closed 15,448, while 9,925 others remained outstanding from before and during those months.[68]

In late 1943, the RCMP and mobilization officials went one step further in their search for defaulters, launching a series of "roundups" in large cities across the country. In each case, constables swooped down on taverns, pool halls, beer parlours, and other "shady establishments" where men tended to congregate, to check their registration certificates and other papers. Records kept by NSS of specific raids indicate that the cities affected in Ontario included Windsor, Hamilton, Niagara Falls, and Toronto, as well as lumber camps in the countryside around Sudbury and North Bay, to which it was suspected that men might have gone to evade the more stringent regimes in urban areas. Every RCMP division in the country carried out similar raids. Out of a total of 39,973 people who were investigated in 1,659 raids between late October and the end of November alone, 105 army deserters and 344 NRMA defaulters were apprehended in the above types of establishments, along with 164 other people who had violated national registration regulations by daring to be unemployed by this point in the war, or to work in non-essential jobs.[69] NSS officials also ordered employers to carry out a "compulsory check-up" of all their workers, and report any who did not possess proof of meeting the requirements of wartime mobilization regulations. Another 10,040 potential NRMA recruits were found in this manner, as well as 258 army deserters and absentees.[70] In at least some ways, these actions were reminiscent of procedures used in police states rather than a democratic country like Canada. But clearly, by the beginning of 1944 the Canadian public was becoming more and more aware of the seriousness of both civilian and military mobilization regulations, and it was getting more difficult to avoid such service. This underscores yet again the extent to which society had been mobilized on all levels.

As the war entered what would turn out to be its last full year, officials faced more and more frustration in their attempts to find and apprehend defaulters. Friends and family often sheltered these men, and in more remote regions it was possible to go for months or even years before being caught. In British Columbia, one defaulter eluded the RCMP for more than a year, fleeing into the bush and at one point diving into a local river to escape officers. He was only taken into custody in June 1946, when he finally decided himself to surrender.[71] In Parent, Quebec, even after the fighting had in Europe had ended in May 1945, a local resident fired several shots over the heads of two military policemen as they pursued a friend of his who was a deserter, yelling (according to the later report of the MPs) "that there was no sons of bitches that were going to take any French Canadians out of this town."[72] Government officials attempted to have concealment of deserters and defaulters made a more serious and easily prosecuted offence under wartime regulations, this time with some success.[73] In addition, large numbers of defaulters from Quebec were alleged to be living across the border in the northern United States, which already had a sizable French-speaking population, or in lumber camps in places like northern Ontario (another reason for the "roundups" described above).[74] Advisers in the Department of External Affairs went so far as to suggest making a formal agreement with the United States to apprehend and return these types of men from each other's countries, but it never got beyond the negotiating stage.[75]

In early 1944 a new series of problems emerged in Quebec, when defence lawyers for men accused of violating the NRMA discovered that by appealing every conviction they could cause further delays for their clients by backing up the cases in higher courts. This time, the province's officials proved to be more cooperative, and even agreed to allow procedures to be altered temporarily by Order-in-Council to cut down on appeals for the duration of the war, probably because in this case it would mean reducing rather than increasing their workloads.[76] Another problem that slowed down the workings of the mobilization system was that sometimes local officials in rural Quebec insisted on police using complicated procedures to arrest defaulters. But in this instance the cause seems to have been a desire to run up bills for the costs of enforcement, which were paid by the federal government, rather than deliberately to hinder enforcement of the NRMA.[77]

Despite all of these measures, evasion of various aspects of the NRMA remained a significant issue throughout the war, and added yet another difficulty to the many that were already worrying both NSS officials and those at NDHQ by the end of 1943. Approximately 21,000 men remained unaccounted for at the end of the war, down from about 200,000 since the Department of Labour had taken over administering the NRMA in late 1942.[78] But even then, the numbers were deceptive. Of that 21,000, only a small proportion turned out to be due to anything other than errors in the records themselves and inefficiencies in administering them. Over the course of 1945–46, NSS personnel located more men, most of whom turned out to be farmers who had not been aware that they were required to apply for postponement when they received their notices, or names that had been accidentally duplicated in compiling registration records. As of the end of June 1946, the total number of defaulters still on the government's books was much lower, at 6,724.[79] According to C.P. Stacey, 7,255 NRMA men were also struck off strength as deserters at the end of the war, a figure that would account for around half the total of 14,835 (both conscripts and volunteers) who remained unapprehended as of February 1946 – a high number but again a relatively small percentage overall, thanks largely to the efforts of NSS. The numbers suggest yet again the large amount of effort that was being expended for declining returns by 1944.[80]

Of the 6,724 defaulters remaining at large under the NRMA at the end of June 1946, almost three-quarters (4,926, or 73.3 percent) came from Quebec. This was larger even than the proportion of 68 percent from that province under the Military Service Act during the First World War. It is also notable that in one study conducted in 1942, men were rejected for medical reasons at almost twice the rate in Quebec as in Ontario, which might suggest a certain bias on the part of local civilian medical boards. But the army's own doctors rejected men from Quebec at the same rates, suggesting that other factors were at work besides deliberate efforts to avoid the regulations.[81] Quebec had only two mobilization districts and a small portion of a third devoted to administering the NRMA during the war, compared to the three districts and a good part of a fourth that covered Ontario, as a result of the historical imbalance between English- and French-speaking militia units that had been used as the basis for organizing them. The lack of co-operation on the part of the provincial police added to the difficulty of dealing with cases in a more timely manner. Lastly, considering the general stereotypes that existed among many English Canadians during the war, it would not be inappropriate to wonder whether officials focused more intently on Quebec than elsewhere when attempting to identify defaulters.

Nevertheless, it seems clear from the numbers of defaulters, first, that by early 1944 French Canadians in particular were not happy with the NRMA, and second, that the country was reaching the last of its manpower reserves. Despite the complaints of Ralston and some of his senior advisers, there indeed remained few "stones ... left unturned" under which to find more men for overseas service.

The only further step that could be taken was to extend the upper and lower agess of men liable for training. By August 1943 those had almost reached the extremes to which authorities were willing to go during the war, when the minimum age for all men, married and single, was dropped to eighteen-and-a-half from nineteen, and the maximum raised from twenty-six to thirty for married men (the maximum for single men had been set at forty-one since the beginning of 1943).[82] Over the winter of 1943–44, the numbers of soldiers volunteering directly from civilian life also began to dwindle, dropping from a high for the year of 12,218 in January 1943 to a low of 2,789 in December, and rising only slightly again in the first months of 1944. Meanwhile, the numbers of NRMA recruits being enrolled for training had fallen pretty much steadily from mid-1942 on, from 6,833 that July to 5,820 in January 1943, and 1,631 that December. Consequently, figures for NRMA men converting to general service after enrolment dropped from 2,526 in May 1942 to 1,003 in January 1943 and to only 295 for all of December. The proportion going active as each new group of recruits entered basic training had slipped from as high as 50 to 60 percent for the country as a whole, in some of the months in 1941 when individual camps had been achieving rates of 90 to 100 percent, to closer to 30 to 40 percent overall by mid-1942, and around 20 percent by late 1943.[83] As the army looked ahead to the increased fighting that everyone expected would come with the long-awaited invasion of France that spring, it was clear that the NRMA was no longer meeting the demands of an organization that would soon be facing casualties even higher than before.

In these circumstances, commanders turned to the one source of men that remained available to them as reinforcements: the thousands of soldiers who were still in uniform as conscripts in the home defence forces. As early as February 1944, planners at NDHQ were clearly worrying about the need to maintain the flow of men overseas for the coming year. Orders arrived in Pacific Command, directing units to scrutinize every general service soldier below the rank of sergeant for possible release, "to ensure that the reinforcement stream be brought to the volume required for maintenance of necessary reserves in the United Kingdom."[84] A month later, instructions were issued for commanding officers to interview every general service NCO and even warrant officer in their units who was of appropriate age and physical category, in an attempt to convince them to serve overseas (large numbers of these men could not be sent unless they voluntarily agreed to revert to the rank of private or corporal). In the absence of men willing to accept such reversions, commanders were told to report anyone they felt was "*not qualified or suited* [*emphasis in original*]" to hold his current rank, so that eligible men could then be demoted for sending overseas (and thus another area where the line became very blurred between willing and less willing reinforcements).[85]

In late March 1944, authorities went one step further by launching a new recruiting campaign in Pacific Command. In an idea that apparently originated in 13th Canadian Infantry Brigade, whose officers had supposedly been told many times by the NRMA men under their command that the latter were prepared to go overseas voluntarily if the brigade went as a unit, officials in Ottawa decided to permit just that. The tactic was clearly patterned on the same types of approaches that had worked so well in the training centres over the past several years. The 13th Brigade was the logical place to begin this campaign, for it had just returned from Kiska, where the two groups of soldiers had worked side by side for months, and had been considered to be at their peak in terms of training and morale – and where they had also perhaps been made more aware of the true seriousness of the war and the army's needs.. For the General Officer Commanding-in-Chief, Pacific Command, Major-General Pearkes, an eager and energetic commander who reportedly had not lost faith that the NRMA men were soldiers like any others, the idea seemed to have great potential, and the brigade quickly got to work.[86]

Unfortunately, there were significant differences between recruiting operations in training centres earlier in the war and the situation in the 13th Brigade. By early 1944, conscripts far outnumbered volunteers in the brigade, ranging from 60 percent in its headquarters staff to 85 percent of other ranks in the Rocky Mountain Rangers and 95 percent in the *Régiment de Hull.* As Brigadier W.H.S. Macklin, the new commander of the brigade after its return from Kiska, noted in his later report on the recruiting campaign,

> Le Regiment [*sic*] de Hull actually had two N.R.M.A. acting warrant officers, and most of its serjeants [*sic*] were N.R.M.A. Other units also had N.R.M.A. serjeants, corporals and Lance Corporals on strength. If there ever had been any outward distinction between the volunteer and the N.R.M.A. soldier in these units it had long since disappeared. I had hoped that it would not reappear but this hope was not fulfilled. The instant the announcement was made that 13 Infantry Brigade would mobilize on a volunteer basis the active personnel mentally ranged themselves in a body on one side and the N.R.M.A. ranged themselves on the other, and the gulf between them widened and deepened daily.[87]

In hindsight, Macklin identified a number of other problems that had not been evident at the time, but which had come to affect the brigade's cohesion and morale. These included the granting of thirty days' leave for all personnel after its return from Kiska, large numbers of senior officers having been rotated out of the brigade after its stay in the Aleutians (among the replacements being Macklin himself), and several junior officers being transferred out in mid-March to serve in the British army as part of the recently established "Canloan" scheme that allowed a number who had been commissioned in earlier years but were now surplus to Canadian needs to serve in British units to help meet deficiencies on their part overseas.[88]

Even at the time, commanders quickly realized that there would be little chance of 100 percent of the brigade volunteering for general service. Arrangements were made for each battalion to also draw men from two other sister units in Pacific Command, and at first the results seemed positive. In the first two days, more than 150 men "went active." But by early April, the numbers volunteering each day had fallen to a few in each unit, and there they remained. Commanders transferred the NRMA men who were most firmly opposed to volunteering out of the brigade, in an attempt to keep them from influencing their colleagues, and took away NCO ranks from many conscripts who possessed them; not surprisingly, for this reason and also because most of the NCOs were NRMA men themselves, the latter were said to be showing "a noticeable lack of leadership" during the campaign.[89]

As the month went on, conscripts were moved to a special "Tent Camp" on the outskirts of the brigade's headquarters in Vernon, and subjected to a series of route marches, assault courses, and night training schemes, as well as "six inches of mud that could hold its own against the Kiska variety."[90] All requests for leave were cancelled, and three successive Victoria Cross winners visited the area to exhort the men to volunteer, including Major Paul Triquet of the *Royal 22ᵉ Régiment*, who had recently won his VC at Casa Berardi during some of the harshest fighting of the Italian campaign around Ortona. Triquet spoke in French to the *Régiment de Hull* and managed to convince twenty-three men to volunteer.[91] Major-General Pearkes, himself a VC winner from the First World War, spoke to the brigade a few days later. And Lieutenant-Colonel John MacGregor, another VC winner from the First World War, who had served again in England in the Second, took command of the "Tent Camp" and spent several days speaking with conscripts individually about his experiences overseas.[92] Almost every method was used to try to find volunteers, although Macklin denied resorting to open coercion. As he put it: "We have used every form of persuasion that could be thought of – interviews, discussions, sermons, films, speeches. We have appealed to their pride, to their manhood, to their patriotism and even to their self-interest. But we have NOT [*capitals in original*] used threats or intimidation nor subjected these men to extra fatigues or menial duties."[93]

According to Macklin, a "Lieut.-Col. Shimnowski," the senior Roman Catholic chaplain in Pacific Command, was another of the many people who conducted personal interviews with NRMA recruits. A clear example of the non-British origins of many Canadian soldiers during the war, he was reportedly capable of speaking to them in a number of different languages. But he "reduced more than one man to tears without succeeding in persuading the man to enlist."[94] As the brigade's war diarist concluded after the first week of the campaign: "The men do not seem interested at all and the thought of being separated from their platoons and buddies has no effect on them."[95]

The methods being used in Pacific Command to convince NRMA recruits to go active attracted interest elsewhere. The Vernon branch of the Canadian Legion, and particularly its president (who also happened to be that city's mayor), criticized Pearkes and the government for demeaning the Victoria Cross by requiring Major Triquet to speak to NRMA recruits. Howard Green of what had been renamed the Progressive Conservative Party in late 1942 (when the Premier of Manitoba and head of a Liberal-Progressive coalition there, John Bracken, was persuaded to take over its leadership), rose in the House of Commons to question J.L. Ralston on the matter, arguing that it was a sign of the need to extend conscription to overseas service.[96] In Quebec City, on the other hand, the municipal council passed a motion calling for a Royal Commission to look into the events on the west coast, seeing the campaign as a less than veiled attempt to force conscripts to volunteer. Allegations of such practices were received from 133 former members of the *Régiment de Hull*, who were among the NRMA men who refused to volunteer and were transferred out of their unit and eventually to the *Fusiliers du St. Laurent* as part of the recruiting campaign. J.S. Roy, the federal MP for Gaspé, questioned Ralston regarding comments reportedly made by Pearkes during the campaign. And somewhat similarly to developments during the First World War, René Chaloult, a strongly nationalist MLA and one of the leaders of the *Bloc populaire canadien* movement that had been formed after the 1942 conscription plebiscite in Quebec, put forward a motion in that province's legislature objecting to any move to send conscripts overseas. Other members of the legislature countered with a separate motion reaffirming the province's support for the broader war effort. But in contrast to the First World War, when Joseph-Napoléon Francoeur had withdrawn his protest motion before it came to a vote, this time both passed with large majorities.[97]

By late April, recruiting in the 13th Brigade was beginning to wind down. In all, 793 men from it and 491 from other west coast units went active during the campaign, compared to 278 general service men who had already been in the brigade, and 1,102 who were posted in from other units. A total of 177 officers and 2,664 other ranks left for overseas from Pacific Command in early May, including "practically every G.S. soldier below the rank of Sergeant."[98] The numbers were not wholly disappointing, since almost half the men were converts, but it was clear that these proportions would decline in future, as only the most firmly opposed NRMA men remained behind. Within a few days, the 13th Brigade embarked for the east coast, from which it sailed for England in late May. There, it became a training formation, similar to the earlier No. 1 Training Brigade Group in Debert, Nova Scotia, but devoted to teaching future reinforcements brigade-level manoeuvres and bringing them up to full combat efficiency after they arrived in England. It added extra overhead to the army's operations in Britain, but that probably seemed worth the cost for the gain of almost 2,700 new reinforcements at that point in the war. Among its tasks that summer, the brigade was assigned to implement the remustering program for non-infantry reinforcements that will be described in the next chapter.[99] Most of its own other rank personnel quickly moved on as reinforcement drafts to various operational units in western Europe, the first being a platoon of men from the *Régiment de Hull*, which left to join the *Régiment de la Chaudière* in June.[100]

Authorities tried a similar recruiting campaign on the east coast in late April and early May. Because by that time no single operational brigade existed in the region, three separate infantry battalions in widely dispersed locations were nominated to go overseas, provided that each managed to raise their strength to five hundred or more volunteers (roughly half or more of the total of an infantry battalion, and higher for a typical home defence unit). In what was either a case of wishful thinking or a result of the fact that French-speaking reinforcements were always in shorter supply overseas and thus urgently needed (and probably some of both), the units selected included two French-speaking battalions, the *Régiment de Joliette* and the *Régiment de Montmagny*, as well as the Dufferin and Haldimand Rifles.[101]

Judging from the war diaries of these units, the efforts made to encourage men to go active in Atlantic Command were less strenuous than on the west coast. This should not be surprising, since the three battalions involved were smaller and much more isolated from one another than in Pacific Command. It also did not help that 150 men from the Dufferin and Haldimand Rifles were permitted to leave on furlough the day after the campaign began.[102] In the *Régiment de Joliette*, officers who were already volunteers themselves were subjected to the efforts of colleagues from the reserve army whose own service was limited to Canada but who had arrived to help interview the men to try to convince them to go active. According to the battalion's war diarist, "they more or less told us that we were slackers and are to blame for our men not signing active."[103] The results were less encouraging than in Pacific Command, and none of the three battalions reached their quota. The Dufferin and Haldimand Rifles managed to persuade 196 recruits to go active, but the campaign of the *Régiment de Joliette* ended almost before it had begun, with only two recorded converts. The *Régiment de Montmagny* did go overseas, despite falling short of its quota, after absorbing general service volunteers from the *Régiment de Joliette.* In August, one further battalion was permitted to try the same experiment. The Victoria Rifles of Canada eventually sailed for England in November, with a strength of 499 other ranks, at least ninety of whom were drawn from other units on the east coast, and including one platoon from the Dufferin and Haldimand Rifles.[104]

A FEW DAYS AFTER THE 13th Brigade arrived in England, Canadian troops joined larger British and American forces in the famous D-Day landings of June 6, 1944. Allied armies in Italy had just completed the capture of Rome. Over the next few weeks, 3rd Canadian Infantry Division and 2nd Canadian Armoured Brigade would be joined in Normandy by 2nd Canadian Infantry Division, 4th Canadian Armoured Division, and the headquarters of both II Canadian Corps and First Canadian Army, under the overall command of H.D.G. Crerar. Meanwhile, 2nd Canadian Corps soldiered on in Italy, with 1st Canadian Infantry Division, 1st Canadian Armoured Brigade, and 5th Canadian Armoured Division under the command of Lieutenant-General E.L.M. Burns. Over the next several months, the plans and arrangements of the past four years would be put to the ultimate test, and everyone, politician and general alike, would find out whether the reinforcement system that had been created would be sufficient to meet the increased demands that would now be placed on it.

Yet by early June 1944 the fate of the army's reinforcement system had already been largely decided. Since mid-1943, the huge home defence forces that had been created earlier in the war had been considerably reduced. In the search for men for the army, air force, navy, and agricultural and industrial production, Canadian society had come to be mobilized on a scale never seen in the country's history, before or since. Unfortunately, these measures had not been sufficient to find the numbers demanded by the army, and by early 1944 the limits were rapidly being reached, by extending the age groups and classes of men liable for training, by calling out residents who were not Canadian citizens, and by making more and more systematic efforts to locate defaulters and deserters who had managed to evade the NRMA up to that point in the war.

No matter how hard commanders pushed, the NRMA's capacity to encourage further voluntary enlistment had been exhausted.

All of this set the stage for the final crisis over conscription in October and November 1944. By early 1944, the NRMA and the way it had been administered by army officials had come to shape not only the character of the country's armed forces but also the debate that would now emerge. As the year went on, all of the factors that had been set in place before that time began to come together, to make the situation increasingly a political rather than a military problem, and one that both sides would eventually have to face head on. In the end it would force both to a decision that they had created the entire compulsory military training system to try to avoid.

8

Revolt or Realization? The NRMA and the Conscription Crisis of 1944

In late 1944, conscription exploded once more onto the public agenda. It resulted in another round of dramatic debates among the country's highest political leaders, in what has come to be known by historians as the "second conscription crisis," in contrast to the earlier one over amending the NRMA in January to June 1942. This time, it was sparked more by difficulties internal to the Canadian army overseas, and it was of more concern to English than to French Canadians, opponents among the latter group having resigned themselves after the plebscite of 1942 to it being brought in eventually. Still, Prime Minister King's central concern remained to avoid dividing the two groups any more than absolutely necessary to end the war. For J.L. Ralston and the senior commanders of the Canadian army, the concern was to find enough men to keep units that were heavily engaged in Europe at least close to the strength necessary to allow them to continue operations. As was noted at the beginning of this book, at the moment of most extreme tension on November 22, 1944, King finally agreed to order 16,000 conscripts overseas. But he did so only after convincing himself that he had been forced to do so by his senior generals, who were on the verge of wresting control of the country's political affairs away from the government. He conveniently forgot that he was also facing a number of pressures from public opinion, as well as from members of his own Cabinet, to extend conscription, and the correspondingly much more real threat of the political collapse of his government. Even Bruce Hutchison, who first reported the notion of the army revolt in a sympathetic biography of the prime minister, suggested that King had created the threat largely in his own mind, to convince himself to do what was politically necessary "to save his Government, his nation, and himself."[1]

King's accusations do raise a number of questions about the actions of senior officers in 1944. In the view of R.M. Dawson,

> while it is true that there was no revolt in the Canadian army, there was a real trial of strength between the civil and the military powers. There is no doubt that

> the soldiers were playing with political gunpowder and the consequences could have been catastrophic if a few matches had been carelessly tossed around by irresponsible participants. In this sense, and in this sense only, there was an army revolt, and it succeeded.[2]

In contrast, C.P. Stacey presented most of the army's actions as correct and proper in his 1970 study of the crisis from the military's point of view. The generals knew what their political superiors did not seem willing to admit: that by that point in the war there was no other option but to send conscripts overseas. So it was not surprising that by late November one senior officer had resigned in protest at the policy and that others seemed ready to do so – the development that King viewed as an impending revolt. In a democracy such as Canada's, resignation was the only alternative open to military or civilian officials who could not in all good faith follow policies that their political superiors ordered them to carry out. In Stacey's words, "the government's military advisors had exercised their constitutional function with complete propriety."[3]

The problem in attempting to understand the events of October and November 1944 is that in practice the situation was not nearly so simple of a matter of right and wrong. Some senior officers did go beyond the strict limits of civil-military relations in the actions they took, breaking down the barrier that many authorities consider should be maintained between the military's role of providing professional advice to its civilian masters, and the latter's right to make all decisions with respect to policy. At no time in a healthy system of civil-military relations is it considered proper for the military to go beyond that point. And the difficulties had been caused by their pressing for such a large army in 1940–42. Yet ultimately the CWC had approved this policy, in spite of some of its members' reservations. Another important part of the civil-military relationship is the politicians' responsibility to consider the military's advice carefully when making decisions.[4] In peacetime Canada the army had never had a strong place in this relationship, but in the circumstances of 1940 and 1941 it had gained enough influence, and H.D.G. Crerar had done such a careful job in proferring it, that its advice was accepted.[5] By 1944, the pendulum had begun to swing back, and in hindsight King was justifiably not willing to go the one further step politically that in his mind would mean his breaking faith with French Canadians. In the particular circumstances of the fall of 1944, what he and some of his colleagues seemed to fail to understand was just how certain some of their senior officers were that the voluntary system had failed. Many had spent years attempting to make the current conscription policies work, with the results and consequences that have been discussed in earlier chapters of this book. By late 1944, in their minds, these efforts were no longer succeeding, and some of them tried in every way possible to convince the government of this fact. In the end, if the federal Cabinet refused to accept their recommendations, the politicians were fully within their right to do so. But in that case it was the duty of generals who could not support the policy to resign and make way for others who were prepared to carry it out.

Thus, the real issue for historians is to try to understand why these senior officers saw the situation in the way they did by late 1944. And in this respect, once again it is vitally important to understand the context set by the NRMA and the system the army had constructed around it. By the time the final crisis came in 1944, the actions of both sides were being shaped in significant ways by the views they had come to hold about the NRMA, and for the army in particular by its last four years of interaction with the tens of thousands of men who had served under that authority. Many of the problems that had emerged by late 1944 had been brought on by the army itself, as a result of the way it had organized the compulsory military training system in previous years so as to make it such an integral part of building and maintaining the "big army." These developments had not necessarily been intended to lead to conscription being extended to overseas service. But by this point, to J.L. Ralston and to almost all of the army's planners, it was clear that the NRMA was no longer operating as intended. It was now their duty to admit that they had been wrong, and to deal with the problem regardless of the personal or professional costs to themselves or to the army as an institution, in order to ensure that the war was concluded as quickly and with as little cost as possible.

Consequently, throughout the events of October and November 1944, what was really going on was a process of educating the army's political masters. Given the short time available in which to act, it is not surprising that in a few cases the military officers who were trying to make their superiors aware of the situation behaved inappropriately. In addition, thanks to the way the NRMA had been applied in Canada over the past four years, thousands of conscripts almost seemed too conveniently available to be sent overseas, and this may have made the army's leaders less willing to compromise and pursue other expedients. Yet, ultimately, it can be said that their actions succeeded. Whether the prime minister justified his change of position as a result of a revolt by his generals or on other grounds, he finally admitted the true seriousness of the problem by late November, and agreed to extend conscription to overseas service. Unfortunately, the army would later pay the price for its actions, losing much of the prestige and influence it had built up among its political superiors for its apparently successful management of the war up until then, and among the Canadian public for the scale of its contributions to the fighting overseas; this

Figure 23 W.L.M. King and J.L. Ralston, the two key protagonists during the second conscription crisis of October–November 1944, speaking upon Ralston's return from a trip to England in October 1942. *Source:* LAC, C-024697.

consequently frustrated the designs of men such as Crerar who had had such high hopes that the military would exercise greater influence in Canada in the postwar years.

This chapter reviews much that is already known about the conscription crisis of October and November 1944. But in doing so, it focuses on the role of the compulsory military training system that had been set up under the NRMA in shaping the debates, and thus the larger context that influenced events on both sides. The Allied invasion of Normandy on June 6, 1944, led to the failure of Crerar's effort to use the NRMA to build up a big army overseas that could survive on a voluntary basis alone. It also marked a watershed for the NRMA. With the invasion came a rise in tensions between NRMA recruits and their general service counterparts, and among the officers who commanded both groups. The latter came to see themselves as carrying out an almost impossible duty as they continued to try to convince more NRMA men to volunteer for overseas service. The result was the developments that took place within the federal Cabinet and across the country in the fall of 1944, and during which King and some other political leaders came to feel that the army was unduly resisting the policies of its superiors, whether or not that was in fact the case.

As HISTORIAN R.H. Roy has noted, the beginning of the Allied invasion of Normandy marked a dividing point in relations between conscripts and volunteers. Before then, there had been little evidence of open animosity between the two groups. Afterwards, tensions increased as people in Canada became more aware of how involved their soldiers were in the fighting overseas.[6] At the same time, authorities launched a new nationwide recruiting campaign, aimed specifically at NRMA men but in a new way, by targeting their friends, families, and the general public to press them to volunteer for overseas service.[7] One of the most immediate results of the invasion itself was a noticeable surge in conversions among conscripts. The number "going active" in June more than tripled to 3,259 from the previous month's total of 1,025, before falling back to the previous level in July – although figures would remain higher throughout the summer than they had been in the early months of 1944.[8] Nevertheless, these numbers were not nearly as high as had been hoped, especially as June wore on and the nature of the fighting in France became more clear. A week after D-Day, Ralston called on his Cabinet colleagues to reduce recruiting for the navy and air force, a request that C.G. Power met by suspending all activities until October.[9] As Power commented to his son in late June: "At the present time Ralston wants a certain number of men for General Service every month and he is just about getting them by the skin of his teeth."[10] Further cuts were also made to anti-aircraft units and other coast defence formations in Canada, now that the threat of attack seemed to be that much lower, in an attempt to release another 4,000 general service soldiers for overseas.[11]

These developments, along with the army's earlier recruiting campaigns among home defence units in April and May, provoked a number of incidents that began to expose more sharply the differences between "A" and "R" recruits. In May, Major-General Pearkes acknowledged that one "very minor brawl" had taken place between a general service and an NRMA soldier during 13th Canadian Infantry Brigade's recruiting drive in British Columbia, although he passed it off as "obviously the result of a glass of beer and ... of an extremely minor nature."[12] In late June, another disturbance involving as many as two hundred men was linked to a fight between an NRMA and a general service recruit at A-1 Canadian Artillery Training Centre in Petawawa, Ontario. Discipline had apparently deteriorated to the point that a sergeant was thrown to the ground and "pick[ed] on" by several men for trying to break up the fight. When another soldier tried to intervene, the participants argued about "whether he was fighting for the General Service or the N.R.M.A." In investigating the dispute, Ralston uncovered evidence of another case two months earlier in the neighbouring A-2 Artillery Training Centre, where a fight had been sparked by one general service recruit objecting to another singing a song in French. This incident may again have been related to anti-NRMA sentiments, and if nothing else it revealed the general strain that existed between some English- and French-speaking soldiers by that stage in the war.[13]

In mid-July, tensions between NRMA and general service men erupted further into the open at Currie Barracks (A-16 Canadian Infantry Training Centre), in Calgary, Alberta. A story carried by Canadian Press reported that a group of 150 general service and NRMA recruits had taken part in a "battle" at the camp, during which "rifles and bayonets were brandished."[14] Further investigation revealed that no weapons had actually been used, and the centre's acting commandant, Lieutenant-Colonel J.O.R. Evans, reported that fewer than one hundred men had been involved. The incident had been sparked by an encounter between two NRMA sentries and an inebriated general service soldier, after the latter had attempted to follow two members of the Canadian Women's Army Corps back to their huts through the sentries' lines and fallen off the bicycle he was riding at the time. Conveniently forgetting the details of the event in his drunken state, he reported to friends that his cuts and bruises had been caused by the sentries. The following night, fifteen to twenty general service men returned to the NRMA men's hut, turning over beds and breaking windows before nearby officers and NCOs arrived to disperse the crowd that had formed outside. The incident proved to be the most serious example of tensions between the two groups during the war.[15] But as Evans suggested in his initial report to Ottawa: "At present, when the friends and relatives of the Active boys are becoming casualties on the several battle fronts, a very bitter feeling exists against N.R.M.A. personnel."[16]

In the investigation that followed, several witnesses confirmed these sentiments. Other slights that were said to have contributed to the tensions were the greater ease with which NRMA men could obtain leaves or take vocational courses, as well as NRMA men being driven in trucks during a field exercise while volunteers marched, or conscripts being served soup in the mess when "G.S." men were not. In both these cases, local officers noted that the events had been blown out of proportion. At the same time, NRMA recruits were not blameless, reportedly referring to general service volunteers as "General-" or "Government-Suckers."[17]

Another illustration of the heightened tensions that existed at this time is a song that was originally thought to have sparked the disturbance in Calgary, and was preserved by authorities at NDHQ in Ottawa and is reproduced as the frontispiece to this book. Called "Salute to a Zombie," it was sung to the tune of "My Darling Clementine" and had been heard in the local canteen a few weeks before the events in Calgary. The copy filed at NDHQ was forwarded by an anonymous soldier in British Columbia, who commented on the bottom of the page that "this is what we find on the table when we go on meal parade."[18] The song emphasized the "shame" of being a zombie and the resentment at NRMA men for sharing the army's benefits but not the costs of serving overseas, and ended with a call for the zombies to go active. It was not the only pejorative work that was produced during the war; several others have been reproduced at the beginning of most of the parts of this book (and see in particular "Seventy Thousand Zombies" at the beginning of Part 4). Undoubtedly, these songs and other wartime pieces of doggerel had an impact on the men subjected to them in training centres and home defence units across the country.

In September 1944, a story appeared in the *Victoria Times* that indicates how greatly tensions had increased between the zombies and the broader public by then, and that provides a good summary of attitudes in the weeks before the second Cabinet crisis over conscription. As the *Times* put it, citizens in Duncan, British Columbia, were "enraged with the home defence men." The report quoted a local citizen and member of the Pacific Coast Militia Rangers, who despite being an army officer did not seem to think it imprudent to comment publicly that:

> "When they first came here ... they were handsomely treated – the Canadian Legion War Services ran a canteen for them and the I.O.D.E. worked hard to entertain them and make them at home."
>
> Now, he said, the men boast they'll never fight, talk disparagingly and insultingly of active service men and are generally provocative in the presence of other soldiers who wear the G.S. badge.[19]

Fortunately, tensions do not seem to have risen beyond that stage before November 1944. But even at this level they were serious, and given such sentiments it is hardly surprising that few remaining NRMA soldiers were willing to change their mind and volunteer for overseas service.

As these events were transpiring in Canada, the fighting intensified overseas. The Canadian army was large enough to be granted sole responsibility for one of the five D-Day beaches, and the RCAF and RCN provided considerable support to various Allied forces. Casualties among ground troops were lighter than expected on June 6. But the campaign quickly degenerated into a costly battle to break out of the early bridgeheads, against strong opposition from German forces, especially in the British and Canadian sectors. Canadians played key roles in some of the toughest battles. Operations ended up lasting much longer than most planners had expected, and some Canadian units fought almost continuously from early June until the end of August. Then, instead of resting, First Canadian Army (with British and other troops under command, in place of I Canadian Corps, which was still in Italy) was assigned the task of liberating the French ports along the coast of the English Channel for most of September, to open them to Allied shipping. They then captured the approaches to the even larger and more vital Belgian port of Antwerp, in what would become known as the Scheldt campaign, and went on until the start of November. Between June and November, the Canadian army suffered approximately 25,000 casualties in northwest Europe, a large proportion in front-line infantry units, and only after the Scheldt were Canadian units finally withdrawn and placed in reserve. The worst part was that after having expected some lulls in the fighting during that period to be able to rest and rebuild but receiving none, Canadian formations in northwest Europe spent from late 1944 until the beginning of the following February away from the main action. This allowed the reinforcement stream to catch up and begin to meet the army's needs once again, just when everybody had been fearing as they debated conscription back home that the numbers would be running out completely overseas. But after having gotten their estimates for expected periods of activity so wrong over the previous six months, and hoping repeatedly for a break that had not yet come, neither Ralston nor his generals were prepared to take any further chances in October and November 1944.[20]

The story of the crisis that emerged in Canada's overseas reinforcement organization in the summer of 1944 has been told elsewhere and does not need to be explored in extensive detail here.[21] But three problems came together by October to help bring the Canadian army to the point where it was facing an imminent shortage of men. In the first place, lacking their own experience with which to estimate casualty rates, Canadian generals had relied on British calculations, which before 1943 had been based almost entirely on operations in North Africa and other theatres around the world, and on largely defensive rather than offensive battles in the early years of the war. As a result, casualties fell short of expectations in Italy and northwest Europe for some non–front-line troops in 1943–44, while those among infantrymen came to be far higher than projected.

This problem was aggravated by a second factor. Like their colleagues in most western armies, Canadian leaders had crafted their formations based on experiences early in the war, which suggested that mechanized operations and firepower would be the key elements in future campaigns. Instead, from the beginning of the Allied operations in which Canada was involved in Italy in 1943, infantrymen bore the brunt of the fighting. They suffered 75 percent of all casualties among Canadian units, rather than the 50 percent upon which reinforcement pools had been based. The figures would be very similar in northwest Europe in 1944.[22] Thus, even before June 1944, surpluses of some types of Canadian soldiers were piling up in overseas depots, while infantry reinforcements fell below the levels commanders considered necessary to sustain operations for a reasonable period.

The third factor that finally brought conscription back to the political level as an issue in 1944 was that the fighting in northwest Europe turned out to be much longer and more intense than officials had predicted. Thanks again to their own lack of direct experience, Canadian army planners had relied on British forecasts, which assumed that the intensity of operations would vary over time, permitting reinforcement pools to be rebuilt between major battles. Instead, after late August 1944 every Canadian formation was actively involved in almost continuous combat, both in Italy and in northwest Europe, and losses began accumulating at an alarming rate, with little relief until November.

Thus, the real difficulty that led to political problems in Canada was shortages not of all volunteers, but rather of very specific types. As early as April, Lieutenant-General Stuart, who had become Chief of Staff at Canadian Military Headquarters in London the previous December, made arrangements to begin "remustering" Canadians in England, and large numbers of surplus armoured troopers, artillerymen, and soldiers from other arms suddenly found themselves posted to infantry establishments for retraining as infantrymen. For some, the change may have been particularly ironic, considering that as we have seen, sizable numbers of NRMA recruits had been encouraged to go active after basic training so that they could join these same corps and arms to avoid infantry service. At least a few such men must have been overseas by 1944 and suddenly found themselves becoming infantrymen anyhow. Along with these efforts in England, authorities in Canada spent the next several months shipping as many infantry volunteers as possible, in place of planned drafts of other arms, a decision that helped lead to the east and west coast recruiting drives described in the previous chapter.[23] By the end of the summer, new policies required all NRMA men of suitable categories who were prepared to volunteer for overseas service to do so as infantry.

By mid-1944, then, a number of efforts were under way to address infantry shortages overseas. Ultimately, over 12,500 other ranks were remustered overseas between late April 1944 and January 1945. Although Stuart would later be criticized for attempting to retrain Canadian soldiers instead of simply announcing his difficulties immediately to the government, at first the policy seemed to make sense, and most men were given sufficient time to prepare fully for their new roles. As C.P. Stacey has noted, the Canadian government had made its position against conscription for overseas service very clear, and Stuart was particularly aware of these views, both personally, and professionally as the former CGS. As a result, he tried to deal with the situation quietly in England – not so much to avoid politicians discovering that the army had miscalculated its needs, as one might conclude in reading his actions, but more likely to try to protect those politicians from having to deal with the issue in the first place. Where Stuart erred was in taking it upon himself to do this without at least informing his superiors more fully of the potential for trouble, or better yet asking explicitly for their permission, a task which it was his duty to do as one of the government's most senior military advisers.[24]

Furthermore, clearly Stuart and other senior figures within DND still viewed the conscripts as a source of manpower of last resort. As early as January 1943, while still CGS, he had written that the continued presence of NRMA men in the home defence forces would "provide us with a strategic reserve available to meet unforeseen future contingencies, not only in Canada but also overseas should the situation so demand ... This might be necessary if voluntary recruiting should fall below the minimum required for overseas reinforcement requirements or in the event of the First Canadian Army suffering casualties over and above the rate of replenishment being provided."[25] In presenting his plans to reduce the size of the country's forces in August 1943, he had again justified retaining some men in uniform in Canada, not only for strategic reasons but as "a potential source of reinforcements for the Canadian Army overseas."[26] By February 1944, Ralston himself was stating publicly in the House of Commons that one reason the NRMA men were being kept in uniform was in case they were later needed overseas.[27] In June, an anonymous adviser (most likely Major-General H.F.G. "Harry" Letson, who had replaced B.W. Browne as Adjutant-General in 1942) was even more open in a private memorandum to Ralston, commenting: "Up to the present, reinforcement demands have been met entirely on a voluntary basis but should this become impossible in the future I have no doubt that the Military Members [of the Defence Council, within NDHQ] will advise you to obtain authority to utilize these N.R.M.A. soldiers as reinforcements on a compulsory basis." Either Ralston or his correspondent later altered the second part of the above sentence to end less explicitly: "should this become impossible in the future these N.R.M.A. soldiers are available and trained as reinforcements on a compulsory basis." As the memorandum added, however, even the number of men enrolled as conscripts under the NRMA had been falling for months. Consequently, "even without any conversions to G.S. status whatsoever current enrollments under the N.R.M.A. would not be more than sufficient to provide for estimated normal wastage," a sign that even relying on the NRMA might not be enough to meet the army's needs for long.[28] Ralston's friend and colleague, A.L. Macdonald, the minister for naval services, recorded Ralston making similar comments to the Liberal caucus a few days later.[29] At almost exactly the same time, Grant Dexter set down his own perceptive observation that although Ralston seemed to be genuinely trying to work within the current voluntary system, he was also acting just as politicians had done before conscription was introduced during the First World War, when they "had known the hopelessness of the situation for months but had delayed action in order that the proof should become 'overmastering' and therefore the country be unified in support of the policy."[30]

In the meantime, events in Canada went on much as before. As Stacey has again noted, Ralston was aware of some of the early warnings of danger overseas, and had appointed Stuart as Chief of Staff in London in December 1943 partly to keep track of the manpower situation there.[31] He also continued to worry about finding men in Canada. Although he does not seem to have been aware of the precise degree of the threat that existed overseas by the end of the summer, he kept track of figures more fully than some previous historians have suggested. In early June, Letson reported that based on current predictions of enlistment in Canada, and conversion rates among the NRMA, there would be enough men to meet existing needs overseas until at least the end of 1944, but only if the rate of volunteering did not fall lower than it already had among either conscripts or the general public, and only by using more men drawn from home defence units to make up the current difference between these figures and the army's requirements overseas. Ominously, by the end of the year suitable general service personnel from those units would "have shrunk to below 20,000, and will be approaching the point where further withdrawals may not be feasible."[32]

Along with these developments in the summer of 1944, Ralston and the rest of the CWC were facing new political difficulties. In mid-June, C.P. McTague, the national chairman of the Progressive Conservative Party, rebelled against efforts by John Bracken and some of its other new leaders to shift it slightly to the left politically and away from some of its more traditional positions, such as support for conscription. In a nomination speech to his riding association (and with Bracken present), McTague publicly demanded that the federal government send conscripts overseas to aid the fighting in Europe. At the same time, the Liberal Party was facing challenges from much further left on the political spectrum in the form of the CCF, which had become the official provincial Opposition party after an election in Ontario in August 1943, and then swept to victory in Saskatchewan in June 1944.[33] By September, Prime Minister King's thoughts had turned to the federal election he would have to call by 1945, and plans for reorganizing his Cabinet to emphasize the tasks of re-establishing civilian society and the economy after the war.[34] In the middle of the month,

Figure 24 The Cabinet War Committee, 1943. Front row, left to right: C.G. Power (Minister of National Defence for Air), T.A. Crerar (Minister of Mines and Resources), W.L.M. King (Prime Minister, and Secretary of State for External Affairs), J.L. Ralston (Minister of National Defence), and J.L. Ilsley (Minister of Finance). Rear row, left to right: A.L. Macdonald (Minister of National Defence for Naval Services), J.E. Michaud (Minister of Transport), C.D. Howe (Minister of Munitions and Supply), and Louis St. Laurent (Minister of Justice). *Source:* LAC, C-026922.

both the Cabinet and the CWC began considering the roles Canadians would play in the Pacific war in 1945, and finalizing demobilization policies for the large numbers of men and women who were expected to be released from the armed forces with the end of the fighting in Europe.[35]

Optimism about the war led to another action that marred relations between individual ministers in Canada, just as problems of manpower were beginning to loom larger overseas. In mid-September, Canada played host to the second Quebec Conference between Winston Churchill and Franklin Roosevelt. During the conference, King and most of his ministers took time to attend a dinner for Liberal Party workers at the Quebec Reform Club, during which the prime minister in his own words "spoke about conscription and how I had maintained the position that there would be no conscription unless it were absolutely necessary. That I never believed it was necessary. Now men saw for themselves those who had served had done so voluntarily."[36] According to A.L. Macdonald, King's words had even more meaning to the others who heard them. As Macdonald described the speech:

> "Have you had conscription," he [King] asked. "If you have not had it up to now, is it likely that you will ever have it when the war in Europe is nearing its end?" What we have said was that we would only apply conscription if it was absolutely necessary. It has not been necessary up to the present, but if it should become necessary, then somebody else would have to enforce it, and he would back out of public life. He hoped, however, that if he did that he would not have to go alone, but that some Liberals would go with him.[37]

Considering that King was speaking in Quebec City, and the informal and partisan nature of the dinner, it is not surprising that he took the opportunity to make such statements. He was also clearly carried away by the emotion of the moment. Moreover, the experiences of the past few days in Quebec City seem to have convinced King and a number of other Cabinet ministers that the war was almost over. But the story of the speech grew with the telling.[38] For Ralston, who had not been present but heard about it from Macdonald and others, the statement was especially offensive, in that the prime minister appeared to be repudiating the entire policy that he had agreed upon in Cabinet in 1942. As a former military man, and in view of the difficulties he had been facing over the past two years trying to keep the overseas army at full strength, he also knew better than to make such assumptions. As Grant Dexter later noted, Ralston discussed the matter with King, but the two could not agree on the exact meaning the words conveyed: "So nothing much happened, except that the Col. hates his guts more than ever."[39]

Yet as the summer came to an end there were few signs of an impending crisis overseas. News of the war's progress seemed positive, as Allied forces finally broke out of Normandy in late August and advanced rapidly across the rest of northern France, and into Belgium, and seized Antwerp at the beginning of September. Unfortunately, German troops had not vacated the approaches to the port, and only later in the month did commanders began to realize that the war might not be won in a matter of weeks, as many people had begun to hope. In mid-September, Field-Marshal Bernard Montgomery launched his famous attempt to end the war before the end of 1944, with Operation Market Garden – the failure of which helped ensure that the conflict would last well into 1945, although it would take the public longer than the generals at the front to become aware of this fact.[40]

In addition, despite early hints of problems in France, Stuart returned to Canada to appear before the CWC in late July, to request permission to raise the strength of the overseas army by another 6,000 men, 1,764 of whom had already been committed to new units. He also recommended establishing a 12th Canadian Infantry Brigade in Italy, an expedient that had been suggested by British commanders there to increase the amount of infantry in 5th Canadian Armoured Division so that it could carry out all of its required tasks in the theatre. Although Stuart proposed using men already in Italy to create the 12th Brigade, including anti-aircraft and armoured car units that were no longer needed for their primary duties, it still meant that yet more infantry would be needed to replace losses once the new formation went into action. As Stuart reported to the CWC in a well-known statement on August 3, "although the Army had been fighting for some twelve months in Italy and two months in France, the reinforcement situation was very satisfactory. At present there were reinforcement personnel available for three months at the intensive battle casualty rate ... The only factor which was causing anxiety was the shortage of reinforcement personnel for French Canadian units."[41] After the reinforcement crisis erupted in October, Stuart was roundly vilified for making these statements, not least by the members of the CWC. But before leaving for Canada in July, Stuart had authorized new efforts to remuster men from various corps overseas, and at that point it was still assumed that First Canadian Army would be able to count on a break from operations by the end of August. Thus, the problem did not seem to be nearly as dangerous then as it does in hindsight. Nevertheless, one has to wonder at Stuart's confidence in requesting yet more men for overseas service even as potential difficulties were beginning to mount.

Six weeks later, in fact, Stuart's assertions came into question in a very public way. On September 18, 1944, Major Conn Smythe returned to Toronto, where he was very well known as the owner of the Toronto Maple Leafs of the National Hockey League, after having been wounded commanding his 30th Light Anti-Aircraft Battery in France. A day later, the *Globe and Mail* published charges by Smythe that the Canadian army was facing a serious shortage of manpower in Europe and that soldiers were entering combat without proper training. Smythe ended by calling for the trained men of the NRMA to be sent overseas. According to his own later account in his memoirs, his view of the situation had been shaped while recovering from his wounds overseas, as he spoke to a number of men about their experiences in both France and Italy. After consulting with the publisher of the *Globe*, George McCullagh, a personal friend and like Smythe a firm opponent of the government's conscription policies, Smythe decided to make his concerns public.[42] At first, his statement attracted little notice in Ottawa, and was assumed to be merely another attempt to turn conscription into a political issue. But as newspaper stories began to increase, eventually ministers were forced to pay greater attention.[43] According to other sources, Ralston had already begun to worry about the tone of recent reports from England related to manpower, and decided to investigate further.[44] In early October he left for Europe to see the situation for himself.

What Ralston found when he arrived in the war zone confirmed Smythe's views, but for somewhat different reasons than Smythe had alleged. After investigating the charges of lack of reinforcements, Ralston concluded that in most cases the men were more than adequately qualified. More significantly for events at the time, during visits to Italy and northwest Europe he began to uncover the more general problems that the army had been facing in maintaining its infantry forces overseas, and that had grown worse in late August and September as reserves fell and efforts to remuster men failed to meet requirements in the field. Stuart now admitted that based on the experiences of the past four months, casualties would be far higher in the future than anticipated. And after remustering and shipping all remaining volunteer infantrymen available from Canada, reinforcements for this arm would be completely exhausted by January 1945. Ralston also heard a number of complaints from men in the field. Some troops, especially in Italy, had now served in Europe for almost five years without receiving a furlough to visit Canada. Others called attention to the government's refusal to send NRMA men overseas, which seemed to them to be a sign of their country's lack of support for its volunteer soldiers.[45] Ralston returned to Canada in mid-October, accompanied by Stuart. On October 19 he presented the disheartening news to the CWC, along with Stuart's recommendation that the government find the men necessary to keep the army's reinforcement pools up to strength by extending the NRMA to include overseas service.[46]

The information came as a shock to several members, and particularly the prime minister. In the face of the overly optimistic reports that were still appearing in his evening newspapers, and some of his more official telegrams reporting war news from the government of Great Britain, King could not bring himself to believe that the situation was as serious as Ralston had made it out to be. Over the next few days, he advanced a number of reasons for avoiding the policy. The change would have to be introduced in the House of Commons, and likely fought out in a general election, and it would have a number of impacts on Canada's allies. At one stage, he even suggested that extending compulsory military service to Europe would prevent world peace after the war, because Canada would not be able to take the lead in creating postwar organizations. As the debates went on it became clear, as he had stated on the first day, that while he "wished to do everything possible to win the war, including overseas conscription were this necessary ... he could not bring himself to say that it was."[47]

In contrast, Ralston and several of his colleagues reminded King of the latter's 1942 promise that if conscription became "necessary" – a definition they had taken to mean militarily – then it would be introduced without delay. They also disagreed with the prime minister's reading of domestic politics. In response to suggestions that Canada cut back its forces overseas, Ralston and Stuart both pointed out that the Canadian army had been organized to fight in the front lines of the western Allies, as one small part of a much larger force, and thus there were few ways to cut troops without directly affecting operations at the "sharp end."[48] King himself made a few tenuous attempts to sound out Churchill and Roosevelt, in the hope that they would be willing to help him out of his difficulties, although even he seems to have recognized the objections that would have been raised had he officially asked British or American soldiers to take on a larger share of the war effort so that Canada could avoid sending conscripts overseas.[49]

Throughout the rest of October, most of the government's key ministers met almost daily to discuss the issue, either in the CWC or the full Cabinet. Despite lengthy deliberations, within a few days it had become clear that neither side would back down. Both were obviously torn over their views of the war effort overseas, and their precise definitions of "necessary." As King pointed out on more than one occasion, there was no reason to assume that the fighting would go on continuously for the rest of the year, as it had up until now (a reading of the situation that later proved to be correct). But, having made such an embarrassing mistake by relying on more optimistic forecasts earlier in the summer, it is not surprising that Stuart took a more pessimistic view, along with Ralston and a few other members of Cabinet.

One of King's most telling criticisms came when he called both Ralston and Stuart to task for coming to him at all with news of a shortage of reinforcements. "Throughout the whole course of the war," he was recorded as saying, "he had always asked in respect of any increase in the size of the Army if the particular increase in question jeopardized the Government's policy in respect to volunteer enlistment for overseas. He had always been assured in this respect by the Government's military advisors."[50] Of course, as we have seen, the difficulty was not a shortage of all reinforcements, but only of infantry, a problem that could not easily have been foreseen before 1944. Still, in a broader sense

King's comments were valid. And in leading things to this stage the NRMA had played a key role. It had helped encourage commanders to create the big army overseas in the first place, and their political superiors to approve it. And by 1944 the army's commanders were relying heavily on the NRMA just to keep these forces up to strength. Even before the shortage of reinforcements began to appear, there was little flexibility built into the system to find yet more men if a problem such as the current one emerged. That it would be likely to cause a major crisis was almost inevitable by this point.

In addition, the knowledge that a large body of NRMA men existed that could easily be sent overseas clearly influenced the actions of opponents on both sides of the issue in late 1944. From the point of view of the pro-conscriptionists, as both Ralston and Stuart noted at different times (although in Stuart's case, only by stepping onto political ground on which it was not properly his place to tread), it would be difficult to convince Canadian soldiers overseas or the public at home that firm measures such as reducing voluntary units were necessary, when such a large, well-trained group of men remained available in Canada.[51] On October 23, Lieutenant-General J.C. Murchie, the current CGS, suggested a number of expedients that might find at least a few more general service infantry reinforcements from among home defence forces in Canada. These included reducing physical standards for infantry; accelerating training by prohibiting embarkation leaves and shipping men directly from advanced training centres to reinforcement organizations overseas; moving surplus men from other arms and shipping them directly to England for remustering there; forcing NCOs and other skilled personnel to go overseas as general duty infantry; and cutting the minimum age for men to serve in Europe from nineteen to eighteen-and-a-half. But all of these steps would add only another 5,500 infantrymen to the army's reinforcement pools by the end of the year, which revealed the true seriousness of the crisis.[52] Such expedients might have delayed the army's difficulties for at least a few weeks and given authorities a little more time to consider other solutions. Most of Murchie's suggestions were in fact approved by the CWC, then quickly forgotten over the next few days as the political crisis in the Cabinet heated up.[53] But because of the ease with which the need for 15,000 infantry could apparently be met by sending NRMA men overseas, Ralston and his supporters continued to press firmly for that action. As King confided to his diary on October 25: "What annoys me about the Defence Dept. is that any proposal made, short of conscription of N.R.M.A. men, meets with instant rejection."[54]

On the other side, as noted at the beginning of Chapter 7, several ministers were shocked when they discovered that 120,000 general service soldiers remained in uniform in Canada. As C.G. Power wrote in his memoirs: "I, for one, found it difficult to understand why it should be necessary, with the great mass of manpower available, to take the drastic steps recommended."[55] As we have seen, the existence of such large numbers was partly the result of the huge organization that had been built up under the NRMA in 1942 and 1943, and that had proven to be much more difficult to cut again afterwards. When Ralston, Power, and A.L. Macdonald were assigned to review the army's figures in late October, to see if any new overseas volunteers could be weeded out of this organization, it quickly became clear that after eliminating men who were already in the training stream and on the way overseas (and thus included in previous forecasts of available reinforcements), and people such as instructors who had to remain in Canada unless the whole training system for future reinforcements was to be shut down, almost every man who seemed to be available to be released from vital duties was too young, too old, or of too low a physical or mental category to be able to serve overseas.[56] Reducing some of that overhead by returning some soldiers to civilian life might at least have freed up other, higher-category men in industry and other occupations to volunteer. Yet that would have required months to accomplish, if not longer, and men seemed to be needed now. In addition, after the years of debate with NSS and other departments over mobilization and leave policies, military leaders were likely reluctant to release what was ultimately a force of last resort that remained under their control should an even greater emergency present itself in the future. At this stage in the war, it was unlikely that Germany would be able to hold on much longer into 1945. But the war with Japan still loomed, and enough conscripts were available who seemed able to meet the immediate need, so that the remaining force could be withheld for possible future contingencies. Nevertheless, the presence of the 120,000 volunteers made it difficult for anticonscriptionists in the government to accept that extending conscription might be necessary to find the required men. Clearly, the way the NRMA had been administered in previous years was coming back to shape all sides of the current debate.

By the end of October, matters seemed to be coming to a head. At that point, Cabinet members were considering one more recruiting drive among NRMA men, a step that King at least was hopeful would produce enough reinforcements to end the crisis. Among the suggestions put forward to improve the chances of the campaign was to alter existing policies to offer NRMA men who volunteered more than the normal war service gratuities and other rewards that they and all volunteers began earning from the time they enlisted, by making them retroactive for several months beforehand. The prime minister also put great emphasis on the impact that he and other ministers might have by making personal appeals and speeches to the NRMA men.[57]

Unfortunately, King's comments only revealed how far he and many ministers remained from understanding the true nature of the situation. During the discussions, Ralston read portions of the report on recruiting in 13th Canadian Infantry Brigade that Brigadier Macklin had prepared earlier in the year. King's response was to note in his diary that "Ralston took up considerable time in reading reports of his officers who had tried to recruit from the N.R.M.A. men. One could see that the officers had been very strongly biased in favour of conscription."[58] As it became more and more clear that an impasse had been reached, Ralston began to threaten more and more firmly to resign if his recommendations were not put into effect without further delay, in the hope of preventing the debate from being drawn out any further.[59] King found a solution to Ralston's threats of resignation in the person of former general A.G.L. McNaughton, who had broken with Ralston and been removed from command of First Canadian Army in December 1943 after opposing sending Canadian troops to Italy. His fall had also come as a result of a loss of confidence in his abilities on the part of his British superiors.[60] King had talked with him several times since his official retirement in September 1944, as he considered making McNaughton the first Canadian-born Governor-General. Then, in mid-October, McNaughton spoke out strongly against conscription for overseas service in a convocation speech at Queen's University. By November 1, after further discussions, the prime minister had decided to make him the new Minister of National Defence.[61]

That decision led to the famous scene of November 1, when King, expecting Ralston to again threaten to resign, suddenly found his opponent softening: Ralston now offered to support one further recruiting campaign among NRMA men, as long as a final deadline was set, after which if it was not successful the decision would be made to send the NRMA men overseas. Instead, the prime minister responded by drawing out the earlier resignation letter that Ralston had delivered to him in 1942, but that he had not accepted at the time, and announcing that he was now doing so. The action was, in the reported words of Cabinet minister Colin Gibson, "cold-blooded," and consequently it has drawn much attention from historians describing the events of October and November 1944.[62]

Another three weeks would pass between McNaughton's accession to power as defence minister and the King government's final decision to institute conscription for overseas service. During that time, commanders across the country were asked to return one more time to the men they had been trying to convince to go active for several years, and make yet another attempt to find volunteers. The events of these three weeks are at the heart of the debate over the alleged army revolt of 1944, for over that period senior officers became involved in a number of incidents that called into question their loyalty in the eyes of politicians (and, later, historians). It was probably understandable that many of them did not have much hope of success, after everything that had gone on in Canada over the previous four years. But they were officers in the Canadian army, and their duty was to serve their political masters to the best of their ability. And many did so, despite their own views that the situation was hopeless. In fact, Ralston had only begun wavering in his own opposition to the idea of another recruiting campaign on November 1, after a telephone call to Major-General Pearkes on the west coast, who seemed to be willing to proceed with another campaign as long as the authorities realized that conversions were not likely to come quickly or in large numbers. Pearkes recommended setting aside a minimum of three weeks to allow any measures to take effect. His support for the campaign came as a surprise to more than one Cabinet minister, some of whom considered him strongly pro-conscriptionist, despite the amount of effort he had put into earlier efforts to find converts among the NRMA men in his command. As King put it on November 1: "In the course of the discussion, MacKinnon [the Minister of Trade and Commerce] came out quite strongly that he thought Pearkes was no good; that he really had not his heart in trying to get the men; he really wanted conscription."[63]

Following the introduction of McNaughton to the Cabinet on November 2, the new recruiting campaign got under way. In the first few days, a Cabinet Recruiting Committee made up of some of the strongest supporters of the proposal prepared a brief report on which to base the effort (and which provided much information on the composition of the NRMA in late 1944, as was referred to in earlier chapters). Members of the committee also received a report on the attitudes of NRMA personnel from the Adjutant-General's office, which summarized the army's views of most of the reasons for resistance to volunteering for general service (and as were discussed in Chapter 6).[64] Thus, the Cabinet was well aware of the challenges that had to be overcome. L.R. LaFlèche, formerly one of the key figures responsible for mobilizing NRMA recruits in the Department of National War Services, and now its minister, prepared a separate report on French Canadian conscripts, and took responsibility for developing special measures aimed at this particular group of men.[65] On November 8, King opened the campaign with a nationwide radio broadcast, and soon afterwards instructions were sent to commanding officers across the country, ordering them to recall the roughly 8,000 NRMA men who were on leave working in agriculture or industry, and to begin concentrating all recruits capable of serving as infantry for retraining in that arm, in order to impress upon them the seriousness of the situation and thus begin the latest effort to find volunteers from among their ranks.[66]

Unfortunately, the A.G.L. McNaughton who took office in November 1944 had had little contact with the country or its home defence forces for much of the war. He had also lost touch with the Canadian army overseas since December 1943. Although outwardly he was still the confident, energetic man whom King and everyone else who came in contact with him had known him to be for a number of years, aside from the very wise expedients mentioned above his campaign relied on little more than his own faith in its success.[67] In McNaughton's view, looking back twenty years later,

> a substantial portion of the N.R.M.A. had been discouraged under the influence of propaganda evidently directed for political and personal motives[,] and with the passing of time and under the pressure to build up a division for employment in the Pacific, the superior recruits and potential NCO's were withheld from the training stream and naturally became increasingly reluctant to accept the liabilities for service in the European theatre and the reduction in rank and pay entailed in the transfer.[68]

In contrast, many Canadians viewed McNaughton almost as a traitor for siding with King against Ralston – an opinion that became clear when he encountered opposition during his first public speech as defence minister in Arnprior, Ontario, on November 5. The following day, he was shouted down when he appeared before a meeting of the Canadian Legion in Ottawa.[69] In the words of Brooke Claxton, who had just entered the Cabinet in October, and who would go on to become defence minister himself in the late 1940s and early 1950s, "I did not like bringing in a general to head off an essentially political difficulty."[70] At least some members of the country's home defence forces also sensed the high degree of animosity that existed between Ralston and McNaughton as a result of the latter's dismissal as commander of First Canadian Army, and assumed that McNaughton had only taken the position to gain revenge on Ralston.[71] McNaughton's animosity extended to Stuart, who had also played a major role in removing him, and one of McNaughton's first acts was to call for Stuart's dismissal (a request Stuart anticipated by submitting his resignation at almost the same moment).[72]

As the days went on, McNaughton took further steps that suggested his lack of understanding of the true situation in Canada, and his assumption that his own popularity and energy would be enough to end the crisis. One of the most well-known was his appearance before a meeting of all District Officers

Commanding (DOCs) and General Officers Commanding from the various military districts and operational headquarters across the country. After summoning them to Ottawa to conduct what most assumed would be a discussion of how to deal with the current challenge of finding further volunteers from among the NRMA, McNaughton merely reviewed the situation, summarized the new policies that would be followed with respect to encouraging the NRMA men to go active, and then reportedly prepared to leave the room. As R.H. Roy has written, in more dramatic fashion than the meeting's official minutes reveal:

> For a moment there was a complete silence. Other officers as well as Pearkes must have wondered whether or not McNaughton had any idea of what had been done already ... He had just about reached the door when several officers rose. Among them was Pearkes who called out "Don't you wish to hear the reports from the District Officers Commanding?" ... McNaughton listened, repeated his declaration that the former generous leave to N.R.M.A. men to work in the farms and fields would be restricted and then left. Certainly his senior officers left him in no doubt whatever about the chances of getting a quick, substantial response which would somehow make the "new" governmental policy a success.[73]

As defence minister, technically McNaughton was correct in his obvious assumption that now that the government's policies had been stated, and he had ordered his subordinates to follow them, it was their responsibility to do so. But his actions gave the impression that he did not even want to hear their advice on the matter. For many officers who not only had taken time out during the current crisis to travel to Ottawa for the meeting but had spent countless hours over the past few years attempting to find ways to convince more NRMA men to go active, it must have seemed clear that none of their political superiors were willing to accept what the government's military servants considered to be the true state of affairs in Canada.

As a consequence, the frustrations of a number of senior officers now began to boil over. Two days after the conference in Ottawa, McNaughton issued a press release implying that the situation was fine, and that as a result of the meeting all of the volunteers needed for overseas would easily be found.[74] That statement sparked Major-General Pearkes and four separate DOCs across the country to write to NDHQ in protest, noting that they had told McNaughton exactly the opposite. Then, on November 20, all of the senior officers in Pearkes's command met in Vancouver for him to pass on the minister's orders from the Ottawa meeting to them. A number spoke to reporters outside the room before the conference began, admitting their own views that the new campaign was not likely to succeed. Although the remarks were made during a time of crisis, and before actually receiving word from Pearkes of McNaughton's views on the situation, the officers went beyond the bounds of acceptable behaviour by expressing such opinions in public. Both McNaughton and King took these men's actions as evidence of a more deliberate attempt to frustrate the government's desire to maintain the policy of voluntary service. On November 22, Brigadier R.A. MacFarlane, one of the DOCs who had challenged McNaughton's press release a few days earlier, followed up on his protests by submitting his resignation as the commander of Military District No. 10 (Manitoba and northwestern Ontario); once again, this was the only acceptable action for an officer to takeif he could not reconcile himself to his government's policies. On the same day, Murchie, the CGS, wrote to McNaughton on behalf of several of the government's senior army advisers to confirm a statement that he had already reportedly made to McNaughton verbally: "After a careful review of all the factors and the latest expression of their views by the District Officers Commanding, I must now advise you that in my considered opinion the Voluntary system of recruiting through Army channels cannot meet the immediate problem."[75]

These events were dramatic. But they do not reflect the behaviour of all senior officers across the country. Even in Pearkes's case, there is evidence that he genuinely intended to make every effort to ensure the campaign's success. As Ralston's son Stuart, who served as an artillery and later a staff officer overseas during the war, reported to C.G. Power in the 1950s,

> I was particularly impressed when I was at Staff College in Kingston in the winter and spring of 1945 to meet Captains and Majors from all over the country and to receive from themselves their accounts as to how hard their commanders from Generals down worked to persuade the Zombies to volunteer and this up to the very last moment. One chap from British Columbia told me that General Pearkes called a meeting of some 2500 officers, being every officer in his command, and that his address to them was absolutely hair-raising in its appeal and urgency that everything possible should be done to make the voluntary system work.[76]

In southwestern Ontario, where the views of NRMA recruits as to why they would not volunteer had been canvassed earlier in the year, the new drive was followed with almost as much attention as the earlier events, and reveals even better some of the difficulties that commanders had faced in most parts of the country up to then, as well as the honest efforts of many officers to find general service recruits. According to records from the headquarters of Military District No. 1, which was responsible for running the November campaign there, it took one week to get organized and begin what its DOC, Brigadier P. Earnshaw, called "a redoubled effort and a new appeal" that would target every individual NRMA recruit suitable for overseas service. Despite being another one of the DOCs who had written to protest McNaughton's press release after the Ottawa meeting of November 14, after returning to London Earnshaw presented his local officers with orders that "I want you to do all possible to get N.R.M.A. soldiers 'to go active.' This appeal can take many forms – to patriotism, to personal gain, etc., etc. You are to ensure that N.R.M.A. soldiers are spoken to either individually or at least in very small groups of 3 or 4, and where possible by yourself." In addition, Earnshaw directed commanders to emphasize Prime Minister King's speech of November 8 in appeals to their men. "In short," he concluded, "I want you, as C.O., to do your very best in every way to get every N.R.M.A. soldier to go active at once, and to ensure that all those fit for it to [*sic*] go into the infantry training stream at the earliest moment."[77]

Over the next few days, reports poured in from commanders throughout the region. But unfortunately the flow of recruits converting to general service remained only a trickle. As one commanding officer put it after noting that only five out of the ninety-three NRMA men in his unit were willing to volunteer, "I can assure you that we made a very fair and strong appeal to these men, and regret to have to report such a poor result."[78] As another officer put it a few days later, his unit contained only one NRMA man suitable for overseas:

> He has been approached regarding "going active" on scores and scores of occasions during the year he has been on strength here. Approach has been made from every conceivable angle, but with no result ... He is of the opinion that he is unfit for service even in Canada, and to that end representations have been made at Ottawa, of which a letter has been received from D.A.A.G. [Deputy Assistant Adjutant-General], M.D. No. 1 today.[79]

Across the country, the results were similar. A meagre 694 NRMA men converted to general service during the first three weeks of November, a relatively large number compared to some of the results in the winter of 1943–44 but still far short of those that the army thought it needed to find in a matter of weeks for overseas.[80]

At the political level, the prime minister was facing another deadline by November 22. The methods King had used to remove Ralston at the start of the month had shocked more than one minister and pushed T.A. Crerar in particular to take an increasingly firm stance in support of conscription as the month went on. He had strongly opposed the growth of the army during the debates of 1941–42, fearing just the difficulties that had now appeared. But by late 1944 he was aware of the strength of calls in English Canada to send NRMA men overseas, and concluded that it needed to be done. So did A.L. Macdonald, J.L. Ilsley, the finance minister, and, by the middle of the month, C.D. Howe ("Howe said he was willing to support any stand Conscription or no Conscription, but for God's sake let us make up our minds").[81] Early in November, both Macdonald and Crerar wrote to King to advocate much the same policy as Ralston had been requesting before he was removed: if the new recruiting drive did not succeed, a firm date needed to be set after which conscripts would be ordered overseas. King's only response was to argue that such views would only weaken efforts to make the drive a success, by assuming in advance that it would fail.[82] But clearly he was beginning to feel more pressure from some of his own Cabinet members to implement conscription for overseas service. And although the pro-conscriptionists remained a minority within the Cabinet, the balance of numbers was beginning to shift. Even Louis St. Laurent, one of the firmest opponents of conscription, and McNaughton himself were beginning to soften on the issue. Macdonald reported St. Laurent as suggesting that now that the initial shock of the shortages had worn off, the situation was much better and conscription might be inevitable, and McNaughton as stating that he wished to pursue the recruiting campaign for two more weeks but after that, "as a soldier, he had an alternative plan in mind ... 'I have put things entrain [*sic*], so that [if] these men have to be moved, they can be moved more quickly than they could have been moved on November 2.'"[83]

By November 22, members of the House of Commons had been recalled from their fall recess, at the request of King, so that his government could explain and defend Ralston's resignation and its current policies. It was now becoming clear that Macdonald, Crerar, and several other ministers were ready to resign, and in fact they met that day and agreed to do so if the prime minister did not accept conscription immediately. The pressures were increasing from every side against his continued adherence to his policy against conscription. In the meantime, McNaughton had telephoned him with Murchie's fateful news about the views of the army's senior commanders. As King described the conversation in an oft-quoted comment, McNaughton "expressed the opinion that it was like a blow in the stomach. He also said that he had the resignation of the Commander in Winnipeg. That if the Commanders, one after the other, began to resign the whole military machine would run down, begin to disintegrate and there would be no controlling the situation." Even more significant is what King then added: "It is apparent to me that to whatever bad management this may have been due, we are faced with a real situation which has to be met and now there is no longer thought as to the nature of the military advice tendered."[84] This settled the issue for him, and for most of the rest of the day he went about preparing the ground for exactly the policy against which he had stood without wavering until that moment. By that evening, the decision had been made, and Cabinet met the next morning to decide on the final form of the Order-in-Council that would send the zombies overseas.

In retrospect, November 22 was clearly the most fateful day of the second conscription crisis. For both McNaughton and King, two of the staunchest opponents of conscription, the developments of the previous few days had seemed to culminate to bring them finally to admit what many of the army's leaders had been trying to get them to understand for some time. In deciding to advocate conscription, both men had clearly been influenced by the actions of a small number of senior officers and by the mounting evidence of the firmness of these men's views. For the prime minister, there were also political considerations: the decision to support the extension of conscription enabled him to head off a political revolt within his Cabinet that, more than an imagined military one, threatened to bring down his government.

In contrast, what was most significant to the army's commanders was simply that the government had finally been brought to see what its military advisers considered to be the reality of the situation. In the end, while at least some of the generals were clearly prepared to follow the precepts of Western civil-military traditions and resign to try to provoke their superiors to see the situation their way, the consequences of their actions were less important to them than the apparent need they saw to send men overseas, to maintain the forces fighting there. As far as they were concerned, the later loss of influence that the army suffered for its behaviour and even charges that they had been plotting against the government were probably acceptable, as long as the result was to keep faith with the men in Europe.

In shaping these views, once again the NRMA had played a significant role. It was not the immediate cause of the crisis in 1944, but it had helped to bring the situation to that point over the longer term. And during the events of October and November 1944, it clearly affected the actions of people on both sides of the debate. For Ralston and several of his senior commanders, there seemed to be little option but to send the conscripts overseas. For King and other opponents of conscription in Cabinet, the crisis marked the point where the army seemed to have betrayed the promises made over the previous few years. The result was a situation where a full month of tension-filled debate had been required before army leaders were finally able to convince the government that conscription really was necessary, in both military and political terms.

Part 5: The Aftermath

The Zombie Prayer[1]

We thank Thee, Lord, for Mackenzie King,
Who keeps his promise not to bring
Such divers[e] trials and tribulations
As making us fight for Allied Nations.
Who looks Canadians in the eye,
and says, "My Zombies shall not die."

We also thank Thee, too, O Lord,
That he provides us with our board,
He gives us lodging, clothes and guns,
But keeps us clear of nasty Huns.

And when our country fights the Japs,
And men are needed to fill the gaps,
And Pray, dear Lord, to spare us boys,
And send those awful G.S. guys.

From Active Service we preserve,
We really haven't got the nerve,
Content we are to serve him well,
Who keeps us from the front line Hell.

Grant us this, O Lord, and we will be,
Always grateful unto Thee.

AMEN

Epilogue: Conscription and Canadians in the Second World War

On November 23, 1944, the federal Cabinet passed Order-in-Council P.C. 8891, authorizing it to send 16,000 Canadian conscripts overseas for service in "the United Kingdom and/or ... European and/or Mediterranean operational theatres."[1] Over the next few weeks, the sense of political crisis in Ottawa lessened. The Liberal government survived the vote in the House of Commons approving its order in the early morning hours of December 8, with the support of a number of its Quebec members. Demonstrations took place in Montreal in the early days, but as *La Presse* noted, the measure was limited to the minimum number of conscripts necessary for the moment, and the focus of the war effort remained voluntary. As Granatstein and Hitsman have added, although many French Canadians felt betrayed by the action, it was also clear by that point that King had done everything he could to avoid taking the step. At the end of the month, the Quebec legislature passed a motion protesting the measure, but for the most part the political crisis was quickly forgotten amidst renewed interest in postwar planning and demobilization, and plans for a federal election as soon as the fighting ended in Europe, in which the Liberals in fact took fifty-three out of fifty-five seats in Quebec that June.[2]

Yet the history of the NRMA did not end with the decision to send Canadian conscripts overseas in November 1944. For the first few days the sense of crisis at the military level was stronger than ever. In British Columbia, where most of the trained NRMA men were located, news of the government's change in policy reached them by radio before it did their officers through more official channels. The result was several disturbances. The most serious came in Terrace, where a sit-down strike by two companies of the *Fusiliers du St. Laurent* led to further protests by most of the men in the camp. For several days, NRMA recruits refused to appear on parade or to obey orders from their officers, and some broke into storerooms and seized ammunition and weapons, including Bren light machine guns and Sten sub-machine guns. Technically, the men were in a state of mutiny, and for a few days the situation was taken very seriously by political and military authorities. The problems were aggravated by the fact that most of the senior officers were away from the camp, dealing with the repercussions of the November 20 conference in Vancouver discussed in the previous chapter. On November 23, Major-General Pearkes had recalled them, after Ottawa ordered him to conduct a full investigation of the comments they had made before the earlier meeting.[3]

Rumours of NRMA men mounting anti-aircraft guns and machine guns around the camp turned out to be much exaggerated, and they continued to carry out fatigues and other duties throughout the "mutiny" in Terrace. Canteens and recreational facilities remained open, and troops viewed movies and played sports much like normal. According to the officers who were still present, most of the men simply insisted that they did not want to be ordered overseas. The comments suggest a different view than that which at least some conscripts had supposedly held in earlier years when they were asked why they refused to volunteer and said that they were waiting for the government to order it. On Saturday, November 25, a large group paraded through the camp, bearing banners with slogans such as "Down With Conscription" and "Zombies Strike Back." As one high-ranking officer described both the sense of order that was maintained among the men and the unreal character of the situation as a whole, "as they passed me a portion of the parade paid their compliments, which I returned and told them as they passed that they were marching damn badly. This parade reminded me rather of an overgrown lot of school boys who had just told the teacher to jump in the lake and she had done it."[4] Two days later another large group of men marched through Terrace itself. The disturbance was clearly a serious breach of military discipline, and in a few cases loaded weapons were openly displayed. Once or twice, soldiers allegedly pointed their rifles at officers who attempted to enter their huts, and threatened violence.[5] When an advance party of the Prince Albert Volunteers (an ironic name for a unit composed almost entirely of NRMA recruits) tried to leave the camp to begin moving overseas on November 28, two-thirds of the men were prevented from reaching the outgoing train by personnel from other units. Armed guards also had to be posted along the rail line after a few threatened to stop the train by force.[6] With units in Terrace numbering as few as six volunteers among their entire other rank personnel, officers could do little except read the relevant sections of the army regulations to their troops, and work on a more personal level to try to convince them to stop their activities. At least one group of twenty-one conscripts even volunteered for overseas service during the Terrace mutiny in protest at their comrades' actions. Eventually, the demonstrations petered out, and by November 30 everyone was back on parade, with almost all ammunition and weapons returned to the camp's stores. Within a few days units of the 15th Brigade had begun leaving the town, on the first stage of their journey overseas.[7]

While the Terrace mutiny has attracted most of the attention among historians, it was not the only protest among NRMA men in British Columbia. In

Figure 25 NRMA troops march as part of the "mutiny" at Terrace, British Columbia, November 1944. *Source:* LAC, C-140120.

Vernon an unrecorded number from 16th Canadian Infantry Brigade paraded through the streets on the evening of November 24, followed four days later by about seventy-five soldiers, who "dispersed after cat calling and shouting."[8] Another group of 130 conscripts from the 14th Brigade marched through Nanaimo on November 26, and the next day "384 men mainly from the 25th LAA Bty RCA [Light Anti-Aircraft Battery, Royal Canadian Artillery]" marched through the city of Prince George, reportedly carrying placards with slogans such as "Win the War in Ottawa Before the War in Berlin," "Conscript Wealth and Industry," and "Down With the Legion – This is Just the Beginning."[9] Further demonstrations were recorded in Courtenay, Chilliwack, and Port Alberni.[10] But in every case the disturbances died down relatively quickly, and by early December units were preparing for their moves east. By January, every immediately available trained NRMA infantryman had left Pacific Command for overseas service, and a large-scale remustering policy similar to what had been operating overseas was introduced for conscripts in other corps and branches.[11]

At the same time, preparations were going on in Ottawa to ship the men to Europe. Instructions were issued to allow NRMA soldiers to continue to volunteer for general service, and many did so during November and December, some even on board ship as they sailed to England. Another 7,800 out of the

16,000 men ordered overseas chose to go absent without leave as their units moved across the country from British Columbia to Halifax. These absences occurred mostly while they were on the standard embarkation leave that was granted to all soldiers before they left Canada, and many later returned to service. As A.G.L. McNaughton reminded the CWC, most of the moves took place over the Christmas holiday, and many men simply took the opportunity to stay home for a few days longer than permitted before returning to their units. But 4,082 remained unaccounted for by the end of March 1945. Both of the numbers noted here are huge, constituting 48.8 percent and 25.5 percent of the total of 16,000. Because newspapers were forbidden to report on sailings of troop convoys, the news did not get out to the general public right away, although when the CWC considered whether to extend the ban on publication on January 17, Louis St. Laurent argued that such a move was drastic and that American papers would report it anyhow. In addition, the first group of zombies to proceed overseas included one NRMA recruit who threw his rifle overboard while waiting to sail from Halifax, and several other men who attempted to organize a "'sit-down' strike" to prevent their boarding. Reports on the various developments caused a flurry during McNaughton's campaign for a seat in the House of Commons in early 1945 (see below). But when the details of the rifle incident were investigated, the man turned out to have taken the action because he was mentally unstable rather than for political reasons. Fortunately for the government, the abortive strike did not attract as much notice.[12]

Once the NRMA men arrived in Europe, their commanders' main concern was to make sure they entered combat as quickly and efficiently as possible. H.D.G. Crerar, who now headed First Canadian Army as a full general, and Lieutenant-General Price Montague, the Chief of Staff at Canadian Military Headquarters (CMHQ), both agreed that the best way to deal with the new recruits would be to break them up and place them in the reinforcement stream as individuals, with the goal of mixing them throughout the army rather than identifying them separately as conscripts. In early December, Brigadier W.H.S. Macklin, who knew them from his months in British Columbia and was now serving at CMHQ, noted in a report that the army could at least be sure that most conscripts would be relatively well-trained, and that many would probably be above the standard of some of the soldiers who had been produced by increasingly desperate remustering programs in England in September and October.[13] Although it would be difficult to disguise fully the identity of NRMA recruits, Crerar tried to ensure that they received the same uniforms, badges, and treatment as other soldiers. The result was that, in his words, conscripts would "stand, or fall, in the eyes of the ranks now here, on how they prove themselves as soldiers."[14]

While that may have been the intention of commanders, more impressionistic evidence suggests that this approach may have sometimes backfired. According to Wray Gardiner, an ambulance driver in No. 411 Squadron, RCAF, who witnessed the arrival of a column of army reinforcements in the Netherlands in mid-March 1945, they were booed lustily by other Canadian troops, who assumed they were all zombies.[15] Yet as sapper Kenneth James Brown commented in a letter home from his own unit in late February: "If any of the N.R.M.A. recruits have landed on the continent, I haven't seen them." A month later he simply mentioned matter-of-factly that "we have one or two N.R.M.A. men with this outfit."[16] As with everything else about the zombies, their experiences in Europe seem to have varied from individual to individual.

Unfortunately, there is very little evidence with which to assess their combat performance. As Montague informed Crerar when the conscripts first began arriving in January, one of his staff officers had seen them and "was well pleased with their appearance and general attitude which seemed cooperative."[17] When the Inspector-General of the Canadian army, Lieutenant-General E.W. Sansom, spoke to reporters a month later, he told the story of one group of recruits at a Canadian training camp in England who had been "reported by the stationmaster as having left the cleanest C[ana]d[ia]n troop train ever to have come into his station."[18] More importantly, according to a brief survey of the attitudes of unit commanders in all three Canadian divisions that were engaged in operations as part of II Canadian Corps in northwest Europe in early March 1945, the NRMA men proved to be the equals of volunteers in a number of categories, including general attitude, standard of training, fighting ability, and morale. As the anonymous author who collated the information noted with respect to 4th Canadian Armoured Division: "Up until the query, unit COs were not aware that any NRMA personnel had been posted to their units."[19] Thus, it would seem that the army had achieved at least one of the goals of its administration of the NRMA, by creating a force of well-trained, competent soldiers who could conduct themselves well in combat. In the end, 9,667 NRMA recruits reached the front as conscripts, two-thirds after the end of hostilities in early May. Of that number, 2,463 saw duty in operational units, 69 were killed, 232 wounded, and 13 taken prisoner.[20] In the meantime, shortages overseas had been met thanks to the break that First Canadian Army had received over the winter months of 1944–45. As Montague informed the CGS in Ottawa in early April, the number of infantry reinforcements available to Canadian units in northwest Europe was "now stronger than at any time since D-Day."[21]

As soon as it became clear that the war in Europe was almost over, federal politicians were eager to end a program that remained unpopular among many Canadians. In mid-March 1945, after the last of the original 16,000 NRMA soldiers had been transferred overseas, McNaughton recommended that the CWC send general service soldiers instead of NRMA men to add to the current reinforcement pool, a policy that was now possible thanks to the respite the NRMA had provided to allow the numbers of general service recruits to be replenished. Even before the fighting had officially ended in Europe, the CWC also temporarily suspended the calling up of further civilians for service under the NRMA. That decision was made permanent at the same time as VE-Day was being celebrated on May 8.[22]

Proceedings against deserters and defaulters continued after the end of hostilities in Europe. In the view of several senior officials, apprehending and prosecuting offenders for such serious violations of the country's laws should not be halted simply because the fighting had ended, and enforcement operations went on well into 1946.[23] Staffs in the Department of Labour also continued to identify incorrect records. By June 1946, the number of delinquents had been reduced to fewer than 7,000; on the same date, the total number of NRMA deserters and defaulters stood at 7,225. By mid-1946, officials were admitting that it would be futile to try to track down every offender, and as the immediacy of the war faded they began to consider forgiving all men who remained at large. On August 14, 1946, all existing civilian and military regulations under the NRMA were revoked, and a general amnesty was proclaimed for all such offenders, to begin as of 11 a.m. the following day.[24] Authorities reconsidered the sentences of men who were already imprisoned for similar violations, although they resisted pardoning offenders who had flaunted the mobilization laws willingly and repeatedly during the war. In one case, three brothers had been involved, all of whom had been born in Canada to English parents, suggesting again that not all conscripts were French Canadians or from non-British ethnic backgrounds. They had reportedly been "aided and abetted by their mother who gave misleading information to police officers which carried out investigations to Washington, D.C."[25] For most Canadians, however, the NRMA soon passed into history.

Militarily and politically, the fallout from the administration of the NRMA, and particularly the crisis of October and November 1944, was significant over the last few months of the Second World War. For generals like Crerar who had harboured such great hopes of creating a large, professional army during the war, so that their views on military matters would be welcomed and even sought by their political superiors after 1945, the result was the exact opposite. The army emerged from the crisis with even less standing in the eyes of the country's civilian leaders, and particularly its prime minister. A.G.L.

McNaughton, the former general and previously Crerar's mentor, was so annoyed by the statements made by George Pearkes and his officers in Vancouver on November 20, 1944, that he sent his Inspector-General, Sansom, to the west coast to conduct an official inquiry into the events. Although the investigation exonerated Pearkes, it was clear that he was now even less trusted in Ottawa than he had been earlier.[26] In late December, he got himself into more trouble when he unburdened himself to the CGS regarding the policies he had been asked to pursue in recruiting for general service among the NRMA during the war. His statements were so forceful that officials within DND considered prosecuting him for violating army regulations by challenging the orders of his superiors. Wisely, legal experts in the Department of Justice recommended against doing so. But Pearkes resigned his commission in disgust in February 1945 and entered politics soon afterwards as a Progressive Conservative. This action was certainly not calculated to dispel any of the doubts that some Liberals had expressed about him in 1944, although he later became Minister of National Defence in the government of John G. Diefenbaker, serving during another turbulent time in the making of Canadian defence policy in the late 1950s.[27] As has been noted, Ken Stuart had resigned his post in early November 1944, if not in disgrace then certainly with the suspicions of many members of the wartime Cabinet hanging over his head. Poor health caught up with him and resulted in his death a year later.[28]

For McNaughton, the result was a very brief term as defence minister. Not yet holding a seat in the House of Commons, in early 1945 he ran in a by-election for the rural Ontario riding of Grey North. Angry at McNaughton for his role in the conscription debates of November 1944, and that he had turned down an offer to enter politics on the side of the Conservatives, members of that party campaigned vigorously against him. Combining personal attacks against him for being married to a Roman Catholic with revelations of the various problems in enforcing conscription since it had been extended to overseas service in November, they succeeded in defeating him on February 5. Four months later, McNaughton again failed to gain a seat in the federal general election in his home riding of Qu'Appelle, Saskatchewan.[29] Ultimately, this was unfortunate, since despite his subordinates' actions in November 1944 he was the highest-ranking former military leader to become defence minister to that time. Considering how favourably King viewed him, had McNaughton been able to retain his position he might have been able to preserve some of the status that the army had gained in political councils during the first half of the war.

Instead, Brooke Claxton was named defence minister in December 1946. Although he proved to be a strong, dedicated, and long-serving advocate for all three services, for him his party's political priorities came first, and in his early years in office that meant cutting the military's budget. For a second time, the army lost influence following a world war during which it had made huge contributions. By 1947 it had been reduced from its wartime total of almost 500,000 men and women to only 16,000 full-time troops, with just one brigade organized for operations in the field (and even that force was not permitted to recruit to full strength).[30] Yet this was still larger than the permanent forces of the Canadian army had ever been before, except in 1914–18 and 1939–45. And given the traditional peacetime apathy of Canadians with regard to military affairs, it is highly unlikely that the army could have remained at anything close to its wartime strength after 1945, even without the blows to its image that it had suffered among the politicians in the later years of the war. Still, its wartime difficulties undermined the hopes of Crerar and some of his successors that it would at least have established a successful tradition of representing the country abroad. As Ken Stuart had put it in recommending a reduced but still sizable and stable home defence force for Canada in mid-1943: "In my opinion the present framework and general composition of the operational troops is one that we should have had before the war. It is now answering our purpose admirably. I sincerely hope that it will be retained after the war."[31] Unfortunately, that did not occur.

Given the degree to which manpower problems had thrust the Canadian army into trouble yet again during the Second World War, what is even more surprising is that it still did not seem to have learned from its experiences afterwards. Senior officers began advocating conscription for the postwar army only two months after the end of hostilities in Europe, long before the heightened tensions of late 1944 had died down. As J.L. Granatstein has noted, they continued to do so until well into the 1950s.[32] Given the divisions to which conscription had again led the country during the Second World War, it is not surprising that most Canadians simply wanted to forget the issue, and it suffered a quick death at the political level. Among the more than 150,000 men who had actually experienced conscription first-hand, there was probably even less support for the idea of subjecting others to a similar policy. Thus, despite some of the positive contributions the NRMA had made in helping organize and maintain larger, more effective and professional military forces during the Second World War, it too soon faded from public memory.

Also forgotten were the positive impacts that the NRMA had had on relations between English and French Canadians, notwithstanding the more negative developments of the war. The training program established under the authority of the NRMA had forced the army to become a somewhat more welcoming place for French-speaking officers and men. For francophones who were inclined towards military service, the greatly expanded organization had offered a number of new opportunities to command troops and deal with other soldiers in their own language. It had also brought great numbers of French Canadians who may not have been so willing to serve, face to face with citizens from many other parts of Canada, and vice versa. In the fervour generated by the broader political tensions that had been raised during the war, and with the general desire to forget conscription afterwards, these experiences were soon forgotten, and remain largely forgotten by historians today. The lessons of dealing with large numbers of men from both backgrounds would have to be relearned when, in the 1960s, the federal government introduced the policy of bilingualism and biculturalism that has helped make the armed forces much more open to francophones today.

The impacts of conscription and the NRMA were largely forgotten in almost every way after the Second World War. For almost five full years, the country had been mobilized to an extent that Canadians had not experienced before (nor have they since). Dozens of training centres and military camps stretched across the country. More than a million men and women served in the armed forces, over 150,000 of them as conscripts. Other men and women were nudged by the NRMA towards volunteering for military service, or affected in other ways by the vast administrative machinery that was established between 1942 and 1945 that regulated almost every aspect of Canadian workplaces. Some even spent parts of the war evading civilian authorities, hiding for months or years with families or friends, made criminals not for acts they had committed but for actions they had refused to take. After the war, most Canadians resumed their traditional disinterest in military affairs. Their lack of concern was probably helped along by memories of the divisiveness that conscription had engendered, and as a result we have lost sight of the huge degree to which our usually peaceful Canadian society was mobilized to contribute to the Second World War. As I hope this book has reminded readers, Canadians' contributions to the war were both voluntary and compulsory, and the war affected people in almost every city and town across the country.

As historians we sometimes forget the individuals who were part of the past about which we write. This tendency is even stronger when one attempts to investigate the NRMA and the men who served under its authority. For much of the time they were in uniform they were seen as little more than an anonymous manpower "resource," to be calculated and estimated in abstract terms. Trying to understand how this system operated forces us to delve into the vast bureaucratic and administrative structures that were created to try to ensure its effective operation throughout the war, and this can distance us even further from the human side of events. Thus, I hope that this book also provides a sense of just who the conscripts were who served their country during the Second World War (even if on some level all of them did so unwillingly), as well as how they spent their months and sometimes years in service, and the impact the war and the NRMA had on them. Furthermore, I hope it brings to light some of the experiences of all Canadian soldiers who went through the Second World War training system, whether they were volunteers or at some point conscripts, and those of their larger families and friends.

Finally, and most importantly, by studying how the NRMA was organized and administered, I hope that this book will offer a new and important perspective on broader political and military developments in Canada during the Second World War. The choices the army made in creating the NRMA, and later in making it reflect more fully its own priorities and needs, shaped the higher political debates that took place around conscription. In particular, H.D.G. Crerar sensed that the NRMA could be used to build up the largest possible and most efficient army, with which not only to fight the war, but to play a greater role in postwar affairs. The result was the big army. During the debates over the creation of the big army, both sides accepted Crerar's recommendations, mainly on the unwritten assumption that the NRMA would allow the government to meet demands for larger ground forces, while at least for the moment avoiding an open break within the Cabinet over conscription and other manpower priorities. Several ministers understood the possible implications of increasing the size of the army, not least among them J.L. Ralston, who pleaded in 1942 for King to signal more firmly in advance what he would do if overseas conscription ever did become necessary. But thanks to the assurances of Crerar, and his successor Ken Stuart, and despite the impacts of the big army plan on political events throughout the first half of 1942, King was able to keep the issue at the level of hypothetical political debate, and thus avoid having to make such a firm commitment unless events later forced it on him.

The problem was that after the plan for the big army was accepted, the war against Japan came to exercise a second, less anticipated expansive influence over military policy. Army planners came to rely on the NRMA to meet the politicians' new demands for home defence forces, but without interrupting the flow of men required for the army in Europe. It is even possible that King may have hoped to stop that flow by encouraging such developments in early 1942. One way or the other, thanks partly to the prime minister's actions, the overall demands made on Canadian manpower increased enormously, and the next two years were largely spent trying to find enough soldiers to meet those demands. This led to heightened tensions between Ralston and several of his Cabinet colleagues, that certainly did not help him in the early days of the second conscription crisis of October–November 1944, when the need to extend the policy to overseas service became a real rather than simply a hypothetical question. By helping to exhaust the country's manpower reserves in earlier years, the combined requirements of the expanded home defence forces and the big army overseas also ensured that there would be few alternatives by November 1944 except to send overseas the only remaining reinforcements, the NRMA men. By then, thanks to the degree to which the army's leaders had organized compulsory military training around pressuring NRMA recruits to volunteer for overseas service, they had made it virtually certain that few of the remaining men would go voluntarily. This led to frustration and tension at the political level on both sides in late 1944.

The consequence of these divisions was King's accusation that key generals had been plotting against him to ensure overseas conscription. While most historians have rejected the idea that the army colluded deliberately to force its wishes upon the government, many have emphasized the degree to which commanders certainly demanded larger forces in the early years of the war, and frustrated efforts to find another solution when the final crisis came in 1944. At the practical level, decision making is a much more complex matter, especially in a country such as Canada where in wartime the influence of the military tends to increase, and that of the politicians (which in the case of Canada, was normally predominant) to decrease. An intricate web of motivations, attitudes, and personalities all came to shape events. In particular, when ministers at the Cabinet level failed to grasp the urgency of the situation and the lack of other options available in 1944, their generals felt compelled to resort to the strongest means available to make their superiors aware of the problem, with the result that one senior general resigned and several others were on the verge of doing so by late November. While this may not have been to King's liking, it was a less "political" action than the generals could have taken had they truly been interested in forcing their own opinions on the government.

Those in the army who helped administer the NRMA were not blameless. As we have seen, the personal and professional ambitions of H.D.G. Crerar and other senior personnel did much to shape the NRMA, especially before 1942, and thus the debates that took place as a result. In the summer of 1944, when difficulties emerged with respect to overseas reinforcements, Ken Stuart's duty was to ensure that his minister and the government as a whole were fully aware of the developments, the actions he had taken to address them, and their implications – and arguably to consult with Ralston before making those decisions in the first place, no matter how hopeful Stuart was that he could help his political superiors avoid controversy by dealing with the situation independently. The behaviour of some of George Pearkes's subordinate officers in British

Columbia during the Cabinet crisis of October and November suggests that they were also beginning to allow their frustrations to become public – something that officers are forbidden to do in most circumstances. Yet as a review of these issues and the overall history of the NRMA during the war makes clear, the actions of senior military commanders in 1944 were not nearly as simple of a matter of right and wrong, as previous authors have suggested.

In fact, the story of Canada's zombies during the Second World War is a reminder of the dangers of generalization, in many ways. As historians, part of what we do is try to find the larger themes that help explain more detailed events, and thereby make complex issues more understandable. But at times, we can simplify things too much. This is true for our understanding of French Canada during the war. Clearly, a large majority of francophones opposed conscription, and had a different view towards the Canadian military and participation in overseas wars generally. But they did not oppose it at every turn, and some did serve willingly in the military, as they had in the past. In writing about conscription as a policy, we have also tended to reduce it to two key political developments in January–June 1942 and October–November 1944, partly because both involve some of the most dramatic and significant events in our political history. But in focusing on King and other politicians, and their debates around the Cabinet table, we have forgotten that there was a much larger story going on in terms of what conscription meant for average Canadians across the country for five long years during the war. Lastly, in attempting to answer the question of why the military behaved in the way that it did, we have tended to reduce complex human beings down to simple answers about their motives and actions. As studying the history of conscription below the political level hopefully reminds us, there are no easy answers, and part of our duty as historians is to try to convey to a wider audience not just the broad themes but also the full complexities of our past.

Appendix:
The National Resources Mobilization Act, 1940[1]

An Act to confer certain powers upon the Governor in Council for the mobilization of national resources in the present war. [*Assented to 21st June, 1940.*]

Whereas by reason of developments since the outbreak of the present war a special emergency has arisen and the national safety of Canada has become endangered; and

Whereas it is, therefore, expedient to confer upon the Governor in Council special emergency powers to permit of the mobilization of all of the effective resources of the nation, both human and material, for the purpose of the defence and security of Canada, and

Whereas it is expedient that the said powers should be conferred upon the Governor in Council during the continuation of the state of war now existing:

Therefore His Majesty, by and with the advice and consent of the Senate and the House of Commons of Canada enacts as follows:-

1. This Act may be cited as *The National Resources Mobilization Act, 1940.*

2. Subject to the provisions of section three hereof, the Governor in Council may do and authorize such acts and things, and make from time to time such orders and regulations, requiring persons to place themselves, their services and their property at the disposal of His Majesty in the right of Canada, as may be deemed necessary or expedient for securing the public safety, the defence of Canada, the maintenance of public order, or the efficient prosecution of the war, or for maintaining supplies or services essential to the life of the community.

3. The powers conferred by the next preceding section may not be exercised for the purpose of requiring persons to serve in the military, naval or air forces outside of Canada and the territorial waters thereof.

4. The powers conferred by this Act shall remain in force only during the continuation of the state of war now existing.

5. Every order or regulation passed under the authority of this Act shall be tabled in Parliament forthwith if Parliament is in Session and a copy thereof

sent to every Member of the House of Commons and of the Senate and if Parliament is not in Session then every such order or regulation shall be forthwith published in the *Canada Gazette* and copies thereof sent to every Member of the House of Commons and of the Senate forthwith; provided that any of the steps specified in this section may be omitted or deferred if the Governor in Council considers such omission or deferment necessary in the national interest having regard to the special circumstances.

6. The Governor in Council may prescribe the penalties that may be imposed for violations of orders and regulations made under this Act, and may also prescribe whether such penalties shall be imposed upon summary conviction or upon indictment, but no such penalty shall exceed a fine of five thousand dollars or imprisonment for any term not exceeding five years, or both fine and imprisonment.

Archival Sources Consulted

Library and Archives Canada, Ottawa, Ontario

Records of Government Departments and Agencies:
External Affairs
Finance
Justice
Labour
National Defence
Statistics Canada

Private Papers:
Burns, E.L.M.
Claxton, Brooke
Crerar, H.D.G.
King, W.L.M.
Lapointe, Ernest
McNaughton, A.G.L.
Pope, Maurice Arthur
Ralston, James Layton
Sansom, Ernest William
St. Laurent, Louis
Stuart, Kenneth

Directorate of History and Heritage, Department of National Defence, Ottawa, Ontario
Kardex Files

Military History Research Centre, Canadian War Museum, Ottawa, Ontario

Private Papers:
Brown, Kenneth James
Davis, Allan Franklin and Russell Earl
Moore, C.T.
Pope, Maurice A.
Rooney, Eugene
Silver, Leonard
Williams, Douglas Morely
Wolstein, Edward

Friends of the Canadian War Museum Oral History Project:
Transcript of interview. Ottawa, Ontario. September 2, 2000
Harper, Burton E.

Queen's University Archives, Kingston, Ontario
Crerar, Thomas Alexander
Dexter, Alexander Grant
Power, Charles Gavan
Rogers, Norman McLeod

Nova Scotia Archives, Halifax, Nova Scotia
Macdonald, A.L.
Military Records

United Church of Canada Archives, Toronto, Ontario
Board of Evangelism and Social Service

Cornwall Community Museum, Cornwall, Ontario
Records related to R. Larose and No. 31 Canadian Army (Basic) Training Centre

Orillia Museum of Art and History, Orillia, Ontario
Records related to No. 26 Canadian Army/Armoured Corps (Basic) Training Centre

The Mackenzie King Diaries, 1932–1949
Transcript – Toronto: University of Toronto Press, 1980. Also available online at http://www.bac-lac.gc.ca/eng/discover/politics-government/prime-ministers/william-lyon-mackenzie-king/Pages/search.aspx

Individual Interviews and Correspondence
Beattie, William E. Interview. Cornwall, Ontario. May 22, 2015
Beattie, William E. Personal e-mail to author. September 3, 2015
Gardiner, Wray. Interview. Guelph, Ontario. May 17, 2015
McVicar, Hugh. Personal letter to author. January 28, 1997
Ripstein, Howard. Interview. Montreal, Quebec. April 22, 1997
Roy, R.H.. Personal letter to author. December 20, 1995
Stanley, George F.G. Personal letter to author. December 18, 1995

Notes

Note: In the pages that follow, I have cited all secondary sources only once, in full, and then used a shortened version thereafter.

List of Abbreviations Frequently Used in the Notes

AA&QMG	Assistant Adjutant and Quartermaster-General
AG	Adjutant-General
CA(B)TC	Canadian Army (Basic) Training Centre
CA(R)TC	Canadian Army (Reserve) Training Centre
CGS	Chief of the General Staff
DAG(M)	Deputy Adjutant General (Mobilization)
DHH	Directorate of History and Heritage, Department of National Defence
DM	Deputy Minister
DND	Department of National Defence
DNWS	Department of National War Services
DOC(s), DOsC	District Officer(s) Commanding
GO(s)C-in-C	General Officer(s) Commanding-in-Chief
LAC	Library and Archives Canada
MD	Military District
OC	Officer Commanding
QUA	Queen's University Archives
RG 13	Records of the Department of Justice
RG 24	Records of the Department of National Defence
RG 25	Records of the Department of External Affairs
RG 27	Records of the Department of Labour

Frontispiece

1 Library and Archives Canada, Record Group 24, Records of the Department of National Defence, vol. 2197, file HQ 54-27-63-38.

Introduction

1 The two best overviews of events related to conscription in the Second World War are provided in C.P. Stacey, *Arms, Men, and Governments: The War Policies of Canada, 1939–1945* (Ottawa: Queen's Printer, 1970), 397–484; and J.L. Granatstein and J.M. Hitsman, *Broken Promises: A History of Conscription in Canada* (Toronto: Oxford University Press, 1977), 133–244.

2 Bruce Hutchison, "Mackenzie King and the 'Revolt' of the Army," *Maclean's*, October 15, 1952, 7–9, 57–70; and Hutchison, *The Incredible Canadian: A Candid Portrait of Mackenzie King: His Works, His Times, and His Nation* (Toronto: Longmans, Green, 1952), 366–83.

3 R. MacGregor Dawson, *The Conscription Crisis of 1944* (Toronto: University of Toronto Press, 1961).

4 For the key works, see J.L. Granatstein, *Conscription in the Second World War, 1939–1945: A Study in Political Management* (Toronto: Ryerson, 1969); Granatstein, *Canada's War: The Politics of the Mackenzie King Government, 1939–1945* (Toronto: Oxford University Press, 1975);and Granatstein and Hitsman, *Broken Promises.*

5 Michael D. Stevenson, *Canada's Greatest Wartime Muddle: National Selective Service and the Mobilization of Human Resources during World War II* (Montreal and Kingston: McGill–Queen's University Press, 2001).

6 Richard J. Walker, "The Revolt of the Canadian Generals, 1944: The Case for the Prosecution," in *The Insubordinate and the Noncompliant: Case Studies of Canadian Mutiny and Disobedience, 1920 to Present*, ed. Howard G. Coombs (Kingston: Canadian Defence Academy Press, 2007), 55–100.

7 E.L.M. Burns, *Manpower in the Canadian Army, 1939–1945* (Toronto: Clarke, Irwin, 1956).

8 This conclusion is hinted at by Granatstein and Hitsman in *Broken Promises*, esp. 158, 185–204; but it is also stated more openly by J.E. Rea in "What Really Happened? A New Look at the Conscription Crisis," *The Beaver* 74(2) (April–May 1994), 10–19; and in David Allan Wilson, "Reflections on Conscription, 1944–45," paper presented to the Sixth Military History Colloquium of the Laurier Centre for Military, Strategic, and Disarmament Studies, Waterloo, Ontario, April 21, 1995, esp. 7–11, 17–20. Stevenson also discusses controls on manpower very critically in *Canada's Greatest Wartime Muddle*, 3–14, 26–36.

9 Stacey, *Arms, Men, and Governments*, 468–69, 471.

10 Ralph Allen, *Ordeal by Fire: Canada, 1910–1945* (Toronto: Doubleday Canada, 1961), 394.

11 On these debates, see Dawson, *The Conscription Crisis*; Stacey, *Arms, Men, and Governments*, 434–74; Granatstein, *Canada's War*, 333–74; and Granatstein and Hitsman, *Broken Promises*, 207–31.

12 For a recent overview of the mobilization of civilian society that also begins to explore the experiences of Canadians in uniform, see Jeffrey A. Keshen, *Saints, Sinners, and Soldiers: Canada's Second World War* (Vancouver: UBC Press, 2004), esp. 228–57.

13 Stacey, *Arms, Men, and Governments*, 422, Pierre Vennat, *Lés Héros oubliés: L'histoire inédite des militaires canadiens-français de la Deuxième Guerre mondiale*, vol. 1: *De la mobilisation au raid de Dieppe* (Montréal: Éditions du Méridien, 1997), 14; Yves Tremblay, *Voluntaires: Des Québécois en guerre (1939–1945)* (Outremont: Athéna éditions, 2006), 17; and Sébastien Vincent, *Ils ont écrit la guerre: La Seconde Guerre mondiale à travers des écrits de combattants canadiens-français* (Montreal: vlb éditeur, 2010), 15.

14 On bilingualism, and the history of French Canadians in the Canadian military more broadly, see K.H. Barry Gallant, "The Development of the Canadian Army as a Unilingual Institution in a Bilingual State," MA thesis, McGill University, 1969; and Jean Pariseau and Serge Bernier, *French Canadians and Bilingualism in the Canadian Armed Forces*, 2 vols. (Ottawa: Directorate of History, Department of National Defence / Minister of Supply and Services Canada, 1988 and 1994).

15 Tremblay, *Voluntaires*, 21. For the most obvious examples, see Robert Rumilly, *Histoire de la province de Québec*, vols. 38–49 (Ottawa: Fides, 1968–69); and André Laurendeau, "The Conscription Crisis, 1942," in *André Laurendeau: Witness for Quebec*, ed. and trans. Philip Stratford (Toronto: Macmillan, 1973), 1–121. In addition, Mason Wade reflects some of the same emphases in his now aged but still very solid English-language overview, *The French Canadians, 1760–1967*, rev. ed., vol. 2: *1911–1967* (Toronto: Macmillan of Canada, 1968), 916–1101.

16 Vennat in *Lés Héros oubliés* (3 vols.) provides the most thorough discussion of attitudes within Quebec that tended to be more supportive towards the Second World War.

17 This challenge began as early as the 1970s with Jean-Yves Gravel's chapter, "Le Québec militaire, 1939–1945," in *Le Québec et la guerre, 1867–1960*, ed. Jean-Yves Gravel (Montréal: Les éditions du boréal express, 1974), 77–108; followed by Jean-Pierre Gagnon's *Le 22e bataillon (canadien-français), 1914–1919: Étude socio-militaire* (Ottawa and Quebec City: Les Presses de l'Université Laval/Department of National Defence, 1986). Among the more recent group are Vennat, *Lés Héros oubliés*; Tremblay, *Voluntaires*; Serge Marc Durflinger, *Fighting from Home: The Second World War in Verdun, Quebec* (Vancouver: UBC Press, 2006); and Sébastien Vincent, who in addition to producing two related books, *Laissés dans l'ombre: Quatorze Québécois racontent leur participation voluntaire à la Seconde Guerre mondiale* (Montreal: vlb éditeur, 2004), and *Ils ont écrit la guerre*, also founded and is the webmaster of an online site devoted to this goal (www.lequebecetles guerres.org).

18 J.W. Pickersgill, ed., *The Mackenzie King Record*, 4 vols. (Toronto: University of Toronto Press, 1960–70); *The Mackenzie King Diaries, 1932–1949* [hereafter King Diaries] (Toronto: University of Toronto Press, 1980). The online version is available through Library and Archives Canada at http://www.bac-lac.gc.ca/eng/discover/politics-government/prime -ministers/william-lyon-mackenzie-king/Pages/search.aspx.

19 Tim Cook, *Warlords: Borden, Mackenzie King, and Canada's World Wars* (Toronto: Allen Lane, 2012), 183–84.

Part 1: The Historical Legacy

1 LAC, MG 27, III, B11, J.L. Ralston Papers [hereafter Ralston Papers], vol. 85, "Resignation, Miscellaneous – Caucas [*sic*] Notes, Diary, Memoranda, Speeches, Correspondence, Statement, 'Zombie Prayers.'"

Chapter 1: Conscription and Canadian History, 1627–1939

1 George F.G. Stanley, *Canada's Soldiers: The Military History of an Unmilitary People*, 3rd ed. (Toronto: Macmillan of Canada, 1974), 4, 21–24; W.J. Eccles, "The Social, Economic, and Political Significance of the Military Establishment in New France," *Canadian Historical Review* 52(1) (March 1971): 1–7.

2 George F.G. Stanley, *New France: The Last Phase, 1744–1760* (Toronto: McClelland and Stewart, 1968), 191–96.

3 Granatstein and Hitsman, *Broken Promises*, 5–6.

4 Stanley, *Canada's Soldiers*, 98–101; Granatstein and Hitsman, *Broken Promises*, 6.

5 Gustave Lanctot provides the fullest discussion of French Canadians' attitudes towards the American Revolution, of their militia service during the war, and of their experience of the conflict more broadly, in *Canada and the American Revolution, 1774–1783*, trans. Margaret M. Cameron (Toronto: Clarke, Irwin, 1967). For desertions during the Saratoga campaign, see esp. 164–66.

6 Mason Wade, *The French Canadians, 1760–1967*, rev. ed., vol. 1: *1760–1911* (Toronto: Macmillan of Canada, 1968), 73.

7 On these developments, see especially Roch Legault, "L'organisation militaire sous la régime Britannique et le rôle assigné à la gentilhommerie canadienne (1760–1815)," *Révue d'histoire de l'Amérique française* 45(2) (1991): 243–47; and Legault, *Une élite en déroute: Les militaires canadiens après la Conquête* (Outremont: Athéna éditions, 2002), 67–72, 127–39, 147–51; as well as Jean-Pierre Wallot, "Une émeute à Lachine contre la 'conscription' (1812)," *Révue d'histoire de l'Amérique française* 18(1) (1964): 112–37.

8 Allan Greer, *The Patriots and the People: The Rebellion of 1837 in Rural Lower Canada* (Toronto: University of Toronto Press, 1993), esp. 100–13, 219–25, 239–57, 300–31.
9 The very general overview of French Canadian society and history given in this paragraph is drawn from various sources, but in particular Wade, *The French Canadians,* vol. 1, which despite its age remains the most detailed English-language review of the subject; and John Dickinson and Brian Young, *A Short History of Quebec*, 4th ed. (Montreal and Kingston: McGill–Queen's University Press, 2008). Other key histories in English include Susan Mann Trofimenkoff, *The Dream of Nation: A Social and Intellectual History of Quebec* (Toronto: Macmillan of Canada, 1982); Paul-André Linteau, René Durocher, and Jean-Claude Robert, *Quebec: A History, 1867-1929*, trans. Robert Chodos (Toronto: James Lorimer, 1983); and Linteau, Durocher, Robert, and Ricard, *Quebec Since 1930*, trans. Robert Chodos and Ellen Garmaise (Toronto: James Lorimer, 1991).
10 Desmond Morton, "The Cadet Movement in the Moment of Canadian Militarism, 1909 –1914," *Journal of Canadian Studies* 13(2) (Summer 1978): 56–68; Daniel Thomas Byers, "The Canadian Officers' Training Corps: Support for Military Training in the Universities of Canada, 1908–1935," MA thesis, Wilfrid Laurier University, 1993, 4–56.
11 James Wood, *Militia Myths: Ideas of the Canadian Citizen Soldier, 1896–1921* (Vancouver: UBC Press, 2010), 4–5. Legault also comments on the influence of memories of Cromwell on British views in "L'organisation militaire," 233; and on English settlers' mistrust of standing armies in North America more generally in *Une élite en déroute*, 53–54.
12 Granatstein and Hitsman, *Broken Promises*, 6–7.
13 George Sheppard, *Plunder, Profit, and Paroles: A Social History of the War of 1812 in Upper Canada* (Montreal and Kingston: McGill–Queen's University Press, 1994), 41–99.
14 On the origins and early evolution of the NPAM and the broader Canadian militia after 1855, see C.P. Stacey, *Canada and the British Army, 1846-1871: A Study in the Practice of Responsible Government*, rev. ed. (Toronto: University of Toronto Press, 1963), 89–108, 118, 149–52, 197, 200; Stanley, *Canada's Soldiers*, 209–14, 233–36; and Granatstein and Hitsman, *Broken Promises*, 8–11. On the relationship of French Canadians to it more specifically, see Pariseau and Bernier, *French Canadians and Bilingualism*, vol. 1, 40–45, 49–53.
15 Both Barry Gallant and Desmond Morton focus on Cartier's emphasis on encouraging French-speaking units in Gallant, "The Development of the Canadian Army," 13–14, 20–21; and Morton, "French Canada and the Canadian Militia, 1868–1914," *Histoire sociale/ Social History* 2(3) (April 1969): 32–34. On French Canadians and the military generally, up to the First World War, see also Morton, "French Canada and War, 1868–1917: The Military Background to the Conscription Crisis of 1917," in *War and Society in North America*, ed. J.L. Granatstein and R.D. Cuff (Toronto: Thomas Nelson and Sons, 1971), 86–95; and Morton, "The Limits of Loyalty: French Canadian Officers and the First World War," in *Limits of Loyalty*, ed. Edgar Denton III (Waterloo: Wilfrid Laurier University Press, 1980), 83–88.
16 Morton, "French Canada and the Canadian Militia," 35–36; Gallant, "The Development of the Canadian Army," 26–27; Jean-Yves Gravel, *L'armée au Québec: un portrait social, 1868–1900* (Montreal: Boréal, 1974), 16, 32–35; Pariseau and Bernier, *French Canadians and Bilingualism*, vol. 1, 51; Granatstein and Hitsman, *Broken Promises*, 11–12.
17 On the experiences of the two French-speaking units, see in particular Desmond Morton, "Des canadiens errants: French Canadian troops in the North-West Campaign of 1885," *Journal of Canadian Studies* 5(3) (August 1970): 28–39. Morton also provides an overview of the campaign as a whole, and its aftermath for French–English relations, in *The Last War Drum: The North West Campaign of 1885* (Toronto: Hakkert, 1972).

18 Gravel, *L'armée au Québec*, 94, 102. On the popularity of urban units in general (and using Montreal as a case study), see Carman Miller, "The Montreal Militia as A Social Institution before World War I," *Urban History Review* 19(1) (June 1990): 57–64. See also Morton, "French Canada and the Canadian Militia," 36–38.

19 Gallant, "The Development of the Canadian Army," 1, 22–24, 40–42; Morton, "French Canada and the Canadian Militia," 44–45, 48–49; and Pariseau and Bernier, *French Canadians and Bilingualism*, vol. 1, 47–48, 64–65. On imperial sentiment among English Canadians generally during this time, the classic work is Carl Berger, *The Sense of Power: Studies in the Ideas of Canadian Imperialism, 1867–1914* (Toronto: University of Toronto Press, 1970).

20 On all of these examples, see Morton, "French Canada and the Canadian Militia," 38–41, 45–47 (quotation from 41); Gallant, "The Development of the Canadian Army," 15, 21–22, 24–26, 29–30, 38, 41; and Granatstein and Hitsman, *Broken Promises*, 13. On the origins and evolution of the Permanent Force more generally, see Stanley, *Canada's Soldiers*, 241–43, 247–49; and Stephen J. Harris, *Canadian Brass: The Making of a Professional Army, 1860–1939* (Toronto: University of Toronto Press, 1988).

21 See Carman Miller, "English-Canadian Opposition to the South African War as Seen through the Press," *Canadian Historical Review* 55(4) (December 1974): 422–38; A. Ross McCormack, *Reformers, Rebels, and Revolutionaries: The Western Canadian Radical Movement, 1899–1919* (Toronto: University of Toronto Press, 1977), 118–19; and Thomas P. Socknat, *Witness against War: Pacifism in Canada, 1900–1945* (Toronto: University of Toronto Press, 1987), 23–28.

22 Granatstein and Hitsman, *Broken Promises*, 14–15; Pariseau and Bernier, *French Canadians and Bilingualism*, vol. 1, 61; Carman Miller, *Painting the Map Red: Canada and the South African War, 1899–1902* (Montreal and Kingston: McGill–Queen's University Press, 1993), 26–30.

23 On the centrality to Laurier of national unity, see H. Blair Neatby, *Laurier and a Liberal Quebec* (Ottawa: Carleton University Press, 1973), esp. 205–31.

24 The most thorough modern account of Canada's participation in the South African War is provided in Miller, *Painting the Map Red*. On the origins of, and decision-making about, participation at the start of the war, as well as the recruiting of the first contingent, see esp. 31–62.

25 On Bourassa's reactions to the South African War, see Neatby, *Laurier and a Liberal Quebec*, 109–14. Joseph Levitt discusses Bourassa's thinking and actions in this time period more generally in *Henri Bourassa and the Golden Calf: The Social Program of the Nationalists of Quebec (1900–1914)* (Ottawa: Les Éditions de l'Université d'Ottawa, 1969); for the point on attracting support because he was seen as standing up for French Canada, see esp. 16. Wade, in *The French Canadians*, vol. 1, also discusses Bourassa and his views at some length; see esp. 495–506.

26 The most thorough English-language overviews of the developments discussed in this paragraph can be found in Gilbert Norman Tucker, *The Naval Service of Canada: Its Official History*, vol. 1: *Origins and Early Years* (Ottawa: King's Printer, 1952), 85–211; Oscar Douglas Skelton, *Life and Letters of Sir Wilfrid Laurier*, vol. 2 (Toronto: Oxford University Press, 1921), 284–383, 392–414; Neatby, *Laurier and a Liberal Quebec*, 182–204; Joseph Schull, *Laurier: The First Canadian* (Toronto: Macmillan of Canada, 1966), 480–533, 544–49; Robert Craig Brown, *Robert Laird Borden: A Biography*, vol. 1: *1854–1914* (Toronto: Macmillan of Canada, 1975), 147–211, 235–47; C.P. Stacey, *Canada and the Age of Conflict: A History of Canadian External Policies*, vol. 1: *1867–1921* (Toronto: University

of Toronto Press, 1984), 126–49; and William Johnston, William G.P. Rawling, Richard H. Gimblett, and John MacFarlane, *The Seabound Coast: The Official History of the Royal Canadian Navy, 1867–1939* (Toronto: Dundurn, 2010), 130–210.

27 On English Canadian militarism before 1914, see Morton, "The Cadet Movement," 56; Berger, *The Sense of Power*, 233–58; and Wood, *Militia Myths*.

28 On the initial reactions of Laurier, Quebec generally, and Bourassa, see Wade, *The French Canadians*, vol. 2, 642–54. See also René Durocher, "Henri Bourassa, les évêques et la guerre de 1914–1918," *Historical Papers* (1971): 248–75. R. Matthew Bray provides an excellent overview of English Canadian opinion towards the war in "'Fighting as an Ally': The English-Canadian Patriotic Response to the Great War," *Canadian Historical Review* 61(2) (June 1980): 141–68.

29 On the initial mobilization and raising of the first contingent (as well as the later difficulties once they reached England), see especially A. Fortescue Duguid, *Official History of the Canadian Forces in the Great War 1914–1919*, general series, vol. 1: *From the Outbreak of War to the Formation of the Canadian Corps, August 1914–September 1915* (Ottawa: King's Printer, 1938), 1–101, 145–50; G.W.L. Nicholson, *Canadian Expeditionary Force, 1914–1919* (Ottawa: Queen's Printer, 1964), 18–32; and Ronald G. Haycock, *Sam Hughes: The Public Career of a Controversial Canadian, 1885–1916* (Waterloo: Wilfrid Laurier University Press, 1986), 177–87. Nicholson also provides a solid overview of Canada's participation in the war as a whole, and especially its experiences overseas. For the best and most recent source on the same subject, see also Tim Cook's two-volume history: *At the Sharp End: Canadians Fighting the Great War, 1914–1916* (Toronto: Viking, 2007); and *Shock Troops: Canadians Fighting the Great War, 1917–1918* (Toronto: Viking, 2008).

30 For a French-language perspective on the early developments in the war, see Gérard Filteau, *Le Québec, le Canada, et la Guerre, 1914–1918* (Montreal: Éditions de l'Aurore, 1977), 13–32. Pariseau and Bernier provide a quite critical but unfortunately very brief overview of French Canadian experiences of recruiting and as part of the military effort throughout 1914–18 in *French Canadians and Bilingualism*, vol. 1, 71–89. (They are also the source of the numbers given here, along with Morton, "The Limits of Loyalty," 82, 88; and Granatstein and Hitsman, *Broken Promises*, 24.) The figure of 1,245 comes originally from the companion volume to Duguid, *Official History*, vol. 1, subtitled *Chronology, Appendices and Maps* [ed. A. Fortescue Duguid] (Ottawa: King's Printer, 1938), appendix 86, "Statistical Information Pertaining to the First Contingent."

31 Regarding the second contingent and the initial raising of the 22nd Battalion, see Filteau, *Le Québec, le Canada, et la Guerre*, 32–34, 72-73; Gagnon, *Le 22e bataillon*, 27–41; and Pierre Vennat, *Les <<Poilus>> québécois de 1914-1918: Histoire des militaires canadiens-français de la Première Guerre mondiale*, vol. 1 (Montreal: Éditions du Méridien, 1999), 29–41, 48–54. On the raising of the second contingent generally, see also Duguid, *Official History*, vol. 1, 160–62, 423–30. On errors made in recruiting of French Canadians overall during the war (and for further references to the recruiting of the 22nd Battalion), see Nicholson, *Canadian Expeditionary Force*, 220–21; Morton, "French Canada and War," 95–99; Morton, "The Limits of Loyalty," 88–92; Granatstein and Hitsman, *Broken Promises*, 24–34; and Haycock, *Sam Hughes*, 212–18.

32 Duguid, *Official History*, vol. 1, 449–52; Nicholson, *Canadian Expeditionary Force*, 213–18; Robert Craig Brown, *Robert Laird Borden: A Biography*, vol. 2: *1914–1937* (Toronto: Macmillan of Canada, 1980), 27–35; Stacey, *Canada and the Age of Conflict*, vol. 1, 183–94.

33 Harris, *Canadian Brass*, 92–138; John A. English, *The Canadian Army and the Normandy Campaign: A Study of Failure in High Command* (Westport: Praeger, 1991), 15–16; Kenneth

Radley, *We Lead, Others Follow: First Canadian Division 1914–1918* (St. Catharines: Vanwell, 2006), 180–313.

34 Brown, *Robert Laird Borden*, vol. 2, 135–37; Stacey, *Canada and the Age of Conflict*, vol. 1, 219–20.

35 Nicholson, *Canadian Expeditionary Force*, 218–19, 230–31 (see also 546 for monthly recruiting figures throughout the war). On the difficulties with the recruiting system generally throughout the war, in addition to Nicholson see Granatstein and Hitsman, *Broken Promises*, 34–42; Robert Craig Brown and Donald Loveridge, "Unrequited Faith: Recruiting the CEF 1914–1918," *Revue internationale d'histoire militaire* 51 (1982): 53–79, and Haycock, *Sam Hughes*, 198–212, 218–22.

36 Gagnon, *Le* 22e *bataillon*, 139–212, provides a detailed summary of the later recruiting of the 22nd Battalion and the histories of all of the French-speaking battalions that later contributed men to it. See also Morton, "French Canada and War," 99–102; Morton, "The Limits of Loyalty," 92–96; Filteau, *Le Québec, le Canada, et la Guerre*, 77–79; Haycock, *Sam Hughes*, 215–16; and Vennat, *Les <<Poilus>> québécois*, vol. 1, 78-85, 163, 169–72, 207–20, 285, 288–322, 331–47. Vennat explores the experiences of French Canadian volunteers during the First World War generally, in "Les 'Poilus canadiens-français': les voluntaires oubliés de la Première Guerre mondiale," in *La Première guerre mondiale et le Canada: contributions sociomilitaires québécoises*, ed. Roch Legault and Jean Lamarre (Montreal: Éditions du Méridien, 1999), 253–67, and Vennat, *Les <<Poilus>> québécois* (2 vols).

37 Canada, Dominion Bureau of Statistics, *Fifth Census of Canada 1911*, vol. 1: *Areas and Population by Provinces, Districts, and Sub-Districts* (Ottawa: King's Printer, 1912), table X, 530; *Sessional Papers: Seventh Session of the Twelfth Parliament of the Dominion of Canada, Session 1917*, 7 George V, A.1917 ([Ottawa?]: [King's Printer?], n.d.), Sessional Paper No. 194, "Return: Male Population of Canada, Census of 1911, between the Ages of 20 and 45, both years inclusive, according to conjugal condition and nativity," 24; M.C. Urquhart and K.A.H. Buckley, eds., *Historical Statistics of Canada* (Toronto: Macmillan of Canada, 1965), series A2–14; Granatstein and Hitsman, *Broken Promises*, 28–29; and Pariseau and Bernier, *French Canadians and Bilingualism*, vol. 1, 84.

38 Granatstein and Hitsman, *Broken Promises*, 24.

39 Robert Craig Brown and Ramsay Cook provide a good overview in *Canada, 1896-1921: A Nation Transformed* (Toronto: McClelland and Stewart, 1974), 252–62. See also Filteau, *Le Québec, le Canada, et la Guerre*, 74–77. A thorough overview of the responses of French Canadians in Quebec to the various events throughout the war, drawn mainly from the press of the time, can also be found in Elizabeth H. Armstrong, *The Crisis of Quebec, 1914–18* (New York: Columbia University Press, 1937); on Quebec generally during the war, see also Robert Rumilly, *Histoire de la province de Québec*, vols. 19–23 (Montréal: Montréal-Éditions, n.d.).

40 Brown, *Robert Laird Borden*, vol. 2, 22.

41 On these developments, see in particular Nicholson, *Canadian Expeditionary Force*, 219–20, 221–22, 340–43; Granatstein and Hitsman, *Broken Promises*, 42–66; Filteau, *Le Québec, le Canada, et la Guerre*, 115–16; and Brown, *Robert Laird Borden*, vol. 2, 60–87.

42 Unless otherwise cited below, the account within this paragraph is derived from Brown and Cook, *Canada, 1896-1921*, 268–74; Granatstein and Hitsman, *Broken Promises*, 66–82; and the following further published biographies and other accounts: Skelton, *Life and Letters of Sir Wilfrid Laurier*, vol. 2, 506–45; Schull, *Laurier: The First Canadian*, 581–601; J. Murray Beck, *Pendulum of Power: Canada's Federal Elections* (Toronto: Prentice-Hall, 1968), 136–46; John English, *The Decline of Politics: The Conservatives and the Party System, 1901–20* (Toronto: University of Toronto Press, 1977), 103–104, 129–203;

and Brown, *Robert Laird Borden*, vol. 2, 46–48, 84–125. For the most recent overview of Borden and his role in wartime events, see also Tim Cook, *Warlords*, 7–161.

43 On Laurier's views towards coalition, see also J.W. Dafoe, *Laurier: A Study in Canadian Politics*, Carleton Library ed. (Toronto: McClelland and Stewart, 1963), 99–105.

44 "The Military Voters Act, 1917" and "The War-time Elections Act," 7–8 George V, Chap. 34 and Chap. 39, *Acts of the Parliament of the Dominion of Canada*, 1917 (Ottawa: King's Printer, 1917), 313–31, 355–74.

45 The Francoeur motion is quoted here from J. Castell Hopkins, *The Canadian Annual Review of Public Affairs*, 1918 (Toronto: Canadian Annual Review, 1919), 634. It is also discussed in several of the other sources cited in earlier endnotes. The statement by Marsil appears in Réal Bélanger, "Albert Sevigny et la participation des Canadiens français à la Grande guerre," *Revue internationale d'histoire militaire* 51 (1982), 93, translated from the original French by me. On all of the developments described so far in this paragraph, more broadly, see also Hopkins, *The Canadian Annual Review, War Series*, 1917 (Toronto: Canadian Annual Review, 1918), 493–99, 607–9 (Martel quotation from 496); Hopkins, *Canadian Annual Review*, 1918, 462–64, 634–36; Wade, *The French Canadians*, vol. 2, 735–36, 747–48, 752–69; Granatstein and Hitsman, *Broken Promises*, 82, 89; Filteau, *Le Québec, le Canada, et la Guerre* 117–19, 156–62; Martin F. Auger, "On the Brink of Civil War: The Canadian Government and the Suppression of the 1918 Quebec Easter Riots," *Canadian Historical Review* 89(4) (December 2008): 503–40; and Vennat, *Les <<Poilus>> québécois*, vol. 2, 55–57, 109–21, 147–82. Lastly, Gagnon, in *Le 22e bataillon*, 212–20, describes the atmosphere for officers attempting to recruit volunteers in various parts of Quebec during 1917–18, as well as the Easter riots; and Jean Provencher provides an even more detailed account of the latter in *Québec sous la Loi des mesures de guerre 1918* (Trois-Rivières: Boréal, 1971).

46 Robert Comeau makes this point, among a number of other significant ones about Quebec's views towards conscription, in "L'opposition à la conscription au Québec," in Legault and Lamarre, eds., *La Première guerre mondiale et le Canada*, 106.

47 On the developments described so far in this paragraph, see J. Castell Hopkins, *The Canadian Annual Review, War Series*, 1916 (Toronto: Canadian Annual Review, 1918), 554–55; Barbara M. Wilson, "Introduction," in *Ontario and the First World War, 1914–1918: A Collection of Documents*, ed. Barbara M. Wilson (Toronto: Champlain Society, 1977), lxx–lxxxiv; W.H. Heick, "'If We Lose The War, Nothing Else Matters': The 1917 Federal Election in North Waterloo," *Ontario History* 72(2) (June 1980): 67–92; and Nikolas Gardner, "The Great War and Waterloo County: The Travails of the 118th Overseas Battalion," *Ontario History* 89(3) (September 1997): 219–25.

48 Ian Hugh Maclean Miller, *Our Glory and Our Grief: Torontonians and the Great War* (Toronto: University of Toronto Press, 2002), 178–82.

49 McCormack, *Reformers, Rebels, and Revolutionaries*, 161–62.

50 On the impacts of the war for farmers, and postwar political developments, see W.L. Morton, *The Progressive Party in Canada* (Toronto: University of Toronto Press, 1950), esp. 57–265; W.R. Young, "Conscription, Rural Depopulation, and the Farmers of Ontario, 1917–19," *Canadian Historical Review* 53(3) (September 1972): 289–320; John Herd Thompson, *The Harvests of War: The Prairie West, 1914–1918* (Toronto: McClelland and Stewart, 1978), 121–53; J. Murray Beck, *Politics of Nova Scotia*, vol. 2: *Murray-Buchanan, 1898–1988* (Tantallon: Four East Publications, 1988), 78–82; David Frank, "The 1920s: Class and Region, Resistance and Accommodation," in *The Atlantic Provinces in Confederation*, ed. E.R. Forbes and D.A. Muise (Toronto: University of Toronto Press, 1993), 236–39; and J.E. Rea, *T.A. Crerar: A Political Life* (Montreal and Kingston: McGill–Queen's University Press, 1997), 35–143. King's efforts to bring Progressives under the wing of the Liberal

Party are also traced through the pages of R. MacGregor Dawson, *William Lyon Mackenzie King: A Political Biography, 1874–1923* (Toronto: University of Toronto Press, 1958); and H. Blair Neatby, *William Lyon Mackenzie King, 1924–1932: The Lonely Heights* (Toronto: University of Toronto Press, 1963).

51 On the war, conscription, and its aftermath for labour, see Martin Robin, "Registration, Conscription, and Independent Labour Politics, 1916–1917," *Canadian Historical Review* 47(2) (June 1966), reprinted in *Conscription 1917*, ed. Carl Berger (Toronto: University of Toronto Press, n.d.), 60–77; McCormack, *Reformers, Rebels, and Revolutionaries*, 119–69; Thompson, *The Harvests of War*, 117–21, 160–62; Desmond Morton with Terry Copp, *Working People: An Illustrated History of the Canadian Labour Movement*, revised (Toronto: Deneau, 1984), 101–24; Gregory S. Kealey, "1919: The Canadian Labour Revolt," *Labour/Le Travail* 13 (Spring 1984): 11–44; Kealey, "State Repression of Labour and the Left in Canada, 1914–20: The Impact of the First World War," *Canadian Historical Review* 73(3) (September 1992): 281–314; and Craig Heron and Myer Siemiatycki, "The Great War, the State, and Working-Class Canada," in *The Workers' Revolt in Canada, 1917–1925*, ed. Craig Heron (Toronto: University of Toronto Press, 1998), 11–42.

52 On women and the war generally, see Ceta Ramkhalawansingh, "Women during the Great War," in *Women at Work: Ontario, 1850–1930*, ed. Janice Acton, Penny Goldsmith, and Bonnie Shepard (Toronto: Canadian Women's Educational Press, 1974), 261–307; Alison Prentice et al., *Canadian Women: A History* (Toronto: Harcourt Brace Jovanovich, 1988), 139–41, 203–10; Joan Sangster, "Mobilizing Women for War," in *Canada and the First World War: Essays in Honour of Robert Craig Brown*, ed. David Mackenzie (Toronto: University of Toronto Press, 2005), 157–93; Linda J. Quiney, "'Bravely and Loyally They Answered the Call': St. John Ambulance, the Red Cross, and the Patriotic Service of Canadian Women During the Great War," *History of Intellectual Culture* 5(1) (2005): 1–19 [online journal: www.ucalgary.ca/hic]; and Sarah Glassford and Amy Shaw, eds., *A Sisterhood of Suffering and Service: Women and Girls of Canada and Newfoundland during the First World War* (Vancouver: UBC Press, 2012), esp. 1–23, 103, 315–22. On their experience as nursing sisters and VADs, see also G.W.L. Nicholson, *Canada's Nursing Sisters* (Toronto: Samuel Stevens Hakkert, 1975), 48–99; Linda J. Quiney, "'Sharing the Halo': Social and Professional Tensions in the Work of World War I Canadian Volunteer Nurses," *Journal of the Canadian Historical Association* 9 (1998): 105–24; and Suzanne Evans, "Coming in the Front Door: A History of Three Canadian Physiotherapists through Two World Wars," *Canadian Military History* 19(2) (Spring 2010): 55–62. And for a direct example of the emotional impact for women left at home, see Barry M. Moody, "Acadia and the Great War," in *Youth, University and Canadian Society: Essays in the Social History of Higher Education*, ed. Paul Axelrod and John G. Reid (Montreal and Kingston: McGill–Queen's University Press, 1989), 154–56.

53 All of the information in this paragraph is taken from H.A.C. Machin, *Report of the Director of the Military Service Branch* (Ottawa: King's Printer, 1919). On the workings of the Military Service Act in 1917–18, see also Granatstein and Hitsman, *Broken Promises*, 83–97.

54 The negative conclusion appeared in particular in Granatstein and Hitsman, *Broken Promises*, 96–98; as well as in A.M.J. Hyatt, "Sir Arthur Currie and Conscription: A Soldier's View," *Canadian Historical Review* 50(3) (September 1969): 295, who argued that the shortage of men in 1918 was in fact met by breaking up the 5th Division in England. The opposite point of view appeared as early as 1956 in A.M. Willms, "Conscription 1917: A Brief for the Defence," *Canadian Historical Review* 37(4) (December 1956), reprinted in Berger, ed., *Conscription 1917*, 1–14. J.L. Granatstein has also reversed his own earlier position, in "Conscription and My Politics," *Canadian Military History* 10(4) (Autumn

2001) 35–38; and "Conscription in the Great War," in *Canada and the First World War*, ed. Mackenzie, 62–75. The most recent reassessment appears in Patrick Dennis, "A Canadian Conscript Goes to War – August 1918: Old Myths Re-examined," *Canadian Military History* 18(1) (Winter 2009), esp. 34.

55 On the Siberian expedition, as well as other forces in which Canada participated in northern Russia in 1918–19, see Nicholson, *Canadian Expeditionary Force*, 517–23; John Swettenham, *Allied Intervention in Russia 1918–1919, and the Part Played by Canada* (Toronto: Ryerson, 1967); Roy MacLaren, *Canadians in Russia, 1918–19* (Toronto: Macmillan of Canada, 1976); C.P. Stacey, *Canada and the Age of Conflict*, vol. 1 277–84; and Benjamin Isitt, *From Victoria to Vladivostok: Canada's Siberian Expedition, 1917–19* (Vancouver: UBC Press, 2010), esp. 72–73.

56 For Duff's comments, see Frederick W. Gibson and Barbara Robertson, eds., *Ottawa at War: The Grant Dexter Memoranda, 1939–1945* (Winnipeg: Manitoba Record Society, 1994), memorandum of December 22, 1941, 237; as well as Granatstein and Hitsman, *Broken Promises*, 98; and David Ricardo Williams, *Duff: A Life in the Law* (Vancouver: UBC Press, 1984), 94–95.

57 Machin, *Report of the Director*, 10.

58 Granatstein and Hitsman, *Broken Promises*, 85–86; Thompson, *The Harvests of War*, 133.

59 Molly Ungar, "Saving the Past: Evidence from Military Tribunal No. 330, October, 1917," paper presented at the Tenth Military History Colloquium of the Laurier Centre for Military, Strategic, and Disarmament Studies, Wilfrid Laurier University, Waterloo, May 4, 1999.

60 Miller, *Our Glory and Our Grief*, 146–51.

61 Amy J. Shaw, *Crisis of Conscience: Conscientious Objection in Canada during the First World War* (Vancouver: UBC Press, 2009).

62 For an introduction to his work, see Dennis, "A Canadian Conscript Goes to War," 21–36. In addition, a record of the final decisions taken for all individuals who came before the tribunal in New Germany, Nova Scotia, is available in Nova Scotia Archives, MG 23, Vol. 87, File #2, November 8, 1917, to January 16, 1918.

63 See in particular Dawson, *William Lyon Mackenzie King*, 65–70, 91–120, 132–269 (quotation from 260), 290–309, 354; Neatby, *William Lyon Mackenzie King, 1924-1932*, 73–74 and 166; Beck, *Pendulum of Power*, 149–90; Granatstein and Hitsman, *Broken Promises*, 112–22; John MacFarlane, *Ernest Lapointe and Quebec's Influence on Canadian Foreign Policy* (Toronto: University of Toronto Press, 1999), 25–27 and 33–38; and Lita-Rose Betcherman, *Ernest Lapointe: Mackenzie King's Great Quebec Lieutenant* (Toronto: University of Toronto Press, 2002), 23–30.

64 King's actions during Chanak and the two Imperial Conferences are discussed especially in Dawson, *William Lyon Mackenzie King*, 406–25, 453–80, Neatby, *William Lyon Mackenzie King, 1924–1932*, 176–91; Stacey, *Canada and the Age of Conflict*, vol. 2, 17–31, 35–44, 66–72, 83–89; and Philip G. Wigley, *Canada and the Transition to Commonwealth: British-Canadian Relations, 1917–1926* (Cambridge: Cambridge University Press, 1977). Stacey's book provides a solid overview of Canada's foreign and defence policies throughout the 1920s and 1930s. On that subject, see also James Eayrs, *In Defence of Canada: From the Great War to the Great Depression* (Toronto: University of Toronto Press, 1964); and Eayrs, *In Defence of Canada: Appeasement and Rearmament* (Toronto: University of Toronto Press, 1965).

65 In addition to the sources cited in the previous note, see James Eayrs, "'A Low Dishonest Decade': Aspects of Canadian External Policy, 1931–1939," in Hugh L. Keenleyside et al., *The Growth of Canadian Policies in External Affairs* (Durham: Duke University Press,

1960), 59–80; J.L. Granatstein and Robert Bothwell, "'A Self-Evident National Duty': Canadian Foreign Policy, 1935–1939," *Journal of Imperial and Commonwealth History* 3(2) (January 1975): 212–33; Granatstein, *Canada's War*, 2–5; and Granatstein and Hitsman, *Broken Promises*, 112–28.

66 Further to the sources listed in the previous two notes, see also H. Blair Neatby, *William Lyon Mackenzie King, 1932–1939*, 190–94; and especially Roger Sarty, "Mr King and the Armed Forces," in *A Country of Limitations: Canada and the World in 1939/Un pays dans la gêne: le Canada et le Monde en 1939* ed. Norman Hillmer et al. (Ottawa: Canadian Committee for the History of the Second World War, 1996), 217–46.

67 Quoted in Stacey, *Arms, Men, and Governments*, 398; and in Granatstein and Hitsman, *Broken Promises*, 127. On Manion's selection as Conservative leader in 1938 and his responses to world events in the fall of 1938 and March 1939, see J.L. Granatstein, *The Politics of Survival: The Conservative Party of Canada, 1939–1945* (Toronto: University of Toronto Press, 1967), 10–18, 20–26. On the events of September 1938 and March 1939, in addition to the various works on foreign policy cited already (and especially Neatby, on King's reactions, in *William Lyon Mackenzie King, 1932–1939*, 273–303), see also Terry Copp, "Ontario 1939: The Decision for War," *Ontario History* 86(3) (September 1994): 269–78.

68 On Lapointe's role in these events, see MacFarlane, *Ernest Lapointe*, 138–46; and Betcherman, *Ernest Lapointe*, 259–67.

69 On relations between the British officers commanding the Canadian army during this period and civilian politicians, see in particular Desmond Morton, *Ministers and Generals: Politics and the Canadian Militia, 1868–1904* (Toronto: University of Toronto Press, 1970). See also Harris, *Canadian Brass*, 3–92, on this and efforts to promote increasing professionalism up to 1914 more broadly.

70 Harris, *Canadian Brass*, 141–48; and Wood, *Militia Myths*, 241–43.

71 J.L. Granatstein, *The Generals: The Canadian Army's Senior Commanders in the Second World War* (Toronto: Stoddart, 1993), 85–87; Paul Douglas Dickson, *A Thoroughly Canadian General: A Biography of General H.D.G. Crerar* (Toronto: University of Toronto Press, 2007), 14–70.

72 Granatstein, *The Generals*, 217–18.

73 Granatstein, *The Generals*, 117–18; E.L.M. Burns, *General Mud: Memoirs of Two World Wars* (Toronto: Clarke, Irwin, 1970), 1–83; Douglas E. Delaney, *Corps Commanders: Five British and Canadian Generals at War, 1939–45* (Vancouver: UBC Press, 2011), 60–62.

74 On Ralston's First World War career, and his behaviour as Minister of National Defence during the Second World War, see Daniel Byers, "J.L. Ralston and the First World War: The Origins of a Life of Service," *Canadian Military History* 22(1) (Winter 2013): 3–16; and Byers, "J.L. Ralston as Minister of National Defence During the Second World War: A Reassessment," *Canadian Army Journal* 16(1) (Spring 2015): 70–95.

75 On Stuart's career, and especially his work as editor of the *Canadian Defence Quarterly* in the interwar period, see Granatstein, *The Generals*, 218–22; Eayrs, *In Defence of Canada: From the Great War to the Great Depression*, 97–102, James H. Lutz, "Canadian Military Thought, 1923–1939: A Profile Drawn from the Pages of the Old *Canadian Defence Quarterly*," *Canadian Defence Quarterly* [new series] 9(2) (Autumn 1979): 40–48; Serge M. Durflinger, "The *Canadian Defence Quarterly* 1933–1935: Canadian Military Writing of a Bygone Era," *Canadian Defence Quarterly* [new series] 20(6) (June 1991): 43–47; and English, *The Canadian Army*, 48–49. Yves Tremblay also discusses the *CDQ* as an element of the larger intellectual development of the Canadian army in the interwar period, more critically in *Instruire une armée: Les officiers canadiens et la guerre moderne (1919-1944)* (Outremont: Athéna éditions, 2007), 70–76.

76 Burns, *General Mud*, 84–96; Granatstein, *The Generals*, 119–26; Lieutenant-Colonel Bernd Horn and Michel Wyczynski, "E.L.M. Burns: Canada's Intellectual General," in *Warrior Chiefs: Perspectives on Senior Canadian Military Leaders*, ed. Bernd Horn and Stephen Harris (Toronto: Dundurn, 2001), 143–49; and Delaney, *Corps Commanders*, 62–70. On Simonds's background and his role in the 1938 debate, see also Dominick Graham, *The Price of Command: A Biography of General Guy Simonds* (Toronto: Stoddart, 1993), 9–36; and Lieutenant-Colonel Roman Johann Jarymowycz, "General Guy Simonds: The Commander as Tragic Hero," in *Warrior Chiefs*, ed. Horn and Harris, 108–9. Tremblay also discusses Burns, and this debate, in *Instruire une armée*, 72, 76–85.

77 On the training of the Canadian army and its officers overall, and more specifically ties between the British and Canadian forces during the interwar period, the Staff College and Imperial Defence College courses, and other exchanges, the most recent and thorough discussion can be found in Tremblay, *Instruire une armée*, 31–44, 55–60. See also Maurice A. Pope, *Soldiers and Politicians: The Memoirs of Lt.-Gen. Maurice A. Pope, C.B., M.C.* (Toronto: University of Toronto Press, 1962), 48–107; Eayrs, *In Defence of Canada: From the Great War to the Great Depression*, 85–104; Burns, *General Mud*, 84–86; Stacey, *Arms, Men, and Governments*, 72–80; Reginald H. Roy, *For Most Conspicuous Bravery: A Biography of Major-General George R. Pearkes, V.C., through two World Wars* (Vancouver: UBC Press, 1977), 79–83; Norman Hillmer, "Defence and Ideology: The Anglo-Canadian Military 'Alliance' in the 1930s," *International Journal* 33(3) (Summer 1978): 596–601; Harris, *Canadian Brass*, 192–209; English, *The Canadian Army*, 23–24, 39–56; Granatstein, *The Generals*, 9–27; and Graham, *The Price of Command*, 25–32 and 43–44.

78 On Crerar's interwar career, see Granatstein, *The Generals*, 87–90; and Dickson, *A Thoroughly Canadian General*, 70–117.

79 See John Swettenham, *McNaughton*, vol. 1: *1887–1939* (Toronto: Ryerson, 1968), 185–87; Gallant, "The Development of the Canadian Army," 50–56; Morton, "The Limits of Loyalty," 97; and Pariseau and Bernier, *French Canadians and Bilingualism*, vol. 1, 92–101.

80 Harris, *Canadian Brass*, 145–46, 166–91; Dickson, *A Thoroughly Canadian General*, 90–91, 99–102, 115–16, 143. See also Eayrs, *In Defence of Canada: From the Great War to the Great Depression*, 70–85; and M.A. Hooker, "Serving Two Masters: Ian Mackenzie and Civil-Military Relations in Canada, 1935–1939," *Journal of Canadian Studies* 21(1) (Spring 1986): 38–56.

81 See especially Granatstein, *The Generals*, 96–97, 103–107; and Dickson, *A Thoroughly Canadian General*, 149–51, 212–25.

82 Dickson, "Visions of Professionalism: General H.D.G. Crerar and the Canadian Army, 1939–1942," paper presented at the annual meeting of the Canadian Historical Association, Charlottetown, 1992, 11–12. See also Dickson, *A Thoroughly Canadian General*, 140–44. The influence of the memory created by the Canadian Corps for McNaughton runs through Swettenham's three-volume biography, but for a succinct statement, see *McNaughton*, vol. 1, 174–75.

Part 2: The National Resources Mobilization Act and the Rise of the Big Army

1 LAC, RG 24, vol. 17194, War Diary, No. 32 CA(B)TC, Peterborough, September–October 1940, Appendix 4, "The Song of the Seventh Platoon," n.d.

Chapter 2: Mobilizing Canada

1 On the first months of the war and the election in Quebec, see Granatstein, *Canada's War*, 1–35; as well as Granatstein and Hitsman, *Broken Promises*, 133–36; Norman Ward, ed., *A Party Politician: The Memoirs of Chubby Power* (Toronto: Macmillan, 1966), 123–30

(quotation from 125); Beck, *Pendulum of Power*, 223–40; Laurendeau, "The Conscription Crisis, 1942," 21–35 (quotation from 33); MacFarlane, *Ernest Lapointe*, 146–58; Betcherman, *Ernest Lapointe*, 271–95; and Vennat, *Lés Héros oubliés*, vol. 1, 78.

2 The various aspects of the early war effort discussed in this paragraph are surveyed in Stacey, *Arms, Men, and Governments*, 12–30; and Granatstein, *Canada's War*, 42–59.

3 Gilbert Norman Tucker, *The Naval Service of Canada: Its Official History*, vol. 2 *Activities on Shore during the Second World War* (Ottawa: King's Printer, 1952), 5–51, 269; W.A.B. Douglas et al., *No Higher Purpose: The Official Operational History of the Royal Canadian Navy in the Second World War, 1939-1943*, vol. 2, pt. 1 (St. Catharines: Vanwell/Department of National Defence, 2002), 27–90.

4 F.J. Hatch, *Aerodrome of Democracy: Canada and the British Commonwealth Air Training Plan, 1939–1945* (Ottawa: Supply and Services Canada, 1983), 6–26, 33, W.A.B. Douglas, *The Creation of a National Air Force: The Official History of the Royal Canadian Air Force*, vol. 2 (Toronto: Supply and Services Canada/University of Toronto Press, 1986), 191–230, 343–47; and C.P. Stacey, *Official History of the Canadian Army in the Second World War*, vol. 1: *Six Years of War: The Army in Canada, Britain and the Pacific* (Ottawa: Queen's Printer, 1955), 42–44, 46–64.

5 Stacey, *Six Years of War*, 4–18, 68–70; Stacey, *Arms, Men, and Governments*, 3–5, 11; Hatch, *Aerodrome of Democracy*, 20; and Sarty, "Mr King and the Armed Forces," 217–46.

6 Stacey, *Arms, Men, and Governments*, 30–31; Granatstein, *Canada's War*, 59–66. Many of these negotiations can be followed in detail in the files of the Economic Advisory Committee, a body that was set up within the Department of Finance to coordinate Canada's economic contributions to the war effort, in LAC, RG 19, Records of the Department of Finance, vols. 4660–64 (in particular, see the voluminous files on pork and wheat in vols. 4662 and 4664). Paul Marsden has also produced an excellent overview of the early war effort from the point of view of the Department of Finance in "The Costs of No Commitments: Canadian Economic Planning for War, 1939," in *A Country of Limitations*, ed. Hillmer et al., 199–216.

7 On the developments described in this paragraph, see Granatstein, *The Politics of Survival*, 38–57 (quotation from 48); Granatstein, *Canada's War*, 72–93; and Granatstein and Hitsman, *Broken Promises*, 136–40. Press opinions on the idea of National Government before and during the campaign can also be traced in clippings collected in LAC, MG 26, Prime Minister W.L.M. King Papers [hereafter King Papers], J6, vol. 234, "W.W. II – National Government, n.d., 1939–1942 (Clippings)," July 15, 1939–February 26, 1940. See also MacFarlane, *Ernest Lapointe*, 125–26, and Betcherman, *Ernest Lapointe*, 302–7.

8 Stacey, *Six Years of War*, 44–45; Pariseau and Bernier, *French Canadians and Bilingualism*, vol. 1, 110; and Vennat, *Lés Héros oubliés*, vol. 1, 15, 17–36, 47–55, and 129–31. According to Florent Lefebvre, *The French Canadian Press and the War*, transl. and ed. J.H. Biggar and J.R. Baldwin (Toronto: Ryerson, 1940), 38, *La Presse*'s weekly daily circulation was 142,417.

9 Stacey, *Six Years of War*, 57–58, 72–76, 112–14, 132–34; Stacey, *Arms, Men, and Governments*, appendix "T," 599; Yves Tremblay, *Instruire une armée*, 87–104, 111–22. See also Granatstein, *Canada's War*, 81, on King's reasons for supporting sending the 2nd Division overseas.

10 King Papers, J4, vol. 353, "Conscription" file, C244224–25, "Summary of Additional War Measures Announced by the Prime Minister," May 20, 1940; Stacey, *Six Years of War*, 76–80. On all of the developments noted in this paragraph, see also Stacey, *Arms, Men, and Governments*, 31–36; and Granatstein, *Canada's War*, 93–96 (where the memorandum noted here is also cited).

11 On the expansion of the RCAF generally, the BCATP, and the experiences of No. 1 Fighter Squadron more specifically, see Hatch, *Aerodrome of Democracy*, 48–59; Douglas, *The*

Creation of a National Air Force, 231–47; and Brereton Greenhous, Stephen J. Harris, William C. Johnston, and William G.P. Rawling, *The Crucible of War, 1939–1945: The Official History of The Royal Canadian Air Force*, vol. 3 (Toronto: Supply and Services Canada / University of Toronto Press, 1994), 182–98.

12 Tucker, *The Naval Service of Canada*, vol. 2, 51–63; Douglas et al., *No Higher Purpose*, 91–95, 104–16, 130–45.

13 "The Emergency Powers (Defence) Act, 1940," 3 & 4 Geo. 6, c. 20, *Halisbury's Statutes of England*, vol. 33 (London: Butterworth & Co., 1941), 541–42; Granatstein and Hitsman, *Broken Promises*, 140. Cf. "The Emergency Powers (Defence) Act, 1939," 2 & 3 Geo. 6, c. 62, *Halisbury's Statutes of England*, vol. 32 (London: Butterworth & Co., 1940), 930–38.

14 *The Canada Gazette*, September 1, 1939.

15 "The National Resources Mobilization Act, 1940," 4 George VI, Chap. 13, *Acts of the Parliament of the Dominion of Canada*, 1939–1940 (Ottawa: King's Printer, 1940), 43.

16 Burns, *Manpower in the Canadian Army*, 116–17. The creation of the NRMA is also discussed in Stacey, *Arms, Men, and Governments*, 32–33; Granatstein, *Canada's War*, 98–100; and Granatstein and Hitsman, *Broken Promises*, 140–44.

17 See King Diaries, June 14–20, 1940.

18 For instance, see memorandum by W.J. Turnbull in King Papers, J4, vol. 353, "Conscription," 244226, "Re: Conscription of Wealth and Manpower," May 23, 1940, which summarizes several telegrams received by the Prime Minister's Office during this period (also noted in Granatstein, *Canada's War*, 96). Further examples are given in Granatstein and Hitsman, *Broken Promises*, 141.

19 Quoted in Granatstein, *Politics of Survival*, 60. For King's similar version of the conversation, see King Diaries, June 17, 1940. The events are also described in Granatstein, *Canada's War*, 98.

20 King Papers, J4, vol. 424, Minutes of Cabinet War Committee [hereafter CWC Minutes], June 17, 1940. Among the ministers and civil servants recorded as speaking in favour of broader measures were C.G. Power (Minister of National Defence for Air, and Acting Minister of National Defence), Ernest Lapointe (Minister of Justice), O.D. Skelton (Under-Secretary of State for External Affairs), C.D. Howe (Minister of Munitions and Supply), and J.L. Ralston (Minister of Finance, and future Minister of National Defence).

21 Pickersgill, *The Mackenzie King Record*, vol. 1, 94; King Diaries, June 14 and 17; King Papers, J4, vol. 424, CWC Minutes, May 22, 23, and 29 and June 17 and 27, 1940.

22 King Diaries, June 17, 1940.

23 Dominion of Canada, *Official Report of Debates of the House of Commons*, vol. 1, 1940 (Ottawa: King's Printer, 1940), 852–976; King Papers, J4, vol. 373, "National Resources Mobilization Act," C258604–605: "The National Resources Mobilization Act, 1940: Notes for use in introducing the Bill, or on second reading," n.d. [June 1940]; and public comments by C.G. Power, Minister of National Defence for Air, in a radio broadcast included in transcript form in RG 24, vol. 2050, file HQ 54-27-1-24, circular letter, Major-General B.W. Browne, AG, to all DOCs, July 15, 1940.

24 King Diaries, June 17, 1940.

25 On all of the developments in Quebec discussed in this paragraph, see Elizabeth H. Armstrong, *French Canadian Opinion on the War, January, 1940–June, 1941* (Toronto: Ryerson, 1942), 8–9, 15–20; Laurendeau, "The Conscription Crisis, 1942," 40–45; Vennat, *Lés Héros oubliés*, vol. 1, 79–86; MacFarlane, *Ernest Lapointe*, 175; Betcherman, *Ernest Lapointe*, 317–19; and Tremblay, *Instruire une armée*, 105–11, 122–27. On Houde specifically, see also Granatstein, *Canada's War*, 101–2; and Granatstein and Hitsman, *Broken*

Promises, 145. On Cabinet's actions (and for the quotations that appear in the text here), see King Diaries, August 3 and 5, 1940.

26 On the work of the Temporary Committee that decided the details of how the registration would proceed and the information that would be collected, see various documents in LAC, RG 31, Records of Statistics Canada, vol. 1414, file 1533, "1940 National Registration for War"; RG 19, vol. 3581, file N-02, "National Registration, Doctor W.A. Mckintosh," reports of the Temporary Committee, June 24 and 25, 1940; and King Papers, J6, vol. 234, "W.W. II – National Registration, 1940–1941 (Clippings)," clipping from *Ottawa Journal* titled "Dr. Coats' Registration Job 'Marvellous' Says Minister," December 27, 1940. A general summary of the registration is also available in LAC, RG 27, acc. 97–98/052, "Historical Record of The National Registration 1940." See also Granatstein, *Canada's War*, 100–2; and Granatstein and Hitsman, *Broken Promises*, 144–46. Lastly, civilian aspects of the operation of the NRMA are dealt with in Stevenson, *Canada's Greatest Wartime Muddle*; on the registration and the later framework that was set up for calling out men, see esp. 18–21.

27 On Rogers's death and the reorganization of Cabinet that followed, see Stacey, *Arms, Men, and Governments*, 36–37; and Granatstein, *Canada's War*, 104–5.

28 King Diaries, September 5 and 13–19, 1939; Pickersgill, *The Mackenzie King Record*, vol. 1, 25–26; and Granatstein, *Canada's War*, 25–26. On the Bren light machine gun, which led to a Royal Commission (and for which J.L. Ralston, who was at that time a private lawyer in Montreal, worked as the government's legal counsel), see Stacey, *Arms, Men, and Governments*, 101–2.

29 Dawson, *The Conscription Crisis of 1944*, 29–31; Granatstein, *Canada's War*, 202; Granatstein and Hitsman, *Broken Promises*, 170; Rea, "What Really Happened?": 10–19; Walker, "The Revolt of the Canadian Generals," esp. 60–66, 70. For a somewhat differing view, see Byers, "J.L. Ralston as Minister of National Defence during the Second World War," 70–95.

30 Stacey, *Six Years of War*, 80–81; Tremblay, *Instruire une armée*, 87–104, 111–22, 127–33.

31 LAC, RG 24, microfilm reel C-5121, file HQC 7959, untitled memorandum, June 25, and following documents to July 5, 1940 (incorrectly dated 5 June).

32 LAC, RG 24, vol. 2050, HQ 54–27–1-24, transcript of radio address titled "Men Wanted."

33 Dickson, *A Thoroughly Canadian General*, 139–40; and Granatstein, *The Generals*, 93.

34 LAC, MG 30, E 157, General H.D.G. Crerar Papers [hereafter Crerar Papers], vol. 1, file 958C.009(D12), "CGS files 1940-1941 – Personal Correspondence Lt-Gen Crerar-Lt-Gen McNaughton. Period Aug 40 to Mar 41," Crerar to McNaughton, September 9, 1940. See also Crerar's comments to the Cabinet War Committee in King Papers, CWC Minutes, July 26, 1940; as well as Granatstein and Hitsman, *Broken Promises*, 144. For another interpretation of Crerar's comments, see Walker, "The Revolt of the Canadian Generals," esp. 62.

35 The final training plan appears in LAC, RG 24, vol. 6570, file HQ 1161-1-5, "Procedure of National Defence Department Mobilization Act," vol. 1, circular letter, AG to all DOCs, August 20, 1940.

36 LAC, RG 24, War Diaries, vol. 13200, Deputy CGS, August 1940, Appendix 1; and vol. 13202, Directorate of Military Training, various entries for period July–September 1940.

37 Excerpt from *La Patrie*, January 19, 1941, in LAC, RG 24, vol. 16913, War Diary, No. 44 NPAM Training Centre [later CA(B)TC], St-Jérôme, January 1941, Appendix 4.

38 Captain A.A.E. Batchelor of No. 131 Canadian Militia Training Centre had lost his left hand while serving in the 5th Battalion, Canadian Expeditionary Force, where he earned several awards for bravery, along with his officer's commission. LAC, RG 24, vol. 17291, War Diary, No. 131 CA(B)TC, Camrose, February 1, 1941.

39 LAC, RG 24, War Diaries, vol. 17306, No. 111 CA(R)TC, Gordon Head, October 7, 1940; vol. 16913, No. 44 CA(B)TC, St-Jérôme, February 1941, Appendix 5, letter, Raymond Lacasse to OC, February 24, 1941.

40 Interview with Howard Ripstein, former corporal, No. 41 CMTC, April 22, 1997.

41 LAC, RG 24, vol. 17254, War Diary, No. 70 CA(B)TC, Fredericton, September 7, 1940. See also C.P. Stacey, *A Date with History: Memoirs of a Canadian Historian* (Toronto: Deneau, n.d. [1982]), 104–5; and Tim Cook, *Clio's Warriors: Canadian Historians and the Writing of the World Wars* (Vancouver: UBC Press, 2006), 98.

42 LAC, RG 24, vol. 17021, War Diary, No. 44 CMTC [later A-12 Canadian Army (Advanced) Training Centre], Farnham, August 13–16, 1940.

43 Ripstein Interview, April 22, 1997.

44 LAC, RG 24, vol. 17233, War Diary, No. 51 CA(B)TC, Chicoutimi, August-September 1940, Appendix II, "A Canadian Militia Training Centre."

45 A summary of strengths at the beginning of the first training period can be found in LAC, RG 24, vol. 6571, HQ 1161–1-5, vol. 3, "Strength of men reported for Training as at 16 Oct. [1940]."

46 LAC, RG 24, vol. 6571, HQ 1161–1-5, vol. 2, telegram, DOC, MD 13, to DND, October 1, 1940; C. Gunning, *North Bay's Fort Chippewa, 1939–1945* (North Bay: 1991), 15, 21.

47 LAC, RG 24, War Diaries, vol. 17269, No. 102 CA(B)TC, Fort William, September 11; vol. 17252, No. 62 CA(B)TC, Charlottetown, September 30, 1940.

48 Ralston Papers, vol. 68, "Construction Projects, 1942: Work carried out since commencement of war," Major-General E.J.C. Schmidlin, Quartermaster-General, to Ralston, March 11, 1941.

49 See various correspondence in LAC, RG 24, vol. 6570, file HQ 1161–1-5, vol. 1, August 23–September 23, 1940.

50 LAC, RG 24, War Diaries, vol. 17264, No. 100 CA(B)TC, Portage la Prairie, September 30–October 11; vol. 17295, No. 132 CA(B)TC, Grande Prairie, September 25–October 9; vol. 17194, No. 32 CA(B)TC, Peterborough, October 9, 1940. Staffs also had to be accommodated in a similar manner for the first few days before training started in Vernon. LAC, RG 24, vol. 17277, War Diary, No. 110 CA(B)TC, August–October 1940, Appendix 3.

51 For two references to snow shovelling during PT periods in particular, see LAC, RG 24, War Diaries, vol. 17220, No. 45 CA(B)TC, Sorel, November 30, and vol. 17194, No. 32 CA(B)TC, Peterborough, December 2–3, 1940.

52 Pariseau and Bernier, *French Canadians and Bilingualism* vol. 1, 125. I have inferred Fredericton from their naming of Lieutenant-Colonel A.J. Brooks and G.F.G. Stanley, both of whom served there, as well as a personal letter to me from Stanley, December 18, 1995, which mentions some of the same information.

53 LAC, RG 27, vol. 631, file 58–2, "National War Services Dept.," schedule dated September 16, 1940. On Dundurn specifically, see also RG 24, vol. 6571, HQ 1161–1-5, vol. 1, Lieut. Colonel G.A.H. Trudeau, T[emporarily]/Commanding, MD 12, to Secretary, DND, September 4, 1940 (as well as documents around that date on general arrangements made in various military districts).

54 Canada, Dominion Bureau of Statistics, *Eighth Census of Canada*, 1941 (Ottawa: King's Printer, 1950), vol. 1, table 38, 700–1.

55 LAC, RG 24, vol. 13202, War Diary, Directorate of Military Training, September 20; LAC, RG 24, vol. 6570, HQ 1161–1-5, vol. 2, DAG(M) to AG, October 14; LAC, RG 27, vol. 631, file 58–2, "National War Services Dept.," schedule dated October 25, 1940. The changes can also be traced at the level of individual training centres through LAC, RG 24, War

Diaries for camps Nos. 40–47 in Military District No. 4, vols. 16912, 17021, 17200, 17205, 17213, 17220, 17225, and 17305, September–October 1940.

56 Vennat also comments on the number of francophones who served on the staffs of training centres in Quebec, and the number of centres that offered training in French. Both issues were followed regularly in *La Presse*; in one case, the paper even highlighted one of the platoons outside Quebec that was able to train entirely in French, in Cornwall. Vennat, *Lés Héros oubliés*, vol. 1, 87–88, 117–19.

57 Granatstein and Hitsman, *Broken Promises*, 147.

58 LAC, RG 24, vol. 6571, file HQ 1161-1-5, vol. 3, Gerard Lacourciere [*sic*], Mayor, Ville de Megantic [*sic*], to Ralston, September 20; see also other documents on file, September 19–November 7, 1940.

59 LAC, RG 24, vol. 6571, file HQ 1161-1-5, vol. 3, DOC, MD 13, to DND, September 28, 1940.

60 "Is Camrose to Be Military Training Centre?," August 7, and other clippings in LAC, RG 24, vol. 17290, War Diary, No. 131 CA(B)TC, Camrose, August 1940, Appendices A to D, and October 1940, Appendices D to G.

61 LAC, RG 27, vol. 631, file 58–1, "National War Services Dept.," Nixon to Gardiner, July 16, 1940. On the unemployment relief camps in the 1930s, see Eayrs, *In Defence of Canada: From the Great War to the Great Depression*, 124–36. On Gardiner, see Norman Ward and David Smith, *Jimmy Gardiner: Relentless Liberal* (Toronto: University of Toronto Press, 1990); on his time as dual minister, see esp. 237–46.

62 LAC, RG 24, vol. 13202, War Diary, Directorate of Military Training, August 15, 1940.

63 LAC, RG 24, vol. 17258, War Diary, No. 71 CA(B)TC, Edmundston, December 1, 1940.

64 LAC, RG 24, vol. 17143, War Diary, No. 10 CA(B)TC, Kitchener, November 22, 1940.

65 LAC, RG 24, vol. 17269, War Diary, No. 102 CA(B)TC, Fort William, October 22, for reference to library, and "Summary" included with war diary for whole period October 1–31, 1940, for quoted comment.

66 LAC, RG 24, War Diaries, vol. 16885, No. 11 CA(R)TC [later S-11 Advanced Driving and Maintenance School], Woodstock, September 29; vol. 17205, No. 42 CA(B)TC, Joliette, September 29; vol. 16912, No. 44 CA(B)TC, St-Jérôme, September 29, 1940.

67 LAC, RG 24, War Diaries, vol. 17143, No. 10 CA(B)TC, Kitchener; vol. 17188, No. 31 CA(B)TC, Cornwall, both October 9; vol. 17243, No. 55 CMTC, Rimouski, October 18, 1940.

68 LAC, RG 24, War Diaries, vol. 17225, No. 47 CA(B)TC, Valleyfield, October 8; vol. 17306, No. 50 CA(R)TC, Valcartier, October 31; vol. 17236, No. 53 CA(B)TC, Lauzon, October 31; vol. 17233, No. 51 CA(B)TC, Chicoutimi, November 3; vol. 17240, No. 54 CA(B)TC, Montmagny, November 4, 1940.

69 Gagnon, *Le 22e bataillon*, 214.

70 Armstrong, *French Canadian Opinion on the War*, 8, 30–31; Vennat, *Lés Héros oubliés*, vol. 1, 141–50.

71 As Vennat notes, in August 1940, Villeneuve had also requested parish clergy to do everything they could to try to help make national registration a success, as a sign of cooperation with the public authorities. Vennat, *Lés Héros oubliés*, vol. 1, 85. See also the discussion of this, as well as Villeneuve's actions in this period more broadly, in Armstrong, *French Canadian Opinion on the War*, 16, 31–33. For a more negative view of Villeneuve's wartime influence, see Laurendeau, "The Conscription Crisis, 1942," 49.

72 Granatstein, *Canada's War*, 102; Granatstein and Hitsman, *Broken Promises*, 147.

73 For example, see LAC, RG 24, War Diaries, vol. 17269, No. 102 CA(B)TC, Fort William, "Summary," November 1–30; vol. 17277, No. 110 CA(B)TC, Vernon, November 1940, Appendix 8, "Report on Training," November 7, 1940, 3.

74 For Hanson's comments, see King Papers, J4, vol. 365 (reel H-1538), "National Resources Mobilization Act," C252399 and C252404, clippings from *Ottawa Journal* and *Ottawa Citizen*, August 2; and vol. 353 (reel H-1532), "Conscription," C244243, clipping from the *Montreal Gazette*, October 12, 1940. For the comment from *Saturday Night*, see editorial titled "Thirty-Day Soldiers," October 12. Another clipping in the same vein appears in King Papers, J6, vol. 234, "W.W. II – National Resources Mobilization Act, 1940–1941 (Clippings)," under the title "Thirty Days Not Enough," *Ottawa Citizen*, October 11, 1940. See also Miles Resartus, "Canada's Democratic Army," *The Canadian Forum* 20(238), November 1940, 242–43.

75 LAC, RG 24, vol. 17200, War Diary, No. 41 CA(B)TC, Huntingdon, September 1–2, 1940.

76 Paraphrased from LAC, RG 24, vol. 17167, War Diary, No. 23 CA(B)TC, Newmarket, October 3, 1940.

77 For all of the comments made here and in the sentences immediately above, see Lucien A. Côté, with Réal Bouvier, *Je les ai vus mourir: Les souvenirs de guerre d'un jeune soldat canadien-français* (Montreal: Éditions Macadam, 1995), 9–20 (quotation from 18), 311.

78 LAC, RG 24, War Diary, vol. 17307, No. 111 CA(R)TC, Gordon Head, January 17, 1941.

79 LAC, RG 24, War Diaries, vol. 17306, No. 111 CA(R)TC, Gordon Head, October 19; vol. 17153, No. 20 CA(B)TC, Brantford, November 6; vol. 17307, No. 121 CA(R)TC, Dundurn, December 18, 1940; vol. 17269, No. 102 CA(B)TC, Fort William, January 28; vol. 17264, No. 100 CA(B)TC, Portage la Prairie, January 29, 1941.

80 LAC, RG 24, War Diaries, vol. 16885, No. 11 CA(R)TC, Woodstock, November 5 and December 18; vol. 17093, No. 130 NPAM Training Centre [later A-20 Canadian Army (Active) Training Centre], Red Deer, November 6, 1940. For another example of exercises being carried out in cooperation with the RCAF, see vol. 17245, No. 60 CA(B)TC, Yarmouth, December 16, 1940.

81 LAC, RG 24, vol. 17220, War Diary, No. 45 CA(B)TC, Sorel, November 5, 1940.

82 See Bruno Ramirez, "Ethnicity on Trial: The Italians of Montreal and the Second World War," in *On Guard for Thee: War, Ethnicity, and the Canadian State, 1939–1945*, ed. Norman Hillmer, Bohdan Kordan, and Lubomyr Luciuk (Ottawa: Canadian Committee for the History of the Second World War, 1988), esp. 73–74; as well as Lita-Rose Betcherman, *The Swastika and the Maple Leaf: Fascist Movements in Canada in the Thirties* (Toronto: Fitzhenry and Whiteside, 1975); and the several articles in Franca Iacovetta, Roberto Perrin, and Angelo Principe, eds., *Enemies Within: Italian and Other Internees in Canada and Abroad* (Toronto: University of Toronto Press, 2000).

83 LAC, RG 24, vol. 16885, War Diary, No. 11 CA(R)TC, Woodstock, September 9–12, 1940.

84 For a good example of shortages in one training centre, see the list of missing items in LAC, RG 24, vol. 17225, No. 47 CA(B)TC, War Diary, Valleyfield, February 1941, Appendix 5, "General Report on Training."

85 For example, see LAC, RG 24, War Diaries, vol. 17182, No. 22 CA(B)TC, North Bay, March 5; vol. 17266, No. 100 CA(B)TC, Portage la Prairie, March 11, 1942.

86 LAC, RG 24, vol. 6570, HQ 1161-1-5, vol. 1, DAG(M) to D[irector]. of Org[anization]., August 28, Lt.Col. A.J. Everett, Org. 2(a), to DAG(M), September 9, and AG, to DOC, MD 6, September 12. See also same file, vol. 2, telegram, AG, to Col. A.A. Magee, September 9; Brigadier J.P. Archambault, DOC, MD 4, to Secretary, DND, October 3; and AG to DOC, MD 4, October 7, 1940.

87 Ralston Papers, vol. 68, "Compulsory Training, 1942: 4 months Training. Order of Call. N.R.M.A. May-June 1941, May 1942," Crerar to Ralston, March 10, 1941.

88 For example, see LAC, RG 24, vol. 17277, War Diary, No. 110 CA(B)TC, Vernon, December 1940, Appendix 6 "Conscientious Objectors: Class of October 9th.–Nov. 22nd, 1940," and

various unnumbered appendices, February 1941, which describe several cases of how conscientious objectors were dealt with during the training period there.

89 On the legal status of Jehovah's Witnesses generally, see LAC, RG 13, vol. 2600, file 142035, "Privy Council. If members of 'Jehovah's Witnesses' exempt from military service. Sec. 18, National War Services Regulations (Recruits) 'Conscientious Objectors.' Defence of Canada Regulations. Unlawful Associations. January 14, 1941." On the particular case described here, see documents in Ralston Papers, vol. 80, "Jehovah's Witnesses, alleged mistreatment of, 1944: Investigation into allegations, May."

90 LAC, RG 24, vol. 17292, War Diary, No. 131 CA(B)TC, Camrose, December 18, 1941.

91 For these numbers, as well as an overview of the men's experiences, see Socknat, *Witness against War*, 227–58.

92 LAC, RG 27, vol. 3022, "Summaries of Mobilization Statistics, 1943," Table 1, "Summary of Mobilization Statistics, first three (Thirty-Day) Military Training Periods."

93 Granatstein and Hitsman, *Broken Promises*, 145–46.

94 LAC, RG 24, vol. 17305, War Diary, No. 30 CA(R)TC, Brockville, November 1940, Appendix 5, "General Report on Training."

95 LAC, RG 24, vol. 16885, War Diary, No. 11 CA(R)TC, Woodstock, October 24, 1940.

96 Ralston Papers, vol. 68, "Compulsory Training, 1942," Crerar to Ralston, March 10, 1941. For similar comments from another source, see Granatstein and Hitsman, *Broken Promises*, 147.

97 LAC, RG 24, vol. 17305, War Diary, No. 30 CA(R)TC, Brockville, February 1940, Appendix 5, "Report on Training."

98 For instance, see LAC, RG 24, War Diaries, vol. 17233, No. 51 CA(B)TC, Chicoutimi, December 1940, Appendix III, "General Report on Training," and February 1941, Appendix I, "General Report on Training;" vol. 17269, No. 102 CA(B)TC, Fort William, Reports on Training in November 1940, Appendix V, December 1940, Appendix III, and February 1941, Appendix IV; and vol. 17277, No. 110 CA(B)TC, Vernon, November 1940, Appendix 8.

99 Such comments appear throughout the "Reports on Training" that are found in most training centre war diaries for this period, and often also in the day-to-day diary entries. For two of the best examples, see LAC, RG 24, vol. 17306, War Diary, No. 111 CA(R)TC, Gordon Head, November 7 and December 21, 1940. The apparent views of trainees were also reported by camp staff in a newspaper (*Kamp Pain*) they created for the men in No. 132 CA(B)TC, Grande Prairie. Particular examples can be found in LAC, RG 24, vols. 17295–96, December 1940, Appendix 8, 17, 19; January 1941, Appendix 7, 14–15; and April 1941, Appendix 9, 6–7, 13.

100 LAC, RG 24, vol. 17290, War Diary, No. 131 CA(B)TC, Camrose, November 1940, Appendix C, "A Nice Little Story about Militia Camp," *Camrose Canadian*, November 20, 1940.

101 LAC, RG 24, vol. 17194, War Diary, No. 32 CA(B)TC, Peterborough, November 1940, Appendix 4, "Trainees Opposed to Camp Life Change Opinions As Time Passes," November 7, 1940.

102 LAC, RG 24, War Diaries, vol. 17295, No. 132 CA(B)TC, Grande Prairie, November 1940, Appendix 5, "Trainees Praised at Grande Prairie," *Grande Prairie Herald-Tribune* [?], November 8; and vol. 16912, No. 44 CA(B)TC, St-Jérôme, November 1940, Appendix 5, untitled newspaper clipping from *La Patrie*, November 10, 1940. The *Edmonton Journal* repeated such comments in connection with the second training period in December 1940, noting in particular that two of the men "would feel 'quite lonely' when they got home." LAC, RG 24, vol. 17093, No. 130 NPAM Training Centre, Red Deer, December 1940, Appendix 4, untitled clipping from *Edmonton Journal*, December 21, 1940.

103 QUA, C.G. Power Papers [hereafter Power Papers], box 70, file D2025, "Military District No. 5," "Survey of Conditions Prevailing in M.D. No. 5 (Based on reports of Unit Intelligence Officers for period from 9th to 22nd Feb. 1941)."
104 Vennat, *Lés Héros oubliés*, vol. 1, 117–18.
105 Gibson and Robertson, eds., *Ottawa at War*, April 19, 1942, 311.
106 LAC, RG 24, War Diaries, vol. 17269, No. 102 CA(B)TC, Fort William, December 1940, Appendix III, "Report on Training," December 22, 1940; vol. 17167, No. 23 CA(B)TC, Newmarket, January 16; vol. 17277, No. 110 CA(B)TC, Vernon, "Report on Formation of Ski Patrol," February 1941.

Chapter 3: Enshrining the NRMA

1 Crerar Papers, vol. 19, file 958C.009(D338), "Personal Correspondence July 1940–June 1941," Crerar to Major-General R.O. Alexander, DOC, MD 2, September 11, 1940.
2 Crerar Papers, vol. 25, file 958C.009(D426), "General Crerar's personal papers – Addresses and Memoranda by General H.D.G. Crerar," speech to Canadian Club titled "The Military Problem," October 23; and report on speech in King Papers] J6, vol. 234, "W.W. II – National Resources Mobilization Act, 1940–1941 (Clippings)," story titled "Victory for Right Sure, Says Crerar," *Montreal Star*, October 23, 1940. For similar statements, see also King Papers, J4, vol. 424, CWC Minutes, July 26, and Crerar Papers, vol. 1, file 958C.009(D13), "CGS files 1940–1941 – Observations on Canadian Requirements in Respect to the Army," E.L.M. Burns, Assistant Deputy CGS, to Crerar, October 29, 1940. On the speech itself, see also Dickson, *A Thoroughly Canadian General*, 153.
3 Gibson and Robertson, eds., *Ottawa at War*, September 13, 1940, 73–74. See also Granatstein and Hitsman, *Broken Promises*, 148–49.
4 Ralston Papers, vol. 37, "Appreciations – Chiefs of Staff," memorandum titled "The Canadian Army," Crerar to Ralston, September 3, 1940. Also discussed in Granatstein and Hitsman, *Broken Promises*, 148–49; Granatstein, *The Generals*, 95; Dickson, *A Thoroughly Canadian General*, 143; and Walker, "The Revolt of the Canadian Generals,", 61–62.
5 Ralston Papers, vol. 37, "Appreciations –Chiefs of Staff," Crerar to Ralston, "Canadian Army Programme for 1941," September 24, 1940. Also Stacey, *Six Years of War*, 87–89.
6 Douglas et al., *No Higher Purpose*, 145–50.
7 Douglas, *The Creation of a National Air Force*, 347–50.
8 King Papers, J4, vol. 424, CWC Minutes, October 1, 3, 9–10, 23, and 31, 1940. On the debates in the CWC over the winter of 1940–41 generally that are described in this and the following paragraphs, see also Granatstein and Hitsman, *Broken Promises*, 148–50; and Dickson, *A Thoroughly Canadian General*, 152–56.
9 A record of the overseas discussions is available in Ralston Papers, vol. 1, "Secret. Diary. November 28, 1940–January 9, 1941," entries for December 17, 1940, and January 2 and 4, 1941, and Appendices "N" and "V." See also Stacey, *Six Years of War*, 90–91. On King's pushing for consideration of a plan for recruiting other men in the new training centres, see King Diaries, October 23 and December 4, 1940.
10 Ralston Papers, vol. 68, "Speech File, 1941: 19 February 1941, Departmental Activities, trip to England, Training Programmes, CWAC, Finances, Feb–Dec 1940, Jan–Feb 1941," telegram, Ralston to Prime Minister and to C.G. Power (Acting Minister of National Defence), January 6, 1941.
11 King Diaries, especially January 27–28 (quotation from 28). On the debates, see also the more thorough account in King Papers, J4, vol. 424, CWC Minutes, November 29 and December 4 and 18, 1940, and January 8, 24, 27, and 28, 1941.

12 Crerar Papers, vol. 1, file 958C.009(D12), Crerar to McNaughton, May 19, 1941. Also noted in Granatstein and Hitsman, *Broken Promises*, 151; Dickson, *A Thoroughly Canadian General*, 160; and Walker, "The Revolt of the Canadian Generals," 65.

13 King Diaries, January 28, 1940.

14 LAC, RG 24, War Diaries, vol. 17269, No. 102 CA(B)TC, Fort William, "Summary" for November; vol. 17249, No. 61 CA(B)TC, New Glasgow, November 7; vol. 17295, No. 132 CA(B)TC, Grande Prairie, Appendix 5, newspaper clippings dated November 8 and 14; vol. 17292, No. 131 CA(B)TC, Camrose, December 1940, Appendix E, newspaper clipping titled "A 'Red Letter' Day at Camrose Basic Centre"; vol. 17252, No. 62 CA(B)TC, Charlottetown, January 1941, Appendix V, and February 1941, Appendix IV.

15 Power Papers, box 70, file D2025, "Military District No. 5," "Survey of Conditions Prevailing in M.D. No. 5."

16 The "Reports on Training" that were regularly included as appendices in the war diaries of many training centres note lectures and other efforts to encourage men to volunteer in New Glasgow, Charlottetown, Chicoutimi, Brockville, and Vernon. Recruiters from the RCAF, Royal Canadian Artillery, and Canadian Armoured Corps are recorded as having visited seventeen different centres (Charlottetown, Rimouski, St-Hyacinthe, Sherbrooke, Joliette, Huntingdon, Brockville, Peterborough, Brantford, Newmarket, Kitchener, North Bay, Portage la Prairie, Camrose, Red Deer, Grande Prairie, and Vernon), between December 15, 1940, and February 7, 1941. In Long Branch, the RCAF was aided by the fact that it had a recruiting station in a school across the road from the camp; 205 members of the training class were apparently gathered together and taken there to submit their applications for service in December (LAC, RG 24, vol. 17304, War Diary, No. 21 CA(B)TC, December 19, 1940). In Gordon Head, thirty-two men were singled out for signifying their willingness to volunteer for active service, and given special arm bands along with a special course of training to encourage their interest in the army (vol. 17307, War Diary, No. 111 CA(R)TC, 11 December 1940).

17 For example, see comments by Major R.H. Huntingdon, OC, No. 102 CA(B)TC, Fort William, in LAC, RG 24, vol. 17269, War Diary, November 1940, Appendix IV, "The 30-Day Training Plan" *Fort William Times-Journal*, November 16, 1940. In Camrose, the centre's commander had a special form prepared, based on his previous experience as a District Recruiting Officer, to provide a tangible record of his trainees' willingness to serve overseas (vol. 17291, War Diary, No. 131 CA(B)TC, January 1941, Appendix K).

18 See various documents in LAC, RG 24, vol. 6571, HQ 1161-1-5, vol. 3, October 19–December 4, 1940 (which also indicate the general thoughts of several senior army officials about encouraging NRMA recruits to volunteer for active service during this period). Evidence of such recruiting also appears in the war diaries of a number of the individual training centres from December 1940 to February 1941.

19 DHH, file 114.1(D87), "PROJECTS 21 & 23 (Compulsory Training)," circular memorandum by Colonel E.L.M. Burns, Assistant Deputy CGS, to CGS, Deputy CGS et al., November 27, 1940.

20 Ralston Papers, vol. 68, "Speech File, 1941," Crerar to Ralston, January 26, 1941. See also Granatstein and Hitsman, *Broken Promises*, 148, on the issue generally.

21 King Papers, J4, vol. 424, CWC Minutes, December 18, 1940, and January 27, 1941.

22 Ralston Papers, vol. 115, "Manpower National Selective Service, miscellaneous material re[.] preparation of Army programme – proposed organization, April 1941–April 1943," Crerar to Ralston, April 23; King Papers, CWC Minutes, April 23, 1941; Granatstein and Hitsman, *Broken Promises*, 150–51.

23 The entire file on LAC, RG 24, reel C-5270, file HQS 8792, "Reaction to Compulsory Service," is devoted to this subject, and includes reports from the DOCs of MDs 1, 2, 3, 4, 5, 6, 7, 10, 12, and 13, and the GOC-in-C, Pacific Command (reporting reactions from M.D. 11), April 29–May 3.
24 LAC, RG 24, vol. 17233, War Diary, No. 51 CA(B)TC, Chicoutimi, April 1941, Appendix II, Lt.Col. J. Landry, OC, to H.Q., MD 5, May 1, 1941.
25 LAC, RG 24, War Diary, vol. 17167, No. 23 CA(B)TC, Newmarket, April 1941, Appendix D, E.B. Dodgson, Capt. and Adj., for R.B. Harkness, Lt-Col., OC, No. 23 (Basic) T.C., to DOC, MD No. 2, April 28, 1941.
26 Granatstein and Hitsman, *Broken Promises*, 151–52 (quotation from 151).
27 King Papers, J4, vol. 353, "Conscription," C244265–70, "Attitude of the Canadian newspapers towards conscription."
28 DHH, file 114.1(D188), "Training Centres," memorandum, Browne to CGS, Quartermaster-General, and Master-General of the Ordnance, July 30, 1940.
29 Gibson and Robertson, eds., *Ottawa at War*, May 7, 1941, 167–68.
30 LAC, RG 24, vol. 6571, HQ 1161-1-5, vol. 4, AG to CGS, March 27, 1941.
31 Ralston Papers, vol. 68, "Compulsory Training – NRMA, 1942," AG to all DOCs, July 17, 1941.
32 Ralston Papers, vol. 68, "Compulsory Training – NRMA, 1942," AG to DOCs, MDs 2, 3, 4, 5, 6, 10, 12, and 13, August 12, 1941.
33 Ralston Papers, vol. 68, "Compulsory Training – NRMA, 1942," AG to all DOCs, September 26, 1941.
34 Ralston Papers, vol. 68, "Compulsory Training – NRMA, 1942," AG to all DOCs, November 4, 1941, and attached Appendix.
35 LAC, RG 24, vol. 17120, War Diary, A-23 Coast Defence and Artillery Training Centre, Halifax, April 1, 1941, and following days.
36 Burns, *Manpower in the Canadian Army*, 83–88, 118. See also Stacey, *Six Years of War*, 121, 134–35.
37 LAC, RG 24, vol. 80, file HQ 1161-1-18, vol. 1, H. DesRosiers, Acting DM of National Defence (Army) to J.R. Hurtibise, July 16, 1941.
38 My findings here agree broadly with those of Pariseau and Bernier in *French Canadians and Bilingualism*, vol. 1, 110–15, 122–27, as well as appendix Z, 331–32 (but which is based on data from later in the war, 1943). See also Gravel, "Le Québec militaire, 1939–1945," 87–92.
39 For example, see LAC, RG 24, vol. 17168, War Diary, No. 23 CA(B)TC, Newmarket, March 5, 1941, which notes the addition of light machine guns to the syllabus, along with lesser items such as map reading and first aid.
40 Gibson and Robertson, eds., *Ottawa at War*, May 20, and June 12, 1941, 169–70, 176–78; Granatstein, *Canada's War*, 201–4; Granatstein and Hitsman, *Broken Promises*, 150–54; Walker, "The Revolt of the Canadian Generals" 63.
41 C.P. Stacey makes this point at the beginning of his description of the campaign in *Six Years of War*, 115–16.
42 King Papers, J4, vol. 424, CWC Minutes, April 23, 25, and 30, and 9 May 9, 1941; King Diaries, April 23 and 30, 1941.
43 LAC, RG 25, vol. 2633, file 715-40, "National Resources Mobilization Act, 1940. Military Service in Canada," pt. 1: "Call for Men for the Army: An Address by Honourable J.L. Ralston, Minister of National Defence, Delivered over a national network of Canadian radio stations, 11th May 1941."
44 Stacey, *Six Years of War*, 116; Granatstein and Hitsman, *Broken Promises*, 154.
45 Such activities are noted for example in LAC, RG 24, War Diaries, vol. 17277, No. 110 CA(B)TC, Vernon, February 28; and vol. 17252, No. 62 CA(B)TC, Charlottetown, May 20, 22, 28, and 31 and June 17 and 23, 1941.

46 LAC, RG 24, War Diaries, vol. 17240, No. 54 CA(B)TC, Montmagny, 30 May; vol. 17236, No. 53 CA(B)TC, Lauzon, June 4 and 10–11; vol. 17243, No. 55 CA(B)TC, Rimouski, June 4; vol. 17233, No. 51 CA(B)TC, Chicoutimi, June 11–13 and June 1941, Appendix II; vol. 16913, No. 44 CA(B)TC, St-Jérôme, June 11 and 15, 1941.

47 For the best examples, see LAC, RG 24, War Diaries, vol. 17291, No. 131 CA(B)TC, Camrose, May 16 and 23; vol. 17296, No. 132 CA(B)TC, Grande Prairie, May 23; vol. 17144, No. 10 CA(B)TC, Kitchener, June 19, 1941.

48 See in particular the various newspaper clippings recording such events in LAC, RG 24, War Diaries, vol. 17277, No. 110 CA(B)TC, Vernon, May 1941, Appendix [31]; and vol. 17252, No. 62 CA(B)TC, Charlottetown, June 1941, Appendix V; as well as the following diary entries in other camps: vol. 17296, No. 132 CA(B)TC, Grande Prairie, May 31; vol. 17265, No. 100 CA(B)TC, Portage la Prairie, June 2; vol. 17291, No. 131 CA(B)TC, Camrose, June 9; vol. 17233, No. 51 CA(B)TC, Chicoutimi, June 12; and vol. 17240, No. 54 CA(B)TC, Montmagny, June 15, 1941.

49 On the various events during the recruiting campaign in Quebec, see Vennat, *Lés Héros oubliés*, vol. 1, 155–65.

50 For a few of the more detailed or notable descriptions of events in individual training centres, see LAC, RG 24, War Diaries, vol. 17180, No. 22 CA(B)TC, North Bay, June 28; vol. 17188, No. 31 CA(B)TC, Cornwall, June 28; vol. 17195, No. 32 CA(B)TC, Peterborough, June 28; vol. 17221, No. 45 CA(B)TC, Sorel, June 28; vol. 17269, No. 102 CA(B)TC, Fort William, June28; vol. 17144, No. 10 CA(B)TC, Kitchener, June 28–29; vol. 17206, No. 42 CA(B)TC, Joliette, June 28–29; vol. 16913, No. 44 CA(B)TC, St-Jérôme, June 28–29; and vol. 17277, No. 110 CA(B)TC, Vernon, June 28–29, 1941.

51 LAC, RG 24, War Diaries, vol. 17202, No. 41 CA(B)TC, Huntingdon, July 12–13; vol. 17206, No. 42 CA(B)TC, Joliette, July 12–13; vol. 17214, No. 43 CA(B)TC, Sherbrooke, July 12–13; vol. 16913, No. 44 CA(B)TC, St-Jérôme, July 12–13; and vol. 17221, No. 45 CA(B)TC, Sorel, July 12–13, 1941.

52 Stacey, *Six Years of War*, 116.

53 For example, see LAC, RG 24, War Diaries, vol. 17133, No. 51 CA(B)TC, Chicoutimi, July 1941, Appendix I, "Distribution des proclamations, 3 juillet, 1941"; vol. 17240, No. 54 CA(B)TC, Montmagny, July 3; vol. 17252, No. 62 CA(B)TC, Charlottetown, July 3; vol. 17265, No. 100 CA(B)TC, Portage la Prairie, July 3, 1941. The French-language version of the proclamation is also reproduced in Pariseau and Bernier, *French Canadians and Bilingualism*, vol. 1, 111.

54 LAC, RG 24, War Diaries, vol. 17202, No. 41 CA(B)TC, Huntingdon, August 22–23 and August 1941, Appendix IV: "Report on Recruiting Activities. Week Commencing 30th August ... [ellipses in original] Ending 6th Sept., 1941"; vol. 17154, No. 20 CA(B)TC, Brantford, August 23–25 and August 1941, Appendix IX (documents related to a tour of the camp by a group of Canadian newspaper editors). Charlottetown (vol. 17252), St-Jérôme (vol. 16913), and Joliette (vol. 17208) all also continued to act as enlistment depots for civilian volunteers.

55 LAC, RG 24, War Diaries, vol. 17226, No. 47 CA(B)TC, Valleyfield, January 1942, Appendix 9, circular letter, AG to GOsC-in-C, Atlantic and Pacific Commands, 4th Canadian Division, all DOCs, et al., December 13, 1941; vol. 17298, No. 132 CA(B)TC, Grande Prairie, entry for January 9, 1942.

56 LAC, RG 24, vol. 17208, War Diary, No. 42 CA(B)TC, Joliette, March 26, 1942; Stacey, *Six Years of War*, 116.

57 LAC, RG 24, War Diaries, vol. 17221, No. 45 CA(B)TC, Sorel, June 16; vol. 17206, No. 42 CA(B)TC, Joliette, June 26; vol. 17206, No. 42 CA(B)TC, Joliette, July 15; vol. 17202, No. 41 CA(B)TC, Huntingdon, unnumbered appendix from August 1941: "Hemmingford,

Athelstan, Huntingdon Enlistment Commendable," newspaper clipping from the editorial page of the *Huntingdon Gleaner*, September 3, 1941. For an example of a similar pessimistic comment from outside Quebec, see also vol. 17153, No. 20 CA(B)TC, Brantford, June 28, 1941.

58 See Granatstein, *Canada's War*, 204, for the various results of the recruiting campaign. In fact, the war diarist in Chicoutimi noted very proudly that MD 5 had surpassed its objective. See LAC, RG 24, vol. 17233, No. 51 CA(B)TC, July 11, 1941.

59 Stacey, *Arms, Men and Governments*, appendix "T," 600. Unfortunately, figures for NRMA recruits volunteering for general service in the army, air force, and navy are listed in this source only by individual months, while the recruiting campaign ended part-way through July. Thus, the low numbers I have given here are from figures for May and June alone (305+1,023 for the army, for a total of 1,328 – and 101+220 RCAF, and 36+65 RCN, for a total of 422), while the higher ones include all of July (which in fact had the highest single number of NRMA who volunteered for the three military services, for the entire year), for an additional, 1,258 army recruits (making a total for the army over three months of 2,586) and 924 RCAF and RCN recruits (for a three-month total of 1,346).

60 For example, No. 10 CA(B)TC in Kitchener recorded separate visits from recruiting officers from the RCAF, the RCN, the Canadian Armoured Corps, "the Canadian Armoured Division Signals," the Royal Canadian Artillery, the local active force ambulance unit (15th Field Ambulance), and a representative looking for candidates for trades training, all between May and July, and all specifically to recruit NRMA men (LAC, RG 24, vols. 17144–45, May 8–July 9, 1941).

61 LAC, RG 24, vol. 17202, War Diary, No. 41 CA(B)TC, Huntingdon, July 8, 1941.

62 Stacey, *Arms, Men and Governments*, appendix "T," 599–600.

63 King Papers, J4, vol. 424, CWC Minutes, May 8 and 14, 1942.

64 For these numbers, see Stacey, *Arms, Men and Governments*, appendix "T," 600–602. Hatch, *Aerodrome of Democracy*, 33 and 181–82, and Douglas, *The Creation of a National Air Force*, 230, both note the RCAF using waiting lists, so that applicants could go through the rest of the selection process and then be ready when an appropriate training spot became available.

65 Charles Messenger, *'Bomber' Harris and the Strategic Bombing Offensive, 1939–1945* (London: Arms and Armour Press, 1984), 191. For this reference I am indebted to David Bashow, who is the author of several works on the history of Canadian military aviation, and in this connection especially *No Prouder Place: Canadians and the Bomber Command Experience, 1939–1945* (St. Catharines: Vanwell, 2005).

66 LAC, RG 24, vol. 17195, War Diary, No. 32 CA(B)TC, Peterborough, July 9–14, 1941.

67 LAC, RG 24, vol. 17221, War Diary, No. 45 CA(B)TC, Sorel, July 16, 1941. Other examples of large numbers of staff members going active in training centres in Quebec can be found in vol. 17225, No. 47 CA(B)TC, Valleyfield, July 19; vol. 16913, No. 44 CA(B)TC, St-Jérôme, June 27 and July 16; vol. 17240, No. 54 CA(B)TC, Montmagny, June 12–13; vol. 17243, No. 55 CA(B)TC, Rimouski, July 9, 1941, and February 10, 1942; and vol. 17237, No. 53 CA(B)TC, Lauzon, July 5, 1941. For references to staff members joining the RCAF, see also vol. 17225, No. 47 CA(B)TC, Valleyfield, August 15, and vol. 17207, No. 42 CA(B)TC, Joliette, December 10, 1941.

68 For example, in Portage la Prairie 43 out of 200 other ranks on the staff had still not volunteered for active service by late June. LAC, RG 24, vol. 17265, War Diary, No. 100 CA(B)TC, Portage la Prairie, June 3 and 21, 1941.

69 On the creation of the Ogdensburg Agreement and the Permanent Joint Board on Defence, as well as later defence planning, see in particular Stacey, *Arms, Men, and Governments*, 336–54; and Granatstein, *Canada's War*, 124–32.

70 On the genesis of the new division, see DHH, AHQ Rpt [Army Headquarters Report] (D7), "The 6th Canadian Division," 1–5; Ralston Papers, vol. 37, "Appreciations – Chiefs of Staff," CGS to Minister of National Defence, document titled "Appreciation: The Nature of the Canadian Army Effort, Mid-Summer 1941 to Spring 1942," May 18; and copy of full Chiefs of Staff Appreciation, dated May 28, 1941. On the CWC meeting itself, see King Papers, J4, vol. 424, CWC Minutes; and King Diaries, both June 5, 1941.

71 King Papers, J4, vol. 424, CWC Minutes, June 5, 1941.

72 On T.A. Crerar's experiences of Union Government in the First World War, and his views on conscription in the Second, see Rea, *T.A. Crerar*, esp. 35–57, 206–8; as well as Gibson and Robertson, eds., *Ottawa at War*, July 30, 1941, 189.

73 Crerar Papers, vol. 1, file 958C.009(D12), "CGS files 1940-1941 – Personal Correspondence Lt-Gen Crerar – Lt-Gen McNaughton. Period Aug 40 to Mar 41," Crerar to McNaughton, June 26 ; vol. 25, file 958C.009(D426), "General Crerar's personal papers – Addresses and Memoranda by General H.D.G. Crerar," vol. 1, press release, "Text of address today by Major-Gen. H.D.G. Crerar, Chief of the General Staff, to a conference of Commandants of Training Centres from all parts of the Dominion," July 8; vol. 19, file 958C.009(D333), "General Crerar's personal correspondence file ... July 1940–June 1941," press release, July 22, containing statement by Lt.-Gen. McNaughton on training in Canada. See also MG 30, E 133, General A.G.L. McNaughton Papers [hereafter McNaughton Papers], vol. 227, file CC7/CRERAR/6, Crerar to Minister of National Defence, June 27; assorted newspaper clippings on the same file; Gibson and Robertson, eds., *Ottawa at War*, July 28, 1941, 186–88; and Dickson, *A Thoroughly Canadian General*, 162.

74 Among many fine sources that discuss the Barbarossa campaign, for a very good, brief introduction see Williamson Murray and Allan R. Millett, *A War to be Won: Fighting the Second World War* (Cambridge, MA: Belknap Press, 2000), 120–42 (see also 101–9 on the Balkan campaign).

75 Granatstein, *The Politics of Survival*, 73–78; Granatstein, *Canada's War*, 203–5.

76 King Diaries, May 20 and 21; King Papers, J4, vol. 424, CWC Minutes, May 20 (source of quotation) and 21, 1941; Stacey, *Arms, Men, and Governments*, 41–42. On both public sentiment and the developments related to the use of Canadian troops overseas discussed in this paragraph, see also Granatstein and Hitsman, *Broken Promises*, 151–53. See also Pickersgill, *The Mackenzie King Record*, vol. 1, 219–27. For J.G. Gardiner's views on conscription, see Ward and Smith, *Jimmy Gardiner*, 282–84.

77 King Papers, J4, vol. 424, CWC Minutes, June 5 and July 15 and 29, 1941 (quotations are from latter meeting). See also Ralston Papers, vol. 52, "Manpower," vol. 2, notes titled "Canadian Formations," July 5, and notes titled "Re. Source of Recruits for 5th and 6th Divisions," July 27; King Diaries, July 29; and Gibson and Robertson, eds., *Ottawa at War*, July 30, 1941, 188–90.

78 Crerar Papers, vol. 19, file 958C.009(D333), "General Crerar's personal papers – Personal Correspondence – Vol. II. July 1941–November 1941," Crerar to Lt.-Col. F.G. Malloch, Commandant, Canadian Signals Training Centre, Kingston, July 16, 1941.

79 Crerar Papers, vol. 19, file 958C.009(D338), "General Crerar's personal correspondence file ... July 1940–June 1941," Crerar to Brigadier E.L.M. Burns, Brigadier, General Staff, Canadian Corps, London, England, May 24, 1941.

80 QUA, Grant Dexter Papers, box 2, file #20, memorandum dated July 25, 1941.

Chapter 4: Creating the "Big Army"

1 *Burns, Manpower in the Canadian Army*, table XXIX, 172.

2 Stacey, *Arms, Men, and Governments*, 48.

3 Stacey, *Arms, Men, and Governments*, 51.
4 *Eighth Census of Canada*, 1941, vol. 1, tables 15, 19, and 20, 622–23 and 640–53;. I arrived at 1,732,546 by taking the number of single men aged 15 to 44 from table 20 of the census (1,506,293), which is the closest it comes to listing single men by ages, and then taking table 15, which breaks down the numbers of Canadian men by each individual age and assuming that all men listed there who were aged fourteen were single (113,124), and that all men aged 45 to 47 (200,873) were single in the same proportion as for the male population as a whole (as listed in table 19 – 3,323,094 divided by 5,900,536, or approximately 0.563), and then multiplying 200,873 by 0.563 to get 113,129, and adding 1,506,293 + 113,124 + 113,129 = 1,732,546.
5 Stacey, *Arms, Men, and Governments*, appendix "O," 587.
6 See Gibson and Robertson, eds., *Ottawa at War*, September 16, 1941, 195, and following memoranda.
7 King Papers, J4, vol. 424, CWC Minutes, April 23 and May 9, 1941.
8 LAC, RG 25, vol. 2633, file 715–40, "National Resources Mobilization Act, 1940. Military Service in Canada," pt. 1: "Call for Men for the Army."
9 For copies of circular letters from the Adjutant-General to various commanders across Canada authorizing the employment of "R" recruits as part of training centre establishments, and as medical orderlies there and in district medical facilities, see Ralston Papers, vol. 68, "Compulsory Training – NRMA, 1942: pressure on recruits to go active, regulations. April 1941–March 1942," May 13 and 19, August 6, September 2, and October 25, 1941.
10 A list of every unit to which Members (HD) were posted by the start of 1942, and the numbers in each location, can be found in Ralston Papers, vol. 72, "Shortage of Military Personnel: Officers and Other Ranks, 1942: January–February, July, October," tables labelled "East Coast Defences," "West Coast Defences," and "6th Division," all dated January 30, 1942.
11 Ralston Papers, vol. 72, "Shortage of Military Personnel," documents titled "6th Canadian Division: Shortages as at 24 Jan 42," January 30; "Coast Defence & Anti-Aircraft: Shortages as at 24 Jan 42," January 31, 1942. See also vol. 37, "Armed Forces Strength, 1941," summary of Canadian army strength dated October 3, 1941.
12 Ralston Papers, vol. 52, "Manpower," vol. 2, "Manpower Memorandum No. 2," AG to Minister, July 24, 1941. A copy of the Department of Munitions and Supply's study, titled "Memorandum on Man-Power Requirements and Supply in Canada," appears in Ralston Papers, vol. 68, "Compulsory Training, 1942: 4 months Training. Order of Call. N.R.M.A. May–June 1941, May 1942" (enclosed with memorandum from H. Carl Goldenberg, Associate Director-General, Economics and Statistics Branch, Department of Munitions and Supply, to Ralston, June 12, 1941). On Ralston's referral of the study to Browne, and Crerar's opinions on it, see Ralston Papers, vol. 117, "Manpower – Sixth Division re manpower – with index, July 1941," correspondence between Ralston, George Currie [one of Ralston's two civilian Executive Assistants], and Crerar, May 26 and July 4, 9, and 28, 1941. See also Granatstein, *The Generals*, 97.
13 Gibson and Robertson, eds., *Ottawa at War*, June 12, 1941, 177. Also cited in Walker, "The Revolt of the Canadian Generals," 64.
14 Gibson and Robertson, eds., *Ottawa at War*, September 16, 1941, 195–96. On Ralston's handling of army affairs, and more particularly his relationship with Crerar and other senior commanders, see also Byers, "J.L. Ralston as Minister of National Defence during the Second World War": 70–95.
15 Crerar Papers, vol. 1, file 958C.009(D12), Crerar to McNaughton, August 11, 1941. This letter is also quoted in greater detail in Stacey, *Six Years of War*, 94; Granatstein, *The Generals*, 97–98; and Dickson, *A Thoroughly Canadian General*, 175.

16 On Pope, see his own *Soldiers and Politicians*, esp. 180 for the quotation; as well as Granatstein, *The Generals*, 207–17, 232–36; and Dickson, *A Thoroughly Canadian General*, 98–99.

17 Ralston Papers, vol. 38, "Army Programme (Secret) 1940–41," Brigadier Maurice Pope, A[ssistant]CGS, to CGS, September 23: "Army Organization: A Survey as of September, 1941." Unfortunately, although Pope discusses his time in Canada in *Soldiers and Politicians*, 160–81, he does not ever mention this report or issue. He has also left papers at both Library and Archives Canada and the Canadian War Museum, but neither collection contains any material related to his time as Assistant CGS.

18 See Ralston Papers, vol. 68, "Reinforcements – Overseas and Canada, 1941: July to October," A.A. Magee, E.A. [the second of Ralston's two civilian Executive Assistants – George Currie is mentioned a few notes above], to Minister, October 4; as well as Ralston's notes on the issue in the same file, titled "Re: Manpower," October 4, 1941.

19 Ralston Papers, vol. 38, "Army Programme (Secret) 1940–41," Crerar to Ralston, September 29, 1941.

20 Crerar Papers, vol. 1, file 958C.009(D1), "CGS files 1940–41 – Canadian Army Programme 1942–1943; Manpower Memorandum No. 3; 'R' Recruits – Financial and Economic Summary 1942–43," memorandum by CGS to Minister, November 18, 1941, titled "Army Programme, 1942–43."

21 As Crerar noted in a private speech in December, being CGS in wartime was "not in accordance with my personal ambitions." With most of his work apparently complete in Ottawa, he gave up the chance to be promoted to Lieutenant-General at that time, after reportedly making it "quite clear to the Minister that I would rather be a Major-General in an overseas command than a Lieut.-General in an office job in Ottawa." Crerar Papers, vol. 25, File 958C.009(D426), "General Crerar's personal papers – Addresses and Memoranda by General H.D.G. Crerar," speech titled "Remarks – Farewell Dinner – 4th December, 1941." On Crerar's efforts to gain promotion as CGS, and his later appointment to overseas command, see also Granatstein, *The Generals*, 96–97, 99–101; and Dickson, *A Thoroughly Canadian General*, 149–51, 178–80.

22 Urquhart and Buckley, eds., *Historical Statistics of Canada*, series C36–46; Stacey, *Arms, Men, and Governments*, 416.

23 Among the various places where copies of the report of the LSIC can be found is Ralston Papers, vol. 113, "Manpower – Labour Supply Investigation Committee's report to the Labour Coordination Committee – with appendix and index, October 1941." See also Ralston Papers, vol. 113, black binder titled "Manpower, vol. 1, Hon. J.L. Ralston," summary of the report by J.E. Wells, November 15; and vol. 116, Manpower National Selective Service and Civilian Work – July–Nov[.] 1941, Feb[.] 1942–March 1943," memo "For Cabinet War Committee" by A.D.P. Heeney [Clerk of the Privy Council and Secretary to the Cabinet and CWC], submitting and summarizing LSIC report, n.d. [October 1941]. For the CWC's discussions related to the LSIC report, see also King Papers, J4, vol. 424, CWC Minutes, October 2, November 6, 19, and 26, and December 1 and 2, as well as King Diaries, October 2, November 6 and 26, and December 1 and 2, 1941; and Gibson and Robertson, eds., *Ottawa at War*, November 18 and 20 and December 3, 1941, 222–24, 227–29. The key secondary accounts appear in Stacey, *Arms, Men, and Governments*, 403–4; Granatstein and Hitsman, *Broken Promises*, 185–88; and Stevenson, *Canada's Greatest Wartime Muddle*, 4–5, 26–27.

24 Crerar Papers, vol. 1, file 958C.009(D1), "CGS files 1940-41," two memoranda, both from CGS to Minister and dated November 26, respectively enclosing manpower tables and commenting on them; AG to Minister, November 26, 1941, titled "Manpower Memorandum No. 3: Army Programme 1942–43" (source of quotation). See also a later version of the

same memorandum, dated November 27, that appears on the same file; as well as AG to Minister, December 4, 1941; and "Memorandum on Canadian Army Programme, 1942–1943," summarizing the above reports, produced by the CGS's office, n.d. [December 1941]. See also Gibson and Robertson, eds., *Ottawa at War*, December 3, 1941, 228–29.

25 Stacey, *Arms, Men, and Governments*, 252–88; and Greenhous et al., *The Crucible of War*, 13–105.

26 As Hatch notes, in *Aerodrome of Democracy*, 101 (as well as 203–5), the BCATP's yearly output would double in 1942 over 1941 and would continue to rise through 1943.

27 Tucker, *The Naval Service of Canada*, vol. 2, 274; Stacey, *Arms, Men, and Governments*, 44–45. The numbers planned for all three services for 1942–43 also come from the same pages of Stacey, as well as King Papers, J4, vol. 424, CWC Minutes, December 3, 1941.

28 On the views of Crerar and Howe generally during these debates, see the Dexter memoranda of November and early December 1941 cited by Gibson and Robertson in previous notes; as well as Rea, "What Really Happened?":14–15; Rea, *T.A. Crerar*, 207–10; and Robert Bothwell and William Kilbourn, *C.D. Howe: A Biography* (Toronto: McClelland and Stewart, 1979), 165–66.

29 King Diaries, December 2, 1941. This exchange was recorded similarly by Macdonald, in Nova Scotia Archives, MG 2, Angus L. Macdonald Papers, vol. 1503, Personal Diaries [hereafter Macdonald Diaries], folder 389, December 2, 1941.

30 King Papers, J4, vol. 424, CWC Minutes, December 2, 1941.

31 King Diaries, December 3, 1941.

32 King Papers, J4, vol. 424, CWC Minutes, December 3, 1941. The same exchange is recorded by Granatstein in *Canada's War*, 209–11; in Granatstein, *The Generals*, 224; and somewhat more dramatically in Granatstein and Hitsman, *Broken Promises*, 157–58.

33 Granatstein and Hitsman, *Broken Promises*, 158.

34 King Papers, J4, vol. 354 (reel H-1532), "Conscription," memorandum titled "Personal View With Respect to 1942–43 Proposed Programme of the Army," December 3, 1941.

35 King Diaries, December 3, 1941. See also Granatstein and Hitsman, *Broken Promises*, 158.

36 Walker, "The Revolt of the Generals," 68.

37 Granatstein, *The Generals*, 217, 224.

38 Gibson and Robertson, eds., *Ottawa at War*, January 12, 1942, 258; Granatstein and Hitsman, *Broken Promises*, 158, Granatstein, *The Generals*, 224; and Walker, "The Revolt of the Canadian Generals," 68. For other examples of similar comments from McNaughton and Ralston, see King Papers, J4, vol. 424, CWC Minutes, February 18, 1942.

39 King Papers, J4, vol. 424, CWC Minutes, March 11, 1942; Stacey, *Six Years of War*, 96–99; and Dickson, *A Thoroughly Canadian General*, 180–82.

40 Granatstein and Hitsman, *Broken Promises*, 158.

41 Evidence that the prime minister was also thinking along these lines can be found in Gibson and Robertson, eds., *Ottawa at War*, November 7, 1941, 218. According to Dexter, King had told friends that war in the Pacific was imminent and would result in two or even three divisions having to be raised in Canada, mostly of NRMA recruits.

42 Murray and Millett, *A War to be Won*, 177–95.

43 Stacey, *Six Years of War*, 173.

44 On Canadian involvement in the defence of Hong Kong, see Stacey, *Six Years of War*, 437–91; Carl Vincent, *No Reason Why: The Canadian Hong Kong Tragedy – an examination* (Stittsville: Canada's Wings, 1981); Brereton Greenhous, *"C" Force to Hong Kong: A Canadian Catastrophe, 1941–1945* (Toronto: Dundurn, 1997); and Nathan M. Greenfield, *The Damned: The Canadians at the Battle of Hong Kong and the POW Experience,*

1941–45 (Toronto: HarperCollins, 2010). On francophones in the Royal Rifles, and their experiences as part of the battle, see also Vennat, *Lés Héros oubliés*, vol. 1, 281–99; and Vincent, *Ils ont écrit la guerre*, 41.

45 Granatstein, *The Politics of Survival*, 79–96; Granatstein, *Canada's War*, 205–6; Granatstein and Hitsman, *Broken Promises*, 158–60, 162–63.

46 King Papers, J4, vol. 424, CWC Minutes, December 10 and 16, 1941; LAC, RG 25, vol. 2793, file 715–40, pt. 2: "Memorandum for the Prime Minister: Re: Manpower-organization," by A.D.P.H[eeney], December 9, "Memo" by H.F.A[ngus], December 17, and E[scott].R[eid]. to Norman Robertson, December 17, 1941; Gibson and Robertson, eds., *Ottawa at War*, December 11 and 15, 1941, 233–35.

47 Granatstein, *Canada's War*, 206–208, 211–15. See also Granatstein, *The Politics of Survival*, 96–97, 105–6. On the death of Lapointe and its impact on King, as well as the recruiting of St. Laurent, see also MacFarlane, *Ernest Lapointe*, 185–89; and Betcherman, *Ernest Lapointe*, 342–45.

48 King Diaries, December 3, 1941.

49 Pickersgill, *The Mackenzie King Record*, vol. 1, 333; and Vennat, *Lés Héros oubliés*, vol. 1, 303.

50 Granatstein and Hitsman, *Broken Promises*, 163–66. Granatstein, *Canada's War*, 213–18.

51 Granatstein, *The Politics of Survival*, 97–105, 106–12; Granatstein, *Canada's War*, 220–21; Granatstein, *Broken Promises*, 167.

52 For Laurendeau's account of the events of early 1942, see "The Conscription Crisis, 1942," 50–95. Mason Wade notes Maxime Raymond's expressing of a similar view in *The French Canadians, 1760–1967*, vol. 2, 948.

53 On the events of the plebiscite, see Laurendeau, cited immediately above; Granatstein, *Canada's War*, 221–28; Granatstein and Hitsman, *Broken Promises*, 168–71; and Pariseau and Bernier, *French Canadians and Bilingualism*, vol. 1, 116–17. See also Gravel, "Le Québec militaire, 1939–1945," 81.

54 Vennat, *Lés Héros oubliés*, vol. 1, 190, 301–15. On the impact of Lapointe's absence, see also MacFarlane, *Ernest Lapointe*, 189–93; and Betcherman, *Ernest Lapointe*, 345–47.

55 See especially Ralston Papers, vol. 54, "Plebiscite, Gen. (Secret), 1942," copies of miscellaneous notes by Ralston on various issues during this period, and particularly a copy of a memorandum prepared by A.L. Macdonald, a confidant of Ralston's, on "Conversation Ralston and I had with P.M., Saturday, January 31." Original also in Macdonald Diaries, folder 390, following entry for January 28, 1942, See also Granatstein, *Canada's War*, 219–20; and Granatstein and Hitsman, *Broken Promises*, 167–68.

56 For example, see the comments of Grant Dexter and J.W. Dafoe, editor of the Winnipeg Free Press, on Ralston's and King's positions, in Gibson and Robertson, eds., *Ottawa at War*, May 7–8, 1942, 315–20.

57 For a very good summary of Ralston's views during this period, see various items in Ralston Papers, vol. 116, "Manpower – notes made by J.L. Ralston for manpower discussions, n.d."

58 Dominion of Canada, *Official Report of the Debates of the House of Commons*, vol. 3 (Ottawa: King's Printer, 1942), 3236; and Granatstein and Hitsman, *Broken Promises*, 177.

59 On developments between April and July generally, see Stacey, *Arms, Men, and Governments*, 401–2; Granatstein, *Canada's War*, 228–43; Granatstein and Hitsman, *Broken Promises*, 172–80; and Rea, *T.A. Crerar*, 211–13. They are also covered in the King Diaries and the King Papers, J4, vol. 424, CWC Minutes, as well as in Macdonald Diaries, folder 390; and in Gibson and Robertson, eds., *Ottawa at War*, April 19 and 30, May 7–13, June 15–25, and July 9–21, 1942, 311–49.

60 King Diaries, December 7 and 10; Macdonald Diaries, folder 389, December 11, 1941; and Gibson and Robertson, eds., *Ottawa at War*, December 8, 9, and 11, 1941, 230–34.

61 On these events, see Ann Gomer Sunahara, *The Politics of Racism: The Uprooting of Japanese Canadians during the Second World War* (Toronto: James Lorimer , 1981), 27–32; and Patricia E. Roy, J.L. Granatstein, Masako Iino, and Hiroko Takamura, *Mutual Hostages: Canadians and Japanese during the Second World War* (Toronto: University of Toronto Press, 1990), 75–88. On the internment of Japanese Canadians generally, see also Ken Adachi, *The Enemy That Never Was: A History of the Japanese Canadians* (Toronto: McClelland and Stewart, 1976); and W. Peter Ward, *White Canada Forever: Popular Attitudes and Public Policy toward Orientals in British Columbia* (Montreal and Kingston: McGill–Queen's University Press, 1978).

62 In fact, American military planners had agreed to this policy several months earlier, and officially confirmed it at the Arcadia Conference in Washington at the end of December 1941. Stacey, *Six Years of War*, 310–11.

63 King Papers, J4, vol. 424, CWC Minutes, February 18 and 20, 1942. See also Dexter's report of events in Gibson and Robertson, eds., *Ottawa at War*, February 26, 1942, 278–79.

64 Gibson and Robertson, eds., *Ottawa at War*, February 13 and 28, March 16, 1942, 276–78, 280–82 (quotations from 281–82), 299–301. In contrast, King's Diary for February 27 only records discussing the overall situation in the Pacific with the two men, in a few sentences. See also King's comments emphasizing concerns about west coast defences in King Papers, J4, vol. 424, CWC Minutes, March 5–6, 1942.

65 King Diaries, March 17; and King Papers, J4, vol. 424, CWC Minutes, March 18, 1942.

66 W.A.B. Douglas, "The Air Defence Dilemma in Canada, 1939–1945," *Canadian Defence Quarterly* 14(2) (Autumn 1984): 43–48; Douglas, *The Creation of a National Air Force*, 351–72.

67 King Papers, J4, vol. 424, CWC Minutes, March 18, 1942.

68 King Papers, J4, vol. 424, CWC Minutes, March 20, 1942.

69 DHH, AHQ Rpt (D11), "The 8th Canadian Division, 1942–1943," 12–13.

70 On these various developments, see RG 24, vol. 6921, AHQ Historical Reports no. 1, "Fixed Coast Artillery Defences on the Pacific Coast," 9–17; no. 2, "The Anti-Aircraft Defences of the Pacific Coast," 6–12; and no. 4, "The Anti-Aircraft Defences of the Atlantic Coast," 14–29; as well as DHH, AHQ Report (D3), "The Employment of Infantry in the Pacific Coast Defences (Aug 39 to Dec 43)," 11–20; AHQ Rpt (D7), "The 6th Canadian Division," 8–11; AHQ Rpt (D8), "The 7th Canadian Division," 4–16; and AHQ Rpt (D11), "The 8th Canadian Division," 4–22.

71 Stacey mentions the expansion of basic training centres in *Six Years of War*, 134–35. A complete list of training establishments across the country as of July 1943 also appears in appendix "D," 528–35. Evidence of "R" recruits transferring directly into operational units can be found in LAC, RG 24, War Diaries, vol. 17215, No. 43 CA(B)TC, Sherbrooke, February 14 and April 6; vol. 17226, No. 47 CA(B)TC, Valleyfield, February 16; vol. 17220, No. 45 CA(B)TC, Sorel, April 6; vol. 17203, No. 41 CA(B)TC, Huntingdon, April 8; vol. 16914, no. 44 CA(B)TC, St-Jérôme, February 16 and March 3; vol. 17208, No. 42 CA(B)TC, Joliette, February 11 and 17–19, March 5, 9–12, 14, 17–18, 24 and 26–28, April 2–3, 6 and 8; vol. 17234, No. 51 CA(B)TC, Chicoutimi, February 16; vol. 17240, No. 54 CA(B)TC, Montmagny, February 17; vol. 17243, No. 55 CA(B)TC, Rimouski, February 17; vol. 17238, No. 53 CA(B)TC, Lauzon, February 18; vol. 17250, No. 61 CA(B)TC, New Glasgow, March 9 and April 1942, Appendix D, monthly returns of outgoing "R" recruits; vol. 17284, No. 120 CA(B)TC, Regina, February 17 and 26 and March 11 and 14; and vol. 17292, No. 131 CA(B)TC, Camrose, February 11 and 14, 1942.

72 LAC, RG 24, vol. 6921, AHQ Historical Report no. 2, "The Anti-Aircraft Defences of the Pacific Coast," 11. According to the same report, at 12, such postings continued from August to December 1942, with 500 "R" recruits per month arriving on the west coast, most of whom were provided with only a rapid four-week course and then posted to operational units. For similar cases of "R" men going straight from induction depots to infantry battalions, see Ralston Papers, vol. 72, "Shortage of Military Personnel: Officers and Other Ranks, 1942: January–February, July, October," Major-General H.F.G. Letson, AG, to Minister, April 20, 1942; and DHH, AHQ Report (D3), "The Employment of Infantry in the Pacific Coast Defences," 15, as well as "Amendments to Narrative," para. 63.

73 LAC, RG 24, War Diaries, vol. 17243, No. 55 CA(B)TC, Rimouski, February 17; vol. 17238, No. 53 CA(B)TC, Lauzon, February 18; vol. 17203, No. 41 CA(B)TC, Huntingdon, February 15, 20, and 25, March 13 and 19, and April 13; vol. 17196, No. 32 CA(B)TC, Peterborough, March 5; vol. 17270, No. 102 CA(B)TC, Fort William, February 11 and March 11; and vol. 17266, No. 100 CA(B)TC, Portage-la-Prairie, February 12, 17, and 27 and March 12 and 19; and vol. 17298, No. 132 CA(B)TC, Grande Prairie, February 11, 1942.

74 DHH, AHQ Report (D3), "The Employment of Infantry in the Pacific Coast Defences," 22; Roy, *For Most Conspicuous Bravery*, 182; Louis E. Grimshaw, "No. 1 Armoured Train," *Canadian Defence Quarterly* 21(2) (October 1991): 40–44.

75 Roy, *For Most Conspicuous Bravery*, 178.

76 DHH, AHQ Report (D3), "The Employment of Infantry in the Pacific Coast Defences," 17.

77 Ralston Papers, vol. 53, "Miscellaneous," CGS to Minister, November 23, 1940: "The Position of Reserve Formations & Units"; vol. 72, "Reserve Army – Reserve Units, 1942: Administrative and Training Staffs, June 1940–September 1940, March 1941," CGS to Minister, February 5; draft circular letters, AG to GOsC-in-C, Atlantic and Pacific Commands and all DOCs, February 8 and March 1, 1941.

78 See Crerar Papers, vol. 19, file 958C.009(D333), Crerar to Brigadier E.L.M. Burns, July 13, 1941.

79 See various documents on LAC, RG 13, vol. 2869, file 143782, "National Defence: Recruiting Committee – Reserve Army, May 13, 1942"; as well as Ralston Papers, vol. 72, "Reserve Army, 1942: Draft Statement: Policy for Recruitment, April"; and a number of other miscellaneous files on the reserve army in 1942 located in the same volume of Ralston's papers.

80 Ralston Papers, vol. 68, "Australia, Token Force for, 1942: also Canadian Home Guard, East & West Coast Reserve Militia, March," CGS to Minister, March 25, 1942; vol. 82, "Reserve Army, 1944: Report, Instructions re[.] attendance, leave, Dates of Summer Camps, July 1942–Jan[.], March, June 1944," excerpt from "Annual Army Estimates, 1944–45," on subject of "Reserve Army of Canada," January 29, 1944.

81 DHH, AHQ Report (D3), "The Employment of Infantry in the Pacific Coast Defences," 23–24; Ralston Papers, vol. 81, "Pacific Coast Militia Rangers, 1944: Rationale for, role of, organization, strength, conditions of service," excerpt from "Annual Army Estimates, 1944–45" on "Pacific Coast Militia Rangers," January 28, 1944; Roy, *For Most Conspicuous Bravery*, 177–78.

82 LAC, RG 24, vol. 6923, AHQ Historical Report No. 30, "Army Participation in Measures taken by the Three Services for the Security of the Gulf of St. Lawrence and the Lower River during the Period of German Submarine Activity, 1942–45."

83 King Papers, J4, vol. 424, CWC Minutes, January 31, 1942; Gibson and Robertson, eds., *Ottawa at War*, January 14, 15, and 28, 1942, 258–62, 269.

84 King Papers, J4, vol. 424, CWC Minutes, February 4, 13, and 26, 1942; Gibson and Robertson, eds., *Ottawa at War*, February 26 , 1942, 279; Stacey, *Arms, Men, and*

Governments, 404–5; Granatstein and Hitsman, *Broken Promises*, 188–90; Stevenson, *Canada's Greatest Wartime Muddle*, 5–6, 27–28.

85 King Papers, J4, vol. 424, CWC Minutes, July 8, 15, 17, 22, 29, and 31, August 19, September 9, 17, and 23, October 7 and 21, November 30, and December 9, 1942. See also Gibson and Robertson, eds., *Ottawa at War*, July 4, 9, 15, 19, and 21, August 2 and 27, September 25, and October 5, 14, 23, 29, 1942, and January 3, 1943, 328–95; Stacey, *Arms, Men, and Governments*, 405–10; Granatstein and Hitsman, *Broken Promises*, 190–96; and Stevenson, *Canada's Greatest Wartime Muddle*, 6–11 (quotation from 10).

86 Stacey, *Arms, Men, and Governments*, 416.

87 Stacey, *Arms, Men, and Governments*, 416; Ruth Roach Pierson, *"They're Still Women After All": The Second World War and Canadian Womanhood* (Toronto: McClelland and Stewart, 1986), esp. 95–113 (and 100–1 for the conclusions about the CWAC noted here).

88 Ralston Papers, vol. 38, "Army Programme (Secret) 1940–41," Brigadier Pope to CGS, September 23, 1941, and other correspondence between those two men and the Minister of National Defence on the same file, October 31–November 6, 1941. Prime Minister Mackenzie King agreed with the move and made the same point about releasing volunteers for overseas in King Papers, J4, vol. 424, CWC Minutes, November 26, 1941.

89 Stacey, *Six Years of War*, 123.

90 Stacey, *Six Years of War*, 123; AHQ Historical Report no. 2, "The Anti-Aircraft Defences of the Pacific Coast," 18. On RCAF participation in the defence of Alaska, see F.J. Hatch, "The Aleutian Campaign," *Roundel*, May 1963 (pt. 1), 18–23, and June 1963 (pt. 2), 18–23; Hatch, "Allies in the Aleutians," *Aerospace Historian* 21(2) (Summer/June 1974): 70–78; and Douglas, *The Creation of a National Air Force*, 410–20.

91 Burns, *Manpower in the Canadian Army*, 123; Stacey, *Six Years of War*, 123.

92 Unless otherwise noted, information in this and later paragraphs is drawn from Stacey, *Six Years of War*, 492–505; Roy, *For Most Conspicuous Bravery*, 184–94; Galen R. Perras, "An Aleutian Interlude: Canadian Participation in the Recapture of the Island of Kiska," MA thesis, Royal Military College of Canada, 1986, 1–121; Perras, *Stepping Stones to Nowhere: The Aleutian Islands, Alaska, and American Military Strategy, 1867–1945* (Vancouver: UBC Press, 2003), esp. 136–52; DHH, file 595.013(D4), "The Canadian Participation in the Kiska Operations," by G.W.L. Nicholson, December 11, 1943; and LAC, RG 24, vols. 14164–65 (reel T-12399), War Diary, Headquarters, 13th Canadian Infantry Brigade, June–August 1943. For American views on these events, see also Stanley W. Dziuban, *Military Relations between the United States and Canada* (Washington: Office of the Chief of Military History, 1959), 256–68; and Brian Garfield, *The Thousand-Mile War: World War II in Alaska and the Aleutians* (Garden City: Doubleday , 1969).

93 DHH, file 595.013(D3), "Report on Kiska Operation (1943) – 13 Cdn Inf Bde – by Commander, 13 Cdn Inf Bde [Brigadier H.W. Foster]," September 3, 1943.

94 Nicholson, "Canadian Participation in the Kiska Operations," paragraphs 11–13.

95 Nicholson, "Canadian Participation in the Kiska Operations," para. 14.

96 On the invasion of Attu, see in particular Garfield, *The Thousand-Mile War*, 208–58 (esp. 256, where he notes that the casualties suffered there – at least 12,500 – were the second-highest of the entire Pacific war for the United States compared to the number of troops committed, behind only Iwo Jima); and Perras, *Stepping Stones to Nowhere*, 111–35.

97 Stacey, *Six Years of War*, 503–4, Garfield, *The Thousand-Mile War*, 271–85; Perras, *Stepping Stones to Nowhere*, 152–56; LAC, RG 24, vol. 14165 (reel T-12399), War Diary, Headquarters, 13th Canadian Infantry Brigade, July 24 and August 9, 1943.

98 LAC, RG 24, vol. 14165 (reel T-12399), War Diary, Headquarters, 13th Canadian Infantry Brigade, August 17, 1943. The names of the four dead soldiers are from Nicholson, "Canadian Participation in the Kiska Operations," para. 196.

99 Of the 3,129 NRMA men serving outside Canada, 2,090 were in Newfoundland, 211 in Goose Bay (Labrador), 664 in Jamaica, and 164 in Alaska. For all figures cited in this paragraph, see Ralston Papers, vol. 76, "Strength Return, 1943: as at 8 May 1943 and 3 July 1943, May–June 1943," weekly strength return for July 3, dated July 12; vol. 73, "Canadian Army – Progress Report on Programme, 1943: 4-10 July 1943," Progress Report no. 136, July 15, 1943; Burns, *Manpower in the Canadian Army*, 134–35; and Stacey, *Six Years of War*, 174–76.

Part 3: Canadian Conscripts and Their Experiences During the War

Note: An earlier version of this and parts of the following chapter appeared in "Les <<zombies>> du Canada: un portrait des conscrits canadiens et de leur expérience durant la Deuxième Guerre mondiale," *Bulletin d'histoire politique* 8 (2–3) (printemps 2000): 184–204; and "Canada's Zombies: A Portrait of Canadian Conscripts and Their Experiences during the Second World War," in *Forging a Nation: Perspectives on the Canadian Military Experience*, ed. Bernd Horn (St. Catharines: Vanwell, 2002), 155–76.

1 LAC, RG 24, vol. 17252, War Diary, No. 62 CA(B)TC, Charlottetown, April 1942, Appendix IX.

Chapter 5: Canada's Zombies, Part 1

1 King Papers, J4, vol. 425, CWC Minutes, draft report on CWC meeting of October 19, 1944, prepared by Major-General Maurice Pope. Also King Diaries, October 19, 1944.

2 DHH, file 322.009(D50), "Brigade Groups – Pacific Comd – Org & Admin – Sep 43/ Sep 44," Brigadier W.H.S. Macklin, Commander, 13th Canadian Infantry Brigade, to GOC-in-C, Pacific Command, May 2, 1944, report titled "Mobilization of 13 Bde on an Active Basis." Also Stacey, *Arms, Men, and Governments*, appendix "S," 596; and Granatstein and Hitsman, *Broken Promises*, 206.

3 Rules governing the collection of this information, as well as a sample of the form used, can be found in LAC, RG 24, vol. 6570, file HQ 1161-1-5, "Procedure of National Defence Department Mobilization Act," vol. 2, draft Order-in-Council, September 6; and formal Order-in-Council P.C. 4904/1940, September 17, 1940. Unfortunately, the statistics themselves were part of a collection of unprocessed material from the army's "Directorate of Records," which I am indebted to Tim Cook and Paul Marsden for alerting me to in the late 1990s. These records had still not yet been formally accessioned or catalogued when I viewed them, and at the time of publication of this book I have so far been unable to find out from LAC where exactly they ended up being placed among the formal accessions of RG 24. But I can provide a complete copy of these statistics upon request, from one that was made for me in the late 1990s.

4 The total number of conscripts listed in the Directorate of Records statistics is 158,056, which represents an error rate of approximately 0.1 percent over the final postwar total of 157,841 provided in Stacey, *Arms, Men and Governments*, appendix "T," 599–602.

5 For good summaries of the various age classes used during the war, see Burns, *Manpower in the Canadian Army*, 146; and Stacey, *Arms, Men and Governments*, appendix "N," 586.

6 *Eighth Census of Canada*, 1941, vol. 1, table 15, 622–23.

7 Figures for all men who had enlisted in the active army up to August 31, 1942 are available in Ralston Papers, vol. 76, "Rehabilitation 1943, Interdepartment[al] General Advisory Committee on Demobilization & Rehabilitation, August, November 1942, January–February 1943," copy of report by Department of Labour titled "Interim Tabulation of Occupational History Forms supplied by the Armed Forces, including those serving on the North American Continent but not including the Reserve Army," dated January 30, 1945. Numbers for early 1943 are available in Ralston Papers, vol. 76, "Statistics – Miss.[*sic*] O.J. Waters 1943, Army – Age Groups, Casualties, C.E.F. Enlistments, Intake,

Strengths, Sept[.] 1914–Dec[.] 1919, Sept[.] 1939–January 1944," table titled "Enlistments by Age Groups as at January 16, 1943."

8 Power Papers, box 39, "General Staff Memoranda ... October–November 1944," memorandum titled "Report of Cabinet Committee on Army Enlistment for General Service," November 6, 1944. Of the 37 percent of NRMA recruits from outside central Canada, 6 percent reportedly came from the Maritimes, 24 percent from the Prairies, and 7 percent from British Columbia.

9 *Eighth Census of Canada*, 1941, vol. 1, table 20, 641–52.

10 LAC, RG 27, vol. 996, file 2–114, pt. 1, "N.W.S. Aliens – Mobilization": "Number of Single Men and Childless Widows 18–30 Years of Age, Both Inclusive, by Provinces, as per National Registration Figures of August, 1940," May 5, 1942.

11 Gibson and Robertson, eds., *Ottawa at War*, December 9, 1941, 231–33.

12 A published report from November 1944 strengthens this assumption, since it provided figures for the languages spoken by NRMA recruits, broken down in a similar manner as here, while noting explicitly that the information denoted only the mother tongues of recruits. LAC, MG 32, B5, Brooke Claxton Papers [hereafter Claxton Papers], vol. 172, "Manpower – Statistics, Clippings," pamphlet by the Wartime Information Board titled "Canada at War," no. 42, November 1944, 47.

13 Ralston Papers, vol. 76, "Statistics – Miss.[*sic*] O.J. Waters 1943," table titled "French Canadian Enlistments, Based on return in House of Commons by three Services – June 24, 1942."

14 For example, together Manitoba, Saskatchewan, Alberta, and British Columbia provided 85.0 percent (5,498) of all German-speaking recruits listed in Table 5, and 63.2 percent (12,208) of the 19,310 men listed as "Other." Roughly half of all Polish Canadian and Russian Canadian NRMA recruits came from the three prairie provinces, while Saskatchewan and British Columbia alone accounted for 96.4 percent (1,760) of recruits stating no religion. LAC, RG 24, statistics from Directorate of Records, Appendix H1, "N.R.M.A. All Ranks by Language by Province on Enrolment."

15 According to LAC, RG 24, statistics from Directorate of Records, Appendix H1, 56.1 percent (1,702) of all Italian Canadian conscripts came from Ontario, and 28.9 percent (876) from Quebec, for a total once again of 85.0 percent.

16 Power Papers, "Report of Cabinet Committee." Also noted in Granatstein and Hitsman, *Broken Promises*, 207. According to figures provided in LAC, RG 24, vol. 14165 (reel T-12400), War Diary, Headquarters, 13th Canadian Infantry Brigade, December 1943, Appendix IX, at that point 42.5 percent of all of its General Service and NRMA personnel were "British," 22.2 percent were "French," 2.5 percent Russian, 12.4 percent Polish and Ukrainian, and 20.4 percent "Others." If these figures indicate the true makeup of this brigade as Macklin was writing a few months later in May 1944, then they may suggest the origins of some of his views as described at the beginning of this chapter.

17 Quebeckers made up 56.4 percent of Roman Catholic NRMA recruits and 60.2 percent of Catholics in Canada as a whole. Corresponding figures for New Brunswick are 5.1 and 4.6 percent, for Ontario, 18.4 and 17.8 percent, and for Saskatchewan, 5.4 and 4.2 percent. LAC, RG 24, statistics from Directorate of Records, Appendix G1, "N.R.M.A. All Ranks by Religion on Enrolment"; *Eighth Census of Canada*, 1941, vol. 1, table 50, 720–27.

18 See in particular the various documents on LAC, RG 13, vol. 2871, file 145384, "National Sel[ective]. Service, Position of Irish Citizens Under the National Selective Service Mobilization Regulations. Proposed Order in Council."

19 LAC, RG 24, statistics from Directorate of Records, Appendix G1, "N.R.M.A. All Ranks by Religion on Enrolment."

20 Ralston Papers, vol. 71, "Questions, Replies to on Order Paper, pgs 1–191, January–April 1942," document titled "Return to Order of the House of Commons No. 51, Dated 23rd February, 1942."

21 On Jewish Canadian attitudes towards both voluntary and compulsory enlistment, and overall statistics related to their military service, see Gerald Tulchinsky, *Branching Out: The Transformation of the Canadian Jewish Community* (Toronto: Stoddart, 1998), 205–17.

22 On these attitudes in the interwar period, see Tulchinsky, *Branching Out*, 172–203; and on resistance of public and governmental officials towards accepting prewar refugees from Nazi Germany particularly, see also Irving Abella and Harold Troper, *None is Too Many: Canada and the Jews of Europe, 1933–1948* (Toronto: Lester and Orpen Dennys, 1983).

23 On policies towards Asian Canadians, see King Papers, J4, vol. 424, CWC Minutes, September 26 and October 1, 3, and 8, 1940; as well as various correspondence in RG 25, vol. 2818, file 1154–40C, "Participation of Orientals in Canada in Military Training Scheme." See also Patricia E. Roy, "The Soldiers Canada Didn't Want: Her Chinese and Japanese Citizens," *Canadian Historical Review* 59(3) (September 1978): 341–58.

24 LAC, RG 24, vol. 17292, War Diary, No. 131 CA(B)TC, Camrose, December 1941, Appendix E, unattributed newspaper clippings, titled "4 Chinese, Lone Japanese Are Camrose Camp Buddies" and "Four Chinese, One Japanese, Enjoying Army," n.d.

25 On the issue of Sikhs in the Canadian military, see correspondence in LAC, RG 25, vol. 2818, file 1154–40C.

26 For these and other references to African Canadians in various training centres, see LAC, RG 24, War Diaries, vol. 17306, No. 111 CA(R)TC, Gordon Head, October 28; vol. 17277, No. 110 CA(B)TC, Vernon, December 13, 1940; vol. 17168, No. 23 CA(B)TC, Newmarket, May 28 and August 3; vol. 16913, No. 44 CA(B)TC, St-Jérôme, August 3; vol. 17149, No. 12 CA(B)TC, Chatham, December 23; and vol. 17202, No. 41 CA(B)TC, Huntingdon, November 12 and 19, 1941, and January 4, 1942. For two recent articles that begin to address the issue of African Canadian enlistment in the armed forces, and particularly the RCAF, see Mathias Joost, "Racism and Enlistment: The Second World War Policies of the Royal Canadian Air Force"; and Simon Theobald, "Not So Black and White: Black Canadians and the RCAF's recruiting policy during the Second World War," *Canadian Military History* 21(1) (Winter 2012): 17–34, 35–43.

27 Ralston Papers, vol. 81, "National Resources Mobilization Act, 1944. Negroes in Canadian Army," extract from "Annual Army Estimates, 1943–44" dated January 28, 1944. On the dispute, see also various correspondence and newspaper clippings in LAC, RG 27, vol. 1486, file 2–162–9, "Exception to N.N.S.S. [*sic*] Mob. Regulations. Negros [*sic*] Chinese Japanese Etd. [*sic*] not acceptable to Army for non-medical reasons."

28 See James W. St. G. Walker, "Race and Recruitment in World War I: Enlistment of Visible Minorities in the Canadian Expeditionary Force," *Canadian Historical Review* 70(1) (March 1989): 1–26 (which discusses the experience of both Aboriginal and African Canadians in the First World War); Timothy C. Winegard, *For King and Kanata: Canadian Indians and the First World War* (Winnipeg: University of Manitoba Press, 2012), esp. 6, 76, 137; and R. Scott Sheffield, "'Of Pure European Descent and of the White Race': Recruitment Policy and Aboriginal Canadians, 1939–1945," *Canadian Military History* 5(1) (Spring 1996): 8–15.

29 King Papers, J4, vols. 424-25, CWC Minutes, May 6 and June 20, 1941, and December 22, 1944; and various correspondence on LAC, RG 13, vol. 2601, file 142069, "Sec. 3, National War Services Regulations, 1940 (Recruits). Application to Indians." For further information

on this subject, see Michael D. Stevenson, "The Mobilisation of Native Canadians during the Second World War," *Journal of the Canadian Historical Association* 7 (1996): 205–26; and Stevenson, *Canada's Greatest Wartime Muddle*, 37–50. Although few direct records have been found of Aboriginal personnel undergoing training in individual camps, there were at least two instances: LAC, RG 24, War Diaries, vol. 17277, No. 110 CA(B)TC, Vernon, January 20–22, and vol. 16913, No. 44 CA(B)TC, St-Jérôme, August 3, 1941.

Chapter 6: Canada's Zombies, Part 2

1 The description in the first part of this chapter is drawn from the war diaries of training centres and operational units across the country where conscripts served during the war, including a complete reading of the diaries for every basic training centre for the first two years of the NRMA's operation (1940–42). I have also read a number of diaries for advanced training centres during the same period, which suggest that the experiences of NRMA recruits were similar, on a day-to-day level, once they went on to serve there.

2 Diet sheets listing the daily menus for recruits can be found in the monthly war diaries of numerous training centres.

3 For brief descriptions of these standards at various points in the war, see Stacey, *Six Years of War*, 112–13; Stacey, *Arms, Men, and Governments*, 451; and Stevenson, *Canada's Greatest Wartime Muddle*, 20–21.

4 In the most extreme example, recruits in New Glasgow, Nova Scotia, suffered through outbreaks of influenza, measles, meningitis, and one case of pneumonia that resulted in the death of a trainee, all during one training period in early 1941. At least three other recruits died in other training centres over the first two years of operation of the NRMA, one of meningitis and two of pneumonia. LAC, RG 24, War Diaries, vol. 17252, No. 62 CA(B)TC, Charlottetown, December 11; vol. 17282, No. 120 CA(B)TC, Regina, November 28 and 30, 1940; vol. 17249, No. 61 CA(B)TC, New Glasgow, January 30–February 8, 1941; vol. 17279, No. 110 CA(B)TC, Vernon, February 28, 1942.

5 Caroline D'Amours, "Reassessment of a Crisis: Canadian Infantry Reinforcements during the Second World War," *Canadian Army Journal* 14(2) (Summer 2012): 82.

6 Burns, *Manpower in the Canadian Army*, 77–78.

7 W. Denis Whitaker and Shelagh Whitaker, *Tug of War: The Canadian Victory That Opened Antwerp* (Toronto: Stoddart, 1984), 212–33 (quotation from 220).

8 Andrew Brown, "New Men in the Line: An Assessment of Reinforcements to the 48th Highlanders in Italy, January–October 1944," *Canadian Military History* 21(3) (Summer 2012): 35–47; D'Amours, "Reassessment of a Crisis," 73–89. For further recent comments on the issue of training and reinforcements overseas especially, see Terry Copp, *Cinderella Army: The Canadians in Northwest Europe 1944–1945* (Toronto: University of Toronto Press, 2006), 143–44, 178–79; and Robert Engen, *Canadians Under Fire: Infantry Effectiveness in the Second World War* (Montreal and Kingston: McGill–Queen's University Press, 2009), 126–33. The first and also most detailed and thorough study of training in the Canadian army as a whole, so far, is Yves Tremblay's *Instruire une armée*; see also his account based on oral histories of Quebec veterans, in *Voluntaires*, 39–57.

9 Interview with William E. Beattie, about his father William L. Beattie, Cornwall, Ontario, May 22; personal e-mail from Beattie, September 3, 2015.

10 For examples of such competitions, see LAC, RG 24, War Diaries, vol. 17306, No. 111 CA(R)TC, Gordon Head, August–November 1940, Appendix 5[?], "Tabloid Sports," October 19; vol. 17148, No. 12 CA(B)TC, Chatham, November 1940, Appendix 4, "Athletic Field Day," November 2; and vol. 17277, No. 110 CA(B)TC, Vernon, December 1940, unnumbered appendix, "Programme of Indoor Sports," December 7, 1940.

11 LAC, RG 24, War Diaries, vol. 17153, No. 20 CA(B)TC, Brantford, November 24, 1940; vol. 17167, No. 23 CA(B)TC, Newmarket, January 17; vol. 17291, No. 131 CA(B)TC, Camrose, January 20; vol. 17021, No. 40 CA(R)TC, Farnham, January 22; vol. 17202, No. 41 CA(B)TC, Huntingdon, October 26 and November 6, 1941.

12 For references to less common sports such as rowing, see LAC, RG 24, vol. 17233, War Diary, No. 51 CA(B)TC, Chicoutimi, August 10, 1941; for curling, see vol. 16970, No. 101 CA(R)TC, Brandon, December 5; vol. 17295, No. 132 CA(B)TC, Grande Prairie, December 8, 1940, and vol. 17246, No. 60 CA(B)TC, Yarmouth, February 14, 1942; and for skiing, see vol. 17264, No. 100 CA(B)TC, Portage la Prairie, January 25 and February 1, 1941.

13 For examples of games against local high schools, see LAC, RG 24, War Diaries, vol. 17153, No. 20 CA(B)TC, Brantford, October 26, 1940; vol. 17202, No. 41 CA(B)TC, Huntingdon, November 24, 1941; and vol. 17279, No. 110 CA(B)TC, Vernon, January 24, 1942. In addition, teams from Fredericton took part in a number of competitions against the nearby University of New Brunswick, including football and track and field, while in July 1941 recruits from St-Jérôme visited Montreal to play a series of exhibition softball games against teams from the US Army and two local women's clubs. LAC, RG 24, War Diaries, vols. 17254–55, No. 70 CA(B)TC, Fredericton, October 26, 1940, and May 13 and October 4, 1941; vol. 16913, No. 44 CA(B)TC, St-Jérôme, July 5 and 17, 1941.

14 LAC, RG 24, vol. 14164 (reel T-12398), War Diary, Headquarters, 13th Canadian Infantry Brigade, January 23, 1942.

15 LAC, RG 24, War Diaries, vol. 17179, No. 22 CA(B)TC, North Bay, October 18, 1940; vol. 17277, No. 110 CA(B)TC, Vernon, October 17, 1940, May 14, 1941, and May 1941, Appendix [32]; vol. 17093, No. 130 NPAM Training Centre, Red Deer, December 1940, Appendix 4, newspaper clipping titled "Military Ring Finals Fought At Red Deer," December 21, 1940; vols. 17269–70, No. 102 CA(B)TC, Fort William, June 18, July 15, and November 28, 1941; vol. 17259, No. 71 CA(B)TC, Edmundston, October 10 and 31 and November 7, 1941, and October 1941, Appendix 6.

16 See LAC, RG 24, vol. 16891, War Diary, No. 52 CA(B)TC, Lac-Mégantic, May 3, 1941, as well as newspaper clippings on Appendix 4 for the same month.

17 For example, LAC, RG 24, vol. 17202, War Diary, No. 41 CA(B)TC, Huntingdon, January 27, 1942 ("The Centre Hockey Team is going to win this Year's Championship").

18 For example, see LAC, RG 24, vol. 17155, War Diary, No. 20 CA(B)TC, Brantford, February 12, 1942. On the impact of compulsory military service on hockey more broadly, see correspondence in LAC, RG 25, vol. 3041, file 4198-A-40, "Status of Hockey Players under United States and Canadian Selective Service Regulations"; R. Bruce McIntyre, "Which Uniform to Serve the War: Hockey in Canada versus Military Service during World War II," *Canadian Journal of History of Sport* 24(2) (December 1993): 68–90; and Douglas Hunter, *War Games: Conn Smythe and Hockey's Fighting Men* (Toronto: Viking, 1996; reprint, Penguin Books, 1997), esp. 63–64, 84–85, 96–98.

19 LAC, RG 24, vol. 17168, War Diary, No. 23 CA(B)TC, Newmarket, February 19; vol. 17196, No. 32 CA(B)TC, Peterborough, March 24, 1942.

20 LAC, RG 24, vol. 13802 (reel T-10560), War Diary, AA&QMG, 6th Canadian Division, April 28, 1943.

21 On these various developments generally during the war, see Hunter, *War Games*, 95–110.

22 LAC, RG 24, War Diaries, vol. 17307, No. 121 CA(R)TC, Dundurn, October 24; vol. 17269, No. 102 CA(B)TC, Fort William, December 17, 1940; vol. 17282, No. 120 CA(B)TC, Regina, January 17; vol. 17144, No. 10 CA(B)TC, Kitchener, January 24, 1941.

23 LAC, RG 24, vol. 17304,War Diary, No. 21 CA(R)TC, Long Branch, January 29, 1941.

24 Among them, the "M.R.T. Tin Hat Review" visited several training centres in Military District No. 4 around Montreal in 1940–41, while the "T. Eaton Co. Masquers," the "Blue Bell Bullets Review," and the "Evans Sisters" did the same in 1941–42. The "'Arf a Mo" concert party visited Gordon Head in October 1940 and January 1941, and the "Lifebuoy Follies" toured parts of Ontario in 1942. Further information can be found in the war diaries of those training centres, as well as in Gunning, *North Bay's Fort Chippewa*, 40–42.

25 LAC, RG 24, vol. 16885, War Diary, No. 11 CA(R)TC, Woodstock, December 11, 1940.

26 LAC, RG 24, vol. 17221, War Diary, No. 45 CA(B)TC, Sorel, January 21, February 6, April 15, and September 11, 1941, and May 24, 1942.

27 For example, see LAC, RG 24, War Diaries, vol. 17304, No. 21 CA(R)TC, Long Branch, December 6, 1940; vol. 17168, No. 23 CA(B)TC, Newmarket, May 10; vol. 17149, No. 12 CA(B)TC, Chatham, October 22; and vol. 17202, No. 41 CA(B)TC, Huntingdon, November 14, 1941.

28 LAC, RG 24, War Diaries, vol. 17269, No. 102 CA(B)TC, Fort William, January 15; vol. 17277, No. 110 CA(B)TC, Vernon, February 1; vol. 17296, No. 132 CA(B)TC, Grande Prairie, April 25, 1941.

29 LAC, RG 24, War Diaries, vol. 17295, No. 132 CA(B)TC, Grande Prairie, November 4 and December 17; vol. 17306, No. 111 CA(R)TC, Gordon Head, December 5, 1940; vol. 17220, No. 45 CA(B)TC, Sorel, November 6; vol. 17225, No. 47 CA(B)TC, Valleyfield, November 13; vol. 17207, No. 42 CA(B)TC, Joliette, November 20; vol. 17214, No. 43 CA(B)TC, Sherbrooke, November 27; vol. 16914, No. 44 CA(B)TC, St-Jérôme, December 11, 1941; vol. 17155, No. 20 CA(B)TC, Brantford, January 7; vol. 17284, No. 120 CA(B)TC, Regina, March 18, 1942.

30 Gunning, *North Bay's Fort Chippewa*, 95.

31 LAC, RG 24, War Diaries, vol. 17306, No. 50 CA(R)TC, Valcartier, December 7; vol. 17233, No. 51 CA(B)TC, Chicoutimi, December 7, and December 1940, Appendix I, "Nos militaires à la radio," *Le Progrès du Saguenay*, December 12; vol. 17243, No. 55 CA(B)TC, Rimouski, December 13, 1940; vol. 17206, No. 42 CA(B)TC, Joliette, July 17; vol. 17221, No. 45 CA(B)TC, Sorel, July 24; vol. 17225, No. 47 CA(B)TC, Valleyfield, July 31; vol. 17214, No. 43 CA(B)TC, Sherbrooke, August 7, 1941.

32 For examples of regular smokers, see LAC, RG 24, War Diaries, vols. 17205 and 17207–8, No. 42 CA(B)TC, Joliette, November 1–5, 1940, September 19, 1941, and February 4 and April 15, 1942. On bingo games for recruits held both inside and outside the training centres, see vol. 17220, No. 45 CA(B)TC, Sorel, October 28, 1940, and April 3, 1941; vol. 17258, No. 71 CA(B)TC, Edmundston, January 22; vol. 17201, No. 41 CA(B)TC, Huntingdon, April 8; vol. 17145, No. 10 CA(B)TC, Kitchener, August 12; vol. 17240, No. 54 CA(B)TC, Montmagny, September 15, 1941, and January 6, 1942; vol. 16913, No. 44 CA(B)TC, St-Jérôme, September 16; and vol. 17234, No. 51 CA(B)TC, Chicoutimi, November 24, 1941.

33 For two particular examples, see LAC, RG 24, War Diaries, vol. 17249, No. 61 CA(B)TC, New Glasgow, December 19, 1940, which records a mess dinner held by sergeants serving in that training centre;, as well as vol. 17282, No. 120 CA(B)TC, Regina, January 28, 1941, which records a dinner held by the officers for the Lieutenant-Governor of Saskatchewan.

34 For examples of recreation centres being established for military personnel in local communities, see LAC, RG 24, War Diaries, vol. 16970, No. 101 CA(R)TC, Brandon, October 24; vol. 17295, No. 132 CA(B)TC, Grande Prairie, November 2; vol. 17305, No. 30 CA(R)TC, Brockville, November 23, 1940; vol. 17205, No. 42 CA(B)TC, Joliette, February

15; vol. 17195, No. 32 CA(B)TC, Peterborough, August 22 and September 18, 1941; and vol. 17203, No. 41 CA(B)TC, Huntingdon, February 11, 1942.

35 Orillia Museum of Art and History, "Military" file, "Camp 26" sub-file, transcript of interview with Evelyn Davis (née Jamieson – a former Canadian Women's Army Corps clerk at the centre), conducted September 16, 2011. See also copy on this file of "Rules" for women participating in "Dance Nights."

36 LAC, RG 24, vol. 17269, War Diary, No. 102 CA(B)TC, Fort William, January 19, 1942. Fredericton's centre also recorded the local Brunswick Street Baptist Gym opening its doors for recruits to participate in various sports (vol. 17254, No. 70 CA(B)TC, December 11, 1940). On support networks provided for Jewish Canadian recruits by local communities, see Tulchinsky, *Branching Out*, 220–21.

37 Although no men were actually undergoing training at Christmas 1940, a few events were held for staff members. By 1941, training centres were operating much more regularly, and activities were also arranged for the men. Numerous centres in Quebec, especially, recorded participation in Catholic midnight mass on Christmas Eve in both years. For particular examples outside Quebec, see LAC, RG 24, War Diaries, vol. 16970, No. 101 CA(R)TC, Brandon, December 14; vol. 17283, No. 120 CA(B)TC, Regina, December 21, 1940, and December 25, 1941; vol. 17292, No. 131 CA(B)TC, Camrose, December 19 and 25; vol. 17278, No. 110 CA(B)TC, Vernon, December 25–26; and vol. 17252, No. 62 CA(B)TC, Charlottetown, December 25, 1941.

38 LAC, RG 24, War Diaries, vol. 17240, No. 54 CA(B)TC, Montmagny, October 17, December 2 and 4, 1940, and January 23, 1941; vol. 17277, No. 110 CA(B)TC, Vernon, November 3 and December 13–17, 1940, January 10 and February 3–5, 1941; vol. 17252, No. 62 CA(B)TC, Charlottetown, September 24, 1941.

39 LAC, RG 24, War Diaries, vol. 17306, No. 111 CA(R)TC, Gordon Head, October 24 and November 4; vol. 17153, No. 20 CA(B)TC, Brantford, November 24, 1940, and February 14 and 19, 1941; vol. 16885, No. 11 CA(R)TC, Woodstock, December 19, 1940; vol. 17296, No. 132 CA(B)TC, Grande Prairie, March 29; vols. 17291–92, No. 131 CA(B)TC, Camrose, March 31 and November 25, 1941; Gunning *North Bay's Fort Chippewa*, 42.

40 LAC, RG 24, vol. 13271, War Diary, Deputy Adjutant-General, November 1940, Appendix IV, "Summary of Information Respecting Activities in the A.G. Branch," November 21, 1940.

41 LAC, RG 24, vol. 17202, War Diary, No. 41 CA(B)TC, Huntingdon, July 7 and August 16, 1941.

42 For various examples of films being shown inside and outside the camps, see LAC, RG 24, War Diaries, vol. 17205, No. 42 CA(B)TC, Joliette, October 12; vol. 17194, No. 32 CA(B)TC, Peterborough, October 16–18; vol. 17179, No. 22 CA(B)TC, North Bay, October 18, 1940; vol. 17258, No. 71 CA(B)TC, Edmundston, October 24, November 6, and December 3, 1940, and April 2, 1941; vol. 17295, No. 132 CA(B)TC, Grande Prairie, December 2; vol. 17220, No. 45 CA(B)TC, Sorel, December 21, 1940; vol. 17168, No. 23 CA(B)TC, Newmarket, July 18, 1941; vol. 17149, No. 12 CA(B)TC, Chatham, March 18, 1942; and Gunning, *North Bay's Fort Chippewa*, 95–96.

43 LAC, RG 24, War Diaries, vol. 17240, No. 54 CA(B)TC, Montmagny, January 15 and March 1; vol. 17306, No. 46 CA(R)TC, St-Hyacinthe, April 9; vol. 17236, No. 53 CA(B)TC, Lauzon, May 2, July 8, August 11 and 18, and September 11; vol. 16913, No. 44 CA(B)TC, St-Jérôme, June 17; vol. 17205, No. 42 CA(B)TC, Joliette, September 25 and December 19, 1941, and January 14, 1942; vol. 17234, No. 51 CA(B)TC, Chicoutimi, January 21; vol. 17243, No. 55 CA(B)TC, Rimouski, March 2, 1942.

44 Copies can be found in the war diaries of the following basic training centres at various times over the first two years of the training: No. 12, Chatham (titled *Chins Up*); No. 42, Joliette (*Le "Petard"* – later changed to *La Hutte*); No. 44, St-Jérôme (*Le Chevalier*); No. 45, Sorel (*Le Fort Richelieu*); No. 100, Portage la Prairie (*The Centurion*); and No. 132, Grande Prairie (*Kamp Pain*).]

45 For example, see LAC, RG 24, War Diaries, vol. 17307, No. 121 CA(R)TC, Dundurn, October 11, 1940; vol. 17277, No. 110 CA(B)TC, Vernon, April 10, 1941.

46 Interview with Howard Ripstein, April 22, 1997; as well as LAC, RG 24, vol. 17201, War Diary, No. 41 CA(B)TC, Huntingdon, March 23 and April 20, 1941. On Levi, and Jewish Canadian experiences of service in the war more generally, see also Tulchinsky, *Branching Out*, 218–34.

47 LAC, RG 24, vol. 17266, War Diary, No. 100 CA(B)TC, Portage la Prairie, March 29, 1942.

48 Ralston Papers, vol. 71, "Questions, Replies to on Order Paper, pgs 1–191, January–April 1942," document titled "Return to Order of the House of Commons No. 50, Dated 23rd February, 1942." (This is also the source for there being only one full-time Jewish chaplain in 1941.)

49 Tulchinsky, *Branching Out*, 226–27. According to another return to Order of the House No. 46, dated February 29, 1944, located in Ralston Papers, vol. 82, "Replies to Questions on Order Paper, Session January 1944," by that point in the war there were 371 Protestant (including two from the Salvation Army – one in Canada and one overseas), 233 Catholic, and four Jewish chaplains serving in the Canadian army. A little more than half of all the Protestant, a little less than half the Catholic, and two of the four Jewish chaplains were overseas. In light of Tulchinsky's example, it is also interesting to note that according to this 1944 document, the army's Jewish chaplains appear to have been lumped in with Protestant ones for ease of administration.

50 LAC, RG 24, vol. 17240, War Diary, No. 54 CA(B)TC, Montmagny, July 7, 1941. Montmagny's chaplain also undertook a number of other activities, including arranging concerts for trainees, a talent show, money-raising events to pay for Christmas celebrations, and a show by the camp for the population of the town. See entries in the same war diary for October 11, 12, 17 and 25, 1940, and December 17, 1941.

51 LAC, RG 24, vol. 17240, War Diary, 17277, No. 110 CA(B)TC, Vernon, November 1940, Appendix 5, Arthur C. Sutton, Lieut. Colonel, Commanding, NPAM T[raining] C[entre] 110, to Headquarters, M.D. No. XI, November 12, 1940.

52 LAC, RG 24, vol. 17201, War Diary, No. 41 CA(B)TC, Huntingdon, February 1941, Appendix VI, letter, Lt.Col. C.C. Brooks, OC CA(R)TC #41, to AA&QMG, MD 4, February 28, 1941.

53 On North Bay, see LAC, RG 24, War Diary, vol. 17180, No. 22 CA(B)TC, April 1941, Appendix 6, R.L. Denison, Lt.Col. Commanding, No. 22 (Basic) T.C., to Major-General B.W. Browne, AG, NDHQ, April 21, 1941, and attached "Report on Behaviour of Troops in North Bay, April 19, 1941," by Capt. D. Younger, Intelligence Officer, April 28, 1941. For Edmundston, see United Church of Canada Archives, acc. 83.052C, Records of the Board of Evangelism and Social Service, box 55, file 194, various correspondence between Mutchmor, E.W. Aitken, and "Major [H. Stanley] Bland, Senior [District] Chaplain, Military District 7," May 16 to June 7, 1941 (the quotation appears in a letter of Aitken to Mutchmor, May 19). I am indebted to Suzanne Morton of McGill University for pointing me to the materials in the United Church of Canada Archives related to these topics.

54 Tim Cook, "'More a medicine than a beverage': 'Demon Rum' and the Canadian Trench Soldier of the First World War," *Canadian Military History* 9(1) (Winter 2000): 7–22. See also Cook, *At the Sharp End*, 242–44.

55 For evidence of wet canteens being established in specific training centres, see LAC, RG 24, War Diaries, vol. 17259, No. 71 CA(B)TC, Edmundston, September 15; and vol. 17154, No. 20 CA(B)TC, Brantford, September 16, 1941.

56 For these incidents, see various documents in LAC, RG 24, vol. 2193, file HQ 54–27–63–20, vol. 1, "Disturbances, C.A.S.F. [Canadian Active Service Force] Troops M.D. No. 5"; vols. 2196–97, file HQ 54–27–63–34, "Disturbance at Sussex Camp between Dufferin and Haldimand Rifles and Les Voltigeurs de Québec," vols. 1–3; and Ralston Papers, vol. 77, "Sussex Camp Disturbances, 1943: 6 May 1943, between Dufferin and Haldimand Battalion and Voltigeurs de Quebec [*sic*], May and June."

57 On these two topics, see Earle Birney, *Turvey: A Military Picaresque* (Toronto: McClelland and Stewart, 1949), 10, 16–18, 32, 40–42, 61. Birney was well-placed to write about the issues, having served as a personnel officer both at home and overseas during the war – in connection with which, see Elspeth Cameron, *Earle Birney: A Life* (Toronto: Viking, 1994), 205–11, 232–36.

58 See, however, the work of Paul Jackson, *One of the Boys: Homosexuality in the Military during World War II* (Montreal and Kingston: McGill–Queen's University Press, 2004), who has managed to reconstruct a number of these men's stories much more fully.

59 For two examples of thefts of smaller amounts of cash, see LAC, RG 24, War Diaries, vol. 16885, No. 11 CA(R)TC, Woodstock, December 7, 1940, which records $115.00 being stolen from a recruit in the barracks of that city's training centre; and vol. 17278, No. 110 CA(B)TC, Vernon, recording the Salvation Army Canteen being broken into on July 14, 1941, and $17.00 and a quantity of cigarettes stolen.

60 LAC, RG 24, vol. 17093, War Diary, No. 130 NPAM Training Centre, Red Deer, December 1940, Appendix 4, unattributed newspaper clipping titled "Charged With Pilfering From Military Camp"; Keshen, *Saints, Sinners, and Soldiers*, 38.

61 LAC, RG 24, vol. 17202, War Diary, No. 41 CA(B)TC, Huntingdon, July 1941, Appendix IV, S. Echenberg, Colonel, Commanding No. 4 District Depot, to OC, [No.] 41 Training Centre, June 11, as well as OC to DOC's Representative, MD 4, July 2, and Lt.Col. K.M. Perry, AA & QMG, MD 4, to OC, CA(B)TC #41, July 4, 1941.

62 LAC, RG 24, vol. 17202, War Diary, No. 41 CA(B)TC, Huntingdon, October 13, 1941.

63 LAC, RG 24, vol. 17277, War Diary, No. 110 CA(B)TC, Vernon, December 15, 1940, and January 8, and 20, 1941.

64 See LAC, RG 24, vols. 17277-78, War Diary, No. 110 CA(B)TC, Vernon, June 2 (source of quotation), as well as June 5 and 7 (where the same wording reappears), and July 14, 1941 (quotation repeated a third time, this time regarding another group of thirty men from a separate training class).

65 LAC, RG 24, vol. 17196, War Diary, No. 32 CA(B)TC, Peterborough, April 6, 1942.

66 LAC, RG 24, vol. 17168, War Diary, No. 23 CA(B)TC, Newmarket, August 16, 1941.

67 Ralston Papers, vol. 74, "Discharges and Deserters, 1943: May," Brigadier A.E. Nash, for AG, to Minister, May 30, 1943.

68 In addition to the source cited there, see LAC, RG 24, vol. 17233, War Diary, No. 51 CA(B)TC, Chicoutimi, April 30, 1941.

69 Ralston Papers, vol. 68, "Compulsory Training – NRMA, 1942: pressure on recruits to go active, regulations. April 1941–March 1942," circular letter, AG to GOC-in-C Pacific Command, GOC-in-C Atlantic Command, and All DOCs, 13 August 1941. For a good summary of cases in one early thirty-day training centre, see also LAC, RG 24, vol. 17277, War Diary, No. 110 CA(B)TC, Vernon, November 1940, Appendix 9, "Supplementary to M.F.M. 86," 3, and unnumbered appendices, December 1940 and February 1941, "Summary of Crime Sheets," December 21, 1940, and February 10, 1941.

70 For example, see LAC, RG 24, War Diaries, vol. 17188, No. 31 CA(B)TC, Cornwall, October 12, 1940; and vol. 17225, No. 47 CA(B)TC, Valleyfield, August 26, 1941.
71 LAC, RG 24, vol. 17221, War Diary, No. 45 CA(B)TC, Sorel, January 26, 1941.
72 LAC, RG 24, vol. 13806 (reel T-10564), AA&QMG, 8th Canadian Division, May 6, 1943.
73 Ralston Papers, vol. 69, "French Speaking Units, Lists of, 1942: 7th & 8th Divisions, April," documents titled "French-Canadian Units in Canada," "French-Speaking Units, 7th Division," and "French-Speaking Units, 8th Division"; all dated April 10, 1942.
74 Donna Spalding, "Zombies in Cape Breton," from *The Reader*, New Brunswick, and posted on the blog "Bread 'N Molasses" (http://www.breadnmolasses.com/2006/07/07/zombies-in-cape-breton).
75 John MacFarlane, "Agent of Control of Chaos? A Strike at Arvida Helps Clarify Canadian Policy on Using Troops against Workers during the Second World War," *Canadian Historical Review* 86(4) (December 2005): 619–40 (esp. 633); as well as MacFarlane, *Ernest Lapointe*, 134–35.
76 LAC, RG 24, vol. 14164 (reel T-12399), War Diary, 13th Brigade, May 1942, Appendix III, unattributed newspaper clipping titled "French-Canadians at Nanaimo; Quebec Outfit Becoming Bi-Lingual," May 11, 1942.
77 Vennat, *Les Héros oubliés*, vol. 2, 362–63.
78 Paul Brisson, *Coq-à-l'âne de mes souvenirs* (Beloeil: Privately published, 2000), 13–35, 43, and unpaginated "portrait" by his daughter Pauline near end of book. I have inferred Long Branch from Brisson's description of having taken a small arms course in the Toronto suburbs ("dans la banlieue de Toronto," 32).
79 On the subjects discussed in this paragraph, see Stacey, *Arms, Men, and Governments*, 420–24; Granatstein and Hitsman, *Broken Promises*, 160–61; Pariseau and Bernier, *French Canadians and Bilingualism*, vol. 1, 113–16, 122–38; Granatstein, *The Generals*, 237–57; and MacFarlane, *Ernest Lapointe*, 131–34. See also DHH, AHQ Rpt (D8), "The 7th Canadian Division," 10.
80 LAC, RG 24, War Diaries, vol. 14169 (reel T-12403), Headquarters, 14th Canadian Infantry Brigade, June 3 to July 23; vol. 14173 (reel T-12406), Headquarters, 16th Canadian Infantry Brigade, July 18–26; vol. 14175 (reel T-12408), Headquarters, 19th Canadian Infantry Brigade, July 23 to August 31; vol. 14175 (reel T-12408), Headquarters, 18th Canadian Infantry Brigade, August 31 to October 15, 1943.
81 For example, see LAC, RG 24, vol. 17180, War Diary, No. 22 CA(B)TC, North Bay, June 1941, Appendix 6, "183 Youths Enlist at North Bay," *North Bay Nugget*, July 11, 1941.
82 On the developments discussed here, see LAC, RG 24, War Diaries, vol. 17292, No. 131 CA(B)TC, Camrose, November 12; and vol. 17259, No. 71 CA(B)TC, Edmundston, December 13, 1941; as well as Ralston Papers, vol. 68, "Compulsory Training – NRMA, 1942," Routine Order No. 1526, December 24, 1941, prohibiting the wearing of Canada badges by NRMA personnel; Ralph Allen, *Home Made Banners* (Toronto: Longmans, Green and Co., 1946), 51; Stacey, *Arms, Men, and Governments*, 429; Gunning, *North Bay's Fort Chippewa*, 62; and Andrew Iarocci, "Side-Steppers and Original-Firsts: The Overseas Chevron Controversy and Canadian Identity in the Great War," *Canadian Military History* 20(3)(Summer 2011), 51–52.
83 Allen, *Ordeal by Fire*, 393–94.
84 Allen, *Home Made Banners*, 38–75; Allen, *The High White Forest* (New York: Doubleday, 1964), 170–94. The characters and situations described in the two books are very similar and obviously based on the same example. For further discussion of this issue, see also Granatstein and Hitsman, *Broken Promises*, 154–56.

85 Conn Smythe, with Scott Young, *If You Can't Beat 'Em in the Alley* (Toronto: McClelland and Stewart, 1981), 147–48.

86 Barry Broadfoot, *Six War Years, 1939–1945: Memories of Canadians at Home and Abroad* (Toronto: Doubleday Canada, 1974), 3–4 (quotation at 4), 334–35.

87 LAC, RG 24, vol. 17144, War Diary, No. 10 CA(B)TC, Kitchener, March 22, 1941.

88 LAC, RG 24, vol. 17168, War Diary, No. 23 CA(B)TC, Newmarket, July 10–11, 1941. For further examples of parades explicitly being used to encourage volunteers, see also vol. 16913, No. 44 CA(B)TC, St-Jérôme, July 8; vol. 17283, No. 120 CA(B)TC, Regina, July 11 and 14; vol. 17246, No. 60 CA(B)TC, Yarmouth, November 15; vol. 17168, No. 23 CA(B)TC, Newmarket, November 17; vol. 17234, No. 51 CA(B)TC, Chicoutimi, December 3, 1941 and January 16, 1942; vols. 17259–60, No. 71 CA(B)TC, Edmundston, December 13, 1941, and March 21 and April 18, 1942; and vol. 17144, No. 10 CA(B)TC, Kitchener, January 14, 1942.

89 LAC, RG 24, War Diaries, vol. 17180, No. 22 CA(B)TC, North Bay, May 1941, Appendix 5, June 1941, Appendices 5 and 6, December 1941, Appendix 7, and January 1942, Appendix 7; vol. 17156, No. 20 CA(B)TC, Brantford, March 1942, Appendix VII; vol. 17266, No. 100 CA(B)TC, Portage la Prairie, February 1942, Appendix I; vol. 17202, No. 41 CA(B)TC, Huntingdon, December 1941, Appendix VI.

90 LAC, RG 24, vol. 17202, War Diary, No. 41 CA(B)TC, Huntingdon, December 4, 1941. See also related entries for December 7–10.

91 In the words of William E. Beattie: "as good of a Canadian as you could get," and "all soldier – a gentleman" (Beattie interview, May 22, 2015). Also personal e-mail from Beattie, September 3, 2015.

92 LAC, RG 24, vol. 17188, War Diary, No. 31 CA(B)TC, Cornwall, June 3, 1941.

93 LAC, RG 24, vol. 17243, War Diary, No. 55 CA(B)TC, Rimouski, January 25, 1942.

94 Ralston Papers, vol. 68, "Compulsory Training – NRMA, 1942," Brigadier F.L. Armstrong, DOC, MD 3, to Secretary, DND, February 9, 1942.

95 Ralston Papers, vol. 68, "Compulsory Training – NRMA, 1942,", Larose to DOC, MD 3, February 5, 1942.

96 LAC, RG 24, vol. 80, file HQ 1161-1-18, "Complaints Generally Reserve Training Centres," vol. 2, statement by Joseph Robert Miville, September 7, 1941. Both the original document in French and an English translation appear in this file, the latter being the source of the above quotation.

97 LAC, RG 24, vol. 80, HQ 1161-1-18, statement by J[oseph]. Albert Lefebvre, September 7, 1941.

98 LAC, RG 24, vol. 80, HQ 1161-1-18, statement by Miville.

99 See in particular LAC, RG 24, vol. 80, file HQ 1161-1-18, L.R. LaFleche [*sic*], DM, to O.M.M. Kay, Acting DAG(M), September 8, 1941; reports from DOC, MD 3, October 3, 8 and 11; AG to DOC, October 30; AG to Ralston, December 12; and Ralston to J.T. Thorson, Minister of National War Services, December 18, 1941.

100 LAC, RG 24, vol. 80, HQ 1161-1-18, Lt.Col. E.M. Ansell, OC, No. 12 Basic Training Camp, to Col. W.H. Kippen, MD 1, February 19, 1942, and attached documents.

101 LAC, RG 24, vol. 17264, War Diary, No. 100 CA(B)TC, Portage la Prairie, March 1941, Appendices 1–2, "Colonel Ackland's Address To Reserve Army Recruits," and "Colonel Ackland's Address To Active Army Recruits," n.d. [both March 21, 1941]. For later examples in the same centre, see vols. 17265–66, May 1941, Appendix 3, "Speech by Lt.Colonel C.M. Ackland, M.C., V.D., to 'R' Recruits of 4th Course" [May 16, 1941]," as well as the main war diary entries for April 18, August 4, and December 8, 1941, and January 12, 1942.

102 Canadian War Museum, Military History Research Centre, Friends of the Canadian War Museum Oral History Project, 31D 1 HARPER, transcript of interview with Burton E. Harper, Ottawa, Ontario, September 26, 2000.

103 Milan (Mike) Bosnich, *One Man's War: Reflections of a Rough Diamond* (Toronto: Lugus Productions, 1989), 6–12. I am indebted to Myron Momryk, former archivist at LAC, for this reference.

104 LAC, RG 24, vols. 17189–90, War Diary, No. 31 CA(B)TC, Cornwall, July 2–5 and August 11, 1941, and April 21, 1942. Entries for January 23–24, 1942, also suggest that very close to 100 percent of "R" recruits went active out of a further group of men who arrived in the camp that month.

105 LAC, RG 24, vol. 17195, War Diary, No. 32 CA(B)TC, Peterborough, July 11; vol. 17168, No. 23 CA(B)TC, Newmarket, July 26 and August 22; vol. 17145, No. 10 CA(B)TC, Kitchener, September 16 and November 26; vol. 17252, No. 62 CA(B)TC, Charlottetown, October 23; vol. 17149, No. 12 CA(B)TC, Chatham, November 26, 1941.

106 LAC, RG 24, vol. 17195, War Diary, No. 32 CA(B)TC, Peterborough, October 26, 1941.

107 LAC, RG 24, War Diaries, vol. 17189, No. 31 CA(B)TC, Cornwall, July 1–3, 1941, January 24 and April 24, 1942; vol. 17195, No. 32 CA(B)TC, Peterborough, July 11; vol. 17168, No. 23 CA(B)TC, Newmarket, August 23; vol. 17145, No. 10 CA(B)TC, Kitchener, September 1, 1941.

108 Bosnich, *One Man's War*, 22–23.

109 Allen, *The High White Forest*, 187–94.

110 Vincent, *Ils ont écrit la guerre*, 48–49, 244–45.

111 LAC, RG 24, vol. 80, HQ 1161-1-18, vol. 1, Camille Chouinard to Hormidas Chouinard, June 27 (source of quotation), Précis of letter from Hormidas Chouinard to Ernest Lapointe, July 2, and A. Tessier, Capt. & Adjut[ant]., for OC, A-13 Infantry Training Centre [Valcartier], to [?],August 27, 1941.

112 LAC, RG 24, vol. 80, HQ 1161-1-18, vol. 2, Armstrong, DOC, MD 3, to DND, 3 September 1941.

113 LAC, RG 24, vol. 80, HQ 1161-1-18, vol. 2, Marcel Lacroix, Adrien Boudreault, Raymond Berube [*sic*], et.al. [to DND], September 9, and Lt.-Colonel J.N. Turgeon, OC Canadian Army Basic Training Centre No. 53, Lauzon, Quebec, to Deputy Assistant Adjutant-General [DAAG], MD No. 5, September 24, 1941.

114 LAC, RG 24, vol. 80, HQ 1161-1-18, vol. 2, M. McCabe and J. Leclair to King, July 25, 1941.

115 LAC, RG 24, vol. 80, HQ 1161-1-18, vol. 1, letter from Camp Borden (author's name severed by censors), July 9, 1941.

116 LAC, RG 24, vol. 80, HQ 1161-1-18, vol. 1, Major W.E. Macklin and Lt.Col. J.P. Girvan, A-10 Infantry (Advanced) Training Centre, to Camp Headquarters, Camp Borden, July 31, 1941.

117 For example, see LAC, RG 24, vol. 80, HQ 1161-1-18, vol. 1, Lt.Col. P.L. Park, OC 15th Field Regiment, RCA, to Headquarters, RCA, 4th Division, December 3, 1941; DM(Army), to AG, March 16, 1942; and Lieut.-Colonel G. Francoeur, OC, Canadian Army Basic Training Centre No. 44, St-Jérôme, to Headquarters, MD No. 4, March 24, 1942. See also LAC, RG 24, vol. 80, HQ 1161-1-18, vol. 3, Robert Phaneuf to Minister of National Defence, January 18, 1942; Major J. Henri Labrie, Commanding Officer, Canadian Army Basic Training Centre No. 55, Rimouski, to DAAG, Military District No. 5, February 2, 1942; Norman Smith, Editor, Ottawa *Journal*, to AG, May 21, 1943, and attached items; anonymous letter from "N.R.M.A. Personel" [*sic*], June 13, 1944; and Assistant Private Secretary, DND, to AG, September 22, 1944.

118 Broadfoot, *Six War Years*, 331. For further comments on the experiences of recruits after going on to home defence units, see Burns, *Manpower in the Canadian Army*, 122–23; and Granatstein and Hitsman, *Broken Promises*, 155.

119 None of the Canadian historians cited earlier in this book who have written about Kiska describe the experiences of the men after the initial landings in any depth. G.W.L. Nicholson did provide a much more detailed account in his early days as a historical officer for the army, which can be found in DHH, file 595.013 (D4), "The Canadian Participation in the Kiska Operations," December 11, 1943. On the experiences of the *Régiment de Hull* in particular, see also Pierre Vennat, *Lés Héros oubliés*, vol. 2, 207–22, and for the Canadian Fusiliers, see Bill Corfield, *Silent Victory: The Canadian Fusiliers in the Japanese War* (Surrey: Timberholme Books, 2003).

120 LAC, RG 24, vol. 14165 (reel T-12399), War Diary, Headquarters, 13th Canadian Infantry Brigade, July 19, 1943.

121 LAC, RG 24, vol. 14165 (reel T-12399), War Diary, Headquarters, 13th Canadian Infantry Brigade, September 15, 1943.

122 LAC, RG 24, vol. 14165 (reel T-12399), War Diary, Headquarters, 13th Canadian Infantry Brigade, October 28, 1943. Roy, *For Most Conspicuous Bravery*, 195, also quotes from various entries in this same source to describe the weather conditions.

123 LAC, RG 24, vol. 14165 (reel T-12400), War Diary, Headquarters, 13th Canadian Infantry Brigade, December 7, as well as January 1944, Appendix IV, "Headquarters 13 Canadian Infantry Brigade (Rear Party Diary)," entries for December 25–26 and 29, 1943, January 2–3 and 10, 1944.

124 LAC, RG 24, vol. 14165 (reels T-12399-400), War Diary, Headquarters, 13th Canadian Infantry Brigade, August 29 and September 27, as well as copies of the *Kiska Volcano* contained in appendices for each of the months from August 1943 to January 1944; Nicholson, "Canadian Participation in the Kiska Operation," paras. 86, 192.

125 LAC, RG 24, vol. 14165 (reel T-12400), War Diary, Headquarters, 13th Canadian Infantry Brigade, December 9, 12, and 14, 1943.

126 For general policies on conscripts serving as NCOs, see LAC, RG 24, reel C-5270, file HQC 7959-3, "Policy re – N.R.M.A. N.C.O.-s," and particularly circular letter by AG, April 22, 1942, along with undated "Draft Memorandum" [July 1944], and "Policy re N.R.M.A. N.C.Os." [Summer 1944].

127 Côté, with Bouvier, *Je les ai vus mourir*, 29–33.

128 These officers were Lt.-Col. Eugène Nantel, who was mentioned in Chapter 1 as the first commander of No. 44 CA(B)TC in St-Jérôme; Lt.-Col. Paul Brosseau, who took over from Lt.-Col. Nantel there in December 1942; and Major L. Younger, the commander first of No. 132 CA(B)TC in Grande Prairie and later of No. 103 CA(B)TC in Winnipeg; as well as Lt.-Col. John Alexander Adamson and Lt.-Col. J.N.E. Grenier for their work as commanders of the Pictou Highlanders and the *Régiment de Montmagny* (which will be discussed in Chapter 7), respectively. I am indebted to Hugh Halliday for this information, which was given to me from a database created by him from a collection of uncatalogued award citations held at DHH.

129 DHH, file 322.009(D50), Brigadier W.H.S. Macklin, Commander 13th Canadian Infantry Brigade, to GOC-in-C, Pacific Command, "Mobilization of 13 Bde on an Active Basis," May 2, 1944, Appendix "A," "Enrolling NRMA. [*sic*] Personnel for Active Service: 1 Bn. Le Régiment de Hull C.A.," n.d.

130 Bosnich, in *One Man's War*, 18–22, explicitly refers to this.

131 DHH, file 322.009(D50), Macklin report, 11–13 (quotation from 13). See also Stacey, *Arms, Men and Governments*, appendix "S," 595–96; and Granatstein and Hitsman, *Broken Promises*, 206.

132 DHH, file 322.009(D50), "Enrolling NRMA. Personnel for Active Service: 1 Bn. Le Régiment de Hull."

133 LAC, RG 24, vol. 2197, HQ 54–27–63–38, "Disturbances Between G.S. and N.R.M.A. Personnel, A-16 Currie Barracks, Calgary, 18-7-44," proceedings of court of inquiry, July 20, 1944.

134 LAC, RG 27, vol. 996, file 2–114, "N.W.S. Aliens – Mobilization," pt. 2, Charles J. Christie, Secretary, Municipal District of Stauffer, quoted in letter, L.R. LaFlèche, Associate DM, DNWS, to J.P. McIsaac, Divisional Registrar "N," DNWS, March 20; see also LaFlèche to Brigadier O.M.M. Kay, Deputy AG, March 30, 1942.

135 These files can be found throughout vols. 253–265 of the McNaughton Papers.

136 Interview with Wray Gardiner, Guelph, Ontario, May 17, 2015; LAC, RG 24, vol. 27352, personnel file for A108336, Charles H. Wilson.

137 Beattie interview, May 22; personal e-mail from Beattie, September 3, 2015.

138 One of the anonymous interviewees in Broadfoot, *Six War Years*, 348, also mentions a man who refused to go active because he had three brothers in the services already and his mother did not want to risk losing all four.

139 Of the twenty-eight NRMA recruits who had not been born in Canada, five (3.5% of the total of 143) were from Great Britain or Ireland, seventeen (11.9%) from Europe, three from (2.1%) the United States, and one from Syria; information was unavailable for two men. Among the ninety recruits whose parents had not both been born in Canada, twenty-nine (20.3% of 141) came from families where at least one had been born in Great Britain or Ireland, fifty (35.0%) from Europe, seven (4.9%) from the United States, and the same man from Syria, whose parents both came from there, and for three men information was not available. Statistics in this paragraph are compiled from DHH, file 161.009(D8), "N.R.M.A. – MD 1 Nov/Dec 1944: Persuasion NRMA," records of interviews and other documents concerning A-29 Canadian Infantry Training Centre, Ipperwash, Ontario, May 9–12, 1944. I am indebted to Carl Christie, the former Senior Research Officer at DHH, who made this restricted personal information available to me on condition that it only be used in anonymous aggregate form.

Part 4: The Fall of the Big Army

1 King Papers, J4, vol. 365 (reel H-1538), "National Resources Mobilization Act."

Chapter 7: "No stone ... unturned"

1 Dawson, *The Conscription Crisis of 1944*, 33.

2 Burns, *Manpower in the Canadian Army*, 11–14, 89–94, 132–33; Stacey, *Arms, Men, and Governments*, esp. 445, 451–52. See also Dawson, *The Conscription Crisis of 1944*, 31–32; and Granatstein and Hitsman, *Broken Promises*, 210, 216–17.

3 Granatstein and Hitsman, *Broken Promises*, 194.

4 Ralston Papers, vol. 76, "Reinforcements, 1943: Authorization for, strength summary, estimates, recommendations, January, March," CGS to Minister, March 28, 1943. See also King Papers, J4, vol. 425, CWC Minutes, January 6 and May 13, 1943.

5 King Papers, J4, vol. 425, CWC Minutes, June 18, 1943; DHH, AHQ Report (D3), "The Employment of Infantry in the Pacific Coast Defences," 28; Ralston Papers, vol. 39, "Army in Canada, General (Secret)," CGS to Minister, August 30, 1943; vol. 82, "Troops, Reduction of Operational, 1944: strength return summaries and decisions, January," excerpt from "Annual Army Estimates, 1944–45: Reduction of Operational Troops in Canada," January 27, 1944.

6 Ralston Papers, vol. 80, "Link Training Plan 1944, Rationale, explanation, organization, January," excerpt from "Annual Army Estimates, 1944–45," January 27, 1944; vol. 83, "War Appropriation Speech 1944 – Feb. 1944, Working Papers – #2, Exclusive of McNaughton Material n.d.," copy of DND press release, August 29, 1943. See also Stacey, *Six Years of War*, 134-35.

7 On the developments discussed in this and the following paragraph, see the primary sources on the July 1943 reorganization cited in the previous paragraph, as well as Ralston Papers, vol. 82, "Training – Brigade Group at Debert, 1944: January," excerpt from "Annual Army Estimates, 1944–45: Training Brigade Group," January 27, 1944; King Papers, J4, vol. 425, CWC Minutes, July 21 and August 31, 1943; DHH, AHQ Rpt (D7), "The 6th Canadian Division," 12–15; DHH, AHQ Rpt (D8), "The 7th Canadian Division," 11, 17–18; DHH, AHQ Rpt (D11), "The 8th Canadian Division,," 17–18, 23–25; LAC, RG 24, vol. 6921, AHQ Historical Reports No. 1, "Fixed Coast Artillery Defences on the Pacific Coast," 10–13, No. 2, "The Anti-Aircraft Defences of the Pacific Coast," 14–27, and No. 4, "The Anti-Aircraft Defences of the Atlantic Coast," 40–70; Stacey, *Six Years of War*, 183–86; Stacey, *Arms, Men, and Governments*, 410–11; and Roy, *For Most Conspicuous Bravery*, 203–5.

8 DHH, AHQ Report (D3), "The Employment of Infantry in the Pacific Coast Defences," 28.

9 King Papers, J4, vol. 425, CWC Minutes, May 13 and August 31, 1943.

10 King Papers, J4, vol. 424, CWC Minutes, July 17, 1942. See also Gibson and Robertson, eds., *Ottawa at War*, August 27, 1942, 365; and Granatstein and Hitsman, *Broken Promises*, 191–92.

11 King Papers, J4, vol. 424, CWC Minutes, esp. September 9, October 28, November 4, 11, 18, and 30, December 9, 1942, and February 10 and 24, 1943. See also Gibson and Robertson, eds., *Ottawa at War*, September 25, 1942, 367.

12 LAC, RG 24, vol. 2915, file HQS 9011–9-5, "Questions from and Reports to the Minister – National Selective Service," statistical table titled "Interim Results of Requisitions Under the National War Service Regulations (Recruits) And the National Selective Service Mobilization Regulations, by Military Training Periods, 20 Mar 1941 to 2 Apr 1943." See also same, by military districts, May 9, 1943.

13 LAC, RG 24, vol. 2915, file HQS 9011-9-5, Brigadier A.E. Nash, Vice AG, to D[irector of]. Req[uirements]., February 20, 1943.

14 Ralston Papers, vol. 78, "Conscription Speech – file 1 1944," flyer titled "A Message to Canadian Farmers," April 17, 1944.

15 LAC, RG 24, vol. 2915, HQS 9011–9-5, A.G. Stewart, Member, Mobilization Board, Division "M," Regina, Saskatchewan, to Gardiner, March 6, 1943. See also similar protest by Lt.-Col. A.W. Pascoe, Dist[rict]. Recruiting Officer, M.D. No. 12, to Lt.-Col. James Mess, Director of Army Recruiting, February 11, and related comments of Col. J.A. deLalanne, Directorate of Mobilization and Requirements, to Vice AG, March 25, as well as those in an earlier memorandum regarding "Matters Discussed with General Riley [Supervisor of Mobilization, NSS] this afternoon," January 22, 1943, all in the same file.

16 LAC, RG 24, vol. 2915, HQS 9011–9-5, Mitchell to Ralston, March 4, 1943, and attached memorandum from Major-General H.J. Riley to Arthur MacNamara, Director of NSS, dated March 2.

17 LAC, RG 24, vol. 2915, HQS 9011–9-5,Nash, for Major-General H.F.G. Letson, AG, to Minister, February 17, 1943. The original of this memorandum, which makes it more clear that it was prepared by Nash as opposed to Letson, can be found in Ralston Papers, vol. 52, "Manpower, Gen. (Secret)," vol. 2.

18 Stacey, *Arms, Men, and Governments*, appendix "T," 599–601.

19 On the attitudes and problems of NSS officials, and responses from the DND, see also various other documents in LAC, RG 24, vol. 2915, HQS 9011–9-5, January 22 to March 23, 1943.
20 For example, see LAC, RG 24, vol. 2915, HQS 9011–9-5, Letson to Minister, March 8, 1943.
21 LAC, RG 24, vol. 2915, HQS 9011–9-5, Ralston to Mitchell, April 1, 1943.
22 LAC, RG 24, vol. 2915, HQS 9011–9-5, April 3, 1943.
23 King Papers, J4, vol. 425, CWC Minutes, April 28, June 24 and 28, July 2 and 7, and September 15; LAC, RG 27, vol. 3057, file 21–14, "N.S.S. Mobilization. Aliens," Ralston to Mitchell, June 4, and Mitchell to Ralston, June 22; Gibson and Robertson, eds., *Ottawa at War*, May 10, 1943, 411–12; and Granatstein and Hitsman, *Broken Promises*, 198–202.
24 Stacey, *Arms, Men, and Governments*, 430–31 (quotation from 431). The April 1 letter is also quoted in slightly altered form ("I can suggest that") in Granatstein and Hitsman, *Broken Promises*, 202; also, Burns refers to information from the same March–April exchange of letters in *Manpower in the Canadian Army*, 120.
25 Granatstein and Hitsman, *Broken Promises*, 203.
26 Hatch, *Aerodrome of Democracy*, 101–12; Douglas, *The Creation of a National Air Force*, 250–66.
27 Greenhous et al., *The Crucible of War*, 638.
28 On the last months of the BCATP, see Hatch, *Aerodrome of Democracy*, 181–87; and Douglas, *The Creation of a National Air Force*, 291–93.
29 Allan D. English, *The Cream of the Crop: Canadian Aircrew, 1939–1945* (Montreal and Kingston: McGill–Queen's University Press, 1996), 137–44.
30 On Canada's lack of participation in strategic decision making, see Adrian W. Preston, "Canada and the Higher Direction of the Second World War 1939–1945," *R.U.S.I. Journal* 110(637) (February 1965): 28–44; as well as C.P. Stacey, "Canadian Leaders of the Second World War," *Canadian Historical Review* 66(1) (March 1985): 64–65, 69–72.
31 See English, *The Cream of the Crop*, 142; and John A. English, *The Canadian Army and the Normandy Campaign*, 110–11.
32 G.W.L. Nicholson, *Official History of the Canadian Army in the Second World War*, vol. 2: *The Canadians in Italy, 1943–1945* (Ottawa: Queen's Printer, 1957), 20–26; Pickersgill, *The Mackenzie King Record*, vol. 1, 494–504. Sources on Hong Kong have already been cited in Chapter 4. On Dieppe, the literature is considerable, but some key starting points are Stacey, *Six Years of War*, 349–412; Brian Loring Villa, *Unauthorized Action: Mountbatten and the Dieppe Raid* (Oxford: Oxford University Press, 1989); and Brereton Greenhous, *Dieppe, Dieppe* (Montreal: Art Global, 1992).
33 LAC, RG 24, vol. 6926, AHQ Historical Section Report No. 63, "Manpower Problems of the Canadian Army in the Second World War," by J.M. Hitsman, August 17, 1953, 143; Burns, *Manpower in the Canadian Army*, 120.
34 LAC, RG 24, vol. 2915, HQS 9011–9-5, Mitchell to Ralston, March 23, 1943.
35 Hugh McVicar, personal letter to author, January 28, 1997. See also Hugh McVicar, "'Backdoor to War': A Canadian Infantryman at Hochwald and Xanten, February–March 1945," *Canadian Military History* 4(2) (Autumn 1995): 75–81.
36 Vincent, *Laissés dans l'ombre*, 177–78, 205.
37 The figures for these calculations are taken from Stacey, *Arms, Men, and Governments*, appendix "T," 599–602.
38 Hitsman, "Manpower Problems of the Canadian Army," 143; Burns, *Manpower in the Canadian Army*, 119. For examples of such comments by C.G. Power, see King Papers, J4, vol. 424, CWC Minutes, February 26; and for J.L. Ralston, see Gibson and Robertson,

eds., *Ottawa at War*, September 27 and October 29, 1942, 371 and 383. Numerous other, more vague allusions can also be found in the minutes of the CWC for various dates, and particularly during the debates over the Canadian army program in late 1941 and early 1942, and those that led to the creation of NSS later in 1942.

39 Stacey, *Arms, Men, and Governments*, 412.

40 Ralston Papers, vol. 68, Compulsory Training – NRMA 1942, pressure on recruits to go active. regulations. April 1941–March 1942," circular letter, AG to GOsC-in-C, Atlantic and Pacific Commands, and all DOCs, March 31, 1942.

41 Ralston Papers, vol. 73, "Agricultural and Compassionate Leave 1943. Regulations, memoranda, Hansard. March, May–July," and similar circular letters, March 17 and 30 and July 5, 1943. On provisions for agricultural, lumber, and mining leaves generally, see also Stacey, *Arms, Men, and Governments*, 411–12.

42 See various documents in Ralston Papers, vol. 74, "Coal Miners – Special Leave to Army. 1943, January, May–June."

43 Ralston Papers, vol. 52, "Manpower, Gen. (Secret), Vol. 2," memorandum by A.D.P. Heeney to CWC, September 7, and Nash to the Minister, September 10, 1943.

44 See esp. Ralston Papers, vol. 79, "Forestry Corps 1944, Summary of Rates of Pay, Leave Regulations, Personnel, Regulations, Application, Civilian Work., Jan[.]–March," excerpt from "Annual Army Estimates, 1944-45"; Stacey, *Arms, Men, and Governments*, 411; and Rea, "What Really Happened?": 17.

45 Ralston Papers, vol. 78, "Conscription Speech – file 1 1944 (during budget debate), Working Papers July," minutes of meeting of "War Manpower Committee of the Cabinet, ... June 21, 1944"; vol. 82, "Replies to Questions on Order Paper, Session January 1944," Orders of the Day No. 36, answer to question by J.-F. Pouliot, February 3; vol. 81, "Port Battalions, 1944, Organization and proposed Employment of Port Companies. January," excerpt from "Annual Army Estimates, 1944–45" dated January 26, 1944. See also Granatstein and Hitsman, *Broken Promises*, 201.

46 King Papers, J4, vol. 425, CWC Minutes, April 7 and 14 and May 5 and 14, 1943.

47 King Papers, J4, vol. 425, CWC Minutes, July 21, August 31, and September 8 and 15, 1943, and January 20, 1944.

48 Ralston Papers, vol. 76, "Strength Return, 1943: as at 8 May 1943 and 3 July 1943, May-June 1943," weekly strength return for July 3, dated July 12, 1943; DHH, File 111.21065(D1), "Reinf. situation – Cdn Army, 1944," document titled "Summary of Personnel on 'Extended Leave' or 'Duty' as at 30 Sep 44," November 2, 1944; Power Papers, box 39, "General Staff Memoranda ... October-November 1944," copy of "Report of Cabinet Committee on Army enlistment for General Service," November 6, 1944.

49 LAC, RG 25, vol. 2633, file 715–40, pt. 1, "National Resources Mobilization Act, 1940. Military Service in Canada," copy of "Memorandum for the Prime Minister," November 14, 1941.

50 LAC, RG 24, vol. 6924, "Historical Report No. 35, Historical Section (G.S.), Army Headquarters: Allied Forces in Canada, 1940–1943."

51 A summary of developments throughout the war can be found in LAC, RG 25, vol. 3498, file 20–3-2–1946/1, memorandum titled "Conscription of Aliens and Non-Canadian British Subjects in Canadian Forces," [no author] July 15, 1948. See also King Papers, J4, vol. 424, CWC Minutes, November 19, 1941, and January 7 and 23, February 13, July 22, and November 18 and 30, 1942.

52 These numbers are compiled from LAC, RG 27, vol. 996, file 2–114, pt. 1, "Statement showing by nationalities and by provinces the number of non-British subjects between the ages of 21 and 45, both inclusive, who registered in Canada in August 1940," Department

of National War Services, September 30 1941; same file, pt. 2, "Number of aliens born in the years 1912 to 1921, both inclusive"; and a second untitled table, both dated May 1, 1942; and pt. 3, "Table showing, by age groups, the number of nationals of European countries, single or childless widowers as of July 15th, 1940," September 21, and two similar tables for "Asiatic" and "European" countries, both dated September 22, 1942.

53 LAC, RG 27, vol. 1478, file 2–117–1, "Delinquents, Police Action," L.R. LaFlèche, Associate DM, DNWS, to "All Chairmen and Divisional Registrars," Circular Memorandum no. 22, September 27, 1940; S.T. Wood, Commissioner, RCMP, to T.C. Davis, Associate DM, DNWS, January 31; LaFlèche, Circular Memorandum no. 159, February 12; and further similar memoranda, no. 219, May 5, no. 235, May 22, and no. 284, July 25, 1941.

54 Ralston Papers, vol. 114, "Manpower, Vol. 3," Ralston to Thorson, March 4, and Ralston to St. Laurent, March 13, 1942. On the reluctance of NSS officials to deal with the issue in greater detail early in the war, see also Gibson and Robertson, eds., *Ottawa at War*, September 25–27, 1942, 369, 372; and LAC, RG 24, vol. 2915, HQS 9011–9-5, J.A. deLalanne, "Matters Discussed with General Riley," January 22, and Vice AG to Minister, February 4, 1943.

55 Examples of various cases can be found in correspondence in LAC, RG 24, vol. 6570, file HQ 1161–1-2, vol. 1, "National Registration Regulations." See also RG 13, vol. 2113, file 145335, W.S. Boyd, Legal Assistant to Chief Registrar, National Registration, Department of Labour, to A. MacNamara, DM, October 12, 1943.

56 For example, see LAC, RG 25, vol. 2633, file 715–40, pt. 1, "R.C.M.P. Reveal Cards Forgery For Vote Fraud," clipping from *Montreal Gazette*, December 9, 1940, as well as RG 24, vol. 2250, file HQ 54–27–98–5, "Forgery and Sale of Certificates Generally," vol. 1, correspondence regarding a corporal stealing documents from No. 44 CA(B)TC in St-Jérôme, for use by a forger, August 1943 to January 1947.

57 Stevenson, *Canada's Greatest Wartime Muddle*, 22–23.

58 For an overview of mobilization procedures that describes how medicals and other steps in the process were carried out, see LAC, RG 24, vol. 2915, HQS 9011–9-5, "Procedure [for] Call-Ups Under N.R.M.A.," no author, March 23, 1943. See also Stevenson, *Canada's Greatest Wartime Muddle*, 20–21.

59 LAC, RG 24, vol. 2915, file HQS 9011–6-0, vol. 5, "Requirements – National Selective Service – Generally," A. de Gaspé Taché, Registrar, Mobilization Division "E," Montreal, to Director, Mobilization Section, NSS, October 16 and November 3 and 23, 1944, as well as later correspondence all related to a doctor in Montreal who was alleged to have taken money to help men get medical rejections. In the same file, see also Col. J.E. MacDermid, D.Admin. [Director of Administration], to Liaison Officer, NSS, December 23, 1944, regarding a lawyer who was investigated for helping people obtain deferments and discharges illegally. Allegations regarding military personnel can be found in LAC, RG 27, vol. 3055, file 21–3-10, "N.S.S. Mobilization. Prosecutions," H.A.R. Gagnon, Assistant Commissioner and Director, Criminal Investigation, RCMP, to M.W. Wright, Legal and Enforcement Division, Mobilization Section, NSS, October 29, 1945, and other documents on that file to April 1946 dealing with possible misconduct by a senior officer at Camp Borden. See also correspondence in Ralston Papers, vol. 75, files titled "Medical Prosecutions – Québec, 1943: General Courts Martial Forfeitures re[.] alleged irregularities in Medical Examinations, February–March," and "Medical Prosecutions – Québec, 1943: Newspaper Clippings + [*sic*] Hansard Extracts, February," both of which document a group of officers and other ranks who were actually convicted of accepting bribes for providing deferments.

60 LAC, RG 24, vol. 2250, HQ 54–27–95–5, vol. 1, report by Constable J.I.P. Poirier, Rivière du Loup Detachment, RCMP, April 28, and later correspondence to July 6, 1945; and vol. 2, report by Constable C.J.F. Georget, Sherbrooke Detachment, RCMP, July 17, 1945, and "P.M.," for DM(Army), to DM, Department of Justice, November 1, 1946.

61 LAC, RG 13, vol. 2871, file 145990, "Labour. Consolidation of the National Selective Service Mobilization Regulations. November 13, 1943," H.R.L. Henry, Private Secretary, Department of Justice, to DM, November 29; W.R.J[ackett]., to DM, December 2; F.P. Varcoe, Assistant DM, to Supervisor of Mobilization, NSS, December 9; Henry to DM, Department of Justice, December 16, 1943.

62 Stacey, *Arms, Men, and Governments*, appendices "O," "P," and "Q," 587–89.

63 LAC, RG 27, vol. 997, file 2–106–303, "Men called out under National War Services Regulations, 1940 (Recruits) (Consolidation 1941) who refuse to take delivery of notices sent by Divisional Registrars," esp. Captain G.R. Benoit, Supervisor of Recruiting for Military Training, DNWS, Circular Memorandum No. 303, August 27; Raymond Ranger, Registrar, Administrative Division "E," Montreal, to Benoit, August 28; Benoit to Ranger, August 30; and Edgar W. Mingo, Registrar, Administrative Division "G," Halifax, to DNWS, August 30, 1941.

64 See correspondence in LAC, RG 27, vol. 1478, file 2–117–1, "Delinquents, Police Action"; and LAC, RG 13, vol. 2600, file 142037, "R.C.M.P. Enforcement of Military Training Regulations. January 15, 1941."

65 LAC, RG 13, vol. 2028, file 144043, "Amendment to National War Services Regulations. Power to 'Peace Officer' to Arrest Delinquent Without Warrant, August 15, 1942," Benoit to F.P. Varcoe, August 14, Jackett to Acting DM, Department of Justice, August 16, and E. Miall, Acting DM, to Benoit, NSS, August 16, 1942; vol. 2615, file 145218, "Labour. Enforcement of National Selective Service Mobilization Regulations, 14-4-43," F.J. Mead, Assistant Commissioner and Director, Criminal Investigation [RCMP], to A. MacNamara, DM, Department of Labour, April 9; Jackett, "Memorandum for the Deputy Minister of Justice," May 10; F.P. Varcoe, DM, to DM of Labour, May 11, 1943; LAC, RG 27, vol. 3055, file 21–2-3, "N.S.S. Mobilization. Delivery of Orders Military Training by Post-Office," MacNamara, Director, NSS, to Commissioner, RCMP, April 19, 1944.

66 On sharing of information between DND and NSS, see LAC, RG 24, vol. 2915, HQS 9011–9-5, Col. J.A. deLalanne, D.Req., to Vice AG, January 15, 1943, and Gibson and Robertson, eds., *Ottawa at War*, January 3, 1943, 394–95. For tracing work and hiring of private companies, see RG 24, vol. 2915, HQS 9011–9-5, Nash, for AG, to Minister, "Call Under N.R.M.A.," May 29; RG 27, vol. 3055, file 21–3-2, "N.S.S. Mobilization. Tracing of Delinquents," Major-General H.J. Riley, to A. MacNamara, September 7 and 28, 1943; Stacey, *Arms, Men, and Governments*, 414; and Stevenson, *Canada's Greatest Wartime Muddle*, 24–25.

67 Specific examples can be found in LAC, RG 27, vol. 1478, file 2–117–1, Captain G.R. Benoit, Supervisor of Recruiting for Military Training, to Superintendent K. Duncan, Assistant Director, Criminal Investigation Division, RCMP, February 15; Benoit to Lorne McDonell, Divisional Registrar, Administrative Division "C," Kingston, Ontario, March 6; and Henri-Paul Drouin, Divisional Registrar, Division "F," Quebec City, to Benoit, 6 June 1941.

68 LAC, RG 27, vol. 3055, file 21–3-7, "N.S.S. Mobilization. Functions & Appointments of Enforcement Officers," Commissioner S.T. Wood, RCMP, to Louis St. Laurent, Minister of Justice, June 5 and 28 and July 23, 1943. See also Stacey, *Arms, Men, and Governments*, 414. For comments about the workload required to identify and deliver notices to men more broadly, see also documents in LAC, RG 27, vol. 1478, file 2–117–1, "Delinquents,

Police Action"; as well as RG 13, vol. 2603, file 142619, "National War Services. National War Services Regulations. If person who leaves his home address immediately after receiving notification to report for military training should be returned to place of offence for trial. August 10, 1941."

69 LAC, RG 27, acc. 1977–78/103, vol. 115, file 21–64, vol. 1, G.H. Preston, DEO [District Enforcement Officer], Windsor, Ontario, to Edward M. Dillon, Regional Enforcement Officer [REO], Toronto, October 1; J.H. Healy, DEO, St. Catharines, to Dillon, November 1; F.F. Sewell, DEO, Sudbury, to Dillon, December 16–17; Commissioner Wood, RCMP, to A. MacNamara, DM, Department of Labour, December 18, and attached statistical return tabulating figures, as well as several newspaper clippings from Windsor newspapers, n.d. [October], and the *Globe and Mail*, October 30, 1943.

70 Stacey, *Arms, Men, and Governments*, 415; Stevenson, *Canada's Greatest Wartime Muddle*, 22.

71 LAC, RG 27, vol. 3055, file 21–3-10, "N.S.S. Mobilization. Prosecutions," Director, Criminal Investigation, RCMP, to Director, Mobilization Section, NSS, June 12, 1945, and various other documents to March 1947. Stacey provides a similar example of a man evading repeated orders to report for training to work on farms in Saskatchewan in *Arms, Men, and Governments*, 414.

72 LAC, RG 24, reel C-8376, file HQS 8815, "Disturbances at Military Training Centres," vol. 1, DOC, MD 4, to DND, May 29, 1945, and attached Investigation Report by "Sgt. Salconi" and "Pte. Brown" (the two MPs).

73 See various correspondence on LAC, RG 13, vol. 2871, file 145972, "National Defence. Concealment of Deserters and Absentees. Suggested Amendment to Defence of Canada Regulations. November 10, 1943," and particularly copy of Order-in-Council P.C. 826, February 11, 1944, putting amendments into effect; as well as vol. 2872, file 147257, "National Defence (Air). Defence of Canada Regulations 31.A.(1)(C) – Concealment of Deserters or Absentees suggested amendment to include 'or harbours or aids or assists in harbouring such member.' June 6, 1944."

74 LAC, RG 25, vol. 2851, file 1539-B-40, "Arrangements between United States and Canada re[.] the return of deserters and draft evaders – General File," pt. 1, confidential memorandum, Office of the Director, Intelligence Division, War Department, forwarded by L.B. Pearson, Chargé d'Affaires, Canadian Legation, Washington, to Secretary of State for External Affairs [Prime Minister King], August 12, 1942; as well as LAC, RG 27, acc. 1977–78/103, vol. 115, file 21–64, F.F. Sewell, DEO, to E.M. Dillon, REO, December 16; and G.E. Fraser, A/[Acting] Enforcement Officer, North Bay, to Sewell, December 17, 1943.

75 LAC, RG 25, vol. 2633, file 715–40, pt. 1, Under Secretary of State for External Affairs [Norman Robertson], to Hume Wrong, Canadian Legation, Washington, November 27; vol. 2793, file 715–40, pt. 2, Wrong to Robertson, December 3, 1941; King Papers, J4, vol. 424, CWC Minutes, April 9, 1942; LAC, RG 25, vol. 2851, file 1539-B-40, "Arrangements between United States and Canada re[.] the return of deserters and draft evaders – General File," various documents January 1942–October 1945.

76 LAC, RG 13, vol. 2621, file 146609, "Labour-National Selective Service. Delay in Hearing of National Selective Service Appeals – Quebec. Amendment to Section 749 – Criminal Code. January 13, 1944," G. Hems, for Associate Director of Mobilization, NSS, to F.P. Varcoe, Department of Justice, January 11, 1944; as well as various later correspondence, March to August; and copy of Order-in-Council P.C. 6713, August 25, 1944, enacting the final changes.

77 LAC, RG 27, vol. 3055, file 21–3-1, "N.S.S. Mob. Enforcement General," F.J. Mead, Deputy Commissioner, RCMP, to A. MacNamara, DM, Department of Labour, July 10, 1944.

78 According to Raymond Ranger, Acting Associate Director, NSS (Mobilization), to Arthur MacNamara, DM of Labour, May 5, 1945, at the end of April the number of men not yet accounted for totalled 21,934, while Stacey, *Arms, Men, and Governments*, 415 and appendix "O," 587, provides a number of 20,591 as of a week later in early May, at the end of the war in Europe. The decline from 200,000 cases at the end of 1942 is noted in LAC, RG 27, vol. 3055, file 21-3-12, "National Selective Service (Mobilization). Enforcement. Check Up and Prosecution of Delinquents After Cessation of Hostilities," Humphrey Mitchell, Minister of Labour, to D.C. Abbott, Minister of National Defence, March 8, 1946.

79 LAC, RG 27, vol. 3055, file 21-3-12, Administrative Instruction No. 117, May 9, 1945, S.H. McLaren, Acting Chief Executive Officer, to A. MacNamara, February 19, and Raymond Ranger to MacNamara, June 19 and July 6, 1946.

80 Stacey, *Arms, Men, and Governments*, 414; LAC, RG 27, vol. 3055, file 21-3-12, Col. A.L. Tosland, D.Liaison, DND, to A. MacNamara, DM of Labour, March 23, 1946.

81 LAC, RG 27, vol. 3055, file 21-3-12, Ranger to MacNamara, July 6, 1946.

82 Burns, *Manpower in the Canadian Army*, 146; Stacey, *Arms, Men, and Governments*, appendix "N," 586.

83 These totals and rough percentages are calculated from figures given in Stacey, *Arms, Men, and Governments*, appendix "T," 599–601.

84 LAC, RG 24, vol. 14166 (reel T-12400), War Diary, Headquarters, 13th Canadian Infantry Brigade, February 1944, Appendix V, A/Comd [Acting Commander] 13 Cdn Inf Bde, "Manpower for Overseas: Withdrawal from 13 Cdn Inf Bde," February 7, 1944.

85 LAC, RG 24, vol. 14166 (reel T-12400), War Diary, Headquarters, 13th Canadian Infantry Brigade, March 1944, Appendix IV, Brigadier i/c [in charge of] Administration, Pacific Command, to Heads of Departments and Services, and O[fficer]'s C[ommanding]., All Units and Formations, Pacific Command, "Pacific Command Circular Letter No. 184," March 3, 1944.

86 On the origins of the recruiting campaign in Pacific Command, see Stacey, *Arms, Men, and Governments*, 428–29; Roy, *For Most Conspicuous Bravery*, 209–10; Granatstein and Hitsman, *Broken Promises*, 204; DHH, file 322.009(D50), "Brigade Groups – Pacific Command – Org & Admin – Sep 43/Sep 44," record of "Conference – Manpower – 1 Apr 44," April 4; and Brigadier W.H.S. Macklin, Commander 13th Canadian Infantry Brigade, to GOC-in-C, Pacific Command, "Mobilization of 13 Bde on an Active Basis," May 2, 1944, 4–5. This last report is reprinted almost in full in Stacey, *Arms, Men, and Governments*, appendix "S," 591–98. Granatstein and Hitsman also include a lengthy excerpt in *Broken Promises*, 205–206, and in addition it was the source of the views of Brigadier Macklin that were noted at the beginning of Chapter 5.

87 Macklin, "Mobilization of 13 Brigade," 9–10. Also quoted in Roy, *For Most Conspicuous Bravery*, 213.

88 Macklin, "Mobilization of 13 Brigade," 1–4; Roy, *For Most Conspicuous Bravery*, 210–11. On the Canloan scheme, see also Stacey, *Six Years of War*, 138–39; C.P. Stacey, *Official History of the Canadian Army in the Second World War*, vol. 3: *The Victory Campaign: The Operations in North-West Europe, 1944–1945* (Ottawa: Queen's Printer, 1960), 633–35; and Wilfred I. Smith, *Code Word CANLOAN* (Toronto: Dundurn, 1992), esp. 1–27.

89 LAC, RG 24, vol. 14166 (reel T-12400), War Diary, Headquarters, 13th Canadian Infantry Brigade, April 11, 1944.

90 LAC, RG 24, vol. 14166 (reel T-12400), War Diary, Headquarters, 13th Canadian Infantry Brigade, esp. April 8–21, 1944 (quotation at April 14). See also Macklin, "Mobilization of 13 Bde," 6–8.

91 LAC, RG 24, vol. 14166 (reel T-12400), War Diary, Headquarters, 13th Canadian Infantry Brigade, April 11 and 13, 1944, and April 1944, Appendix X: "Hero of Italian Battlefronts, Major Paul Triquet, in Vernon," *Vernon News*, and "Quick Response To VC Winner's Appeal," *Vancouver Sun*, both dated April 13, 1944. On Triquet's actions at Casa Berardi, see Nicholson, *The Canadians in Italy*, 310–14; Daniel G. Dancocks, *The D-Day Dodgers: Canadians in Italy, 1943–1945* (Toronto: McClelland and Stewart, 1991), 167–70; Bill McAndrew, *Canadians and the Italian Campaign, 1943–1945* (Montreal: Art Global, 1996), 75–76; and Mark Zuehlke, *Ortona: Canada's Epic World War II Battle* (Toronto: Stoddart, 1999), 202–11.

92 On Pearkes, see LAC, RG 24, vol. 14166 (reel T-12400), War Diary, Headquarters, 13th Canadian Infantry Brigade, April 20, as well as Appendix XIX: "General's Appeal to Recruits," *Vancouver Sun*, and "Gen. Pearkes Asks Troops To Go Active," *Vancouver Daily Province*, both dated April 21, 1944. For descriptions of the visits of all three of the VC winners, see also Macklin, "Mobilization of 13 Bde," 6–7; and Roy, *For Most Conspicuous Bravery*, 211–13.

93 Macklin, "Mobilization of 13th Bde," 14.

94 Macklin, "Mobilization of 13th Bde," 6. See also LAC, RG 24, vol. 14166 (reel T-12400), War Diary, Headquarters, 13th Canadian Infantry Brigade, April 4, 1944.

95 LAC, RG 24, vol. 14166 (reel T-12400), War Diary, Headquarters, 13th Canadian Infantry Brigade, 10 April 1944.

96 DHH, file 322.009(D50), "MEMO for G.O.C.-in-C.," by Brigadier i/c Administration, April 21; Ralston Papers, vol. 82, "Triquet, Major Paul V.C., 1944: re[.] use of Triquet, Victoria Cross, for recruiting, April," two undated documents recording statements of President of Legion Branch in Vernon, and statement by Ralston in reply; vol. 81, "Recruiting for Overseas, 1944: Camp Vernon, B.C., Pacific Command, April–June," excerpt of speech from *Hansard* by H.C. Green, n.d., 2348, and following documents; Dominion of Canada, *Official Report of Debates of the House of Commons*, vol. 1, 1944 (Ottawa: King's Printer, 1944), 2283; various newspaper clippings in LAC, RG 24, vol. 14166 (reel T-12400), War Diary, Headquarters, 13th Canadian Infantry Brigade, April 1944, Appendix XXVIII. On the changes within the Conservative Party, see Granatstein, *The Politics of Survival*, 113–50.

97 LAC, RG 24, vol. 14166 (reel T-12400), War Diary, Headquarters, 13th Canadian Infantry Brigade, April 1944, Appendix XXVIII: "Ralston Backs Gen. Pearkes," *Vancouver Sun*, April 28, 1944; Ralston Papers, vol. 81, "Recruiting for Overseas, 1944: Camp Vernon," various documents; vol. 78, "Conscription, 1944: Hansard References 1942, Jan[.], March, May–July 1942," telegram, Cmdg 13 Cdn Inf Bde [Macklin], to AG, May 23, and point-form notes by Ralston, "RE: Recruiting – Pacific Command," May 30; vol. 81, "Recruiting for Overseas, 1944: in British Columbia. Newspaper Clippings, April-May," clippings from *Globe and Mail*, April 27, and *L'Action Catholique* and *Le Soleil*, both May 13, 1944. On Chaloult and his actions during the Second World War, see also his own *Mémoires politiques* (Montréal: Éditions du jour, 1969); Wade, *The French Canadians*, vol. 2, 929, 933, 959; and Laurendeau, "The Conscription Crisis, 1942," 17–18, 43, 73–75, 100–3. On the Bloc generally, see Paul-André Comeau, *Le Bloc populaire: 1942–1948* (Montréal: Éditions Québec/Amérique, 1982); Michael D. Behiels, "The Bloc Populaire Canadien and the Origins of French-Canadian Neo-nationalism, 1942–8," *Canadian Historical Review* 63(4) (December 1982): 487–512; and Behiels, "The Bloc Populaire Canadien: Anatomy of Failure, 1942–1947," *Journal of Canadian Studies* 18(4) (Winter 1983–84): 45–74.

98 DHH, file 322.009(D50), Major-General Pearkes to Major-General H.F.G. Letson, AG, May 13, 1944.
99 Stacey, *Arms, Men, and Governments*, 438.
100 On the 13th Brigade's move overseas and later developments, see LAC, RG 24, vol. 14166 (reel T-12400), War Diary, Headquarters, 13th Canadian Infantry Brigade, esp. April 26, May 1–5, May 25–June 1, and June 8 and 18, 1944.
101 DHH, file 322.009(D50), Major-General J.C. Murchie [Vice CGS], personal letter to Pearkes, April 26, 1944.
102 LAC, RG 24, vol. 15054, War Diary, Dufferin and Haldimand Rifles, May 3–4, 1944.
103 LAC, RG 24, vol. 15184, War Diary, Régiment de Joliette, May 10, 1944.
104 For developments during the campaign on the east coast, generally, see LAC, RG 24, War Diaries, vol. 15054, Dufferin and Haldimand Rifles, April–May 1944; vol. 15184, Régiment de Joliette, April–May 1944; vol. 15189, Régiment de Montmagny, April 1944; and vol. 15279, Victoria Rifles of Canada, August–December 1944. See also Hitsman, "Manpower Problems of the Canadian Army," 149–51; and Stacey, *Arms, Men, and Governments*, 430.

Chapter 8: Revolt or Realization?

1 Hutchison, *The Incredible Canadian*, 7.
2 Dawson, *The Conscription Crisis of 1944*, 92.
3 Stacey, *Arms, Men, and Governments*, 471.
4 The classic work on civil–military relations, particularly for Western democracies, is Samuel P. Huntington, *The Soldier and the State: The Theory and Politics of Civil–Military Relations* (Cambridge, MA: Harvard University Press, 1957). On these ideas in connection with Canada in particular, see also Harris, *Canadian Brass*, 3–7.
5 Paul Dickson develops this notion most explicitly in "The Politics of Army Expansion: General H.D.G. Crerar and the Creation of First Canadian Army, 1940–41," *Journal of Military History* 60 (April 1996): 271–98; see also his *A Thoroughly Canadian General*, 139–40.
6 See Reginald H. Roy, "Morale in the Canadian Army in Canada during the Second World War," *Canadian Defence Quarterly* 16(2) (Autumn 1986): 40–45.
7 Roy, "Morale in the Canadian Army," 44; Granatstein and Hitsman, *Broken Promises*, 207.
8 Stacey, *Arms, Men and Governments*, appendix "T," 601.
9 Stacey, *Arms, Men and Governments*, 417–18.
10 Power Papers, box 1, "Political Jottings," vol. 3, C.G. Power to "Pen[dleton]" [Power], June 27, 1944. See also King Papers, J4, vol. 425, CWC Minutes, June 14, 21, and 28, 1944.
11 King Papers, J4, vol. 425, July 26, 1944; LAC, RG 24, vol. 6921, AHQ Historical Reports No. 2, "The Anti-Aircraft Defences of the Pacific Coast," 28, and No. 4, "The Anti-Aircraft Defences of the Atlantic Coast," 33–34, 70.
12 DHH, file 322.009(D50), "Brigade Groups – Pacific Command – Org & Admin – Sep 43/Sep 44," Pearkes to Major-General H.F.G. Letson, AG, May 13, 1944.
13 Ralston Papers, vol. 81, "Petawawa Disturbances, 1944: Statement on incident, Court of Inquiry, Documentation for the Court Inquiry, July," draft "Statement – Petawawa Disturbances," for delivery in the House of Commons, July 20, 1944.
14 See various clippings in Ralston Papers, vol. 79, "Currie Barracks Disturbances, 1944: Report, Messages, Orders, Clippings, July," all dated July 20; as well as LAC, RG 24, vol. 2197, HQ 54-27-63-38, "Disturbances Between G.S. and N.R.M.A. Personnel, A-16

Currie Barracks, Calgary, 18-7-44," newspaper clipping titled "Song Blamed for Trouble," *Globe and Mail*, July 21, 1944.

15 Unless otherwise noted, the story of these events is taken from various reports in LAC, RG 24, vol. 2197, HQ 54–27–63–38, and particularly the proceedings of the Court of Inquiry that investigated the incident, July 27, 1944. See also the published account by Dean F. Oliver, "'My Darlin' Clementine'? Wooing Zombies for $6.50 a Night: General Service–NRMA Relations in Wartime Calgary," *Canadian Military History* 7(3) (Summer 1998): 46–54.

16 LAC, RG 24, vol. 2197, HQ 54–27–63–38, Evans, A[cting]/Commandant, A16 Can[adian]. Inf[antry]. Training Centre, to Headquarters, M[ilitary]. D[istrict] [13]. July 13 and 20, 1944.

17 LAC, RG 24, vol. 2197, HQ 54–27–63–38, Court of Inquiry.

18 LAC, RG 24, vol. 2197, HQ 54–27–63–38, "Salute to a Zombie," forwarded to AG by O.J. Waters, Private Secretary to the Minister of National Defence, July 18, 1944.

19 DHH, file 322.009(D39), "PCMR, Duncan B.C. – Org & Admin – 13 Mar 44/29 Oct 45," story from *Victoria Times*, September 13, quoted in correspondence, Major H.C. Bray, G[eneral] S[taff] O[fficer] 2 Intelligence (Security), Pacific Command, to Staff Officer, P.C.M.R. [Pacific Coast Militia Rangers], September 25, 1944. This correspondence was in fact created by officers inquiring as to whether charges should be laid against the officer for making such public statements.

20 On Canadian involvement in the campaigns of 1944 in northwest Europe, see in particular Stacey, *The Victory Campaign*; English, *The Canadian Army and the Normandy Campaign*; Bill McAndrew, Donald E. Graves, and Michael Whitby, *Normandy, 1944: The Canadian Summer* (Montreal: Art Global, 1994); Bill McAndrew, Bill Rawling, and Michael Whitby, *Liberation: The Canadians in Europe* (Montreal: Art Global, 1995), 13–34; Terry Copp, *Fields of Fire: The Canadians in Normandy* (Toronto: University of Toronto Press, 2003); and Copp, *Cinderella Army*.

21 See especially Stacey, *Arms, Men, and Governments*, 424–41, on which the information in this and the following paragraphs is based.

22 For a discussion of these issues, see also LAC, MG 30, E 537, Ernest William Sansom Papers [hereafter Sansom Papers], vol. 2, "Report on Survey of Reinforcement Situation – Canadian Army Overseas," March 29, 1945, 2–3.

23 Ralston Papers, vol. 81, "Recruiting for Overseas, 1944: Camp Vernon, B.C., Pacific Command, April–June," point-form notes by Ralston, n.d. [late April], and "Draft Statement" on recruiting in 13th Brigade, April 27, 1944.

24 On Stuart's actions, as well as the remustering program in general, see Stacey, *Arms, Men, and Governments*, 433–34, 437–41; Granatstein and Hitsman, *Broken Promises*, 210–11; Granatstein, *The Generals*, 227–31; and Sansom Papers, "Report on Survey of Reinforcement Situation," 4, 10–11, and Appendix no. 18. For a contrary view of the significance of the miscalculations of casualties, see also Walker, "The Revolt of the Canadian Generals," 71.

25 Ralston Papers, vol. 38, "Army Programme 1943–44, General," document titled "Draft Memorandum on Canadian Army Programme 1943–44" by Stuart, January 17, 1943.

26 Ralston Papers, vol. 39, "Army in Canada, General (Secret)," Stuart to Minister, August 30, 1943. See also King Papers, J4, vol. 425, CWC Minutes, August 31, 1943.

27 *Official Report of Debates of the House of Commons*, vol. 1, 1944, 462. See also Ralston Papers, vol. 45, "Enlistments, General," extract from Hansard, February 14, 1944.

28 Ralston Papers, vol. 86, "Resignation – Reinforcement – ," unknown author, to Minister, June 26, 1944.

29 Macdonald Diaries, Folder 392, June 29, 1944.
30 Gibson and Robertson, eds., *Ottawa at War*, June 23, 1944, 467–70 (quotation at 470).
31 See DHH, file 312.009(D52), "Stuart Corresp File – Personal – rec'd [sic] from General Foulkes, 3 Jan ? [sic]," Ralston to Stuart, March 26; as well as other correspondence on this file between the two men, tracking the issue between January and June 1944; and Stacey, *Arms, Men, and Governments*, 424–27.
32 Ralston Papers, vol. 86, "Resignation – Reinforcement – figures, allocations, overseas situation, candidates bulletin," Letson to Minister, June 7, 1944. See also King Papers, J4, vol. 425, CWC Minutes, June 14; and Gibson and Robertson, eds., *Ottawa at War*, June 22, 1944, 465–66.
33 On the rise of the CCF and other domestic political developments after 1943, and the actions of McTague in 1944, see Granatstein, *The Politics of Survival*, 160–78; Granatstein, *Canada's War*, 264–88, 335–36; and Granatstein and Hitsman, *Broken Promises*, 208–9. See also Gibson and Robertson, eds., *Ottawa at War*, June 24, 470–73; and DHH, file 312.009(D52), Ralston to Lieutenant-General Stuart, June 25, 1944.
34 King Diaries, September 5, 7–8, and 26–29 and October 5–6 and 12–13, 1944; Gibson and Robertson, eds., *Ottawa at War*, September 17–25 and October 6, 1944, 481–85; Granatstein, *Canada's War*, 335–36.
35 King Papers, J4, vol. 425, CWC Minutes, September 22–23; King Diaries, September 6–7, 20, 22–23, and 28–29 and October 5 and 11; Macdonald Diaries, folder 392, September 22 and October 5 and 11, 1944. On plans for participation in the war against Japan, see also Stacey, *Arms, Men, and Governments*, 54–65, 482–84.
36 King Diaries, September 14, 1944.
37 Macdonald Diaries, folder 392, September 14, 1944.
38 For example, see Grant Dexter's second-hand account of it in Gibson and Robertson, eds., *Ottawa at War*, September 22, 1944, 481–82.
39 Gibson and Robertson, eds., *Ottawa at War*, September 25, 1944, 484. On Ralston's meeting with King in Quebec City, see also King Diaries, September 15; and Macdonald Diaries, folder 392, September 21, 1944.
40 On the developments of late August and September, see Stacey, *Six Years of War*, 279–322; McAndrew, Rawling, and Whitby, *Liberation*, 13–34; and Copp, *Cinderella Army*, 15–44.
41 King Papers, J4, vol. 425, CWC Minutes, August 3, 1944. See also King Diaries, and Macdonald Diaries, folder 392, both August 3, 1944; as well as Stacey, *Arms, Men, and Governments*, 436; and Granatstein and Hitsman, *Broken Promises*, 210. On the formation of 12th Canadian Infantry Brigade, see also Nicholson, *The Canadians in Italy*, 479–81.
42 Smythe, with Young, *If You Can't Beat 'Em in the Alley*, 140, 147, 160–67. See also Stacey, *Arms, Men, and Governments*, 440–41; and Hunter, *War Games*, 121–40.
43 Hunter, *War Games*, 140–50, 165–83; King Papers, J4, vol. 425, CWC Minutes, October 11, 1944.
44 QUA, Grant Dexter Papers, box 5, file #37, "Correspondence General 1950 Jan[.]–June," memorandum by George S. Currie [previously Executive Assistant to Ralston and then DM of DND from September 1942 until late September 1944, and who also returned in October to help guide Ralston through the crisis], dated November 4, and sent by Currie to Dexter on January 18, 1950. See also same file, Richard S. Malone, confidential memorandum to Dexter, January 19, 1950; as well as Malone, *Missing from the Record* (Toronto: Wm. Collins and Sons, 1946), 151–53; and Granatstein and Hitsman, *Broken Promises*, 210–11.

45 On Ralston's trip see Stacey, *Arms, Men and Governments*, 440–42.
46 King Papers, J4, vol. 425, CWC Minutes, October 19, 1944. See also Stuart's official recommendation to Ralston, October 19, 1944, in Ralston Papers, vol. 57, "Reinforcement Situation 1944, (Ralston resignation)" [black binder containing key documents on fall 1944 crisis]; and Ralston's own notes of October 21, in the same source, which seem to have guided his presentation of the issue to the full Cabinet a few days later; as well as Stacey, *Arms, Men, and Governments*, 443–44.
47 King Papers, J4, vol. 425, draft report on CWC meeting of October 19, prepared by Major-General Maurice Pope [who was by then serving as a personal staff officer to Prime Minister King and military secretary to the CWC]. For the various arguments advanced by King during the debates, see also King Diaries, October 13, 15, 18–19, 24–27, and 30; Macdonald Diaries, folder 392, October 19–20, 24, and 26–27; Power Papers, box 12, "Conscription Crisis, November 1944," set of "Notes" by Power recording events of October–December [hereafter Power Notes], October 19 and 26; Claxton Papers, vol. 253, "Memoirs, World War II" [hereafter Claxton Memoirs], 646; and QUA, T.A. Crerar Papers, box 119, "King, W.L.M. ... Jan 1942–Dec 1947[,] July 1963," "Notes for the record on the recent crisis in the Government over reinforcements" [hereafter Crerar Notes], December 26, 1944, 1, 3.
48 For these counter-arguments, see the same sources cited in the previous note.
49 On King's attempts to get Churchill to provide a statement against the need for conscription, see his Diaries, October 21–22 and 25–27, 1944; and on his approaches to US officials, see Pope, *Soldiers and Politicians*, 252–54. On both subjects, see also Stacey, *Arms, Men, and Governments*, 466–67.
50 Draft report on CWC meeting, October 19, 1944, cited above. For similar comments, see also King Diaries, October 18–19 and 24; and Power Notes, October 19, 1944.
51 Draft report on CWC meeting, October 19, 1944.
52 Ralston Papers, vol. 57, "Reinforcement Situation 1944, (Ralston resignation)," Murchie to Minister, October 23, 1944.
53 On the discussion of Murchie's recommendations, see King Papers, CWC Minutes, October 24; King Diaries, October 24; Macdonald Diaries, folder 392, October 24 and 26; and Power Notes, October 24, 1944.
54 King Diaries, October 25, 1944.
55 Ward, ed., *A Party Politician*, 153. For similar comments, see King Diaries, October 25–26, 1944; and Claxton Memoirs, 643.
56 See in particular figures in Power Papers, box 39, "General Staff Memoranda Notes re[.] War Committee Meetings, October and November 1944," memorandum titled "Approximate Analysis of Strength of General Service Other Ranks – Canada and Adjacent Territories, 27 Sep 44." On the meeting to review these figures, and their presentation to the CWC the following day, see also Power Notes and Macdonald Diaries, folder 392, both October 26–27; King Papers, J4, vol. 425, CWC Minutes, October 27; King Diaries, October 27; and Crerar Notes, October 2 and 18–19, 1944.
57 On the origins and discussion of the recruiting plan, see King Diaries, October 20–21, 24–26, and 30–31; Power Notes, October 20; Ralston Papers, vol. 57, "Reinforcement Situation 1944, (Ralston resignation)," Murchie to Minister, and copy of memorandum, A.D.P. Heeney to Prime Minister, both October 23, as well as notes by Ralston, titled "Timetable"; King Papers, J4, vol. 425, CWC Minutes, October 24, 26 and 30–31; Macdonald Diaries, folder 392, October 24, 26, and 30–31; and Claxton Memoirs, 651.
58 King Diaries, October 26, 1944. See also Macdonald Diaries, folder 392, October 26; and King Papers, J4, vol. 425, CWC Minutes, October 26, 1944.

59 On Ralston's threats to resign, and particularly King's thoughts on the issue, see King Diaries, October 20, 24–28, and 31; Power Notes, October 21–22; and Macdonald Diaries, folder 392, October 26 and 31, 1944.

60 On the events surrounding McNaughton's removal as commander of First Canadian Army, see John Swettenham, *McNaughton*, vol. 2: *1939–1943* (Toronto: Ryerson Press, 1969), 271–350; Stacey, *Arms, Men, and Governments*, 231–47; Granatstein, *The Generals*, 53–80; Bill Rawling, "The Generalship of Andrew McNaughton: A Study in Failure," in *Warrior Chiefs*, ed. Horn and Harris, 73–90; and John Nelson Rickard, *The Politics of Command: Lieutenant-General A.G.L. McNaughton and the Canadian Army, 1939–1943* (Toronto: University of Toronto Press, 2010), esp. 187–216.

61 On King's discussions with McNaughton, and the origins of his consideration of placing McNaughton in the defence portfolio, see King Diaries, September 22–23, October 21, 23–24 and 31, and November 1; as well as McNaughton Papers, vol. 267, "McNaughton. A[ppointmen]t. to Cabinet et seq. 2 Nov. 1944," McNaughton's handwritten notes, October 31 and November 1, 1944; and John Swettenham, *McNaughton*, vol. 3: *1944–1966* (Toronto: Ryerson Press, 1969), 38–48. On McNaughton's Queen's speech, see also King Diaries, "McNaughton Creed Bars Compulsion," the *Montreal Gazette*, October 23, 1944 (newspaper clipping follows diary entry for October 21).

62 Colin Gibson, Minister of National Revenue, as quoted in Macdonald Diaries, folder 392, November 1, 1944. See also King Diaries for the same date; as well as Crerar Notes, November 2–3; Power Notes, November 12; and Claxton Memoirs, 656–59. On the events of the end of October and the first of November more generally, see also Stacey, *Arms, Men, and Governments*, 453–60; Granatstein, *Canada's War*, 350–54; Granatstein and Hitsman, *Broken Promises*, 218–21; Rea, "What Really Happened?" esp. 18–19; and T. Stephen Henderson, *Angus L. Macdonald: A Provincial Liberal* (Toronto: University of Toronto Press, 2007), 129–38.

63 King Diaries, November 1, 1944. Macdonald's description of the same discussion, and of his and Ralston's call to Pearkes, appear in his own diary on the same date, and records of the Pearkes conversation can also be found in Ralston Papers, vol. 57, black binder on conscription crisis, "Telephone Conversation Mr. Ralston – General Pearkes, November 1, 1944," and "Notes of Telephone Conversation between Honourable A.L. Macdonald and Major General Pearkes, 2 p.m., November 1/44."

64 Power Papers, box 39, "General Staff Memoranda ... October and November 1944," memoranda titled "Report of Cabinet Committee on Army enlistments for General Service," and "Attitude of N.R.M.A. Personnel," both November 6, 1944. Copies of the first report can be found in the papers of most key participants in the events of November 1944, including A.G.L. McNaughton, Brooke Claxton, and T.A. Crerar. See also various documents recording the work of the committee in McNaughton Papers, vol. 255, file 892–10, "Gen. (Secret) Recruiting Committee of Cabinet."

65 QUA, T.A. Crerar Papers, box 176, "Military Secrets," copy of "Memorandum Re: Reinforcements for French-Canadian Infantry Regiments now Overseas," by L.R. LaFlèche, November 6, 1944. See also Macdonald Diaries, folder 392, November 7, 1944.

66 DHH, file 161.009(D8), "N.R.M.A. – MD 1 Nov/Dec 1944: Persuasion NRMA," copy of "Canada's Support of the Army Overseas: Broadcast by Right. Hon. W.L. Mackenzie King, M.P., Prime Minister of Canada, Ottawa, November 8, 1944," as well as circular letter, AG to GOsC-in-C, Pacific and Atlantic Commands, et al., November 8, memorandum titled "Future Policy N.R.M.A.," November 10, and telegram, CGS to GOsC-in-C, Atlantic and Pacific Commands, November 11, 1944. See also Swettenham, *McNaughton*,

vol. 3, 50–51, Stacey, *Arms, Men, and Governments*, 460–63; and Granatstein and Hitsman, *Broken Promises*, 224–25.

67 As Power described McNaughton in his Notes, October 20, "He was convinced that he could break down the core of resistance in the Zombies and get them to enlist. He seemed to be full of vim and vigour."

68 McNaughton Papers, vol. 358, "'Reinforcement Crisis' of 1944 ... Made in 1964 + [sic] 1966," copy of "The Reinforcement Crisis 1944 (Statement by General A.G.L. McNaughton, 12 February, 1964.)"

69 Swettenham, *McNaughton*, vol. 3, 51–54; Stacey, *Arms, Men, and Governments*, 463; Granatstein, *Canada's War*, 358–59; Granatstein and Hitsman, *Broken Promises*, 225.

70 Claxton Memoirs, 661. On Claxton's actions and views during the conscription crisis of 1944, see also David Jay Bercuson, *True Patriot: The Life of Brooke Claxton, 1898–1960* (Toronto: University of Toronto Press, 1993), 129–32.

71 For an example of such views, see Claxton Papers, vol. 137, "Conscription – A," Major And.H. [*sic*] Stott, Royal Canadian Artillery, Com[man]d[ing] 122nd F[iel]d.B[at]t[er]y., R.C.Arty, to Claxton, November 6, 1944.

72 On Stuart's resignation (or dismissal), see Swettenham, *McNaughton*, vol. 3, 50; and Granatstein, *The Generals*, 232–33.

73 Roy, *For Most Conspicuous Bravery*, 224. Also noted and discussed in Swettenham, *McNaughton*, vol. 3, 54–55; Stacey, *Arms, Men, and Governments*, 463–64; and Granatstein and Hitsman, *Broken Promises*, 225–26. On the meetings themselves, see DHH, file 111.21065(D1), "Reinf. situation – Cdn Army, 1944," copy of "Minutes of a Conference of GOsC and DOsC held in the Defence Council Chambers at 0900 hrs, 14 Nov 44," and "Minutes of Afternoon Meeting of GOsC-in-C & DOsC held ... 14 Nov 44"; Macdonald Diaries, folder 392, November 14–16; and McNaughton Papers, vol. 270, House of Commons, #4, "D.Os.C. Conference – Press Statement, November 15, 1944," copy of "Outline of Address to DOsC and GOsC by Minister," and attached documents, n.d. [November 13–14, 1944].

74 For a copy of the document, see McNaughton Papers, vol. 270, House of Commons, #4, "D.Os.C. Conference – Press Statement, November 15, 1944," press release, November 16, 1944.

75 DHH, file 111.21065(D1), CGS to Minister, November 22, 1944. See also Swettenham, *McNaughton*, vol. 3, 55–60; Stacey, *Arms, Men, and Governments*, 464–71; Granatstein and Hitsman, *Broken Promises*, 226; and Roy, *For Most Conspicuous Bravery*, 225–28.

76 Power Papers, box 8, "Ralston, Stuart," Stuart Ralston to Power, August 6, 1952.

77 DHH, file 161.009(D8), Earnshaw to All Commanding Officers (Active Force Units), MD 1, November 17, 1944.

78 DHH, file 161.009(D8), Colonel R. Bland Crouch, Commandant, S-5 Canadian Driving and Maintenance School, Woodstock, to Headquarters, MD 1, November 17, 1944.

79 DHH, file 161.009(D8), Major W.E. Weekes, Royal Canadian Army Medical Corps, OC Woodstock Military Hospital, to DOC, MD 1, November 20, 1944. For other examples, see further correspondence from commanders of local units in this file, dated November 17–23, 1944.

80 Dawson, *The Conscription Crisis of 1944*, 78. Some views of these numbers were more optimistic. For example, see Brooke Claxton's comments in Claxton Memoirs, 652.

81 Power Notes, November 21, 1944. On Crerar's views during this period, see Rea, *T.A. Crerar*, 226–30; for Howe, see Bothwell and Kilbourn, *C.D. Howe*, esp. 165–68, 191; and on these two mens' views as well as more particularly those of his own subject, see Henderson, *Angus L. Macdonald*, 140–47.

82 QUA, T.A. Crerar Papers, box 119, "King, Hon. W.L.M ... Jan 1942–Dec 1947[,] July 1963," King to Crerar, November 18, 1944. See also Crerar Notes, 3; Macdonald Diaries, folder 392, November 13; and Power Notes, November 13, 1944.

83 Macdonald Diaries, folder 392, November 20, 1944. See also Power Notes, November 20–21; and Crerar Notes, 4.

84 On the events of November 22, see entries for that date in King Diaries (source of quotations); Macdonald Diaries, folder 392; and Power Notes; as well as Crerar Notes, 5–6; and more generally Stacey, *Arms, Men, and Governments*, 469–73; Granatstein, *Canada's War*, 362–70; and Granatstein and Hitsman, *Broken Promises*, 226–31.

Part 5: The Aftermath

1 Ralston Papers, vol. 85, "Resignation, Miscellaneous – Caucas [sic] Notes, Diary, Memoranda, Speeches, Correspondence, Statement, 'Zombie Prayers.'"

Epilogue: Conscription and Canadians in the Second World War

1 A copy of this Order-in-Council can be found in DHH, file 112.3S2009(D326), "Reinforcements – Cdn Army, d/15 Mar 42/19 Jun 45."

2 Beck, *Pendulum of Power*, 241–58; Granatstein, *Canada's War*, 370–402; Granatstein and Hitsman, *Broken Promises*, 234–38; and Vennat, *Lés Héros oubliés*, vol. 3, 244–45.

3 On the events noted in this and the following paragraph, generally, see DHH, file 341. PR009(D27), "Court of enquiry into disturbance or riot by NRMA at Terrace, BC – Dec 44," and particularly the proceedings of the court of inquiry into the disturbances, dated December 7, 1944; DHH, file 746.009(D8), "PA Vol[unteer]s reports on disturbances by NRMA at Terrace, d/Nov 45"; Stacey, *Arms, Men, and Governments*, 474–78; Reginald H. Roy, "From the Darker Side of Canadian Military History: Mutiny in the Mountains – The Terrace Incident," *Canadian Defence Quarterly* 6(2) (Autumn 1976): 42–55; Roy, *For Most Conspicuous Bravery*, 229–33; Granatstein and Hitsman, *Broken Promises*, 231–34; Daniel German, "Press Censorship and the Terrace Mutiny: A Case Study in Second World War Information Management," *Journal of Canadian Studies* 31(4) (Winter 1996–97): 124–42; and Peter A. Russell, "BC's 1944 'Zombie' Protests against Overseas Conscription," *BC Studies* 122 (Summer 1999): 49–76. See also Walker, "The Revolt of the Canadian Generals," 89, for once again a different interpretation of these events and their relationship to larger civil–military issues in the fall of 1944.

4 DHH, file 341.PR009(D27), proceedings of court of inquiry on Terrace disturbances, testimony of Lt.-Col. W.B. Hendrie, Commanding Officer, Mountain Warfare School, Terrace.

5 DHH, file 746.009(D8), "Report on recent disturbance Terrace Military Camp," December 20, 1944, statement by Acting Captain G.A. Anthony, 2 i/c [second in command], "C" Company, Prince Albert Volunteers.

6 DHH, file 341.PR009(D53), "Sitreps on Terrace incident by NRMA in Nov 44," Capt. G.W. Burrell[?], for Lt-Col G.F. Paulin, OC, Prince Rupert Defences, to GSO I Op[eration]s, GSO 2 Int[elligence] (Security), and Off[ice]r i/c Adm[inistration], Pacific Command, November 29, 1944.

7 For further information on the events in Terrace, see also LAC, RG 24, vol. 14172 (reel T-12405), War Diary, Headquarters, 15th Canadian Infantry Brigade, November 24–30, 1944, and Appendix I, "Special Brigade Orders," by Brigadier A.R. Roy, Comd 15 Cdn Inf Bde, November 28, 1944.

8 LAC, RG 24, vol. 14173 (reel T-12406), War Diary, Headquarters, 16th Canadian Infantry Brigade, November 24–25 and 28, 1944.

9 LAC, RG 24, War Diaries, vol. 14169 (reel T-12403), Headquarters, 14th Canadian Infantry Brigade, November 26; vol. 13803 (reel T-10561), AA&QMG, 6th Canadian Division, November 27, 1944.

10 Roy, *For Most Conspicuous Bravery*, 230.

11 DHH, file 112.3S2009(D326), CGS to AG, Quartermaster-General, and Master-General of the Ordnance, November 25, 1944.

12 For figures on the NRMA and the description of the rifle being thrown overboard, see Stacey, *Arms, Men, and Governments*, 479. The record of the sit-down strike as well as other information on NRMA men going absent without leave or deserting before proceeding overseas appears in King Papers, J4, vol. 425, CWC Minutes, January 8 (source of quotation), 17 and 24 and February 7, 21 and 28, 1945. On press reaction to the events, see also Granatstein and Hitsman, *Broken Promises*, 233.

13 Crerar Papers, vol. 5, file 958C.009(D129), "GOC-in-C file 6-2. Reinforcements; French-Cdn Reinforcements; Reinforcement Programme; NRMA Reinforcements. Period 5 Apr 44 to 24 Jun 45," Macklin, D[eputy].C.G.S., CMHQ, to Chief of Staff, December 1, 1944. I am indebted to Paul Dickson for pointing me towards records on the reception and treatment of conscripts in the Crerar Papers. See also his own discussion in *A Thoroughly Canadian General*, 369–70.

14 Crerar Papers, vol. 5, 958C.009(D129), Crerar to Lieutenant-General P.J. Montague, Chief of Staff, CMHQ, December 11, 1944. On the treatment of NRMA men overseas, see other correspondence in the same file, as well as King Papers, J4, vol. 425, CWC Minutes, December 22, 1944.

15 Gardiner interview, May 17, 2015.

16 Canadian War Museum, Military History Research Centre, 58A 1 235.26, "Brown, Kenneth James, Sapper," letters home of February 21 and March 31, 1945.

17 Crerar Papers, vol. 5, 958C.009(D129), telegram, Montague to Crerar ("Canmilitry" to "HQ First Cdn Army"), January 12, 1945.

18 Crerar Papers, vol. 5, 958C.009(D129), Sansom to McNaughton, February 21, 1945.

19 Crerar Papers, vol. 5, 958C.009(D129), untitled table attached as Appendix "A" to correspondence, General Officer Commanding, 2nd Cdn Corps, to First Canadian Army, March 9, 1945.

20 Stacey, *Arms, Men, and Governments*, 481–82; Granatstein and Hitsman, *Broken Promises*, 234.

21 Crerar Papers, vol. 5, 958C.009(D129), telegram, Montague to Lieutenant-General J.C. Murchie, CGS ("Canmilitry" to "Defensor"), April 4, 1945.

22 King Papers, J4, vol. 425, CWC Minutes, March 14 and May 1 and 8, 1945.

23 See in particular King Papers, J4, vol. 425, CWC Minutes, March 14 and 22, 1945; as well as documents in LAC, RG 27, vol. 3055, file 21–3-12, "National Selective Service (Mobilization). Enforcement. Check Up and Prosecution of Delinquents after Cessation of Hostilities."

24 LAC, RG 27, vol. 3055, file 21–3-12, as well as LAC, RG 13, vol. 2122, file 151133, "Labour. National Registration Regulations, 1940 and the National Selective Service Mobilization Regulations, 1944. Revocation of Regulations. Draft Report to Council, August 13, 1946," W.R.J[ackett]., "Memorandum for the Deputy Minister," August 10, and draft Order-in-Council, August 10, 1946.

25 LAC, RG 27, vol. 3055, file 21–3-7, "N.S.S. Mobilization. Prosecutions," S.B. Picken, Custodian of Mobilization Records, Division "K," Vancouver, to Raymond Ranger, Assistant to the DM, November 8, 1946.

26 Roy, *For Most Conspicuous Bravery*, 227–29; Sansom Papers, vol. 3, "Scrapbook, 1939–1971," newspaper clipping, "General Arrives to Probe Officers' Draftee Remarks," *Vancouver Sun*, November 24, 1944.

27 LAC, RG 13, vol. 2628, file 148600, "National Defence (Army). Major-General G.R. Pearkes, VC, CB, DSO, MC, February 17, 1945," and particularly R.F. [?], "Memorandum for the Deputy Minister: Re: Major-General Pearkes, G.R.," February 19; as well as F.P. Varcoe, DM, Department of Justice, to Brigadier A.C. Spencer, Acting AG, March 1, 1945. See also Stacey, *Arms, Men, and Governments*, 480–81; and Roy, *For Most Conspicuous Bravery*, 235–39, 284–342; and J.L. Granatstein, *Canada, 1957–1967: The Years of Uncertainty and Innovation* (Toronto: McClelland and Stewart, 1986), 101–19.

28 Granatstein, *The Generals*, 235.

29 Swettenham, *McNaughton*, vol. 3, 71–80, 89–96; Granatstein, *Canada's War*, 389–94, 409; and Granatstein and Hitsman, *Broken Promises*, 236–38.

30 On Claxton and defence policy in the early postwar period, see Bercuson, *True Patriot* esp. 153–74; as well as James Eayrs, *In Defence of Canada: Peacemaking and Deterrence* (Toronto: University of Toronto Press, 1972); and Granatstein and Hitsman, *Broken Promises*, 247–49.

31 Ralston Papers, vol. 115, "Manpower," vol. 5, Stuart to Minister, June 29, 1943.

32 J.L. Granatstein, "'Strictly on Its Merits': The Conscription Issue in Canada after 1945," *Queen's Quarterly* 69(2) (Summer 1972): 192–206; Granatstein and Hitsman, *Broken Promises*, 245–63. See also Walker, "The Revolt of the Canadian Generals," 71–73.

Appendix 1: The National Resources Mobilization Act, 1940

1 4 George VI, Chap. 13, *Acts of the Parliament of the Dominion of Canada*, 1939–1940 (Ottawa: King's Printer, 1940), 43–44.

Index

Note: "(f)" after a page number indicates an illustration; "(t)" a table; and "(m)" a map

STUDIES IN CANADIAN MILITARY HISTORY

John Griffith Armstrong, *The Halifax Explosion and the Royal Canadian Navy: Inquiry and Intrigue*

Andrew Richter, *Avoiding Armageddon: Canadian Military Strategy and Nuclear Weapons, 1950–63*

William Johnston, *A War of Patrols: Canadian Army Operations in Korea*

Julian Gwyn, *Frigates and Foremasts: The North American Squadron in Nova Scotia Waters, 1745–1815*

Jeffrey A. Keshen, *Saints, Sinners, and Soldiers: Canada's Second World War*

Desmond Morton, *Fight or Pay: Soldiers' Families in the Great War*

Douglas E. Delaney, *The Soldiers' General: Bert Hoffmeister at War*

Michael Whitby, ed., *Commanding Canadians: The Second World War Diaries of A.F.C. Layard*

Martin Auger, *Prisoners of the Home Front: German POWs and "Enemy Aliens" in Southern Quebec, 1940–46*

Tim Cook, *Clio's Warriors: Canadian Historians and the Writing of the World Wars*

Serge Marc Durflinger, *Fighting from Home: The Second World War in Verdun, Quebec*

Richard O. Mayne, *Betrayed: Scandal, Politics, and Canadian Naval Leadership*

P. Whitney Lackenbauer, *Battle Grounds: The Canadian Military and Aboriginal Lands*

Cynthia Toman, *An Officer and a Lady: Canadian Military Nursing and the Second World War*

Michael Petrou, *Renegades: Canadians in the Spanish Civil War*

Amy J. Shaw, *Crisis of Conscience: Conscientious Objection in Canada during the First World War*

Serge Marc Durflinger, *Veterans with a Vision: Canada's War Blinded in Peace and War*

James G. Fergusson, *Canada and Ballistic Missile Defence, 1954–2009: Déjà Vu All Over Again*

Benjamin Isitt, *From Victoria to Vladivostok: Canada's Siberian Expedition, 1917–19*

James Wood, *Militia Myths: Ideas of the Canadian Citizen Soldier, 1896–1921*

Timothy Balzer, *The Information Front: The Canadian Army and News Management during the Second World War*

Andrew B. Godefroy, *Defence and Discovery: Canada's Military Space Program, 1945–74*

Douglas E. Delaney, *Corps Commanders: Five British and Canadian Generals at War, 1939–45*

Timothy Wilford, *Canada's Road to the Pacific War: Intelligence, Strategy, and the Far East Crisis*

Randall Wakelam, *Cold War Fighters: Canadian Aircraft Procurement, 1945–54*

Andrew Burtch, *Give Me Shelter: The Failure of Canada's Cold War Civil Defence*

Wendy Cuthbertson, *Labour Goes to War: The CIO and the Construction of a New Social Order, 1939–45*

P. Whitney Lackenbauer, *The Canadian Rangers: A Living History*

Teresa Iacobelli, *Death or Deliverance: Canadian Courts Martial in the Great War*

Graham Broad, *A Small Price to Pay: Consumer Culture on the Canadian Home Front, 1939–45*

Peter Kasurak, *A National Force: The Evolution of Canada's Army, 1950–2000*

Isabel Campbell, *Unlikely Diplomats: The Canadian Brigade in Germany, 1951–64*

Richard M. Reid, *African Canadians in Union Blue: Volunteering for the Cause in the Civil War*

Andrew B. Godefroy, *In Peace Prepared: Innovation and Adaptation in Canada's Cold War Army*

Nic Clarke, *Unwanted Warriors: The Rejected Volunteers of the Canadian Expeditionary Force*

David Zimmerman, *Maritime Command Pacific: The Royal Canadian Navy's West Coast Fleet in the Early Cold War*

Studies in Canadian Military History
Published by UBC Press in association
with the Canadian War Museum.